dancing Class

D1176078

Gender, Ethnicity, and Social Divides in American Dance, 1890–1920

Linda J. Tomko

INDIANA UNIVERSITY PRESS

BLOOMINGTON & INDIANAPOLIS

This book is a publication of

Indiana University Press
601 North Morton Street
Bloomington, IN 47404-3797 USA

http://www.indiana.edu/~iupress

Telephone orders   800-842-6796
Fax orders   812-855-7931
Orders by e-mail   iuporder@indiana.edu

© 1999 by Linda J. Tomko

All rights reserved

No part of this book may be reproduced or utilized in any form or by any means, electronic or mechanical, including photocopying and recording, or by any information storage and retrieval system, without permission in writing from the publisher. The Association of American University Presses' Resolution on Permissions constitutes the only exception to this prohibition.

The paper used in this publication meets the minimum requirements of American National Standard for Information Sciences—Permanence of Paper for Printed Library Materials, ANSI Z39.48-1984.

Manufactured in the United States of America

Library of Congress Cataloging-in-Publication Data

Tomko, Linda J.
   Dancing class : gender, ethnicity, and social divides in American Dance, 1890–1920 / Linda J. Tomko.
   p.   cm.
   Includes bibliographical references (p.   ) and index.
   ISBN 0–253–33571–X (cl. : alk. paper). — ISBN 0–253–21327–4 (pa. : alk. paper)
   1. Dance—Social aspects—United States—History—20th century. 2. Dance—Anthropological aspects—United States—History—20th century. 3. Dance—Sex differences.   I. Title. II. Series.
GV1588.6.T66   1999
306.4'84—dc21   99-18556

1 2 3 4 5 04 03 02 01 00 99

The photograph "Fifteen Acres of Dancing Girls" is from *Dances of the People: A Second Volume of Folk Dances and Singing Games,* collected by Elizabeth Burchenal. © 1913 (Renewed) by G. Schirmer, Inc. (ASCAP). International Copyright Secured. All Rights Reserved. Reprinted by Permission.

Material in Chapter 6 appeared in Linda J. Tomko's "Fete Accompli: Gender, 'Folk-Dance,' and Progressive-era Political Ideals in New York City," in *Corporealities: Dancing Knowledge, Culture and Power,* ed. Susan Foster (London: Routledge, 1996).

CONTENTS

ACKNOWLEDGMENTS

If graduate study doesn't change the way you think, I tell students, then you haven't gotten what you came for. The conception of this book was profoundly influenced by my doctoral study in History at UCLA. I owe a great deal to Alexander Saxton, Kathryn Kish Sklar, and Thomas Hines, but especially for the rigor of their thinking and their receptivity to dance as a subject for investigation. On another campus, Nancy Ruyter gave the same commitment to my research.

I've come to treasure archives as crucial and fragile sites for leaving to ourselves reflections upon ourselves. I am grateful for the assistance rendered me so generously by a number of curators and reference professionals at the following institutions: David Klaassen, Social Welfare History Archives, Walter Library, University of Minnesota, Minneapolis; Alice Owen, the Neighborhood Playhouse, New York City; Madeleine Nichols and Monica Moseley, Dance Collection of the New York Public Library for the Performing Arts; Billy Rose Theatre Collection, New York Public Library for the Performing Arts; David Ment and Lucinda Manning, Special Collections, Milbank Memorial Library, Columbia University; Diana Haskell, the Newberry Library, Chicago; Kitty Keller, Early Archives Coordinator for the Country Dance and Song Society; Elizabeth Mock, University of Massachusetts/Boston, Harbor Campus; Archie Motley, the Chicago Historical Society; Sue Berger and Bernard Crystal, the Ethical Culture Fieldston School, New York City; Mary Ann Bamberger, Special Collections, the University Library, at the University of Illinois, Chicago; Hollee Haswell, the Columbia University Archives and Columbiana Library; Malcolm Taylor, Vaughan Williams Memorial Library, Cecil Sharp House, England; University Research Library, UCLA; Janet Moores, Rivera Library, University of California, Riverside. I am especially grateful to Charles F. Woodford for facilitating the publication use of Doris Humphrey materials held by the Dance Collection, New York Public Library for the Performing Arts. Funding from UC Riverside Academic Senate faculty research grants helped support research and publication preparation for this book.

Many friends made my research trips possible. I thank Norma Adler, Janelle Travers, Tom Travers, Judith Brin Ingber, Pete and Astrid Stewart, Kitty and Bob Keller, Vicky Risner Wulff, Charles Koster, Rachelle Friedman, and Sandra and Jon Spalter, who made their cities, and their homes, home to me. I am profoundly grateful to Matthew Lee, David Lehman, and Rachelle Friedman for intellectual companionship at several stages. The DOMUS study group, and Erik Monkkonen's mobilizing, were important to me. I have been lucky in my colleagues at UC Riverside, dialogue with whom has been pivotal: Christena L. Schlundt, Susan Foster, Sally Ness, Marta Savigliano, and Heidi Gilpin. And I thank individuals whose encouragement about *writing* buoyed me at key points: Judith Chazin-Bennahum, Judy Van Zile, Judith Brin Ingber, Meredith Little, Wendy Hilton, and Margaret Graham Hills.

Finally, I thank Dorothy Overby and Charles Paul Johnston, whose words gave me ears for words, and Diane Goins, who helped me continue. And I thank Steve Tomko, for more than I can say.

INTRODUCTION

In the 1890s and the first two decades of the twentieth century, Loie Fuller, Ruth St. Denis, and Isadora Duncan created new kinds of artistic dance in the United States. Claiming the roles of choreographers as well as performers, these women won national and international recognition and stirred new consideration of dance as a serious form of artistic expression. In the decades that followed in America, the dominant figures of Martha Graham, Doris Humphrey, Helen Tamiris, and Hanya Holm led in the construction of the new genre of modern dance. Colleges and universities both supported and changed in response to the stimulus offered by the newly pioneered dance practices, beginning in the late 1910s to add dance courses to the curriculum for women's physical education. These courses created new academic positions which women teachers filled and a new disciplinary field that students pursued. In all these areas of innovation, women not only were heavily represented but also forged leadership roles in constituting new dance practices.

How can we account for the predominance of women in new forms of artistic dance pioneered in the United States between 1890 and 1920? The new dance practices initiated in this period provided women with leadership roles as choreographers, producers, and trainers of other dancers, roles traditionally occupied by men in two other contemporary American dance genres: classical ballet and show or Broadway dancing. Since the 1860s, these genres had typically confined women's employment opportunities to performance. Although women could and did make substantive and even international careers for themselves, rising as lead dancers to the top of ballet and showgirl ranks, creative, directorial, and management roles in these enterprises were occupied primarily by men.

Such sexual division of labor in dance was the product of more than two centuries of change and development in European and American theatrical dance. And the nature of the division of labor was made manifest both in the forms of the dance itself and in institutional practices. Even before the end of the seventeenth century, "professionals" had begun to dance beside courtiers in ballets staged by and for the pleasure of Louis XIV's court. Professionals became increasingly distinguished from noble and middle-class amateurs in eighteenth-century France and England, and women, joining the ranks later than men, became equally well represented as professional dancers. The Baroque movement vocabulary and choreographies required almost identical skills from male and female performers alike. To be sure, men performed more complicated aerial beats of the legs and a greater number of turns than women in solo choreographies. This variation in step vocabulary is not a small difference, but choreographies for male-female couples demanded the same highly developed skills of movement articulation and rhythmic phrasing from both parties. The great number of extant choreographies notated between 1700 and 1730—more than 335 in all—are the work of male dancing masters. Dancing masters in the early eighteenth century both composed dances and trained students, working as private individuals or in royal and commercial theatres. At the Paris Opera or at London's Drury Lane Theatre and Lincoln's Inn Fields Theatre the posts for dance and music composition were filled by men. A rare exception, popular French dancer Marie Sallé enjoyed individual success not only as a performer but also as a choreographer of works that she danced. Other female professionals were unable to duplicate her achievement.

Late-eighteenth-century dance developments brought revision in the largely similar demands placed on male and female performers. Choreographers began to experiment with partnering, a technique in which one dancer renders physical support to another in the execution of a step or series of steps. A supporting dancer, for example, might lift a partner off the ground or provide a steadying hand for a long-held balance. At first performed by couples of men in character or grotesque scenarios, partnering techniques were carried further in Romantic ballet of the 1820s to the 1850s. Men began to support women in balances and multiple turns, and caught them in leaps. In addition, and for the first time, male dancers took a subordinate role to women, both numerically and as foci for thematic development in the dance work.

For choreographers as well as dancers, Paris was the leading center for European development of the Romantic ballet. The Paris Opera, newly divested of full royal support and forced to operate as a commercial undertaking, was under male direction. Most choreographers employed there were men. One exception occurred in the case of Fanny Elssler, a dancer the Opera management promoted as a rival to Marie Taglioni in order to stimulate box office revenues. Elssler's sister Thérèse is thought to have arranged individual *pas* for her more famous sibling. It was far more typical, however, for Jules Perrot to choreograph for his wife Carlotta Grisi, or for Marie Taglioni's father to compose his daughter's featured sequences.

In Czarist Russia at the end of the nineteenth century, male dancers returned in more equal numbers to the ballet stage, where they continued to be assigned the choreographic task of partnering women. In the later, as in the earlier, nineteenth century, ballet aesthetics shaped females as ethereal, otherworldly creatures, or as voluptuous seductresses from exotic climes. These latter female forms, however, were positioned as alien, orientalized others whose contrasting nature illuminated the chaste evanescence of the former. Men were figured as the stronger sex and as unalterably earthly figures. Choreographies thus lent plastic and thematic support to a nineteenth-century gender ideology that identified women as domestic, modest, and conciliating creatures while it characterized men as worldly, sexually charged, and aggressive competitors in work and public activity. Continuing the pattern of sex-specific employment largely unbroken since the seventeenth century, men filled the bulk of positions as choreographers, teachers, and administrators of theatrical institutions in the Imperial theatre system.

Stereotyping of female dancers was much the same in the vaudeville, music hall, and musical theatre productions of nineteenth-century Europe and America, where performers were often called "ballet girls." Display of the female body was a featured aspect in this genre. While Romantic ballets had certainly exposed the female form, costuming it in gauzy skirts and tight-fitting bodices, many choreographies had promulgated images of chasteness and veiled voluptuousness as well. Late-nineteenth-century American musical theatre productions capitalized on more straightforward display. In these musical theatre contexts women typically worked as performers, executing male theatrical creations and following male direction. English burlesque performer Lydia Thompson proved a very visible exception. She both directed and headlined her own troupe of "British blondes" in American tours during the late 1860s and 1870s, and members of her company tried to emulate her example. Following the Civil War, with the mobility offered by new railroad networks, American musical theatre production was increasingly controlled through syndicates like the Keith or RKO circuits, male enterprises again.[1]

Commencing at different times in the period from 1890 to 1910, emerging dance artists Isadora Duncan, Loie Fuller, and Ruth St. Denis had already begun to challenge such sex segregation of theatrical dance opportunity as they forged careers first as soloists and later as leaders of their own groups. Women constructed still other new practices as alternatives to contemporary ballet and show dancing, asserting the new meanings and forms which expressive dance could contribute to American life. These new practices included aesthetic, folk, and gymnastic dance, introduced in the curricula of settlement houses and in the after-school folk dancing offered to New York City schoolchildren. Conceived as "artistic"—as expressing aesthetic values—such dance activity offered women a purchase on shaping American community and polity, a process through which to constitute a new art form, and a means by which to define themselves as women.

By the 1930s, the new genre of modern dance emerged, built in important respects on the foundations erected in the Progressive era. This artistic dance practice continued to sustain women's roles as vital constitutors of dance practice. Martha Graham, Doris Humphrey, Helen Tamiris, and German émigré Hanya Holm created new movement vocabularies and repertoires of choreographies, trained legions of performers, and negotiated the difficult task of winning audiences. In the same era, women were predominant in fledgling workers' dance groups, whose history has only begun to be re-examined in the academy. Men were not excluded from modern dance, to be sure. Having broken with St. Denis in the 1920s, Ted Shawn in the 1930s directed and toured a company of men dancers. Charles Weidman worked as a choreographer in his own right and with Humphrey as co-director of their company. Erick Hawkins would join Graham's company as the first male member in 1938. Male students were represented among the participants at the Bennington Summer School of the Dance, the most prestigious summer workshop for modern dance in the 1930s. Seminal figures like Merce Cunningham, Paul Taylor, Alwin Nikolais, Daniel Nagrin, and José Limón are only the best-known male choreographers and dancers to establish careers as modern dancers in subsequent decades. But the predominance of women—numerically as choreographers, teachers, and performers, and substantively as shapers of the content and choreographic practices of modern dance—has gone unchanged into the 1990s.[2]

Women's constitution of themselves as creators in addition to executants (and employers as well as employees) and their construction of a new *kind* of dance practice in which to take charge, to take power, was clearly the start of something new in the Progressive era. Their predominance cannot be explained as a simple continuity with Euro-American ballet, vaudeville, or musical theatre dance. How did such predominance come to be? And to what effects did this predominance operate? This book poses and seeks to answer these questions at the site of intersection between two academic disciplines: dance studies and United States history. On one hand it brings historical methods and rigor to bear on dance studies, formulating new questions not traditionally posed by dance historians. On the other hand it brings dance to the attention of United States historians, arguing that they have much to gain from sustained consideration of dance, a cultural practice through which participants have kinetically constructed social, political, and gendered identities and ways of being in the world. It is as these two hands clasp each other, so to speak, as they interleave and finger each other's methodologies and concerns, that a fortified and nuanced dance history may be made, one that positions dance as a social and cultural process operating in the midst, and not at the margins, of American life — indeed, as American life.

What History Brings to Dance Studies

Studies of Euro-American dance's past, and dances past, have carried with them the burden of analyzing a process and entity that leaves few material traces of its primary characteristic — its motion. While biographical materials, costume and production materials, musical scores, and even photographs have provided one kind of access to dance not currently being performed, historians have grappled with the difficult project of imagining, reconstructing, or imaginatively reconstructing the dancing that took place as a kinetic phenomenon. The twentieth-century advent of film, video, and recently the more systematic use of dance notation systems has improved the situation. Now historians are able to study specific past instances of the kinetic phenomena of dancing, though not for every dance form nor abundantly for any single form. Given such problems of evidence as a condition of the field, it is perhaps not surprising that many scholarly accounts of dancing have focused intently on sustaining a record of evanescent dance practices, concentrating on the "internal history" of the art. Closely related to this focus has been the conceptualization of dance as an autonomous field, one which holds its questions and answers within itself, and for which a surround of "context" supplies a complementary, not fundamental, way of comprehending dance artists and activity. This point of view is imminently visible in canonical works of twentieth-century modern dance and ballet history alike. It partakes of a "modernist" view of art making articulated in the early decades of this century, and it has had the effect of positioning theatrical dance as "high art" and as a subject for rarefied tastes. It has also had the effect of marginalizing theatrical dance as a subject of academic inquiry, distancing dance from theorizations about how societies operate and change over time.

Social history perspectives in use since the 1960s offer a compelling alternative for framing and studying American dance in the early twentieth century. Put simply, social history methods direct historians to scrutiny of lived behaviors as indexes of people's identities, beliefs, and agencies. Applied in dance studies, analysis can be directed to dance as a field of activity and to its practitioners as a particularized cohort of people. This means that dance can be considered as a practice that marks, and is marked by, gender, race, age, class, and sexuality. And dance can be explored as a practice that develops varied forms for its own production or support, ranging from family organization to voluntary associations and professional academies. That is, dance too can be assessed in terms of the social categories that divided and united Americans, that provided nexuses of conflict and affiliation, innovation and conservation of tradition. That this capability is not alien to dance studies can be seen in the substantive attention that gender has recently garnered in dance analyses. Other categories and social positions offer equally potent access to comprehending dance, however. An example, developed at length in succeeding chapters, will be suggestive here. Focus on early-twentieth-century immigration flows into the urban center of New York City pinpoints the timing and causal factors involved in the introduction of European "folk dancing" in contemporary public school physical education curricula. Here dance is intimately implicated in the highly charged Progressive-era issues of assimilation and immigration restriction. Applying social history methods to dance analysis brings dance "in" from the margins of U.S. historical and critical inquiry and locates it among other social modalities through which people operated in American society.

Methods from cultural history have much to offer dance studies, as well. Cultural history analyses direct scholarly attention to "culture" as the ways and means by which people make meanings for and about themselves in society, with these ways and means ranging widely from the symbolic to the concrete, the semiotic to the structural. Certain cultural history analyses have turned an intense beam on the activity of art making itself, assessing the status attributed early in the twentieth century to art as the suprasocial product generated by a creative genius. The status of the art work, in other words, derived from the unique sensibility of the creator, and in this take on art making, the born genius was usually male. Cultural history analyses have rejected the universal claims of this theory of art making and the artist. They have historicized it instead as a strategy, forged from Romantic roots and wielded effectively in modernist art battles, particular to an era, to the goals and demands of a specific cultural group. Work like that of Griselda Pollock demonstrates cultural history efforts to think outside the modernist ideology of art making and to comprehend art making as a cultural practice. In this view, correct evaluation and consumption of aesthetic objects are discarded as goals of art historical scholarship. They are replaced with at least two drives: investigation of art as a process for making meanings (and of the conditions which make possible this process, this practice); and assessment of the meanings that particular practices are making, of how the meanings are being made, and of those for whom meanings are made.[3]

Applied to dance studies, such cultural history methods promote consideration of dance as practice that makes social and cultural meanings as it "makes" and remakes itself, changing over time. Dance creators and creations can be understood as unavoidably taking part in contests over the construction of gender and race, conflicts among classes and age-groups, struggles between political theories and regimes—meaning-making systems all. Here dance studies are impelled to test assumptions about individual creative genius as the motor force in dance innovation. To view the activity of dance as a cultural practice encourages dance historians to frame their analyses as at least three-way intersections among the ongoing practice itself; the individual biographies of practitioners and innovators; and the complex of social, political, and economic struggles to make meaning and wield power at particular historical moments. The danced works—the meanings made through dance representations—can be assessed in the same way. This kind of triangulated approach lends the classic task of historical analysis—study of change over time—new and newly enriched materials with which to theorize causation in dance history.

Social history methods and cultural history methods alike provide means and models for dance studies to apply in scrutinizing the discipline's own practice and in framing new analyses. The first of these forays is just as important as the last. As dance studies claims a central rather than marginal place in humanities and interdisciplinary scholarship, it must study itself, take a historiographical view of past writing of its own history. By recognizing and reflecting on the character of its previous analytical models, dance studies can more self-consciously estimate the relationship between the meanings it makes for dance and the questions it frames to guide inquiry.

How Dance Studies May Inform History Writing

Dance has not gone without mention in studies of U.S. history. When Morton White formulated the notion of a "revolt against formalism" to describe Progressive-era America, he advanced a rubric that was capable of embracing the innovations of Isadora Duncan, a rebel and come-outer beyond question. Yet the same rubric provided little incentive to extend consideration to Duncan's peers Ruth St. Denis and Loie Fuller, nor to the legions of showgirls peopling musical theatre and Follies stages in the first several decades of the century. Nor have characterizations and investigations of other periods lent themselves easily, or at all, to dance practices. Rhys Isaac, for example, shrewdly comprehended that something was afoot in pre-Revolutionary Virginia dance practice, and he asserted that some significance must lie in the social recurrence of "jigging." Yet Isaac proved largely unable to theorize that significance. Studies of still another area of American life—eighteenth- and nineteenth-century slave culture—have consistently acknowledged the importance of singing and dancing within the slave quarters, but no systematic inquiry of the phenomenon has been undertaken. Dance has been alternately a neglected and an elusive subject for American history analysis.[4]

Yet a dance focus can bring much to the study of American history, and for no period more so than the Progressive era. Focus on and through dance can illuminate the Progressive era, a time notoriously resistant to historiographical interpretation. To deal with dance is to take as fundamental, to acknowledge as substantive, the enormous interest and energy Americans focused on the body in the years 1890 to 1920. To proceed from a dance focus (to pursue dance as part of the period's meaning-making practices) is thus to see a new linkage among disparate developments in Progressive-era labor activism, immigration flows, domestic architecture, and women's legal rights. For all of these developments involve statements about the body. They constitute attempts to capture the body; to make the body stable for a moment; to address its (knowable) needs; to impose disciplines upon it or mitigate their force.

These insights are worth tracing out briefly here. The struggle for women's protective labor legislation, for example, culminated in the 1908 *Muller v. Oregon* decision, which successfully argued for limiting the length of women's (but not men's) workday. The grounds for the argument were that too long a workday threatened women's reproductive capacities. Hence, the case for workday limitation was successfully argued on the basis of gender and women's bodily needs, where previously it had made little headway when argued in terms of working people's needs as a group—that is, on the basis of class.

New strategies for domestic architecture can also be seen as turning on Progressive-era concern with bodies. Tenement construction in cities like New York swelled to accommodate the influxes of immigrant peoples, and tenement reform drives took as points of departure the sanitation and health of human bodies inhabiting these structures. Here a public health conception of the body turned the wheels of housing reform. The dangers of disease that crowded tenement bodies posed to the bodies at large in the city prompted code writing and regulation at the metropolitan level.

Period struggles over married women's property laws, and also change in divorce proceedings and possibilities, hinged on questions of men's legal possession of women's bodies and properties. And contemporary birth control advocacy provoked questions about women's control of their own reproductive bodies.

The list of Progressive-era body politics is long. What consideration of dance brings to history writing, then, is the cry to recognize bodies as powerful sites for social and political contestation. This consideration of dance equips historians to recognize an expanded repertoire of ways in which people produced meanings in and representations about their lives. It seriously challenges our understanding of arenas in which people contested social categories and struggled for agency, as individuals and within institutions. To study dance is to illuminate conceptions of the body politic as these were put into motion, into play, by particular bodies embodying and bodying forth constructions and protests, changes and continuities in social and political ways of being in the world, United States style. And it aids historians in asking why some modes of meaning-making, and not others, proved crucial at certain times and not others.

The analytical findings generated by dance studies will of course vary with the period being examined. But for studies of the Progressive era, to study dance will point to dance's salience for constructing gender and for worrying issues of immigration, ethnicity, and national identity in the years

1890 to 1920. Scrutiny of dance will point to the constitution of "culture" as a site of contest between men and women. Focus on dance will illuminate the changing and unstable identities of "dance" itself as it serves differing class and ethnicity and aesthetic projects, as it pours forth in what early-twentieth-century people called "a renaissance of dancing."

dancing Class

One Bodies and Dances in Progressive-era America

If dance practices have seldom figured in historical studies of the Progressive era, turn-of-the-century America has itself eluded easy generalization or theoretical condensation. The period was one of unremitting change: few things seemed to be stable; many were in flux. At this conjuncture, human bodies offered potent sites for figuring identities and configuring social relations in the United States.[1]

By the 1890s, accelerating changes in the organization of American economic life were altering the nature of work, the identity of workers, and the spheres in which producers and products circulated. Industrialization had proceeded unevenly, at different paces in different businesses and regions throughout the nineteenth century; now it also comprised the implementation of mass production technologies and the growth of large integrated corporations. Beer, beef, and steel were but three items manufactured by these new means. Their production processes were rationalized and broken into component parts, workers repetitively executed one or only a few parts of the fabrication cycle, and speed in execution of less skilled labor replaced previous emphases on special skills and trained workers. Manufacturing processes were carefully plotted by a new corps of managers, who sought through vertical integration to amass the resources needed for production at one end of the process, and to direct the marketing of the final product at the other. This managerial corps itself offered new job opportunities to middle-class workers in the paid labor force. It also spawned a rapidly growing clerical sector which proved to be a significant employer of female labor.[2]

New technologies of production in turn created demands for labor that were met by wide-open immigration flows into the United States. Turn-of-the-century immigrants were different, however, from people who arrived on American shores earlier in the nineteenth century. Those people had hailed predominantly from western and northern Europe, including the Irish from the 1840s on, and the Germans at midcentury. The new immigrants traveling to East Coast ports of entry came from central and eastern Europe; Chinese and Japanese immigrants entered western ports with the advent of mineral strikes and railroad construction. The new immigrants, in short, looked visibly different from their predecessors. Their number and concentration in urban centers meant that, in 1900, immigrants or children of immigrants constituted two-thirds of the population in cities like Chicago and New York.[3]

Demographics changed in another way as more and more Americans took up residence in expanding urban areas. By 1920, more than half of Americans would live in cities; the rural-to-urban transition was well underway in the Progressive era. At the same time, American farmers found themselves competing for the first time in an international agricultural market, as other countries bid to supply the demand for grains and beef that the United States had successfully targeted. Prices and production of farm crops fluctuated correspondingly and in relation to variables operating at a greater distance from the American scene.[4]

In all, the pace of industrialization, immigration, urbanization, and the shifting contours of rural production meant that children born in 1890 would experience work and social realities indelibly different from those known to their parents. As social and economic pressures changed the pattern of everyday life, native-born and immigrant Americans alike faced the challenge of constituting their identities. Many traditional patterns had to be rethought or adjusted; new circumstances had to be comprehended as well. The values and hierarchies that had guided past activities no longer offered people sole, or infallible, frameworks for operating in the present.

How should these changing circumstances be met? Who could or would direct the responses to them? These questions demanded answers because contemporary political and electoral responses seemed to constitute part of the problem. Indeed, sentiment was strong in several quarters that, little more than a century after the republic's founding, governmental response to the popular will had become distorted. Through contributions to political campaigns, corporations and business interests wielded considerable influence on members of the Senate and the state legislatures which elected them. Cities teeming with newcomers positioned political "bosses" to mediate the needs of immigrants in exchange for their support of "machine" politics; meanwhile urban problems of sanitation, disease control, and food quality received inadequate attention. Thus Progressive-era politics were marked by vigorous and successful campaigns to inaugurate direct election of senators, and initiative, referendum, and recall mechanisms. City manager structures and municipal ownership of utilities were introduced in a number of areas as well, and communities increasingly had recourse to nonelective "commissions" of experts to address pressing public problems. Political corrections and adjustment through bureaucratic management techniques had limits, to be sure. In the South, for example, disfranchisement of black male voters proceeded apace in the aftermath of Reconstruction. Quotidian segregation and a surge of lynchings was consolidating the subordinate position of blacks in all their contacts with whites. And although women in some states enjoyed restricted rights to vote in school or municipal elections, suffrage was denied to women as a group until 1919.

Not just the government's responsiveness to citizens, but also the extent and character of its intervention in the economic realm were debated with new heat beginning in the 1890s. The Populist movement, for example, sought to involve the government more deeply in tempering unstable circumstances that beset farmers and agricultural production. Populists ran a third-party campaign in the 1892 national election and supported the Democratic nominee William Jennings Bryan in 1896. Among its demands, the Populist movement urged government sponsorship of "free silver," an inflationary measure that favored debtor farmers. It also called for government ownership and operation of railroads (since access to and pricing of transportation critically affected movement of agricultural products to market), and formation of "subtreasuries," or means for storing grains and offsetting annual product price fluctuations. The Populists failed to achieve these and other demands, which constituted unprecedented bids for government involvement in the economy at a time of pro-business, hands-off Republican party domination of federal politics. Only with time would features of the Populist platform be incorporated by mainstream political parties. Government regulatory intervention did increase in other areas, however, such as certification of food quality (Pure Food and Drug Act) and conservation of public lands. By the end of the period, too, the nature of Americans' participation in the political process had changed. Party loyalties weakened, and voting began a long-term decline, even though women achieved the vote in 1919. And pressure groups assumed increasing importance as channels for affecting government policies.[5]

For people living between 1890 and 1920, the period this study takes to be the Progressive era, the challenge was not simply to correct governmental abuses nor to reinvigorate old mechanisms.[6] To deal with changed and changing circumstances of economic and social relations, people had to reassess the bounds and possibilities of those networks, and their own place within them. Where once local communities had afforded people necessary and adequate venues for their social, political, and work lives, shifts toward national and international organization in business and agriculture meant that older hierarchies of power and privilege did not obtain, previous frameworks of meaning did not suffice. People had to readjust their sense of self, community, and nation; they had to comprehend each other as parts of a changed whole. Indeed, historians have theorized the concepts of status anxiety and a search for order to explain the behavior of various groups of people in the Progressive era. The very terms in which these theories are framed confirm our awareness that identity formation was at stake in a fundamental way at the turn of the century.[7]

Studies of "commodity capitalism" and a burgeoning Progressive-era "culture of consumption" confirm that the push and pull of identity formation operated in many registers. William Leach has argued, for example, that department stores promoted female shoppers' imaginative reconstitution of themselves. These emporia textured the shopping experience with sensuous new applications of light, color, and glass technologies. Introducing novel forms of service, stores endeavored to shape consumption as a comfortable and leisurely rather than a wearying activity. Staging brightly dressed show windows on the exterior, and festive atmospheres on the interior, department stores offered their predominantly female shoppers a potent sense of possibility. That is, department store contexts positioned women to imagine themselves in new ways, by virtue of their contact with arrays of goods not previously accessible or perhaps even envisioned. Driven by advertising, this culture of consumption countered older ways of being that operated in a noncredit world, ways that stressed frugality, scarcity, and the practical value of objects and purchases.[8]

As with studies of consumption, scrutiny of women's organizational activities has demonstrated that gender constituted a primary field or locus for identity contest and formation in the Progressive era. A "separate spheres" ideology crested in the United States as the nineteenth century drew to a close. This ideology assigned men and women different gender identities on the basis of physiological differences between the sexes, allocating the private world of domesticity and piety to women, the public world of work and politics to men.[9] To be sure, this ideology conflicted with the lived experiences of working class people, immigrants, and people of color. Within these groups, women and adolescents participated along with men in the paid labor force to help sustain family survival. At the same time, organized voluntary activity by middle- and upper-class women pressed at the limits of the gendered division of social space articulated by separate spheres norms. They justified their public sphere incursions with claims of protecting the home, of guarding vulnerable women, children, and families from behaviors and practices that threatened them. These women took collective action to urge moral reform, secure temperance, and provide charity to poor and unemployed people. They founded a number of settlement houses, and staffed others, to interact with new immigrants in their dense and congested neighborhoods and to lobby for municipal remediation of poor conditions.[10]

Women also organized to secure suffrage. As historians have recently recognized, suffrage marches and outdoor meetings made explicit the link between the political and the expressive in the Progressive-era politics of gender. These strategies put women's gendered bodies on the line as they claimed the right to electoral participation. Closely related to this, women's labor uprisings also plied the body to demand changed conditions in industrial work. In 1909, for instance, female makers of ladies shirtwaists walked picket lines on New York's Lower East Side in a strike against garment factories for better wages, shorter hours, improved shop-floor conditions, and union representation. Women workers suffered verbal abuse by police and hired hecklers; they were arrested and jailed as well. Susan Glenn argues persuasively that these demonstrators claimed a dignity and identity as women workers that differed from conceptions their bosses entertained. What is equally salient is that women pressed these claims through bodily perseverance, during bitterly cold winter months, and marshaled physical resources to meet and march, to argue a distinctive identity.[11]

Studies of gender have prepared us, I maintain, to now consider the importance of the body as a ground for the reworking(s) of identity that proved so central to the Progressive era. The gender roles constructed by

Women from Massachusetts and other states marching in the "Great Women's Suffrage Parade" in New York City, 1912. THE SCHLESINGER LIBRARY, RADCLIFFE COLLEGE.

separate spheres ideology were rooted in the physical differences between men's and women's bodies. In the New York City garment industry, allocation of job categories to men and women were frequently linked to physical attributes presumed unique to one gender, such as strength for men and dexterity for women. Support for women's protective labor legislation also drew on conceptions of women's special nature and physical needs. Louis Brandeis's brief for the 1908 *Muller v. Oregon* case justified "hours" legislation by arguing that long working hours posed potential harm to women's childbearing capabilities. In both these instances, the body or its biological determinants supplied a basis for conceiving workplace identities, that is, for formulating gendered constructions of labor and its limits in a rapidly industrializing society. Conversely, techniques of subdivided labor, deskilling, and, subsequently, promotion of "efficiency" inscribed workers' bodies, male and female, with shifting notions about class relations and the limits of worker agency and autonomy. Gender fused with race in still another body discipline, one imposed with fresh vigor in the early-twentieth-century South. There, Jim Crow politics wrote on black male bodies with the physical instrument of lynching. While disfranchisement secured voting as a white male domain, lynching gave palpable expression to modes of subordination, difference, and sexual stereotyping—race identity—that whites were constructing for black males.[12]

The body was clearly linked to issues of gender and sexuality for Progressive-era people. Consideration of the body as a site for identity formation can help us see as connected such disparate factors and fields as labor protests and women's suffrage strategies, theatricalized consumer culture and innovative dance practices, evolution theory and a burgeoning physical culture movement. Further, focus on the body can help us situate the flourishing of dance interest and dance practices in the first decades of the century. At that time, people, and women in particular, forged ways of comprehending their changing experiences through a variety of danced embodiments.

Body Issues/Building Bodies

What were the bodies like that new movement practices put so thoroughly into motion? They were constructed in important ways through a discourse of nature, or evolutionary development, that achieved prominence at the end of the nineteenth century. When Darwinian theory reached the United States, it fell on ground that had been prepared by the earlier circulation of Herbert Spencer's writings. Darwin's work on evolution theorized the human body as a wholly natural entity, its development governed completely by biological processes. Supporters and opponents of evolution theory argued furiously, seeking to sustain or qualify this view and the implications for political and social policy that flowed from it. Arguments on all sides, however, had to deal in some way with an emphasis on the primacy of the natural world over the cultural or social. It was the materiality of human bodies that commanded increased scrutiny and recognition during the Progressive era.[13]

LABORING BODIES

As contemporary commentators were quick to note, material bodies were imprinted by the sweated character of industrial labor and the cramped conditions of urban living. Industry, in its steady pursuit of rationalization, reshaped the physical circumstances of work to narrow and intensify the repertoire of body skills a laborer performed. Upton Sinclair's fictional *The Jungle* vividly renders the subdivision and speedup of labor that characterized mass production industries in 1905. Newly hired by a packing house, the immigrant Lithuanian Jurgis observes men at work in the killing beds:

> The manner in which they did this was something to be seen and never forgotten. They worked with furious intensity, literally upon the run — at a pace with which there is nothing to be compared except a football game. It was all highly specialized labor, each man having his task to do; generally this would consist of only two or three specific cuts, and he would pass down the line of fifteen or twenty carcasses, making these cuts upon each.

After the carcasses bled, they moved down the line

> and there came the "headsman," whose task was to sever the head, with two or three swift strokes. Then came the "floorsman," to make the first cut in the skin; and then another to finish ripping the skin down the center; and then half a dozen more in swift succession, to finish skinning.[14]

Making a limited range of motions, and laboring at top speed with few breaks during ten-hour workdays, workers in this industry were routinized and pushed to the limits of their endurance. Garment work was no less arduous even though many workers labored while seated. Here too, production processes were fragmented into small, repetitive tasks: workers stitched seams or made buttonholes, ran lace or set sleeves. And they worked bent over sewing machines, tables, or goods held in their laps. Often crowded tightly together, with machines sounding in their ears, these bodies were shaped to routine, to sameness and circumscription.[15]

URBAN BODIES

Working-class and immigrant groups were particularly at risk of imprinting by labor processes. Urban living conditions for these groups further exacted a toll, on children as well as adults. In the late 1890s, immigrant flows and expanding industrial labor left cities like Chicago and New York congested with swelling populations. In working-class quarters particularly, tenement housing provided little light or air. Families of six and more people frequently lived squeezed into a single room; use of space and motion through it were correspondingly cramped. Neither dwellings nor public schools

Milliners working on a balcony above the store. Photograph by Lewis W. Hine. LEWIS W. HINE COLLECTION, UNITED STATES HISTORY, LOCAL HISTORY AND GENEALOGY DIVISION, THE NEW YORK PUBLIC LIBRARY, ASTOR, LENOX AND TILDEN FOUNDATIONS.

Children dancing to music of a hurdy-gurdy, Thompson and Third Streets, New York City. KEYSTONE-MAST COLLECTION (X104080), UCR/CALIFORNIA MUSEUM OF PHOTOGRAPHY, UNIVERSITY OF CALIFORNIA, RIVERSIDE.

provided adequate resources for children's play and bodily development. Row house blocks in working-class neighborhoods afforded few internal play areas. Streets in these neighborhoods doubled as commercial space for vendors and as clogged, dusty thoroughfares for horses, carts, trolleys, and pedestrians. When not impossible, it was seldom safe for children to run freely or collect for group games on these streets. Both domestic and public domains, then, curbed and blunted negotiations of space.[16]

City schools were similarly hard put to meet the demands of their bulging enrollments. The design of schoolroom desks, plus classroom protocols that bound children to their desks for five hours a day, made for postural habits that physical training reformers decried. Desks and behavior protocols, they argued further, produced imbalance in paired muscle groups and poor development of internal organs. Schools had for some time mounted physical training programs, but this body work frequently had to be conducted in the aisle space of classrooms. Gymnasiums were not universally available as school facilities; sometimes paved rooftop playgrounds provided the only significant open space available for children's play.[17]

Educators and physical training innovators protested these body-hedging circumstances. They were joined by several contemporary reform groups that aimed to right the inadequate distribution of fundamental urban resources. Felix Adler and Lawrence Veiller led New York City campaigns to protest tenement building design and construction. They recommended models which promised greater access for each dwelling unit to sunlight, moving air, and sanitation facilities. Also in New York City, the Outdoor Recreation League mobilized to claim park space located squarely within densely populated neighborhoods in the city's several boroughs. It insisted upon spaces that permitted users to walk and play on the grass, not simply skirt it in defined paths. Settlement houses like the Henry Street Settlement in New York and Hull-House in Chicago built gymnasiums for recreation by users of all ages. They also established children's clubs and provided meeting rooms for their activities. At the national level, educators, reformers, and new physical training professionals joined in founding the Playground Association of America, aiming to supply and expand public resources for directed recreation activities. These housing, park, and recreation initiatives may be seen as efforts to unbridle working-class bodies, to offset (though not finally remove or restructure) the compacting, containing, and routinizing effects on bodies of labor and life in urban industrial cities.[18]

PHYSICAL CULTURE BODIES

A variety of physical culture systems already in play in the late nineteenth century also constructed American bodies. If the body-blighting effects of labor processes and urban living only slowly won recognition and calls for recuperation, systems of bodily exercise took as a postbellum given that American bodies needed assiduous cultivation.[19]

Physical training systems were developed and utilized in several domains of American life, including ethnic communities, commercial gymnasiums, public schools, domestic or social gatherings for middle-class enthusiasts, colleges, and normal schools. And they shaped at least four distinctive types of bodies in the latter half of the nineteenth century. What might be called "extensive" bodies were shaped by a physical training system that German émigrés brought to America in the 1820s. Based on the work of Ludwig Jahn, this physical training had been implicated in construction of the new sense of German nationalism and nationalist German bodies in the years immediately following Napoleon's defeat at the Battle of Leipzig. In the United States, the Jahn system came to be widely practiced around midcentury in *turnvereine*, associations that provided German immigrants with mutual assistance services, social and intellectual networks, and recreation facilities. German physical culture thus actively buttressed ethnic identity in America, especially in the Midwest. Awareness and practice of the German system subsequently reached beyond the borders of *turnvereine* contexts, informing through several kinds of physical activity the construction of what may be called "extensive" bodies.[20]

EXTENSIVE BODIES

The German system placed heavy emphasis on apparatus work. Men, women, and children exercised using specialized equipment like the vaulting horse, rings, horizontal bar, parallel bars, vaulting pole, ladders, and stairs. People used such apparatuses as stationary bases for building muscular strength and projecting—extending and propelling—their bodies into space, radiating centrifugally from points of attachment to apparatuses. Gymnasiums typically housed numerous apparatuses in a common space, which allowed for communal use. Nonetheless, the fundamental relationship constituted during equipment use was the human-apparatus dyad.[21]

The German system also called for calisthenic exercises (frequently performed with weights), which embraced the swinging of Indian clubs (bowling pin–shaped objects) when these gained popularity in the 1860s. These sorts of exercise quite possibly required practitioners to stand in orderly rows and attempt unison execution. Equally as important as apparatus work were games and the large motor activities of wrestling, running, jumping, fencing, marching, rope jumping, hopping, and stair and ladder climbing. These activities, easily framed as competitions, also launched bodies into and through space. They challenged endurance, strength, and quickness as well as skill, attention, and alertness. In these several ways, then, the Jahn-based German system produced "extensive" bodies. It cultivated the strength and specific skills that enabled bodies to lengthen out in space, stretch away from the trunk's core toward their periphery, yet remain securely linked to their originating launch points. It also promoted external focus and linkages among practitioners. While calisthenics practice probably treated bodies as singular units, featured apparatus work equipped bodies to connect with feat-facilitating devices. The system's emphasis on games and locomotor action certainly directed bodily attention outward toward others in the group, at times sustaining friendly competitions.

POISED BODIES

The German-derived production of "extensive" bodies differed in several respects from the construction of "poised" bodies effected by the Dio Lewis and the Swedish (Ling) gymnastic systems. A lecturer on health and temperance as well as a deviser of gymnastic exercises, Lewis styled himself a medical doctor although he possessed no professional credential. In the 1860s he aimed his gymnastics system at family users, published books to spread his views, and operated normal schools for teachers of physical training. Historian Harvey Green has pointed to the lean, only slightly muscled physique of male exercisers as the ideal developed by systems like Lewis's in the postbellum era. Anterior to this body image, I suggest, and pertinent to exercise performed by either sex, is the production of self-contained, alert bodies poised to move in any direction required, at a moment's notice. Thus, Lewis system classes proceeded by placing individual exercisers at carefully spaced intervals in orderly rows, each person working as an autonomous individual, everyone performing the same tasks simultaneously.[22]

Lewis eschewed the fixed apparatuses of the German system and added or adapted lightweight, handheld, specially designed apparatuses to calisthenic work. For stretching exercises, class work replaced heavier iron

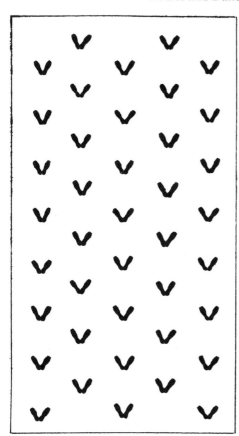

Dio Lewis recommended marking gymnasium floors in this way to ensure appropriate spacing among students during exercises, and also correct placement of the feet. FROM *THE NEW GYMNASTICS FOR MEN, WOMEN, AND CHILDREN* (BOSTON: TICKNOR AND FIELDS, 1862).

dumbbells with lighter wood models. Exercises for hand-eye coordination replaced weightier rubber balls with beanbags tossed from hand to hand. Lightweight wooden wands were also used for joint articulation and stretching exercises. Like the beanbags, they caused gymnasts to negotiate space to the sides and back as well as the front of the body. Instead of the muscular strength and special skills developed by the German system, the Lewis system promoted suppleness and quick reflexes. Performed to music, Lewis calisthenics radiated the limbs away from the body's center but then returned them as well; limbs not only extended in space but also orbited the trunk. While these pinlike bodies traversed little ground at all during

Figure 21. Figure 22.

Figure 23.

Figure 4.

Illustrations for Dio Lewis
exercises showed both women
and men using dumbbells, but
only men using Indian Clubs.
FROM *THE NEW GYMNASTICS
FOR MEN, WOMEN, AND
CHILDREN* (BOSTON: TICKNOR
AND FIELDS, 1862).

Figure 5. Figure 6.

calisthenics, organized games required running and object transfer, foster-
ing fleetness and dexterity in the process. The Lewis system, then, cultivated bodies poised for mobilization, nerves prepared for quick changes,
muscles geared to agility and adeptness.

While the German system only gradually diffused outward from the
turnvereine, Lewis's system enjoyed a vogue in the 1860s. His death in the
1870s opened the door to a resurgence of the German system, again
especially in the Midwest. It also left room for Swedish gymnastics, based
on the work of Per Hendrik Ling and, subsequently, his son Hjalamar
Frederick Ling. Their work was popularized in the United States by Hart-
vig Nissen and Baron Nils Posse; Claus Enebuske published one of the
son's texts in the U.S. in the 1890s. The Swedish system, too, cultivated
"poised" bodies, if anything heightening the preparation of autonomous
bodies finely tuned to receive and respond to external direction. In contrast
to both the Lewis and the German systems, the Swedish system made no
use of music. Teachers put students through their paces by voicing sharp
commands, the cast of which struck many at the time as militaristic.
Directed calisthenics constituted the primary emphasis, with lighter and
less frequent apparatus use than Lewis had employed. The Swedish system
also made some use of gymnastic dancing, which combined ballet stances
and limb positions with calisthenics. As with the Lewis system, the Swedish
method positioned exercisers as single operators, working as fundamentally isolated individuals despite the concurrent focus of classmates intent
upon accomplishing the same goals.[23]

Common to these systems, and perhaps unremarkable to late-twentieth-
century eyes, was acceptance of special, loose-fitting dress for gymnastic
exercise. While men certainly benefited as well, women in particular were
released from corsets laced to attain several distinctive silhouettes during
the nineteenth century. Middle- and upper-class women from the 1830s
through the 1850s tightly laced their corsets to achieve a slender, wasp-
waisted figure. Corset lacings that superseded this fashion, according to
historian Lois Banner, produced "voluptuous women," whose curvy, ample
bosom balanced their hefty, well-rounded hips. The "Grecian bend" silhouette, imitated at one point by voluptuous women, bunched and distrib-
uted these body parts in the sagittal plane, reinforcing the image of ripe
pressure exerted against the constraining container of clothing. With its
absence of stays and more generous cut, gymnastic dress for women promoted full inspiration of the lungs and an enlarged range of movement
through the torso and arms. Gymnastic dress also sported shortened skirts,
few (if any) petticoats, and flat or low-heeled shoes, amplifying the ease and

range of movement in the hips and legs as well. These modifications in exercise dress helped to inject mobility into, and to increase the internal volume of, bodies constructed by the German, Lewis, and Swedish systems.[24]

These systems also shared a unitary conception of the bodies they built. That is, within these systems, exercises and movement goals were directed to gender groups and age-groups without making distinctions *among* members of those groups. A short, fat twenty-year-old, for example, would perform the same Swedish calisthenics that her taller, thinner neighbor executed standing alongside her in a class of thirty other women. The same situation would have obtained in a Lewis or German system calisthenic class; none of them attended to differences among class members in conditioning, body proportions, and individual movement characteristics. What of apparatus work in the German system? It is quite possible that vaults of different heights were used for children and adults, and that rings and parallel bars were adjusted for clusters of males and females as well as for age-groups. What is not clear is whether vaults and rings and horizontal beams were adjusted to individual users. In the main, then, these systems pursued cultivation of bodies that, delimited by age or gender, were treated as largely similar in kind.

WELL-ROUNDED BODIES

Adaptation to individual users was the hallmark of an "American" system devised by Dudley Sargent. Because Sargent sought to fit exercise programs to the needs and features of particular bodies, the system does not readily lend itself to "typing" or specifying a characteristic cultivated body. Trained as a medical doctor and experienced in directing commercial and university gymnasiums, Sargent developed an "anthropometric" approach to the physical training work he directed at the all-male Harvard University beginning in 1879. Each college student presenting himself for voluntary physical training received measurement and diagnosis of his individual strengths and weaknesses, body proportions, general health, and "inherited" tendencies. Sargent then devised a program of "developing" work tailored to capitalize upon or remedy specific features of the student's physical person. Sargent was eclectic and fashioned individual regimens from a wide array of apparatuses and exercise materials then available. He adapted and invented new equipment as well, in response to the needs of his students. Students returned three and six months later for follow-up diagnoses. They were re-examined and re-measured, changes in their body dimensions and physical capacities were carefully noted, and prescription was made for continued work. While the Sargent method produced no single characteristic body type, it may also be understood as endeavoring to shape "well-rounded bodies." Put differently, the Sargent system aimed to heighten and balance capabilities inhering in individual bodies, capabilities as they were articulated in the physical training domain and at the same time differentiated from exhibition-oriented body work and new commercial and collegiate sports. Thus, Sargent-trained bodies comported with the period's physical culture ideal of a toned but not bulky look. They competently managed muscled "extension" in space but eschewed strongman weight lifting. They also achieved a measure of "poised," flexible alertness, yet stopped short of the hair-trigger responsiveness that contemporary track athletes pursued.[25]

Sargent's individuated construction of bodies was entirely consistent with emphases on individual agency and entrepreneurship that permeated conceptions of maleness and economic striving in nineteenth-century America. And, as an "American" system, Sargent's work signaled the advent of new disciplinary, and newly nationalistic, concern for physical training as a professional domain in the United States. Sargent himself had inaugurated a normal school for female teachers in Cambridge in 1881, and the Harvard Summer School for Physical Education, which he launched in 1887, trained both male and female teachers. Dio Lewis before him conducted a normal school for women from 1864 to 1867; this was in addition to another normal school, enrolling both sexes, that he operated for about a decade beginning in 1861. The North American Gymnastic Union, established in 1866 and relocated several times, provided staff for the German community *turnvereine,* as did the YMCA College established in 1886 in Springfield, Massachusetts, for its associations. With backing by Mary Hemenway, Amy Morris Homans founded the Boston Normal School of Gymnastics in 1889 to train (mostly female) teachers in the Swedish system.[26]

This flush of normal schools, first in the 1860s and especially in the 1880s, channeled teachers to several kinds of outlets. Instructors in the German system found employment in ethnic communities, and YMCA teachers flowed to urban venues specific to the Y network. Teachers in either of these systems could also find employment in "unaffiliated" commercial gymnasiums that sprang up in cities beginning in the 1860s. Teachers prepared by the Lewis, Sargent, Homans, and Harvard Summer School normal programs created the supply that met a swelling demand for systematic public school physical training work. This demand surged in the late 1880s as demographic pressures mounted on city school systems.

These were the same years in which the Swedish system gained a foothold in the United States, confronting school administrators, reformers, and the career-minded physical training professionals with the need to make hard choices among several tenable systems. Reform leader Hemenway and normal school director Homans brought this issue to a head in 1889 by initiating a Boston conference on physical training. Chaired by the U.S. Commissioner of Education William T. Harris, the conference drew together advocates of the Swedish, German, Sargent, and gestating "American" systems of gymnastics in an effort to determine which system should be approved for use in the Boston public schools. Perhaps not surprisingly, given the allegiance of Homans and Hemenway, the Boston schools subsequently implemented the Swedish system. But the question was hardly resolved on a national basis, and the conference appointed a commission to continue studying and to make recommendations at some future date. The next three decades would witness substantive shift and experiment as professionals in physical training—now called physical education—tested and weighed the "bodies" and ideologies that flowed from practices like team sports, folk dancing, walking clubs, and even aesthetic dancing.[27]

RELAXED HARMONIOUS BODIES

A fourth example of systematic bodily cultivation helps illuminate the class and ethnic distinctions that permeated physical culture systems. Producing a "relaxed and harmonious" body, an Americanized Delsarte system took its underpinnings from the voice culture work of Frenchman François Delsarte. American theatre innovator Steele MacKaye incorporated aspects of Delsarte's teaching into "harmonic gymnastics," the system he developed for training actors. Genevieve Stebbins, actress and onetime collaborator with MacKaye, made a career in the 1880s of developing and promoting Delsarte-derived materials as a system of physical culture particularly suited to women. Stebbins limned the approach in her 1885 *Delsarte System of Expression*, a copiously illustrated manual reprinted six times by 1902. The system required no apparatus or handheld equipment and was capable of presentation wherever free space was available. Its exercises promoted three fundamental activities: decomposing, or learning how to relax; establishing poise, or learning how to achieve easy equilibrium and readiness to move; and energizing, or learning to efficiently mobilize for action. As historian Nancy Ruyter has shown, deep breathing was fundamental to Delsarte movement. Students also learned to use oppositional movement, to trace spiral patterns with body gestures, and to perform successional movement.[28]

Stebbins essentially equipped what may be called "relaxed and harmonious" bodies to modulate the energy required for any desired action, and to perform it in kinesiologically economical ways. The *Delsarte System of Expression* asserts that she was familiar with the Swedish Ling system as well as yoga breathing exercises; Ruyter suggests that she also drew on numerous other sources in elaborating the Delsarte system. In its emphasis on poise and relaxation, Stebbins's Delsarte system implicitly critiques several features of the Swedish system in particular. While both systems advocated poise in the form of readiness to move, Swedish executants focused their attention on receiving sharp, urgent commands. With poise formulated as "equilibrium," the Delsarte mover remained as ready for stasis as for motion. When moving, the latter also aimed to selectively contract the necessary muscles and to invoke specific quantities of desired energy, efficiently leaving other muscles and energies relaxed and untapped. This, too, contrasted with the angular or jerky movements attributed to Swedish system movers. Delsarte work, we might say, attuned bodies to their kinetic potentials, laying out a continuum but, in contrast to the Swedish system, privileging no vector or direction on that continuum.

That Delsarte physical culture offered instruction in graceful methods for reclining and prostrating oneself (or in popularized derivatives—fainting) may give late-twentieth-century readers cause for amusement.[29] But while this management of the body's ultimate enervation is quite consistent with the Delsarte interest in relaxation, the technique of fainting also signals the gendered and middle/upper-class orientation of the system. Gymnastic systems were introduced in Progressive-era schools to combat the enervating effects of industrial and urban living felt by boys and girls alike. These children were likely, however, to be sons and daughters of immigrants or poor parents, living in crowded working-class neighborhoods. *Turnvereine* members most certainly included middle-class exercisers, a group also specified by its ethnic identification. Male clients who patronized commercial gymnasiums were typically working-class men, while college and university physical training enthusiasts belonged to upper-middle-class and elite families. It was the mastering, mobilizing, empowering features of physical culture systems that would equip members in all these groups to compete in nineteenth-century American laissez-faire economic arenas and ethnically stratified political and cultural networks. The steady-state, if not sanguine, readiness inculcated by the Delsarte system was suited to practitioners not striving in the front lines of entrepreneurship and economic competition. It was to upper- and middle-class white women, for whom the ideology of separate spheres prescribed a distinct realm of female action, that Stebbins provided paid instruction in private and domestic settings, or at young ladies' academies. Relaxed, harmonious bodies, it would seem, could be constructed most readily by those who possessed economic and demographic security. Galvanized, flexible bodies were cultivated by or for those whose class, ethnic, or gender locations demanded pursuit of "the main chance" in unstable work and cultural arenas.

A Renaissance of Dancing

Sweated industrial labor, gendered divisions of that labor, racial disfranchisement, urban residential density, new modes of consumer culture and physical training: these are typical Progressive-era themes that worked themselves out through and upon human bodies. They bear out the centrality of bodies as sites wherein Progressive-era people configured and contested issues of identity. The concurrent fascination with dancing should thus strike historians not only as unsurprising, but also as yet another facet of the period's absorption with and investment in instrumentalizing bodily discourse. Long marginalized in scholarly discourse, the renaissance of dancing that Americans enjoyed in the first two decades of the twentieth century opened up protean spaces for negotiating and worrying identities in a time of flux.

The burgeoning of dance practices in the early twentieth century proceeded in both social dance and theatrical dance arenas. Spurred on by development of new venues and new choreographic styles, social dance practices changed for working-class as well as middle- and upper-class participants. Theatre dancing, at the same time, experienced a resurgence via engagements by touring Russian dancers and the much-debated performances of emerging American artists such as Isadora Duncan and Ruth St. Denis. Traversing the divide between these two vectors of innovation were newly constituted exhibition ballroom dancing teams like Vernon and Irene Castle. The excitement that these new dancing practices generated was both amplified and attested to by newspaper accounts, periodicals, and books devoted to new dance developments. Aspects of both the social and theatre dance innovations drew censure as well. Thus, the contemporary locutions "renaissance" and "dance craze" capture two poles of the reception granted the changing terpsichorean terrain. Dancing bodies provided compelling templates and models for working through issues of autonomy and dependence, gender roles and heterosexuality.[30]

RE-LOCATING SOCIAL DANCE

Experiences of and contexts for social dancing surely differed between urban and rural areas, between long-settled and more recently settled regions of the country, and by race and ethnic groups as well. But it is the innovation that flourished in New York that has received some of the most nuanced analysis by historians. Like other port cities, New York was a crucible for demographic change in the Progressive era; in addition, it served as a national center for theatrical dance performance and new developments in "nightlife," or commercial dining, dancing, and drinking. These several factors render shifts in New York's social dance practices a useful, and admittedly partial, ground for theorizing the sociable dancing bodies produced by the American renaissance of dancing.[31]

New developments in venues for dancing changed the face of social dance for urban working-class and for middle- and upper-class people alike in the first decades of the twentieth century. Dance halls had long supplied contexts for working-class and ethnic community sociability during the nineteenth century. While these spaces are sometimes described as male preserves that were frequented by prostitutes, historian Kathy Peiss has illuminated the use working-class people made of dance halls in New York City for "lodge affairs": balls programmed by and for benefit societies and fraternal organizations. Such affairs were typically held in neighborhood dance halls rented specifically for the occasion, and brought together members of both sexes and several generations from the community. Providing occasions for bodily pleasure, these balls also reinforced family and community ties.[32]

A variation on this mode of organizing balls emerged in the "rackets" of the 1890s. These affairs were organized, by social clubs or amusement societies, solely for the purpose of dancing. They opened admission to any and all, catering to mixed populations of dancers unconnected by family, ethnic, or neighborhood ties. This practice flourished with the expansion of commercial New York dance halls, from 130 in 1895 to 195 in 1910. Most of these were located in working-class districts and held 500 to 1,200 people each. At the same time, many saloons added rooms for meetings and dancing. The sale of alcohol was intimately connected with the commerce of dance halls, and in these contexts, time allocated for dancing was structured to alternate with periods for rest and drinking. In time, racket formats and club sponsorship were dispensed with, and dance halls simply offered opportunities for dancing to anyone who could pay the price of admission. Further expansion in New York occurred between 1910 and 1920 with the opening of six commercial dance halls variously accommodating between 500 and 3,000 people each. Located in commercial amusement zones, these large venues attracted clerical workers and factory laborers; middle-class people turned to restaurants and cabarets.[33]

Prior to the vogue for cabaret formats that commenced in 1911 and 1912, elite and middle-class contexts for dancing centered on carefully structured events usually scheduled as part of an annual "season" for social events. Balls, dinners, and presentations of debutantes were produced for closed or private groups—in other words, as a form of social rather than commercial exchange. Like dress, decorum and dancing styles were closely scrutinized at balls; they required careful preparation in consultation with dancing masters. The venues themselves consisted of ballrooms in large private dwellings or space rented in major restaurants, as were the Patriarch's Balls sponsored annually by Mrs. Astor and mounted at restaurant venues like Delmonico's and Sherry's.[34]

These controlled and delimited contexts for dancing were rivaled by the advent of cabarets as venues for nighttime entertainment. Historian Lewis Erenberg has documented the rise of cabarets in New York City, built upon the brief, failed experiment by moviemaker Jesse Lasky and theatre manager Henry B. Harris in 1911. While their theatre-cabaret quickly folded, by 1912 numerous New York restaurants remodeled their dining floors to place diners' tables in close proximity to bands and exhibition dancers who performed at the center of the floor. Cabarets thus departed from traditional theatre auditorium layouts where proscenium arches separated performers from spectators arrayed in receding rows. With tables ranged round the floor, cabarets promoted a sense of intimate contact between patrons and performers. They also afforded diners the physical space to take to the floor themselves, dancing "publically" for all to see. The price of cabaret meals and drinks (and occasional cover charges) effectively constituted a barrier to entry that only the "prosperous" elite and upper-middle-class people could consistently cross. Within that economic range, however, cabarets mixed together men and women from diverse occupational groups. This in part sparked certain of the objections to "public dancing," for in cabarets entertainers, sporting people, even expensive prostitutes mixed with what Erenberg calls "respectable" people. The "in-group" dimensions of earlier elite and middle-class balls were being rapidly effaced in cabarets.[35]

The 1912 advent of *thés dansants* or "tango teas" also contributed to the transformation of the social composition of dance events. These afternoon functions, while often emulated by private hostesses, were commercially structured to provide unescorted women customers with contexts for taking refreshments and dancing with male partners employed by café owners. Women who could pay the admission price chose partners from unknown and varied class and ethnic backgrounds; accounts critical of tango teas termed these male dance professionals "tango pirates." Tango teas thus positioned women as the consumers of dance services supplied by men. They reversed the roles, the flow of power, in the economic relation that usually obtained when male patrons purchased entertainment provided by dancing girls.[36]

RE-FASHIONING SOCIAL DANCING BODIES

For working-class as well as for elite and middle-class people, then, changes in venues for social dancing removed certain oversights traditionally exercised by community, class, and kin groups. Offering increased elbow room for contact and exchange between the sexes and among occupational groups, commercial dance halls, cabarets, and *thés dansants* afforded as well the opportunity to experience new dance styles, new mobilizations for dancing bodies. These new mobilizations may be more readily grasped when seen in context with the waltz, a dance type common to working-class as well as elite and middle-class balls at the end of the nineteenth century.[37]

Waltzes had been staples throughout the 1800s, changing over time from difficult to more simple maneuvers. In the early 1800s, for instance, the complex five-step waltz required couples to complete one 360-degree revolution in every two measures of music as they danced counterclockwise around the ballroom, advancing along a designated line of direction. By the start of the twentieth century, couples completed the same revolution on a circular path in twice the time—four measures of music; this slackening of pace afforded much more leisurely progress around the dance floor. It should be noted that the waltz itself had aroused furor at the time of its introduction. The round dance position which partners used—man facing woman, his right hand circling the woman's waist, her left hand atop his shoulder, their other hands clasped outward at the side—had at the start of the nineteenth century brought partners closer together than they had ever danced before. And, the vertigo or potential loss of control produced by fast-paced revolutions had excited considerable criticism as well. These features had lost their threatening aspect, or had been tamed, by the start of the twentieth century, with manuals like Allen Dodworth's 1885 *Dancing* (updated and reissued in 1900) carefully stipulating the correct body positions that partners should assume. For all the effort expended by dancing masters and instruction manuals to demark and contain the experience of waltzing, reconstructions of period waltzing make available to historians and dancers in the 1990s still other indexes of what was afoot in the practice of waltzing. Particularly remarkable is the sensation of ongoing flow achieved through coupled bodies, pursuing but not driven along the line of direction in the ballroom, bodies matching the ongoingness of the music's rhythmic drive, emphasizing affects of lightness and moderately sustained initiations of effort. These were among the experiences that turn-of-the-century waltzing afforded as the conventional standard for ballroom dancing.[38]

However, young, working-class women and men in New York City readily forsook the waltz for "spieling"—also known as "pivoting"—and "tough" dancing, the name given to new "animal dances." These generated a lively public discourse about disreputable dancing and spurred the formation in New York City of dance hall investigators and reform groups, a subject that will be treated in chapter 5. Reporting the conduct of a spieling couple at a Coney Island dance hall, Julian Ralph noted in *Scribner's* that, "instead of dancing with a free, lissome, graceful, gliding step, they pivot or spin, around and around with the smallest circle that can be drawn around them." Peiss emphasizes the loss of control and the sexual charge conferred by the "wild" spinning characteristic of spieling. While acknowledging the sexualized proximity spieling offered to couples who performed it, I read spieling as requiring even more control and focused attention than did waltzing. As described by Ralph and Peiss, spieling resembles a dance called zweifachers still performed today by social dancers who frequent "traditional dance" events. Zweifachers uses the step scheme of "pi-vot pi-vot waltz–2–3 pi-vot pi-vot waltz–2–3 waltz–2–3"; spatially the dance puts couples into ever-revolving patterns. Repeated insertion of the two-count pivot step "ups the ante" of waltzing. It requires intense concentration from the partners, drawing them together in strict attention to rhythmic demands and the tightly trimmed spatial path of nonstop turning. While the speed and centrifugal force of zweifachers can be exhilarating when done well, loss of control would defeat execution of this dance type. To be sure, spieling and zweifachers did counter the values associated with waltzing: for lightness and buoyant, steadily flowing steps carving elongated, curved swaths through space, spieling exchanged strong use of body weight, bound flow of energy, sudden initiations of steps, and tightly enfolding semicircles of motion. Difficult of execution, spieling bound partners one to another, as they worked together to master its kinetic challenge. If anything, then, spieling afforded an intensification of bodily effort and reinforcement of the heterosexual dyad in working-class dancing.[39]

Animal dances, popular with working-class as well as elite and middle-class dancers, broke open the coupled position of waltzing and spieling and put a stop to continuous circling of the ballroom following an agreed-upon line of direction. To the tunes of newly popular ragtime music, animal dances like the turkey trot, bunny hug, and grizzly bear called upon dancers to assume bodily postures that imitated animal shapes or motions. These postures were probably assumed while standing in place, with dancers resuming some course around the dance floor, although not necessarily the waltz's counterclockwise circumnavigation. Some animal dances combined imitative postures with specific locomotor profiles: in the turkey trot, dancers utilized a polka-based step scheme while pumping their arms and shrugging their shoulders. Emphasizing body postures, turkey trotters formed or shaped space as well, in contrast with waltzers who coolly arced and sliced through space, riding the waves of the regular downbeat.[40]

Animal dances thus allowed for temporary lapses from the pattern of male leading and female following in traditional ballroom dancing. It provided opportunities for individuals to stylize their own versions of the bunny hug or the grizzly bear. In splitting apart the dancing couple, however provisionally, animal dances thus seated agency in each individual, female and male. Such autonomy was undergirded by transmission of animal dances through word of mouth and by magazines rather than through instruction (and regulation) by established dancing masters and their published manuals.

Circulating in American cities by the years 1908 and 1909, the vogue for animal dances and their expansiveness met a countering force with the arrival of "exhibition dancers," professional ballroom dancers hired to perform at cabaret venues after 1911. Couples like Vernon and Irene Castle or Maurice Mouvet and Florence Walton proffered polished, staged versions of the popular "tough" dances. They replaced the two-step with the softer pedaling of the one-step, to which the Castles in turn added a springy quality to devise the "Castle Walk." Exhibition dancers also presented the South American tango, but as a French-filtered style, one characterized by smoothness rather than passion, and capable of numerous variations requiring no little practice to master. These and other newly introduced dances like the fox-trot and maxixe edged out the imitative animal dances and reaffirmed the couple as the primary unit for social dancing. Exhibition dancers facilitated direct imitation as yet another mode for transmitting new dances. The prosperous teaching enterprise that the Castles developed indicates something of the variety of modes and thus the reach of social dance transmission at the time. They performed at their own cabaret, Sans Souci, and at those belonging to others. They offered dance advice through newspaper and magazine articles, and published the manual *Modern Dancing* in 1913. That same year they founded Castle House, on 46th Street in New York, to offer instruction to elite students. There Vernon supplied the teacher-pupil contact in class or private lessons.[41]

SOCIABLE BODIES

Changes in venues and social dance styles furnished important opportunities for modeling sociable bodies: embodiments that people utilized in their congress with others while pursuing pleasure in corporeal motion. The impact exerted by such changes was felt differently by different class groups, and there is much still to be researched in terms of racial and ethnic group experiences. Working-class spielers reaffirmed the male lead/female follow formula and couple format of nineteenth-century ballroom dancing. However, this group established a public sociability, or venue etiquette, that afforded women a certain autonomy. As Peiss has shown, young women and men typically arrived at commercial dance halls in same-sex groups—"dates" were not required, and they escaped as well the family and community chaperonage that would have obtained at neighborhood dance events. Once inside the dance halls, males and females coupled up on the dance floor, where "breaking" or "cutting in" on couples was customary. Or people coupled up at tables removed from the floor, where alcohol could be consumed. People moved freely from table to table, greeting friends or making new ones, raucously entertaining each other. Male "treating" of females, or buying drinks and food, was an important way in which young working women could sample pleasures their own wages could not have provided. Receipt of such treating always required delicate negotiation, for women thereby incurred obligations to men, satisfaction for which was frequently requested in the form of sexual favors. It was the lexicon of behaviors that commercial dance halls proffered that empowered working-class women to act as operators independent of male escorts, coming and going as free agents, choosing to couple up for spieling or to break apart for animal dances. Extracting pleasures and autonomies in these contexts, working-class women also realized that a cost had to be paid.[42]

Middle-class and elite people, on the other hand, tried on new dancing and sociable bodies in cabarets that regulated venue behavior to a substantial degree. Patrons were encouraged to attend as couples and to maintain the integrity of groups seated at individual tables. Cabarets firmly discouraged not only table hopping but "cutting in" on the dance floor as well. The heterosexual coupling reinforced by cabaret etiquette could be temporarily offset by patrons who took to the dance floor situated amidst a scatter of customer tables. Dancing in close proximity to one's eating and drinking neighbors, men and women capitalized on the temporary openness to experiment and improvisation that animal dances afforded, provisionally prying apart the male-female dyad to mold and maneuver space as individual agents. This modeling of autonomous sociable bodies was increasingly closed down by the refinement and polish that exhibition dancers applied to "tough dancing," and by their continuing manufacture and introduction of new dances to replace the old. For a brief period, *thés dansants* offered unescorted women the upper hand in selecting partners and changing partners as they organized the couple dyad with paid male dancers. Dance hall investigators and popular anxieties motivated periodic closures of tango tea cafés, however, and by 1916 they were on the wane.[43]

What remains important in the cabaret and tango tea contexts is the spectacularization of social dancing. Cabaret settings in particular blurred the line between professional and amateur dancers. Patrons watched the exhibition dancers' performances from their seats, and then stepped onto the same floor that the professionals had only recently vacated. Patrons themselves thus became the subjects for examination, evaluation, and possibly emulation by other observing diners. Slipping from viewer to doer, patrons tasted the difference between passive and active seeking of pleasure in bodily motion and the shifts in kinesthetic awareness that must have accompanied such a translation from audience to performer. The sheer mutability of the situation, the capacity for changeableness that it afforded, for plural and changing identities, was arresting. This was a context that rendered quotidian dancing an instance of performance, while performance came to be an activity available to any sociable body.[44]

Drawn from the working, middle, and upper classes, sociable bodies pursuing pleasure in dancing traversed terrain quite unlike that of gymnasiums or school exercise regimens. Practicing improvisation and absorbing new dances through word of mouth and magazine communiqués, these sociable dancing bodies distanced themselves from the advice and regulation of experts, at least to some degree, and explored their bodies' motion as registers of their own pleasure. In the autonomy of women's attendance at working-class commercial dance halls, and in the initiators' role afforded women by *thés dansants*, changing social dance practices offered room to renegotiate gender roles, however temporarily. In the adoption of spieling and animal dances, men and women performed critical commentaries on nineteenth-century middle- and upper-class constructions of dancing bodies. The deployable bodies that physical culture regimens readied were rendered by social dancing into observable, performing bodies in public dance venues. Bodies that were molded by other contemporary means to economic uses turned to self-initiated production of the body's pleasure, a production that could be danced out nightly if one had the time and money. In the first decades of this century, new social dance practices wrought "performance" as a bodily capacity within reach of anyone who wished to pursue it.

EXHIBITION DANCING; TRAVERSING A DIVIDE

The models for ballroom dancing and decorum promulgated by exhibition dancers like the Castles retain striking parallels with the movement qualities and aesthetic values of ballet as it had been developed in the nineteenth century. In the Castles' 1914 manual *Modern Dancing*, for example, opening chapters remind readers time and again that modern ballroom dancing is both "the personification of refinement, grace, and modesty," and a means of ". . . acquiring grace, elegance, and beauty." These were claims that contemporary ballet could have pressed. Ballroom dancing is characterized by "graceful measures tripped to the lilting rhythm of fine music," the Castles maintained. Its grace consists in stateliness and dignity of movement; it constitutes a poetry of motion and builds visual pictures that realize the music in a different form. Here ballroom dancing parallels the partnership with music and the pictorial approach characteristic of ballet since the early nineteenth century. A capsule summary closes the book with "suggestions for correct dancing," defining by process of negation the upright, columnar stance requisite for ballroom dancing—one that typified academic ballet as well. Do not wriggle the shoulders, it instructs; do not shake the hips; do not twist the body; do not flounce the elbows; do not pump the arms; do not hop—glide instead. The summary reiterates the need for a light touch when making contact with one's partner—ballet aesthetics required the concealment of the body's efforts, in partnering as well as solo dancing—and, yet again, for grace.[45]

When the Castles urged refinement, lightness, and adherence to the models they themselves provided, they aimed to steer ballroom dancers away from the crude models of animal dances. Their ballroom aesthetics arguably prepared contemporary audiences for reception of touring European ballet dancers, yet another dimension of the Progressive era's renaissance of dancing. Not unlike the skill required of aspiring ballroom dancers, ballet dancers' fine bodily control—won through the discipline of daily training—was the key to creating an appearance of refined bearing, graceful motion, and superbly attenuated line or silhouette of the body in space. Ballet further resembled ballroom dancing in privileging the male-female couple as structural element. In the Castle ballroom dyad as in the pas de deux, the man guided and "led"; the woman, put into motion, "followed."[46]

NEW INFUSIONS OF BALLET

Americans in the Progressive era had seen all too little of ballet on native stages until Anna Pavlowa and Mikhail Mordkin appeared on the Metropolitan Opera stage in 1910. Prior to that time, ballet had been produced largely as an adjunct to opera; the Met itself had only in 1909 established a training school of its own. It is true that, following French ballerina Fanny Elssler's visit to the United States in the 1840s, several individuals had struggled to pursue ballet as a high-art practice. There is evidence as well that ballet masters itinerated in frontier towns as far afield as Colorado. These various efforts came to little, and ballet fell into disrepute. Thus, Pavlowa and Mordkin's appearance caused a sensation. They opened their winter 1910 engagement by appearing in the full-length ballet *Coppelia*, assisted by the Met's corps de ballet. Carl Van Vechten, a music stringer covering the performances for the *New York Times*, wrote with elation about Pavlowa's dazzling technique, supreme ease, and lightness. On the dancers' return engagement in October, this time assisted by a company of Russian dancers, Van Vechten wrote long and feelingly about their presentation of *Giselle*. Pavlowa's conception of the heroine in the "mad scene" was both poetic and very close to tragic, he noted, while Mordkin "had no dancing to do in this ballet, but in appearance and action he was superb." Presenting these repertory staples, Pavlowa and Mordkin stirred in audiences a new awareness of what academic ballet could be in the early twentieth century: a practice of exquisite bodily rationalization, apparent ephemeralization, and persistent striving for perfection.[47]

Pavlowa and Mordkin introduced as well something of the coming vogue for expressive Orientalism in ballet. Trained in the Imperial Russian system, they had both participated in the breakaway venture called the "Ballets Russes" that Serge Diaghilev had constructed to breach the confines of the state-supported, traditional Russian approach to choreography and production. Drawing dancers, choreographer, composers, and designers from the motherland, Diaghilev inaugurated the Ballets Russes with a May 1909 ballet season that stunned Paris audiences. With its careful choice of subject matter, décor, composition, and movement values, the Ballets Russes would change ballet irrevocably in the 1910s. It produced ballets of potent Orientalism; works infused with Symbolist ideals; examples of retrospective classicism; and later, more "modernist" ballets. In choreographers Michel Fokine, Vaslav Nijinsky, and Léonide Massine, it introduced new plasticity of gesture and pressed limits within the academic canon of movement. Although the Ballets Russes did not tour the United States until 1916, shrewd imitations of its sensuous exoticism were staged by Gertrude Hoffman and mounted in vaudeville by 1911.[48]

Pavlowa and Mordkin parted company with the Ballets Russes after its first season. Nonetheless, their 1910 performances introduced to American audiences something of the languor and daring that would be more emphatically and more fully developed by the Ballets Russes in its 1916 and 1917 U.S. tours. To their repertoire of classical standards Pavlowa and Mordkin added divertissements which showcased solos and pas de deux imbued with a kind of suggestive sensualism. Their rendition of *Autumn*, to music by Glazunow, struck Van Vechten as venturesome, almost tumultuous. "The Bacchanalian finale, in which Pavlova was finally swept to the earth," he marveled, "held the audience in tense silence for a moment after it was over, and then the applause broke out again." Mordkin dressed "as a savage" in another divertissement, which included his dance with a bow and arrow, shot using a behind-the-back gesture. That divertissement closed with "Pavlova, supported by Mordkin, flying through the air, circling his body around and around. The curtain fell. The applause was deafening." The reviewer's remarks make it almost painfully clear that such dancing proffered barely sublimated markers of desire, markers that a startled audience did not fail to applaud. That works evidencing orientalist strains owed a debt to the Diaghilev model was not lost upon Van Vechten, either; he made explicit in one review the connection between Pavlowa and Mordkin's *The Legend of Aziyade* and the Ballets Russes' *Schéhérazade*.[49]

These works clearly excited viewers with their abandon and their references to barbaric or less civilized peoples, body movements, and couplings. They also provided a provocative reworking of the lead male dancer's role.

Mordkin's bow-and-arrow dance and the rousing finish to the *Bacchanale* thrilled viewers with their manly vigor and athleticism. Such movement qualities were traditionally associated with "character dancers," those performers who represented national types and movement styles within multi-act classical choreographies. Leading male dancers, those termed "danseurs nobles," deployed greater restraint and smooth polish as cavaliers supporting and displaying their patrician female partners. Mordkin's roles as "noble savage" transferred the character dancer's movement qualities to those of the lead dancer, thereby introducing American viewers to an alternative embodiment for principal male dancers. Surely Pavlowa must have unbent a bit as well if she indeed flew through the air, circling round and round Mordkin's body. The large structure that framed ballet practice, however, still affirmed the heterosexual couple as organizing unit.[50]

FEMALE SOLOISTS AS (SELF-SUFFICIENT) INNOVATORS

Pavlowa and Mordkin were but two riders on the wave of theatrical dance innovation that seized American imaginations, inciting both criticism and adulation. Particularly compelling was the surge of "barefoot dancers" that took the stage in the first decade of the twentieth century. Variously called Greek dancers, classic dancers, and interpretative dancers, these innovators were predominantly female. Females had long enjoyed employment as dance performers or executants, of course, but these women constituted themselves as choreographers of their own material as well as performers. Their vogue was set in motion by the movement practices of Isadora Duncan.

In pursuit of dancing that was not "artificial," Duncan shed corset, shoes, and tights; she draped herself in Greek-inspired tunics and dressed her hair loosely. Film-shy, she left no recorded moving images of her dancing, but sketches, photographs, and the recollections of peers indicate that she sent waves of motion outward from the motional center of her solar plexus. She massed her body in ways that acknowledged gravity and the attraction of its pull; she also skipped, walked, and ran with a skimming lightness and joy in rhythm. She dressed her stages simply, using blue-gray cloths and warm-colored lighting. Duncan's relative undress gave audiences pause; her dancing to the music of Beethoven and Wagner, as well as Chopin and Brahms, caused them consternation. As the author of her own movement designs, she was a radical, and after a brief American period of self-fashioning in the late 1890s, she made her career primarily in

Europe. But she returned to the U.S. for performances in the first three decades of this century, and consistently troubled viewers' notions of what might appropriately be recognized as dance.[51]

Duncan slipped and surged through the air, sometimes with weight, sometimes almost impalpably, dancing what one historian has called "a lyric outpouring of passion." Her peer Ruth St. Denis constructed quite a different dancing persona. St. Denis garbed herself in the costume of Asian and Middle Eastern dance cultures and fashioned settings and musical accompaniments to suggest these locales. She, too, bared legs, arms, and feet, deftly wedding her undeniable sensuous appeal with an equally driving aspiration towards things spiritual or transcendent. Thus she combined deep back bends and high leg kicks from the skirt dancer's repertoire with undulating arm gestures and book-derived body postures, setting them in motion with torso spiralings and rhythm-marking footwork, the former impelled in part by exposure to Genevieve Stebbins's Delsartism. With these materials St. Denis created dance dramas of orientalist customs and religion, launching a solo career in 1906 via salon performances and commercial theatrical appearances. Set beside St. Denis's intricate self-presentation, Duncan might look almost debrided. Both, however, staked out new ground for dancing as an artistic practice, that is, an activity of serious intent, productive of beauty and some kind of truth.

A third American, Loie Fuller, put light and motion visibly into play in a career that began with temperance lecturing and proceeded through stock melodrama. Experimenting with electric lighting and diaphanous silk fabrics, she discovered the affective and kinesthetic possibilities of extending her body's reach with handheld wands, thereby manipulating great lengths of fabric into shapes of flowers or suggesting natural phenomena like fire. Like Duncan, Fuller won recognition as an imaginative artist in Europe, where from 1892 she based her work and sometimes headed a company. With its surging, undulating lines, hers was a dance practice that rendered the body's effects instead of its materiality.

Each of these choreographers inspired numerous imitators, through which some flavor of their innovations reached nationwide vaudeville and nascent film audiences, as well as Broadway viewers. In their different ways these dance makers unbridled the capacities for bodily movement shaped and sculpted in other arenas of American life. And they modified in no uncertain terms the customary use of the male-female couple as the structural unit common to social dancing as well as to ballet. Works by Duncan, St. Denis, and Fuller proposed that women could stand alone, that they could author their own movement as well as perform it, and that women could successfully take on the male-gendered role of artistic creator.

The allure that these performers unquestionably exerted brought audiences to realize that a renaissance of dancing was indeed spilling across their country, a renaissance that feted human movement capacity at the same time that it problematized contemporary issues of gender roles, sexual division of labor in the theatre business, access to spirituality, and aesthetic styles. As with workplace practices, urban living, and physical culture systems, the renaissance of ballroom, ballet, and barefoot dancing worked the powerful ground of the body to negotiate a number of Progressive-era meanings and identities.

BODILY INSCRIPTION IN THE
PROGRESSIVE ERA

In the 1990s our access to the "renaissance of dancing" derives in part from period books like the Caffins' *Dancing and Dancers of Today* (1912) and the Kinneys' *The Dance* (1914). Written by husband-wife teams, beating excitedly with partisan fervor, these volumes treat the renaissance in distinctive terms. The Kinneys aim to establish dance's "place in art and life," and they write dance's significance as the large story of a genre—ballet. Yes, dance had a history in ancient Egypt and Greece; people danced in Rome, during the Middle Ages, and in the Renaissance. But in this telling the eighteenth century was dance's—ballet's—golden age; its subsequent decline was reversed by the Romantic Revolution, which included the innovations of Isadora Duncan and the Ballets Russes. National dances of the Occident and Orient, and European folk dance in general, supply the second term of the Kinneys' conceptual dyad; it is to Oriental dancing that soloist Ruth St. Denis is assigned. The Kinneys later disavowed a chapter on ballroom dancing; "it was written under coercion, against the wishes of the authors," they declared in 1926.[52] What frames the Kinneys' analysis is concern with dance as beauty, and as art; dance features the body's skill and grace, its line and postures. The Caffins, in contrast, articulate neither scale nor aesthetic ranking for the dance of their day. Though they write of dancing as an art, and peg ballet as important, they still speak most fervently of dancers, of individual artists. Engaged by fluent bodies, committed to "expressional interpretation of the dance," they distinguish folk, court, and eccentric dance practices of their decade that the Kinneys' analysis disdained or otherwise assimilated. Common to both books is the sense of abundance, of burgeoning plenitude in dance that augurs a fecund future for a revivified dance. For both books, the reinvigorated practice is dance as an "art."

Already coursing through these accounts is the modernist myth of dancing as a rarefied realm, a domain apart from everyday life and accessible only to the few. The Kinneys press choreographic innovations into service to exalt the extant ballet tradition. The Caffins laud dance that speaks to the imagination, but they can't quite sort out the shifting terrain of dance innovation. Old model or no model, the Kinneys and the Caffins cling to "dance as an art" for the explanatory rubric to use in their time. The Caffins, writing about public school girls' folk dancing, draw nigh to the realization that a dance awareness in the Progressive era crossed not just genre lines but class lines as well. Still, this realization does not inform the book as a whole. As paeans to the period, these books must be read for the partial accounts they all too vividly offer.

We should see the Progressive era instead as vibrating with an expansive sensitivity to the body and its movement as registers of changing experience. This sensitivity operated at a variety of class and ethnic positions as well.

In America, with accelerated intensity, manufacturing processes, urban habitation, and ethnic and race relations *shaped* human bodies, or required bodies to *fit themselves* to a priori spatial and energy configurations. Who did the fitting, and how, became the subject of labor contest, racial conflict, physical culture systems, suffrage campaigns, social dancing, and café culture. People in varying class positions *staged* themselves, just as Russian ballet choreographers ruptured and remade the canon of ballet embodiments, and American soloists parsed new inscriptions of femaleness on the dancing body. Movement performance became a bodily capacity open to females and males, lower as well as upper classes, immigrant as well as native-born peoples, amateurs as well as professionals. Never did the modernist model of "art" dancing subside; indeed Fuller, Duncan, and St. Denis burnished it to their own purposes. But it co-existed with alternative perceptions and practices of dancing as bodily performance relevant to people occupying a variety of economic, political, and social positionalities. This expansive bodily practice promised vehicles for writing new selves in a time when shift and change figured more immanently than continuities with the past.

We may see the Progressive era, then, as a complex of disciplines for the body. These became at once the province of settlement houses and schools, of commercial gyms and professional sporting events, of salons and concert stages. Bodily practices functioned as active agencies, not simply as the effects of initiatives felt first in other, more fundamental realms. Dance in the Progressive era would prove capable of worrying urgent issues of immigration, ethnicity, and class. And it would prove especially effective for mobilizing the woman question, for problematizing the gendered divide between public and private spheres of human agency.

Two   Constituting Culture, Authorizing Dance

Among the several dance forms that comprised the "renaissance" of dancing—the felt burgeoning of dance events, experiences, and personalities—two types of dance warrant particular attention, because it was in them that women had come to predominate. In the new practice of expressive dancing, Americans Loie Fuller, Ruth St. Denis, and Isadora Duncan had won, and continued to receive, international recognition as choreographers as well as performers of new theatrical dance styles. In settlement house dance curricula and in folk dancing programs for New York City schoolgirls, women like Irene Lewisohn, Mary Wood Hinman, and Elizabeth Burchenal gained recognition for creating and teaching lyric and movement materials that addressed the physiological and imaginative needs of immigrant children. Unabashedly theatrical, the dancing of Fuller, St. Denis, and Duncan were built on a conception of the dancer-choreographer as Romantic artist, a visionary, gifted individual articulating insights available only to the few. Settlement house activities and school-related folk dance programs, in contrast, conceived of dance as a practice for communal participation by the many, all of whom were believed capable of deriving the joys and benefits therefrom. Despite the different conceptions of dance from which they proceeded and which they developed, these two dance practices were alike in terms of the female agency that drove them. What were the sources of this agency? How can we account for it? This chapter explores ways in which women's "cultural practices" empowered them to forge new dance practices in turn-of-the-century America, focusing on the theatrical dance innovations of Loie Fuller, Ruth St. Denis, and Isadora Duncan. It also investigates the ways in which these changing dance practices helped contest and negotiate concepts of gender at a time when the powerful "separate spheres" ideology of women's roles reached a zenith in the United States.

Women's Cultural Practices

In framing these questions about Progressive-era dance as questions about gender, I depart from the way in which dance historians have traditionally structured their inquiries. Indeed, the framing of these questions as issues of gender has been conditioned by the interpretive insights advanced in women's history, a field established only since the 1960s within the academic discipline of United States history. Pronouncing gender to be a category of historical analysis, scholars of women's history have sustained the claim with tidal waves of articles, books, and monographs. Women's history has thus provided a different framework within which to ask questions about women's numerical and substantive representation in the dance profession, a majority position taken for granted and sometimes even bemoaned by dance professionals. It also provides the concept of a "women's culture," a notion I do not adopt but use instead as a springboard for theorizing something we might call women's "cultural practices."

Briefly stated, the concept of a "women's culture" has been suggested most frequently by historians investigating nineteenth-century subjects. That century's separate spheres ideology charged women with responsibility for child rearing, upholding morality, and maintaining the home as haven. It characterized women as pious, pure, domestic, and obedient, and it consigned them to the private sphere, a realm separate from the world of work and politics. Seen with late-twentieth-century eyes, separate spheres ideology appears to emphasize limitation and to constrain women's scope for action and identity formation. Yet historians have postulated that this ideology actually stimulated the growth of a widely subscribed women's culture: a matrix of values and patterns of behavior which centered on the home but also impelled large numbers of women to take action in the public sphere to protect the home. Women's culture was thus dynamic; acting on its imperatives, women created a number of voluntary organizations through which to attack problems caused by nineteenth-century demographic, economic, social, and political change.[1]

Historians have thus posited women's culture as an orientation and a source of values shared by all women. However, most scholars who utilize women's culture as an explanatory device qualify their analysis at the outset, noting that they theorize a women's culture on the basis of a particular group of women. Typically, the groups so investigated have been middle-class, white, and—frequently—New England women. Thus the concept of a "women's culture" stresses the values and identity women share by virtue of their gender but sidesteps the differences which distinguish them, such as race, class, and region. As it has been put into practice, the notion of a commonly held women's culture exhibits serious theoretical inconsistencies, if not limitations.[2]

Rather than continue to use the notion of a "women's culture," I propose an alternative concept, and a corresponding historical process: women's "cultural practices" that empowered Progressive-era females to innovate in dance. Women's cultural practices can be defined as those activities by which women construct their gendered identity. In these acts of construction, women respond to the ideology of gender proffered in a given period and place, accepting, rejecting, contesting, qualifying, or changing concepts and prescriptions for female identity. In this formulation, women's cultural practices are constructionist; that is, they actively make, question, or remake ideas, behaviors, and embodiments of what it means to be female. And women construct and challenge concepts of gender in ways that are particular to their racial, class, and geographical positions.

In the locution "women's cultural practices," "practices" emphasizes constitution and construction as ways in which people obtain the values and views they espouse, ways equal in importance to accepting tradition or maintaining conventional wisdom. The word "practices" also foregrounds women's investment of their bodies in the experiences through which they shape and form their identity. Such experiences include the legwork of gathering signatures for antislavery petitions in the antebellum period, the post–Civil War prayerful temperance "sit-ins" at taverns, the schedule of home visits performed by charity organization society members, and women's marching in suffrage parades.

The word "cultural" is used for specific reasons as well. Historians have readily borrowed meanings for the concept of "culture" from the discipline of anthropology, where Clifford Geertz's *The Interpretation of Cultures* (1973) offered an influential definition of culture as the webs of signification that people spin. Developing the concept in their own field, historians in the 1970s and 1980s articulated and explored the idea of culture as it bore on groups as diverse as African American slaves and industrial workers.

Embedded in uses that anthropologists and historians alike have made of the culture concept has been the notion of identity assertion or definition of self. Paula Baker has theorized nineteenth-century male political culture as offering men a self-definition formed against the negative reference group of women. Consumer culture has been analyzed as offering people certain bearings in the new plenitude of the marketplace. Through work culture, historians maintain, laborers carved out areas of autonomy — areas of *self*-powering behavior. Constitution of our identity as human beings not only engages each of us, but also requires effort throughout our lifetimes, the more so in times of economic and social change. Such was the case in nineteenth-century America with the rise of a capitalist economy, formation of two different male-only political party systems, the elaboration of transportation and communication networks, a wrenching civil war, and end-of-the-century shifts toward national economic, governmental, and social organization. Women, like men, Native Americans, freed slaves, waves of immigrants, and the steadily increasing number of people experiencing urban life, faced the challenge of constituting identity in changing circumstances.[3]

Central to nineteenth-century women's experience was the need to deal with both the trope and the ideology of separate spheres. In relation to this prescription for behavior, women faced the task of accepting, rejecting, adapting, or qualifying the gender role that a separate spheres ideology meted out to them. I thus use the word "cultural" to signal the identity-constituting capacities of the practices they performed, which included voluntary charitable and benevolent work, campaigns for women's rights and suffrage, promotion of temperance, antislavery activity, formation of women's clubs, and efforts to secure educational opportunities. As the separate spheres ideology crested in the early twentieth century, the challenge to constitute gender identity remained constant for women. They sought and finally secured the right of electoral participation, entry into some new professions, and steadily growing participation in the labor force.

It should be noted that the activities I discuss as women's cultural practices have been assessed previously by historians analyzing women's culture. The shift in focus is all-important, however. Women's cultural practices can vary with the class, race, ethnic group, and region of the women studied. They can take multiple forms and change over time; multiplicity rather than homogeneity informs women's cultural practices.

"Cultural" is deliberately chosen for another reason as well. It is used to distinguish the identity-fashioning processes which I propose, and to capitalize on historians' rather flexible use of the word "culture" to mean, variously, concern with the arts and learning, the complex of values and significations which characterize a society, or both. Historians of the U.S. extend the word "culture" to embrace the arts when they so desire, but this usage is not regularized. My use of the term "women's cultural practices" seeks to emphasize the pertinence of arts activities to women's processes of self-definition.

Among those historians who include the arts as an element in their analysis of political, intellectual, or social change in the United States, the arts most consistently and comfortably examined have been literature and drama. Henry May's *The End of American Innocence* is but one excellent example among many works that focus on literary producers and products.[4] Ambitious studies which successfully relate the arts to analysis of social processes include T. J. Jackson Lears's *No Place of Grace* and Eileen Boris's *Art and Labor*. Both are unusual in evaluating the Arts and Crafts movement in the United States (and other phenomena, in the case of Lears), assessing its instrumentality and consequences for people attempting to redirect change. The arts in Chicago have received scrutiny by Helen Horowitz and Kathleen McCarthy. Horowitz focuses on the founders and institutions of cultural philanthropy such as the Art Institute, Symphony, Crerar and Newberry Libraries, Field Columbian Museum, and the University of Chicago. McCarthy's *Noblesse Oblige* covers the same terrain as part of a larger chronological study of philanthropy, but where Horowitz probed male institutions and their founders, McCarthy details women's attempts to exert cultural power in the Gilded Age by initiating decorative arts work.[5]

As shown by this selective survey of works which factor the arts into analyses of social, political, or economic change, historians have begun to extend the pool of arts and expressive practices which they consider germane. It is instructive, though, that none considers dance. This book argues that dance is intimately connected to Progressive-era issues of gender, democracy, and industrialization. It demonstrates that women's cultural practices provided a ground for women's innovation in dance, and that such innovation helped to constitute women's gendered identity. My articulation of "women's cultural practices" thus also aims to reinstall dance as part of the culture—the terrain—that scholars consider to be subject matter of U.S. history.

Finally, I use "cultural practices" to shift the terms in which dance historians have typically framed their investigation of dance innovators Loie Fuller, Isadora Duncan, and Ruth St. Denis. These women are variously described in historical accounts as visionary trailblazers or pioneers of American modern dance. One guide to modern dance choreographers and their works even charts a genealogy of modern dance which traces ties among "extended choreographic families." What such models emphasize is the role of singular geniuses and their originary insights in the founding and continuity of modern dance as a genre. What such models neglect, however, is the institutional means, the practices, and the milieus through which Fuller, St. Denis, and Duncan constituted their careers. I link women's cultural practices to Fuller, Duncan, and St. Denis to demonstrate that these choreographers functioned not simply as singular geniuses, but amidst and by means of women's self-constituting activities.

Sponsors, Performers, and Spectators; or, Spaces, Bodies, and Vision in New Progressive-era Dancing

In the early stages of their careers, Fuller, St. Denis, and Duncan took advantage of resources and instrumentalities offered them by the women's temperance movement and by women-sponsored society and charity events. These cultural practices provided the developing artists with platforms for performance and with important early models for public presentation of the self. In St. Denis's and Duncan's cases, sponsorship by society and charity women in turn helped to consolidate a new identification for women sponsors as arbiters of the arts. Sponsors for dancing and spaces in which to dance: these were crucial forms of production support. Leaning on women-generated supports, Fuller, St. Denis, and Duncan would go on to produce new constructions of the dancing body and raise new possibilities for viewing female dancers.

LOIE FULLER

An American in Paris, Loie Fuller (1862–1928) brought new uses of fabric and lighting to the Folies-Bergères stage in 1892. She wedded these materials with human motion to create images of a violet, a butterfly, even a "serpentine" form. Drawing on movement precedents from the popular English skirt dance, she also extended that form's kinetic, visual, and imaginative possibilities. She captivated audiences, students, and writers with swirling clouds of rippling, shimmering cloth that billowed, rose, and fell around her diminutive body. Her popularity with the French public endured and a special art nouveau theatre was built for her for the 1900 Paris Exhibition Universelle. Indeed, Fuller's new type of dancing seemed to embody the luminous surfaces and sinuous, twisting line of art nouveau design. Its construction of kinetic visual imagery certainly resonated with Symbolist concern for suggestive atmospheric essences.[6]

Fuller's smashing success in Paris took place after she had only recently changed careers from acting to dancing. Her dancing triumph at age thirty followed more than seventeen years of hard work in the United States trying to make her way into, and then up the ladder in, commercial theater. As she proudly pointed out in the autobiographical *Fifteen Years of a Dancer's Life*, she took the opportunity as a two-and-a-half-year-old to speak her piece at a Sunday afternoon Methodist lyceum she attended with family members. Living in and near Chicago as a young girl, she appeared at age twelve as Little Reginold, a breeches role, in *Was She Right*. A year later, she gave her first "temperance lecture," and toured small towns in Illinois for periods during 1875, 1876, and 1877. She may have performed the role of Mary in productions of the temperance melodrama *Ten Nights in a Barroom and What I Saw There*. Her mother encouraged Fuller's theatrical ambitions, and the aspiring actress probably participated in the informal entertainments which were characteristic events in taverns like the one run by her father Ruben.[7]

Long on self-confidence, Fuller moved from these beginnings to employment in the late 1870s and the 1880s in stock melodramas and musical burlesque. She worked as a singer in *Faust* in Chicago in 1885 and obtained theatrical employment in London in 1889 and 1890. After returning to the U.S. Fuller began experiments with the use of stage lighting and fabrics, which resulted in her American success as a featured dancer in *Uncle Celestin*. Launched on a career as a solo dancer that lasted until the turn of the century, she developed a dance company and started a school in 1908. She made her home in Europe, where audiences acknowledged her distinctive dance practice as artistic. Fuller continued to choreograph and experiment with lighting techniques, winning the friendship of Marie and Pierre Curie and respect from the scientific community.[8]

Fuller's formative experiences in the 1870s show just how resourceful she was in trying to gain a stage career. Until historian Sally Sommer wrote about these efforts, Fuller's foray into temperance lecturing had been noted by scholars but not pursued further. Sommer has drawn attention to nineteenth-century American temperance lecturing and dramas as apt vehicles for the socially acceptable combination of suspect theatricality with moral instruction. She also astutely notes that Fuller was conscious of and valued the power she could exert through the act of performance. The temperance connection bears still further examination, particularly in relation to the timing of Fuller's stint as a temperance lecturer.[9]

LOIE FULLER

949 BROADWAY, N.Y.

Loie Fuller circa 1892. Photograph by Falk. DANCE COLLECTION, THE
NEW YORK PUBLIC LIBRARY FOR THE PERFORMING ARTS, ASTOR, LENOX
AND TILDEN FOUNDATIONS.

Loie Fuller circa 1900. Photograph by Langfier. DANCE COLLECTION,
THE NEW YORK PUBLIC LIBRARY FOR THE PERFORMING ARTS, ASTOR,
LENOX AND TILDEN FOUNDATIONS.

Thirteen years old at the time, Fuller staged her temperance debut in 1875, a little more than one year after the dramatic "Woman's Crusade" for temperance was launched in Hillsboro, Ohio. Temperance concern was not absent in Ohio and Illinois towns at that time. It had been stimulated by post–Civil War continuity with antebellum temperance movements, returned soldiers' lapses from temperance, real changes in the kinds and volume of postbellum liquor consumption, and the recent poor results of a postbellum temperance strategy focused on political change and support for the Prohibition party. Hillsboro residents asked traveling lecturer Dio Lewis, physical culture promoter and sometime temperance speaker, to present a second speech, on temperance, on December 23, 1874. He galvanized the townspeople, especially the women. They met the next day to pray and organize, and subsequently employed the tactic Lewis had recommended in his talk. That is, they descended upon sellers of liquor (pharmacists as well as saloon keepers fell into this category), urging them to cease and desist; if met with a negative response, they were prepared to occupy the premises and pray. From Midwest origins this women's prayer and sit-in tactic spread like wildfire. At a national Sunday School teachers institute in August 1874, temperance women decided to convene a conference to form a national women's temperance league; at the November 1874 conference in Cleveland, Ohio, the national Women's Christian Temperance Union was formed. By 1893, the WCTU became the largest grassroots women's organization in nineteenth-century America, an organization in which women engaging in temperance activity constituted their identities as public workers for American social welfare.[10]

WCTU organizations formed at the local and state level, and Chicago—home of the national WCTU's first Corresponding Secretary, Frances Willard—had an active branch. The WCTU focused in particular on gospel temperance strategy in the first years. It worked to establish speakers' bureaus, create programs for children and adolescents, found temperance reading rooms and "friendly lodges," and publish a news organ. With the motto of "Do Everything!" introduced by Willard, president from 1879 to 1893, the WCTU endorsed woman suffrage "for home protection" as early as 1881, and the organization worked for myriad kinds of improvement in men's, women's, and children's social condition and living environments. Thus, beginning in December 1873, women's enthusiasm for temperance activity burned across the Midwest and took extremely well-organized shape in the WCTU. It was in this climate of heightened public awareness of and women's participation in temperance that Fuller staked her claim as a temperance lecturer.[11]

The temperance identification offered Fuller something that employment in a stock play or burlesque could not—control over presentation of her self. As described in unpublished autobiographical writings, her first outing sprang from one day spent scouting the town of Monmouth, Illinois, to which her family had recently moved. Discovering an available lecture hall, she borrowed money from her father to book it and to pay for posters advertising a lecture by Loie Fuller. Without forethought or planning, she claimed, she walked onto the stage before a capacity crowd which evidenced some surprise at her youthfulness. She extemporized on everyday occurrences, and then this tavern keeper's daughter segued into temperance talk. At one point in her spiel she expanded the usual range of issues considered, questioning the limitation of concern about "intemperance" to drink. She wondered why, for example, the actions of saucy children, devious debtors, and intolerant temperance people were not also dealt with as forms of intemperance. After speaking for two hours, Fuller concluded her remarks, to what she described as appreciative applause. She cleared $85 from the event and gave the sum to her father for his use.[12]

While much about Fuller's autobiographical account may be self-serving, the fact remains that performance as a temperance lecturer placed control of the event in her own hands. She set the date, selected the topic, as it were, and reaped the profits. These were the responsibilities of managers, writers, and producers in the commercial theatre world. While Fuller could gain performance experience in either context, it was as a temperance lecturer that she could set her own agenda, learn crowd management, and taste the economic realities of producing herself.

Further, by presenting herself as a temperance lecturer she was able to capitalize on growing public recognition of temperance work as appropriate to middle-class women. This public receptivity represented a change from temperance work of the 1830s, when women were valued for their moral suasion while men filled leadership roles and spoke from public platforms. Public speaking by women was highly unusual in the 1820s. Disagreement over abolitionist Angelina Grimké's public speaking, for example, excited public censure and fractured the antislavery movement. In the 1840s, women began to speak publicly from temperance platforms for the first time in the newly established Washingtonian movement, which was supported by artisans and working-class people. Female speakers were members of female, self-help "Martha Washington" societies that existed parallel to male Washingtonian groups. The Washingtonian movement faded before the end of the 1840s, but middle-class women participated strongly in 1850s temperance movements. In addition to their critical staffing of petition drives, many women also conducted "vigilante" attacks, destroying the liquor stocks of saloon keepers. Some women also demanded equal rights within the temperance organizations, including the right to speak publically at annual conventions. Some historians maintain that by the mid-1850s it was common for women to address public temperance meetings, yet the reminiscences of Mother Stewart, a Springfield, Ohio, leader of the "Woman's Crusade," indicate that women's public speaking could still be an unusual occurrence as late as 1872. An antebellum temperance group in which women were welcome as speakers, the Order of Good Templars, continued activity in the post–Civil War era and helped sustain the propriety of women's more equal public participation in temperance organizations. With the establishment of the WCTU in 1874, the organization's efforts to establish speakers' bureaus, and Frances Willard's subsequent speaking tours to the South in the early

1880s, the seemliness of middle-class women's temperance participation, even when it involved public speaking, was confirmed.[13]

Fuller's family may have teetered precariously between working- and middle-class status, and her parents' apparent approval of their daughter's theatrical hopes did not square with contemporary middle-class values. She would have profited, nonetheless, in her maiden appearance as a lecturer, from the listeners' attribution to her of middle-class reform intentions. New in town, she *held* this audience with her verbal skills and, it may be said, by virtue of women's newly confirmed authority in temperance leadership. It did not matter that her father kept a tavern or that young Loie probably sang and danced with or for the customers there. And although she claimed to have joined a "Temperance League of Children," it was not temperance conviction so much as the potential theatrical opportunity that made Loie Fuller constitute herself as a lecturer and draw on contemporary temperance discourse for her subject.[14]

The aspiring actress continued to make the most of this theatrical instrumentality. During the Illinois tours of 1875 to 1877, she presented Shakespeare readings and sang, in addition to giving temperance lectures. Her father accompanied her and, an able fiddler himself, probably also played for audiences. In the late 1870s she began to secure commercial dramatic work, and obtained even more in the 1880s. With her success as a solo dancer in the 1890s and the formation of her dance company a decade later, a far more mature and sophisticated Fuller again took charge of the presentation of her self and her creative work. But for a significant, brief period in the 1870s, the burgeoning postbellum women's temperance movement provided role models, subject matter of substantial contemporary interest, and validation for the young aspirant's self-constitution as a lecturer.[15]

RUTH ST. DENIS

Ruth St. Denis (1879–1968) benefited from a related but even more substantive kind of support by women. Born sixteen years after Fuller, St. Denis, too, spent a difficult apprenticeship trying to break into and then ascend in late-nineteenth-century show business. She tried from the first to win work as a dancer. The opening wedge in a paying theatrical career was the job she secured as a skirt dancer in 1894; she performed six times a day at New York City's Worth's Family Theatre and Museum. Subsequent jobs included stints at the Metropolitan Opera's Vaudeville Club (a high-toned outlet for the curiosity of the Met's regular patrons), at Manhattan roof garden entertainments, with touring road shows, and in vaudeville. She obtained a role in 1899 in Augustin Daly's musical farce A *Runaway Girl*, and from 1900 to 1905 found work in David Belasco's realistic, spectacularly staged melodramas *Zaza*, *Madame DuBarry*, and *The Auctioneers*. None of these opportunities in standard theatrical vehicles and venues of the day raised her much above the level of bit part player or chorus girl, and none satisfied her ambition. Possessed of a long-standing interest in literature and things oriental, she found her imagination further fired when she participated in a production of *Sakuntala* mounted by the Progressive Stage Society in 1905. St. Denis began to experiment with *Radha*, a dance drama of her own making. *Radha* drew on the skills of her family and friends, and the performance ultimately required the presence of several "Coney Island hindoos." The chief difficulty, however, lay in finding a venue and a sponsor for the new type of dance fare she was preparing. It was at this point that female sponsors began to lend important support to St. Denis.[16]

St. Denis and her mother had made the rounds of producers and managers since the mid-1890s, so she was well known to them as one kind of performer. But *Radha* was a different undertaking—despite bare midriff and feet, it was not a "leg show." This "Dance of the Five Senses" was staged with a temple set and emphasized connections to religion and spirituality as well as to the sensuous. Mother and daughter looked hard until they found in young producer Henry B. Harris someone willing to book St. Denis on a trial basis. Harris presented her in a showcase concert for theatrical managers at the Hudson Theatre, the venue he managed. The gentlemen were perplexed by *Radha*; finally one of them offered St. Denis a spot in his theatre doing *Radha* for a Sunday evening smokers concert. This New York Theatre engagement was followed by one at Proctor's Theatre where she performed twice a day. St. Denis's art-dance aspirations were a round peg being forced into the square hole of vaudeville, and context here was everything: vaudeville presentation limited the possibility that her work would be understood as "art." Into this situation came Mrs. Orlando Rouland, the wealthy wife of a painter and an avid Orientalist herself. She saw St. Denis's "hindoo" dance drama at Proctor's and was impressed, but the monkey acts which preceded St. Denis's appearance disgusted her. Rouland offered to sponsor a matinee for St. Denis at a "proper uptown theatre," to pave the way for more lucrative bookings. St. Denis put her in contact with Harris. Rouland and twenty-five female friends rented the Hudson Theatre from Harris for a fee and invited a select

Ruth St. Denis, circa 1896, in a pose suggestive of Delsarte exponent Genevieve Stebbins. Denishawn Collection. DANCE COLLECTION, THE NEW YORK PUBLIC LIBRARY FOR THE PERFORMING ARTS, ASTOR, LENOX AND TILDEN FOUNDATIONS.

Ruth St. Denis, 1904–1905, in *Radha*. Photograph by Alice Boughton, Denishawn Collection. DANCE COLLECTION, THE NEW YORK PUBLIC LIBRARY FOR THE PERFORMING ARTS, ASTOR, LENOX AND TILDEN FOUNDATIONS.

group of their friends to a matinee performance for St. Denis on March 23, 1906. In addition to *Radha* St. Denis danced *Incense* and *The Cobras*. After the performance reporters mingled with guests and the patronesses in the theatre lobby, where incense burned and tea was served.[17]

The patronesses included Mrs. Otto H. Kahn, Mrs. Richard Watson Gilder, and Mrs. Eliot Norton. These were women whose husbands made policy at the Metropolitan Opera and *Century* magazine; Mrs. Norton's father-in-law was a notable academic. The invited audience included club and society women and several men as well. Mrs. James Speyer, involved with her husband in New York City education and settlement house reform work, was among them. So was Mrs. Jacob Schiff, whose husband worked on a number of projects to improve conditions for communities of Lower East Side immigrant people. The few men included artist John La Farge, sculptor Homer St. Gaudens, and editor Gilder. Audience response was largely enthusiastic and press coverage was substantial. Pleased, Harris himself booked St. Denis for a series of March and April matinee performances, open to the public, at the Hudson Theatre. In a fundamental way, sponsorship by elite women had won a level of recognition for St. Denis's dancing which Harris, hosting the showcase concert several months earlier, had been unable to catalyze among male producers and booking agents. How had this happened?[18]

Newspaper commentary about the March 23 matinee reveals that the women acted with confidence in their position as arbiters of taste. Patroness Mrs. Charles C. Worthington explained that St. Denis was "a genius and too imaginative and original for the vaudeville, it seemed to us, though if our taking her up gives a boost — is that what you call it? — in the business way, why we are more than pleased."[19] Moving boldly where the more conservative theatre men had hesitated to go, the women created a performance platform for St. Denis. Furthermore, the women were quite conscious that they were taking a leadership position in sponsoring St. Denis's material, unstamped as yet by any other approval. "It's such fun to be in on something absolutely new —" added Mrs. Worthington, "as this certainly is, for she has gotten it all up herself, out of books and things. I believe she has never been abroad."[20] That the patronesses were claiming art status for St. Denis's work was eminently clear to the *New York Times*, whose feature article on St. Denis the following Sunday reported with a somewhat jaded air,

> Society has discovered something new under the limelight. Out of the
> jaws of vaudeville a group of New York women who still keep a weary eye

out for up-to-date novelties have snatched a turn which they hope to make more or less of an artistic sensation. A set of Hindu dances performed by a New Jersey girl with a rather convincingly clear notion of what she is doing, constitutes this latest find.[21]

This female sponsorship conferred immediate legitimacy on both St. Denis and the new, serious dance drama she had introduced. The prominence of the patrons and their guests brought newspaper coverage of the event which, reciprocally, confirmed the women's identification as taste makers or "lady patronesses of the arts," as one column put it. These women succeeded where Harris had failed because of the clout they wielded as new "custodians of culture."

No consensus exists among historians about just who actually were the constitutors, the maintainers, or the "custodians" of culture in turn-of-the-century America. Henry May's analysis of the "genteel" tradition in literature prior to the Great War identifies men as the custodians of culture. Helen Horowitz observes that while women are conventionally associated with arts patronage, she discovered men to be the active founders and institutional guides of Chicago's late-nineteenth-century museums, libraries, symphony orchestra, and university. Two studies of the Arts and Crafts movement paint different pictures of male leadership. While most leaders of the Arts and Crafts movement named by T. J. Jackson Lears were male, Eileen Boris shows that male leaders worried about women's growing prominence, fearing it would trivialize the craftsman ideal and hinder their own ability to define the movement.[22]

That the situation was not clear-cut is revealed by studies of other endeavors such as music making, philanthropy, and the women's club movement. Frank Rossiter links the choices Charles Ives made about his composing activity and business career to a negative perception of classical music as the province of women. Ives associated "genteel" music with things feminine, claims Rossiter, in no small part because women were closely connected to the practice and dissemination of classical music in his own community. Rossiter provides tantalizing grounds for speculating that women had begun to contest male practice and control in some domains of music in the late 1800s. Kathleen McCarthy argues that, while Chicago men asserted cultural leadership by building monuments of mortar and stone, Gilded Age women slowly and gradually took on public arbitership through work in the mediums of philanthropy and decorative arts societies. Perhaps the boldest claim of all is advanced in Karen Blair's study of the late-nineteenth-century women's club movement. "Clubs enabled women to become so closely associated with culture," she asserts, "that they expropriated the previously male world of literature and the arts as their own."[23]

The decided lack of agreement among historians about the gendering of cultural patronage and authority signals that Progressive-era processes of "taste making" and sponsorship were being contested and, I believe, recast. The sponsorship and platforms that society and reform functions provided Duncan and, especially, St. Denis powerfully positioned women to claim the function and status of cultural arbitership in the emergent field of women's innovative dance. This cultural positioning did not die with the Progressive era but flourished in the backing that women like Bethsabee de Rothschild would give to modern dance choreographer Martha Graham, and that Rebecca Harkness supplied to the fledgling Harkness Ballet in the 1960s.

St. Denis's matinee offers compelling evidence of women's burgeoning cultural leadership. Moreover, the *New York Times* article on St. Denis made explicit connection between the sponsors' support and the women's club movement in the United States. "The fascination of the Orient is eternal," it noted. "Women's clubs that have sipped tea over pretty much everything from Sun Worship to Mental Science generally fall back on Eastern lore for things to be enthusiastic about. The 'Road to Mandalay' is ankle deep with the papers of progressive reading societies." Two of the first women's clubs in the United States, Sorosis and the New England Women's Club (NEWC), were formed in 1868 and can be seen as one kind of women's response to nineteenth-century separate spheres ideology. Sorosis was peopled largely by professional women, especially writers, while NEWC members tended to be women deeply involved in reform efforts. Both, however, were founded to help women improve their education in an era when few opportunities for postsecondary or professional training were available to them. The examples of Sorosis and NEWC spawned hundreds of imitations across the country and the club movement became one of primarily middle-class, nonworking women. Aiming at self improvement, club women studied and listened to and wrote papers on traditional humanities subjects like painting, literature, drama, and music. Club activity combined sociability with doses of intellectual work and generated little tension with women's domestic duties and identification. In the 1890s, program emphasis shifted to club involvement in municipal reform affairs, although many clubs never lost their interest in culture study. By then, Karen Blair argues persuasively, the association of women with "culture" was, if not consolidated, at least well enough established to challenge assumptions of male leadership. While the culture study clubs of the 1870s and 1880s had refined women's capacities as appreciators or consumers of culture, the St. Denis matinee demonstrates that women with the financial resources to do so could extend their roles as cultural arbiters to include programming, the active providing of venues for up-and-coming performers.[24]

The matinee example stimulated emulation. On April 6, Mrs. Herbert Saterlee, daughter of J. Pierpont Morgan, sponsored St. Denis's appearance at the Saterlee home for a meeting of the elite Thursday Evening Club, an arts and literature study club. Members of this club included the Sanford Whites, the Joseph Choates, and Mrs. Cadwalader Jones. St. Denis appeared along with other vaudeville performers, and moving pictures were shown as well. It is St. Denis's dancing, however, that a New York *American* illustration captures, with seated society women leaning forward eagerly, drinking in the spectacle. On this occasion, too, the prominence of the sponsoring body drew newspaper attention to St. Denis's new work. Providing a venue and necessary financial support, the sponsors also confirmed the cultural leadership of club members.[25]

Successes like these brought St. Denis additional society engagements, several of which coupled aesthetic appreciation with fund-raising for reform causes. On April 24 she performed at the Waldorf-Astoria in a benefit for the People's Symphony; on April 27 in Washington, D.C. at a benefit sponsored by Mrs. A. C. Barney at the Belasco Theatre; and on May 2 in Boston for a benefit given at Mrs. Jack Gardner's Fenway Court home. In New York the six-year-old People's Symphony had amassed a $6,000 debt providing chamber and orchestral concerts "of the highest character at prices within the reach of students and wage earners." At least several of the People's Symphony Trustees had been in attendance at St. Denis's Thursday Evening Club performance. The Washington, D.C., affair benefited the Barney Neighborhood Club (a settlement house) and the Hospital for Incurables. *The Washington Times* connected St. Denis's impending performance there to her recent spate of society-sponsored appearances. St. Denis's appearance at Fenway Court was similarly part of a benefit for the Holy Ghost Local Hospital for Incurables in Cambridge. The *Boston Post* cited as event patrons the Rev. Samuel Crothers; Charles Eliot, President of Harvard; and Charles Eliot Norton, vice president of the hospital. Mrs. Gardner placed Fenway Court at the disposal of "the friends of the hospital," and suggested that St. Denis be secured to perform. Norton's daughter Elizabeth organized the evening; an extant program lists a contingent of women patronesses, including Mrs. R. H. Dana, Mrs. William Wharton, Mrs. Rudolphe Agassiz, and Mrs. J. J. Storrow.[26]

The elite fund-raising entertainments for reform causes at which St. Denis performed were linked to a larger context of women's social welfare work in turn-of-the-century America. Middle-class and elite women had a solid record of voluntary activity in antebellum charitable and benevolent work, and in the antislavery and temperance movements. Following the Civil War, changing industrial conditions and waves of economic depression sustained the need for women's public voluntary action. By the 1890s, still more systematic charity and reform enterprises were undertaken, such as the New York City Charity Organization Society, the WCTU, and urban settlement houses. By doing this public social welfare work, women stretched the boundaries of—while capitalizing on—the domestic responsibilities and sensibility assigned to them by separate spheres ideology. The venues for St. Denis's performances illuminate the ways women's charitable and reform work supplied women—as patrons or performers—with platforms from which to exert their cultural leadership. Women's reform and arts sponsorship activities mutually reinforced each other as elements of a gendered identity that by the Progressive era was resisting the limitations on women's self-constitution implicit in separate spheres ideology.[27]

St. Denis's Fenway Court appearance was her last before sailing to Europe in June 1906. For the next two years she toured the continent extensively, was received by heads of state, and excited the enthusiasm and respect of poets like Hugo von Hofmannsthal. When she returned to the U.S. in 1909, Harris scheduled evening performances for her at his Hudson Theatre, "the first time in that era when a dancer was able to hold the stage of a New York theatre as an evening attraction." She also toured a cycle of East Indian solo dances to Midwest and East Coast cities between December 1909 and April 1910. With backing by Harris, she presented a new, full-length dance drama, *Egypta*, in New York City matinee performances. Then she performed selected solos from *Egypta* in a 1911–12 cross-country tour. Harris lost money on both undertakings, and to repay him St. Denis returned to vaudeville. St. Denis lost her most important backer when Harris died on the Titanic. To make money, St. Denis turned to vaudeville once more and ultimately took society jobs again. Although she had won recognition in Europe for the artistic status of her dancing, St. Denis found it difficult in the United States to secure, on a consistent basis, appropriate theatrical venues, and with them, audiences for her work. Her return to vaudeville and society jobs signals the awkward fit between St. Denis's concept of art dance and the platforms available for it in commercial theatre, and illuminates the fundamental, continuing importance of women-sponsored venues to her career.[28]

Some of the "society" dates St. Denis performed were for strictly social occasions. She appeared in January 1913 in Mrs. Philip Lydig's private staging of the drama *Judith*. At Louis Tiffany's February 1913 dress ball, where guests wore costumes appropriate to the Egyptian theme and participated in a pantomime, she danced a solo before the woman portraying "Cleopatra." In August, at Mrs. Ogden Armour's Melody Land country estate, her solo dancing was featured in an evening that included dancing for both children and adults. The culture club connection continued to serve as well: she appeared before women's music study clubs in Kansas City and Chicago. Women patronesses in York Harbor, Maine, engaged her to perform at an annual benefit for their town's Historical and Improvement Society. Charitable causes, too, continued to solicit her appearances. In 1909, while performing her East Indian solos in Chicago, she agreed to appear at Mrs. Potter Palmer's annual charity ball at the Chicago Auditorium. Although she donated her services in this instance, the press notice was overwhelming. The $26,000 net proceeds were to benefit a host of social welfare enterprises, including the Chicago Refuge for Girls, Model Lodging House, the Home for Destitute and Crippled Children, the South Side Free Dispensary, Jackson Park Sanitarium, the Chicago Public School Art Society, and the Chicago Orphan Asylum and Friendly Visitors (Stockyard District). In December 1913, in New York City, she took part in a benefit performance for the *New York American*'s Christmas fund. Patronesses for the entertainment, which raised money for Christmas Fund toys and dinners, included Mrs. Stuyvesant Fish, Mrs. John Jacob Astor, and Mrs. James Speyer, the latter having attended the People's Symphony benefit and the St. Denis matinee of March 23, 1906.[29]

A final example shows that cultural sponsorship for St. Denis's dancing proceeded on at least one occasion from women engaged in the campaign for woman suffrage. On March 2, 1914, St. Denis performed at a birthday party given for suffrage leader Anna Howard Shaw at the Hotel McAlpin in New York City. Shaw had broken an ankle and therefore missed the party scheduled for her at the Biltmore Hotel on February 1; one "barefoot" dancer, Florence Noyes, had been engaged to dance there. Shaw attended the March party seated in a wheelchair and reportedly enjoyed performances by dancers St. Denis, Shadwell Morelly, and Isabelle Morton; singer Viola Gillette; and pianist Mrs. Stuart Kohn. Of the dancers, St. Denis was the only one to come down on the ballroom floor to dance directly in front of Dr. Shaw, and "so greatly did Dr. Shaw and the other grave and serious suffragists admire the bare-limbed nymph that they recalled her again and again," the *Tribune* reported. When Shaw sighed, "Dear Me! I wish I could dance like that," Mrs. Henry Villard replied "in doubtful tones," eyeing a just-completed high kick by St. Denis, "Would you dance like that?" "I'd like to be able to," Shaw responded. The leader of the National American Woman's Suffrage Association also admired Morton's silver trousers — not for their beauty but "because they looked so emancipated."[30]

Officers and office staff for the NAWSA were present, and the 150 women at the event represented a mixed middle- and upper-class audience, one intimately concerned with extending women's opportunities for participation in the nation's political and public life. These women apparently enjoyed the entertainment. Shaw's remarks about the dancers' range of movement and sartorial freedom suggest that the new forms of artistic dancing could be read through the political lens of dress reform initiatives.[31]

Shortly after this performance, St. Denis forsook a solo career and took Ted Shawn as her partner. Even in this endeavor she never seemed to achieve financial security. Together or with separate companies of Denishawn dancers, she and Shawn made a number of cross-country tours, sometimes with vaudeville backing. The Denishawn School the two had founded in Los Angeles in 1915, which Shawn managed, provided one source of income, but efforts in the 1920s to expand the school also required more vaudeville touring. In this light of continually precarious finances, the significance of women's sponsorship during St. Denis's early solo career becomes clear. As did other social events and benefits at which St. Denis had performed, the Shaw birthday party provided the artist with needed financial support and offered a performance format in which her work was taken seriously. Moreover, benefits from the arrangement accrued to both parties. While women sponsors provided venues and legitimation for St. Denis's new artistic dancing, they simultaneously confirmed their own identities not simply as consumers of culture but also as active definers and agents of it. Further, women-sponsored events supplied important supplements and periodic alternatives to the conventional theatrical presentation managed by male professionals. These events demonstrate that to forge careers as independent artists, dancers like St. Denis had to have recourse to networks of resources larger than themselves. Far from being singular geniuses, they generated themselves and their artistic dance practices by weaving back and forth between commercial institutions and the networks and relationships supplied by women's cultural practices. The project of dance innovation was, for Isadora Duncan as well as for St. Denis, necessarily a situated endeavor.

ISADORA DUNCAN

In the 1990s, Isadora Duncan is perhaps the best-known figure among Progressive-era innovators of new American dance practices. And this despite the fact that from 1900, Duncan largely made her career in Europe. In the pantheon of American modern dance, Duncan (1877–1927) holds a prominent place for exploring "natural" dance, and for eschewing the artifice and discipline of ballet training and movement vocabulary. In the early twentieth century, Duncan's solo dancing was variously labeled as interpretative or antique Greek dancing, although she specifically disclaimed any intent to reconstruct or reconstitute classic Greek dance. Duncan saw movement as proceeding and unfolding from the solar plexus. Especially in the early phases of her career, when joined with music by the likes of Chopin, Gluck, and Beethoven, dancing issued from her body in waves of motional impulse. Performed on stage spaces hung simply with velvet curtains, her new stagecraft departed from the ornament and realism of St. Denis or the organic simulacra Fuller created with carefully devised lighting effects. Duncan's turn-of-the-century dancing figured liberatory possibility, accomplishing a freedom from "formalism" that resonated strongly with contemporary viewers.

America, however, supplied ground primarily for the launching of Duncan's career. Impoverished and deserted by the father—Joseph Duncan—her family struggled in Oakland and San Francisco to keep its head above water in a period of frequent economic recession. Duncan gained early experience with physical culture via the Oakland *turnvereine*, and also with ballroom dances. She turned these resources to account as a teacher of dancing, as did her sister Elizabeth. In 1895, Duncan journeyed with her mother to Chicago to find theatrical, and better-paying, employment. She secured work as a dancer at the Masonic Roof Garden and was auditioned and hired by theatrical manager Augustin Daly to appear in a New York production. The family removed to New York, and Duncan maintained the connection with Daly through about 1898: she danced in pantomimes and plays, toured with Daly's company in America, and traveled with the company to England. By 1898 she'd experienced ballet training and gained familiarity with Delsartian ideas about movement.[32]

Documentation is slender for Duncan's activity during 1898 and 1899, but available materials show that women's sponsorship and patronage proved fundamental to Duncan's transition from Broadway performance and to her self-constitution as an art dancer. Duncan left Daly's employ and by February 1898 had begun presenting herself as a soloist. She also taught in her sister Elizabeth's dancing school, which catered to children of the wealthy and socially prominent.[33]

The engagements Duncan secured were primarily for social occasions given by or targeted at women from the highest stratum of New York's social elite. For example, the Carnegie Lyceum, a performance space affiliated with Carnegie Hall, was "well-filled with fashionable people" for pianist and composer Ethelbert Nevin's March 24 matinee performance. As one of several supporting artists, Duncan danced three "water scenes" to Nevin's music: *Narcissus, Water Nymphs,* and *Ophelia.* Duncan asserts in *My Life* that in the wake of this concert, many society women who had been in the audience engaged her to appear in their drawing rooms. That Duncan's vogue was established by March, if not a month earlier, is confirmed by *The Director,* a dance magazine aimed at students as well as teachers. *The Director*'s March 1898 issue allows that "Miss Duncan is a professional entertainer, and she has been taken up extensively by well known society women." It also reports repertory not in evidence at the Nevin concert.[34]

Duncan's own account claims that Mrs. [William] Astor invited her to dance at her villa in Newport, prestigious Rhode Island summering site for wealthy East Coasters, and that she danced at other villas too. Clear evidence exists for at least one such Newport engagement, at the end of the season in September. Miss Ellen Mason, a Boston dweller, provided the lawn of her Newport residence for the first of three planned recitals by Duncan. The fare for September 8 was the *Rubaiyat of Omar Khayyam,* "done into dance by Isadora Duncan." Elizabeth Duncan recited the text, with piano and violin accompaniment by her mother and John C. Mullaly. The patrons named in the program booklet—all female—spell out the prestigious support of Mrs. William Astor and Mrs. Potter Palmer, doyennes of New York and Chicago society, respectively. Fifteen socially prominent Newporters listed their names as well, among whom the September *Director* identified Mrs. Calvin Brice as a moving force in introducing "'a dance recital,' the very newest fad in Newport society."[35]

Duncan again danced the *Rubaiyat* in March 1899, amidst a "revival of Khayyam" that winter season, as one newspaper put it. Society figure Mrs.

Robert Osborn managed the event at the Carnegie Lyceum, which was "under the patronage of a number of well-known women." Justin Huntly McCarthy, friend of Augustin Daly and spouse to Broadway performer Cissie Loftus, offered the prefatory lecture on Khayyam, and Duncan danced to McCarthy's prose rendering of the *Rubaiyat*. Cabinet cards by J. Schloss publicizing the *Rubaiyat* capture Duncan in tights and ribboned slippers, free-hanging tresses, and a knee-to-calf-length gown. The release of neck and head, the stretch and deep bend of the torso, are anything but balletic, although stances taken by the feet echo an arabesque, a coupé derrière, or a relaxed lower leg nestled on a turned-out supporting leg. The audience for this experimenting dancer "was quite a fashionable one," according to one performance report. A preview piece made clear that Duncan had "been identified with society for some time," dancing "first at the residences of Mrs. John J. Wysong and Mrs. A. M. Dodge in this city," and that "she entertained fashionable Newport last summer at a fete champetre." Duncan's vogue with society women did not prevent about forty of them from walking out during the program in response to the bared limbs exposed by one of the dancer's costumes.[36]

Duncan and her family lost their belongings in the Windsor Hotel fire three days after this performance. Her society patrons rose in support on at least one occasion. Sixty-seven women — "from the inner ranks of the 150 of New York, San Francisco, Tuxedo [*sic.* Toledo?], and Chicago" — sponsored a benefit performance for her in April at the Lyceum Theatre. Her brother Augustin's melancholy readings and the doleful music reportedly stimulated "giggles and blushes" from some viewers, but at the conclusion all sixty-seven trooped onto the stage to kiss the fire victim and wish her well in her planned journey to England.[37]

It was in London that Duncan would continue her metamorphosis into an art dancer, exploring new music, changing her costuming, eventually shedding spoken texts. From May 1899, when she sailed to London, Duncan primarily made her career in Europe. She returned to America for brief tours in 1908, 1911, 1915, 1916, 1917, and 1922. Thus Europe, not America, catalyzed the period of her greatest artistic transgression and transformation. But Duncan lived and lives in Americans' imaginations as well, and her brief vogue as a "society-dancer" illuminates the way in which female patrons created conditions of possibility for the dancer to begin to construct her transformation.[38]

It should be noted that the events of 1898 and 1899 in which Duncan performed were predominantly "society gigs." While the slender data available prevent a definitive conclusion, the absence of reform or charity-

Isadora Duncan in a "carte de visite" photograph, 1899. Photograph by
Schloss. DANCE COLLECTION, THE NEW YORK PUBLIC LIBRARY FOR THE
PERFORMING ARTS, ASTOR, LENOX AND TILDEN FOUNDATIONS.

linked events marks Duncan's American trajectory as somewhat different from St. Denis's. Duncan's patronesses were prominently married women, the bulk of whom lived in New York City. A June 1899 *Broadway Magazine* article takes sly aim at just such prestigious sponsors. It matches the lead photo of a dreamy, throat-bared Duncan with a caption consisting of the sycophantic "How I love my friends, the Vanderbilts." The caption for a second photo, showing Duncan with downcast eyes focused on a flower-strewn floor, reads, "Isn't Mrs. Highuppe kind to throw flowers," ridiculing the dancer's high-ranking connections. In this mocking article, but also in printed program data and newspaper reports, the linkage of Duncan with the Astors, Vanderbilts, and Palmers suggests that patronage was caught up in, constituted a strategy within, a larger and longer-lasting struggle to recast class status and social position, a struggle dating from the Gilded Age in New York City.[39]

In the nineteenth century, New York grew to be the predominant East Coast entrepôt. The city's wealthiest stratum—the Knickerbocker elite—included families of Dutch and pre-Revolutionary provenance. As the city, its shipping, and its financial markets grew, membership in the wealthiest strata expanded as well. New men and their families, hailing from varied geographical sites, joined the city's economic leadership. This was a product of emigration in search of perceived opportunity as well as overseas immigration; in but one example of the latter, German Jewish immigration in the mid-nineteenth century brought new enterprise and seeded new fortunes in Gotham. The wealth compiled by the Knickerbocker elite, while persisting and holding, declined as a percentage of the city's wealth, and the participation by Knickerbocker families in the city's enterprises declined proportionally. In a real sense, the Knickerbocker patriciate waned; the very success of New York as a metropolis rendered fluid and unstable the city's class leadership. This situation contrasted with the solid grasp enjoyed by Boston's Brahmins on city leadership—financial, civic, and cultural. The decline of Knickerbocker leadership was bemoaned by its members as early as the 1840s. In a similar vein, families that ascended to wealth and social position at midcentury looked askance at competing arrivistes toward the turn of the century. Thus Mrs. Astor, in the 1880s and 1890s the social leader of New York's "Four Hundred" best families, bitterly complained that Mrs. Stuyvesant Fish's entertainments had disintegrating effects in society. Far from dismissing this last data, I take it quite seriously: a primary register for the inscription of city leadership at the highest wealth levels was Society, or the conduct of social intercourse—its rankings, etiquettes, and events.[40]

Mrs. William Astor herself illuminated social leadership as a battle-ground for class leadership. She was born Caroline Webster Schermer-horn, and her family derived from early New York Dutch roots; she thought her Schermerhorn pedigree superior to the arriviste Astors and Vanderbilts. Mrs. Astor outbid her sister-in-law Mrs. John Jacob Astor III for leadership of the "Four Hundred," a term coined by her assistant Ward MacAllister. In the same vein, Mrs. William K. Vanderbilt (later Mrs. O. H. P. Belmont) in 1883 forced Mrs. Astor to recognize her claims to New York's class aristocracy. Mrs. Vanderbilt celebrated the opening of her Fifth Avenue mansion by giving a party during which Mrs. Astor's daughter was scheduled to dance a quadrille; to secure an invitation to watch her daughter dance, Mrs. Astor first had to "call" on Mrs. Vanderbilt, which she did. Another comer, Mrs. Stuyvesant Fish, set her sights on Newport society leadership in 1889; she won recognition as a member, along with Mrs. Vanderbilt and Mrs. Hermann Oelrichs, of the "Social Strategy Board." Mrs. Fish also challenged Mrs. Astor's New York eminence through the vehicle of style. Countering Mrs. Astor's ponderous, three-hour, many-course dinner parties, Mrs. Fish paced her dinners rapidly and invited popular entertainers to amuse her guests. In the 1910s these entertainers included opera singer Nellie Melba and the exhibition dancers Vernon and Irene Castle.[41]

With this brief account of key protagonists and strife among New York's wealthiest women, I argue that Society competition may be seen as a vehicle for class inscription and contest within a mythos and scenario of long-term Knickerbocker decline. Period analysts like Thorstein Veblen were certainly accurate in pointing to Progressive-era women's expanded consumer roles and conspicuous consumption as effects of industrial capitalism. So too should elite women's Society competition be read for its instrumentality in ordering, subordinating, and parsing new and old players and social relations among Gotham's economic leadership. Describing Duncan "as the only real society pet," *Broadway Magazine* snidely documented the power of that female class leadership to direct attention and concern to selected persons and practices. The force of elite women's interest secured for Duncan *as a dancer* performance platforms, receptive audiences, and a level of media visibility she was unable to mobilize in commercial theatre circles. Society patronage constituted an alternative, if small-scale, producing network, and it is perhaps not surprising that the magazine, clearly an exponent of the theatre industry, would both remark and belittle the star-making capacity of such a competing network. Further, the fluid ranks of New York City's economic leadership positioned wealthy women not just to bid for class leadership but to re-define their gender role as well. As patrons of Isadora Duncan, Society women combined consumption and home entertaining—indisputable provinces of women's sphere—with setting standards for aesthetic taste. Deploying a nose for the new, they simultaneously constituted themselves adequate and appropriate judges of talent and innovative practice. Confirming and contesting class leadership through the conduct of high-profile sociability, Duncan's female Society patrons expanded their performance of women's gender role to include cultural arbitrage. As they did for St. Denis, female patrons took unto themselves the work of cultural custodians and created conditions of possibility for new dance at a crucial point in Duncan's career.[42]

SPONSORS AND SPACES

It should not be surprising to find that cultural arbitership for new dance practices was bound up with women's complicated negotiation of the public and private spaces assigned them by separate spheres ideology. While that ideology would seem to have confined women to the distinct and limited domains of home and family, the divide between public and private was far more porous in practice than the prescriptive ideology would admit. And as women's sponsorship of new dance practices confirms, diffusion across the boundary between public and private could flow in more than one direction.

Women's nineteenth-century consignment to "the home" positioned them as managers of the household, as organizers and producers of the spatial resources that it provided to family members and that were serviced by domestic laborers. Karen Halttunen's scrutiny of Godey's Lady's Book suggests that a subtle geography of domestic space was urged upon nineteenth-century middle-class homes. Prescriptive literature like Godey's carefully distinguished parlors and rooms for receiving visitors—the public—both from the rooms dedicated to family members and also those spaces in which domestic help produced the household's food and comforts. Further, advice books and ladies' journals articulated instructions for correctly negotiating domestic space when performing rituals of "calling" on social acquaintances, entertaining at home, even mourning deaths and conducting funerals. In performing these "lexicons of behavior," to use the term coined by Joseph Roach, women traversed a complex of public and private spaces; they communed with the personal family circle but also with the external public world of visitors and employees. With their own persons, then, they threaded through the boundaries segregating public and private space, shuttling with their motion across highly permeable membranes.[43]

I want to argue that women managing households can be seen as producers of public and private spaces within their own homes, in much the same way that commercial theatre managers plotted attractions, engaged performers, and solicited viewers to attend theatrical events. The functions and spaces that women orchestrated were diverse, ranging from the most intimate personal processes to quite widely witnessed displays. Indeed, as early as the 1850s, the manners and social procedures recommended by period advice literature expanded to include promotion of parlor theatricals. Numerous guides detailed charades, tableaux vivants, proverbs, and shadow pantomimes for enactment in home entertainment. Guidebooks explained how to build parlor stages, rig curtains, arrange lighting devices, and devise special effects. Matters of costuming and makeup received attention as well, and *Godey's Lady's Book* coached readers on melodramatic gesture. These entertainments simply added another register to the production and maintenance of household spaces and functions conventionally allotted to women under separate spheres ideology.

The vogue for parlor theatricals that Halttunen identifies was borne out by women's adoption of Delsartian movement practices in the later nineteenth century. Genevieve Stebbins introduced her Delsartian physical culture system in the 1880s to a broad stratum of middle- and upper-class adult white women who studied her movement materials largely in private settings. Stebbins's students deployed their new knowledge in the performance of statue posing and tableaux vivants, selecting their subjects from Greek statuary, classic paintings, and sometimes scenes from literature. Whereas both men and women participated in the parlor theatricals described in midcentury entertainment guides, women alone were the executants in home entertainments comprising Delsartian tableaux and statue posing. Stebbins herself performed in private homes, and also parlayed her considerable skills into appearances at commercial theatre matinees in the 1890s. As a child, Ruth St. Denis viewed one of Stebbins's matinees and derived early inspiration from it. But Stebbins and St. Denis were exceptional in this regard. The "Delsarte system of expression" remained a home-centered practice for the bulk of Stebbins's students.[44]

Parlor theatricals and home Delsartian performance blurred the borders separating public and private presentation spaces. Home productions of dramatic and movement entertainments, performed *by* family and friends in the nineteenth century, fashioned a "public" within the "private" of the family, and this public was "performance." Thus when Duncan and St. Denis found sponsors and venues in the homes and fetes of female society and reform leaders, they capitalized on a transgression of boundaries already set in motion. The difference was that Duncan and St. Denis earned a fee as they traversed that tenuous public/private divide. Where family and friends as amateurs had previously embodied the public of "performance" in the permeable privacy of the home, Duncan and St. Denis brought aspiring professionalism and the cash nexus to their negotiation of liminoid venues. St. Denis's sponsors were implicated too. Newspaper ridicule of the lady patrons for her 1906 matinee confirmed the trespass they were committing: the sponsors were redirecting established routes for exchange and circulation of new performers. At the same time, they rerouted their own currency as cultural custodians. The sponsors staked emerging dance practices as a domain for cultural leadership; they amplified a connection among dance, the feminine, and the corporeal.

WOMEN/PERFORMERS/BODIES

Twentieth-century performers have garnered most of the attention that scholars pay to dance in the United States. Connections among notions of the feminine, matters of the body, and dance have yet to be systematically analyzed for periods preceding the Progressive era. Nonetheless, it is not unreasonable to surmise that dance practices are gendered, even re-gendered, for every period in which they circulate. Among the forces that drive this re-gendering, I speculate, are the changing social and scientific constructions of human bodies over time. Certainly "things corporeal" were re-sorted and re-valued in the Progressive era. That period's devotion to athletics, for example, for males as well as females, indexes a much larger discourse of the body that worried and struggled with conceptions and placements of masculinity and femininity in a rapidly industrializing and urbanizing society. With the dancing practices that they innovated, Isadora Duncan and Ruth St. Denis participated in a re-sorting of the bodily and the feminine, seeking at the same time to win valuation different from that which was accorded ballet girls of their day.

Ballet girls, or broilers as they were sometimes called, were prized for their physiques as much as for the dancing skills they possessed. A buxom figure and willingness to wear very scanty garb were requirements that this cadre of working women shared with female burlesque performers. The latter were expected to sing or speak as well, at least until the 1890s when, as Robert Allen maintains, the voice along with its transgressive potential was stripped from burlesque. Dancers aspiring to vaudeville employment developed tricks of coordination and strength such as dancing while whirling a chair clenched with the teeth. Infusions from Europe occasionally shifted emphases in performance requirements. Skirt dancing techniques developed by English music hall dancers, for example, quickly made their way into American repertoires, including that of Ruth St. Denis.[45]

At bottom, though, what female dancers achieved was circulation of their spectacularization. Theatrical vehicles focused on the dancers' sexuality framed as spectacle, as the "given to be seen" of the performance. Works like *The Black Crook*, first mounted in 1866, combined the spectacularization of the female dancer's body with the increase and elaboration of transformation scenes. Spectacles of the body and of staging comprised a standard for postbellum lyric theatre.

At the turn of the twentieth century, theatrical dancing qualified as entertainment rather than artistic dancing. It did not merit regard as aesthetic. The career progress of Carrie Meeber, Theodore Dreiser's protagonist in *Sister Carrie* (1900), captures the equivocal place that dance occupied as a form of work for women. After journeying to New York City with the besotted but still-married Hurstwood, she leaves him and pursues a theatrical career. Carrie gradually rises from a shield-bearing, sword-toting chorus girl to stardom in a Broadway show and luxurious living in a posh city hotel. The sexual corruption that commenced when she fled Chicago is compounded as she ascends the theatrical ladder, offering up her body in kinetic and histrionic guises for the pleasure of viewing audiences.

As circulated through theatre dance, then, femaleness was constrained as the bodily and the sexual. The innovations by Duncan and St. Denis in the United States may be understood as contesting what the "given to be seen-ness" of women comprised. The new dance practices that they developed did not always or in all ways excise the spectacularization of women. But it did complicate that spectacularization and offer counters to it. Without doubt, Duncan and St. Denis labored hard to displace the demeaned and demeaning status allocated to professional dancers. They strove to produce other meanings for women's dancing, to escape equation of things corporeal with "the sexual" and only the sexual. One of their strategies for doing so was to frame their endeavors as "artistic" and to assume the posture of gifted artists possessing special sensibilities. But while they contested the status, meanings, and movement vocabularies available to professional dancers, they never simply eclipsed the status quo. Rather, their work had the effect of making multiple the possibilities for dancing, for movement practices gendered feminine.

Both Duncan and St. Denis drew upon Delsartian ideas and practices as they forged independent dance careers. St. Denis also mined a vein of imagery associated with the Orient. An Egyptian Deities cigarette poster had captured her imagination when she was still touring with David Belasco's theatre company; this seed helped germinate *Radha*. And as Suzanne Shelton has shown, both St. Denis and her mother moved in circles of people fascinated with Indian literature and mysticism. St. Denis was a voracious reader and steeped herself in contemporary literature about Egypt and India. She took pains so that the scenarios and choreographies that she developed not only evoked the physical settings of these foreign cultures, but alluded to their spiritual, mystical, and religious practices as well. Thus the solo *The Yogi* presented the dancer in meditative states. In *Radha* she fashioned her role as a temple dancer, first indulging the senses through dance and finally renouncing them.[46]

By bringing aspects of the spiritual or transcendent into play through associations with the Orient, St. Denis exploited a widely presumed connection between gender and piety in nineteenth-century America. Separate spheres ideology had assigned child nurture and moral leadership of the family to women, and the perfectionism of the Second Great Awakening spurred women to walk afield to ready society for the millennium. Thus, women organized in voluntary societies early in the 1800s both to prepare for the Second Coming and to protect the family from threats brought home to it by rapidly changing society. It should be remembered that the postbellum WCTU included the word "Christian" in its name. The Social Gospel movement supplied important impetus to women's public activity at century's end. Women's charity causes throughout the century were driven by religious motivation as well as by class identifications.

Thus when St. Denis evoked with her dances things spiritual and of transcendent moral purpose, she tapped into a widely acknowledged realm of female cultural leadership in America. To be sure, her bare feet, her scanty costumes, and aspects of her movement style continued to link her work with the erotic and sexual meanings that had attached to other professional dancers of the day. But St. Denis knit the erotic and sensual with the exalted. She brought together, in other words, the two "bodies" located at the poles of nineteenth-century female morality. At one pole stood the professional dancer, defined primarily by her sexuality. At the other pole stood the mother, whose reproductive, maternal body positioned her as compass star for the family, the source and index of its piety, morality, and nurture. St. Denis's dancing twinned these two bodies in an alliance that remained always uneasy, ever shifting in its kinetic distributions of sensuality and mystical transport. Yet in this twinning she produced "transcendence" as a second, complicated signification for female dancing; she thus fragmented the singularity of sexual meaning that had previously obtained for dance.

Duncan twined her Delsartian background with movement materials culled from early German physical culture exercises, social dances, and the ballet girl vocabulary she performed while in Augustin Daly's employ. Like St. Denis, she clothed herself in the raiment of cultural icons, although these references alluded to imagery of different provenance. In photos from the late 1890s, she conveyed something of a Pre-Raphaelite aura. With loosened tresses and languid mien, standing with or amidst strewn flowers, she looked kin to the muse immortalized by England's Pre-Raphaelite brotherhood. Remaking herself in London and Paris, she came to favor Greek-styled tunics that bared her limbs and throat. From these draperies flashed her legs, moved her magisterial arms, massed her body's weight. Like St. Denis yet again, she incorporated the sensuous presentation of her self as a matter of course in her choreography.

Further, Duncan put into motion a freedom from artifice and a sympathy for natural forms that resonated with values circulating in both the English and American Arts and Crafts movements. Ideas about "truth to nature" and "organic form," developed earlier in the work of John Ruskin and William Morris, were studied widely in certain American circles, including the women's club movement. Associations with the erotic, however, prevented the easy assimilation of Duncan's work to late-nineteenth-century Arts and Crafts aestheticism, even as she strove to distance herself from the "unnatural" techniques of ballet. The cut of her garb and the appropriation of concert-grade music for her choreographies disturbed audiences. Her sexual liaisons in the 1910s, widely reported, provoked them. Like St. Denis, Duncan brought together conflicting affects in her work, but the new meanings she produced for dance also sprang from the very way in which she danced. Ann Daly has persuasively argued that Duncan's early dancing was marked by its ongoingness. Waves of motion emanated from her body's center and flowed to the periphery. In choreographic sequences, one movement melted into the next, and the dancer deployed her body's weight and temporality in response to the music's rhythmic elasticity. Duncan's ongoing movement, Daly asserts, struck the audience as dissolving the dancer's body. Her dancing thus functioned as a metaphor for becoming a self, for working out the subjectivity of the person rather than displaying the body.[47]

The capacity for identity formation is not unique to Duncan's choreography, I submit. This book takes as fundamental the capacity for dance to worry, assert, argue, or confirm identities of many kinds; this capacity operates broadly, underpinning diverse Western dance practices that have been categorized as "theatrical," "social," and "popular." Particularly in its earlier Progressive-era incarnations, Duncan's dancing acted to create fluid subjectivity for the female dancer. Duncan and St. Denis, with their distinctive movement practices, asserted new meanings for the female dancing body at the turn of the twentieth century. They freed that body from fixity and from an essentialized sexuality. They afforded that body fluid subjectivity as well, and St. Denis aligned the physical with the spiritual, conjoining their radically opposite moral valences. Just as female patrons for emerging choreographers intervened in the circulation of dancing, so the female dance makers intervened, to constitute and live new significances for movement practices. As they made new meanings for dance, as they proposed new significances for female bodies, they participated at the same time in new viewing relationships with contemporary spectators.

VISION AND SPECTATORS

Female patrons and choreographer-performers of the new Progressive-era dance practices can be understood as occupying two positions in a triangular relationship of production. Patrons produced the events and the venues, even the linkages to audiences, that emerging dancers sorely needed. Choreographer-performers produced at least two things: the plan and design for the dancing—the choreography itself; and the live rendering, or the embodiment, of the choreography—the performance. And as indicated above, both patrons and choreographer-performers produced distinct meanings or significances for their undertakings. The third position in this triangular relationship was occupied by spectators of the danced presentations. Of course, patrons often also occupied spectator positions. But as spectators, I will argue, they constituted still other meanings for the dancing they viewed, meanings different from those produced at other points in the triangular circulation of new twentieth-century dance practices.

Dance scholarship has only recently begun to consider the issue of spectatorship from a theoretical perspective. Works by Ann Daly and Susan Manning, for instance, reference the substantial literature on "spectatorial positions" that, since the 1960s, has emerged from or been inspired by film studies. Theories of spectatorship developed in film studies have been grounded in study of Hollywood films produced in the "golden age" of the 1930s, 1940s, and 1950s. These films featured a binary logic in which male characters took the active roles and moved the narrative along, while female characters enacted passive roles, existing as the object and source of men's pleasure and desire. Theorist Laura Mulvey has pointed to cinematic techniques such as framing, angle, camera movement, and editing as the means used to create active male and passive female characters within narrative film structures. These same means offered viewers scopophilic pleasure and two kinds of viewing positions: voyeurism or identification with male characters. Female viewers could identify with passive female characters, and desire to be the desired, or they could take on a male viewing position. As theorized in classic studies of film's golden age, then, power and pleasure accrued to the male spectator and the "male gaze"; the "female spectator" found herself inscribed as object, and never subject, in a masculine economy of pleasure and desire.[48]

Why were the cinematic means in Hollywood films used to such ends? Mulvey and others say that structures of Hollywood films were reinforced by pre-existing psychical structures in individual viewers *and* by the larger social structure of patriarchy. The picture that emerges from such film-based theorizing is that viewing positions are fixed and largely invariant, and that they are reinscribed by patriarchy, itself a social relationship without variation or opposition to its authority. This "inelasticity" renders "gaze theory" largely static. Further, we may fairly ask whether a structure for meaning-making that emerged in specific connection to 1930s social and technological contexts can be read backward into other periods or applied to different performance modes. These considerations of inelasticity and historical specificity should caution us against transhistorical application of gaze theory. Its usefulness would seem to be limited for the Progressive era, for instance, since aspects of patriarchy *were* being contested, and since the demographics of patrons, creators, and viewers of dance were changing so fundamentally.

Reception theory and post-structuralist ideas about the "death of the author" have equipped scholars to acknowledge the role that readers play in producing the texts they consume. That is, different communities reading or consuming the same literary products can be expected to derive varying significances from them. In a related vein, art theorist Jonathan Crary has explored the nineteenth-century conception of vision as a fluid, responsive, and malleable activity. He argues that vision itself was rethought early in that century to embrace the "corporeality" of vision. Previous theories of vision had located the substance and the meaning of an image in objects external to the human body. Eyes, and vision, acted as blank slates that were simply written upon by an externally given reality. This view was challenged by scientists in the 1830s and 1840s. Research on the nervous and sensory systems led them to understand the human body as producing a physiological response to, and thus creating the image of, an external object. Such different stimuli as heat, physical blows, and chemicals, for example, all registered their impact on vision in the same way—as "light." Not external sources but the body itself supplied the source of "light." Thus, the body was understood to be the source of vision. With vision made corporeal, it followed that the constitution of meaning was a human process; meaning or "truth" did not reside objectively in external objects. As Crary notes, this vision of vision raised unsettling questions about the existence of exterior reality, questions that were downplayed. But the logic of "corporeal vision" conferred on the body the capacity to produce new forms of the "real." This body-based vision assigned agency and meaning-making power to the viewer; it wrote the spectator into the process of vision. The nineteenth-century currency of corporeal vision lends strong historical support to theorizing new female patrons—new spectators—as intimately involved in producing meanings for the dance and movement practices they viewed. As the viewers changed, as the locations and occasions for viewing changed, so too would the meanings for dance change.[49]

Susan Manning has concluded that, for all her efforts in other directions, Isadora Duncan proved unable to avoid reinscribing images of the erotic female body in her dances. Not until the likes of Martha Graham and Mary Wigman came on the scene were female choreographer-performers able to blunt or redirect the male gaze. Early modern dancers like Duncan did succeed, she maintains, in promoting a female viewing position which allowed women to see themselves as something other than objects of desire.[50] Female spectators could relate their own movement experiences in social dance and physical culture to the movement materials early dance innovators employed in their choreography: Delsartian statue posing, waltz rhythms, and physical culture exercises. Manning's deductions are indeed plausible; they reinforce, I believe, the large point I advance about spectator production of meaning in dance, indeed of the dance itself. For if we take vision to constitute the image perceived, then women's Progressive-era cultural practices positioned them to constitute meanings for dance practices not confined to voyeurism or erotic identification. Women's reform and charity work were premised on the separate spheres recognition of women's moral superiority and religious inclinations. It was these tenets that helped launch women into public sphere activity and that sustained their claims in that domain. From the socially elite to the middle class, St. Denis's "private patron" spectators were well primed to register the spiritual aspirations that informed her work. Her middle- and upper-class culture club and society patrons would have readily received the references her dance dramas made to the historical lore and ritual practices of "oriental" cultures. The sensuousness of St. Denis's self-presentation should not be denied, but I maintain that it did not constitute her sole attraction to viewers.

These strands of sensuousness and serious purpose continued to animate St. Denis's dancing practice some twenty years later, when the young Jane Sherman danced with the Denishawn troupe. Writing retrospectively about those days, Sherman criticized St. Denis for making artistic "compromises" such as shortening her skirts for vaudeville audiences. Countering this view in an article jointly authored with Sherman, Christena Schlundt emphasized St. Denis's repeated declaration of high-minded aspirations. Both historians read St. Denis correctly; the two strands entwined in St. Denis's work. In the Progressive era, the private patronage which St. Denis garnered brought her into contact with spectators quite different in class and ethnic statuses from the audiences she encountered in vaudeville engagements. Her patrons' investment in charity and reform work, even Society sociability, allowed them to constitute St. Denis's dancing as a movement practice they were pleased to sponsor, one that could comport with their views of womanly qualities even as it capitalized on the sensuous appeal long associated with theatre dancing.[51]

The extent to which viewers formed Isadora Duncan's dancing can be seen just as clearly, at the point of her transfer to England and Europe — the primary staging ground of her career. Duncan's New York matinees and Newport dancing featured her in poetry "done into dance." Having been taken up by American society women, Duncan crossed the Atlantic to

England hoping to secure work from female leaders of London society.[52] "Discovered" in Kensington Park by the actress Mrs. Patrick Campbell and entertained at some of her gatherings, Duncan drew to herself a cadre of mostly male supporters, including gallery manager Charles Hallé, critic J. Fuller-Maitland, music professional Sir Hubert Parry, and theatre professionals Joe and Alice Comyns Carr. These people advised Duncan consistently for a period of months, suggesting different music and revising her costuming. Duncan accordingly began to develop programs using the music of Chopin and Renaissance composers, and largely abandoned spoken text as accompaniment for her dancing. These London counselors—her personal spectators—were crucial to this, her second remaking, and to her ultimate success on the Continent.[53]

Duncan's London remaking, along with St. Denis's vogue in New York, suggests the power of new visions to constitute new possibilities and new meanings for dance. Instead of eradicating the sensuous and the sensual, these women countered or bound it up with a second kind of signal. The intertwining of the two signals, the multivocality of their presentations, was intimately connected to the structuring of the events at which they performed, hence to new "looks" or gazes. Their new dance practices depended in part on their new patrons' ability to "see" them differently, to bring to bear different sets of references for making meaning out of the dancers' bodily practices. In the United States this ability to see differently sprang from the patrons' constitution of womanliness, their organizational commitments, their culture club agendas, and the status competition among the wealthiest female members of New York's elite. Middle- and upper-class white women's cultural practices in the Progressive era positioned them to envision dancers and dance as more than simply erotic bodies in motion.

A literary corollary for this production of vision, and of dance, may be found in the tale of public speech and women's rights campaigns told in Henry James's *The Bostonians*. Serialized in 1885 and published in 1886, *The Bostonians* focuses on the postbellum upsurge in women's rights organizing. Olive Chancellor, the bluest of Boston blue bloods, strikes up a friendship with Verena Tarrant, the young, lower-middle-class woman who speaks inspiringly about women's rights when placed under hypnosis by her mesmerist father. Struck by Verena's potential and repelled by the father's exploitative conduct, Olive removes Verena from her parents' home. She launches her on a program of serious reading and discussion; she polishes Verena's social skills and builds her self-esteem. With deliberate speed, she presents Verena as a speaker to carefully selected audiences at choice salons.[54]

Like female dancers at the turn of the century, however, Olive and Verena can never be certain that it is Verena's speaking talents which attract listeners. Certainly Olive's cousin, the impoverished Southerner Basil Ransom, can listen to her without hearing, admiring the tilt of her head, the color in her cheek, her beguiling figure. In a contest of wills, Basil wins Verena away from Olive and the sisterhood the two enjoy in pursuit of their women's rights work. On the eve of Verena's formal "debut" as a women's rights public speaker in the vast Boston Music Hall, Ransom persuades her to walk away from the waiting audience. Olive, compelled by this disaster to do what would otherwise be, for her, unthinkable, steps to the podium herself to save the moment.

James's Bostonians illuminate a spectrum of opinion about the propriety of Verena's speaking and bodily presentation in lectures made before invited, though nonpaying, audiences. Early in their acquaintance, Ransom views Verena's public speaking as amusing and temporary; he thinks of her variously as an inspirational speaker, public character, little prophetess, *improvisatrice*. He notes her air of being on exhibit while speaking and ponders whether her verbal gifts are real or instilled. As he grows increasingly enamored and impatient to win her away from lecturing, he muses that she is a touching, ingenuous victim, or a ranter and sycophant, albeit an engaging one. He is convinced throughout that she is meant for him and "made for love."[55] Olive's sister Mrs. Luna, who hopes to snare Ransom for herself, judges Verena more harshly. Casting aspersions on a New York society matron who presented Verena in her mansion's music room, Mrs. Luna opines,

> I must say I call it a very base evasion of Mrs. Burrage's, producing Verena Tarrant; it's worse than the meretricious music. Why didn't she honestly send for a ballerina from Niblo's—if she wanted a young woman capering about on a platform?[56]

Comparison with a ballerina is meant to insult. Mrs. Luna further describes Verena as a fifth-rate *poseuse* and predicts she will run off with a lion tamer or marry a circus man. Other characters in the novel counter such negative views of women as public speakers, but never fully nor satisfactorily. Olive expresses hopefulness and approval of Verena by calling her a "gifted being"; she places public speaking beyond the pale of women's quotidian activities. In the same vein of exceptionalism, an eager lecture agent asks Mrs. Luna at the fateful Music Hall assembly, "don't you regard her [Verena] as a wonderful genius?" Not only does Mrs. Luna vehemently disagree, but the agent's glowing construction of Verena's activity is also immediately negated when the conflicted speaker absconds.[57]

James demonstrates that the position of the viewer is all-important when evaluating the female public speaker in the novel's 1870s setting. Verena can strike men and women alike as a charming adventuress, but she can also be read quite differently by men and women who hear in her words the prophecy of women's emancipation. In the eyes of Ransom and Mrs. Luna, Verena amounts to little more than a ballerina or an actress, those professionals who make an exhibition of themselves, who are *trained* to look transparent but really aren't, who though engaging are ultimately misguided. Indeed, the sharpest rebuke that Olive levels at Verena is to urge the young woman, "Well, then, go in and speak for them—and sing for them—and dance for them!" What then could induce patrician Olive to step to the podium herself when Verena deserts the swollen and impatient crowd gathered at Boston's most prestigious venue? Only the cause of women's emancipation and the mobilization of women's organized energies, energies which Olive herself had tapped to mount the engagement and attract listeners. Only the expectations of that gathered audience could transform the self-restrained Olive into a public lecturer, one who exhibited herself for all to see, regardless of their motives in looking.[58]

The triangulated processes of patronage, spectatorship, and choreography-performance wrought several kinds of connections among womanhood, dancing, and female bodies in Progressive-era America. From the supply side of the relationship, women's dance patronage challenged the boundary between public and private spheres for women's and men's activities, and it blurred the line between commercial and "private" venues as viable platforms for performers' careers. Women's dance patronage thus established an important new linkage of female bodies and dancing with women's conduct of "booking," or the commercial nexus.

From the demand side, new performing venues mobilized by female patrons afforded spectators opportunities to entertain revised, changed, or enlarged views of females dancing. That Duncan and St. Denis satisfied contemporary thirsts for "culture," in its nineteenth-century sense of things aesthetic and noble, is indexed by the registration of middle- and upper-class daughters in schools operated by the Duncan family (in New York) and by St. Denis with Ted Shawn (the Denishawn school opened in Los

Angeles in 1915). Here were laid foundations for the gendering of modern dance study as female, a gendering that paralleled the female study of ballet, but differed substantially in the movement repertoires and meanings made available for female dancers. Female spectatorship for new dance practices, catalyzed during the Progressive era, wedged open the domain of meanings and gazes that had obtained for theatre dance in the preceding century even as it confirmed the study and performance of dance as a female-gendered activity. The three female choreographer-performers discussed here hailed, strikingly, from the precarious border of the lower middle class, as in Fuller's case, or from the lapsed middle class, in Duncan's and St. Denis's cases. Veterans of contemporary theatre, all three knew firsthand the prevalent association of female dancers with sexual display and libertinage. From the choreography-performance or production side of the triangle, St. Denis capably brought together in her dancing the sensuous qualities of the "pleasurable" dancing body with the religious and moral affinities assigned to the nineteenth-century maternal body. Duncan in her early American career managed to articulate the materiality of the dancing body with a filtered Ruskinian or fin-de-siècle aestheticism and the respect accorded Greek art, an inspiration she referenced and that others attributed to her. What must be understood here is that Duncan and St. Denis succeeded in budging the categories into which dancing female bodies had previously been placed. At the time when separate spheres ideology crested in the United States, these dancers proved able to muddy the waters of women's gender roles. They complicated the routine association of theatre dancing with circulation of sexualized female bodies. To introduce multiplicity and ambiguity where singularity had previously obtained—that was significant. It placed dance in a newly equivocal position, one as fraught with possibility as with traditional meanings. The danger that never lapsed, the potential that would strengthen as the Progressive era waned, was the possibility that *as* a gendered practice, the emerging modern dance could be shouldered aside, subordinated, as a performance form linked to bodies rather than texts, to women rather than men.

Fuller, St. Denis, and Duncan fashioned careers as special individuals, artists of a distinctive sensibility. This was but one approach to innovation in dance in the late nineteenth and early twentieth centuries. Women's cultural practices also furthered development of dance as an artistic activity of which all people were thought to be capable. The Progressive-era settlement house movement supplied an important arena for women's constitution of themselves as social scientists and social welfare workers. And, although they are seldom recognized as such, settlement houses offered an empowering environment for women's innovation in dance. Stellar evidence of this potentiality would be demonstrated in dance and drama work at the Henry Street Settlement in New York City, work which Irene and Alice Lewisohn would parlay into the Neighborhood Playhouse.

Three The Settlement House and
the Playhouse: Cultivating
Dance on New York's
Lower East Side

When the Neighborhood Playhouse opened its doors on the Lower East
Side in Manhattan, the inaugural performances of *Jephthah's Daughter*
excited a decidedly mixed reaction from its audience. Alice Lewisohn, co-
founder of the Playhouse with her sister Irene, remembered that

> Our orthodox Jewish neighbors were scandalized at the free interpreta-
> tion of the Bible text. Caricatures of us appeared in the Yiddish press
> showing "Miss Neighborhood Playhouse" slamming the door in the face
> of the Yiddish playwright. The radically inclined were disappointed that
> the Old Testament was used as source, rather than Andreyev or Gorky,
> and the conventionally minded were shocked at the bare feet of the
> dancers. Still another chorus raised its voice in behalf of strictly Ameri-
> can culture, protesting that only poor material and no good could come
> from this East-Side venture. Notwithstanding the criticism and the pro-
> duction's many imperfections, *Jephthah's Daughter* concluded its sched-
> uled run. Whatever it lacked in finish was compensated by its fervor and
> originality.[1]

The querulous reception accorded the Neighborhood Playhouse's 1915
production indexes the fraught situation of dance and drama work during
a high point of immigration to and through industrial New York City early
in the twentieth century. For ten years preceding the Neighborhood Playhouse debut, the Lewisohn sisters had worked with children's clubs and
classes at the Henry Street Settlement, located in the same Lower East Side

neighborhood. There, dance and drama work constituted one among many strategies through which the Settlement reached out to its immigrant neighbors, attempting to mitigate the ravaging experiences of urban industrial life. Empowered in the settlement context to innovate in dance and drama, the Lewisohns subsequently constructed the Neighborhood Playhouse to secure larger, permanent production facilities. Ensconced in this venue, Playhouse productions participated in the critique of commercial theatre practices known as the "little theatre" movement of the 1910s. Like the Henry Street Settlement House, the Playhouse created a space in which to address issues of immigration and ethnicity through movement modalities. At the same time, the hierarchy of functions and the structuring of production processes developed first at the Settlement and then at the Playhouse acted sometimes to bridge, sometimes to inscribe class and power differences among settlement residents, nonresident workers, and neighborhood participants. The Festival Dancer, that dancing body nurtured from Henry Street Settlement days and refined in the Playhouse era, brought together in her gendered person a complex of immigrant, ethnic, class, and gender identities being negotiated on the Lower East Side. The terms of this negotiation, in turn, suggest much about the elevation of "modernist" sensibility that infused modern dance in the 1920s and 1930s. Valorized by master narratives of modern dance's history, this modernist sensibility privileged aesthetic goals and marginalized, if it did not put under erasure, dance's instrumentality as a form of direct political or social engagement.

The Settlement House Movement

The settlement house movement originated in England in the 1880s and quickly spread to the United States. In both these countries, the movement tried to remedy the problems of poor, working-class people living in industrial cities. In England, the settlement workers' ideal of personal service to the poor was often impelled by religious conviction, and the native-born urban poor formed the object of settlement attention. In America, settlement work was generally secular in character and focused on the waves of immigrants arriving in port and industrial cities.[2]

Immigrants were crucial to the expanding, relatively unskilled labor force required by mass production industry in the late nineteenth century. Between 1870 and 1920, American cities sustained successive waves of immigration. Among more than twenty-six million immigrants were some

two million Jews, propelled by pogroms and circumstances at home but
also drawn by American labor markets; a majority of these located in New
York City. As new workers thronged industrial cities, they exerted enormous demographic pressure. Inadequate housing forced crowded and
unsanitary living conditions on working people who could not afford
needed health care. Working-class children too young to labor in mass
production factories or in the sweating system attended schools sorely
under-equipped to handle the numbers of students. The seasonal nature of
employment in sweated industries such as garment work, and the compe-
tition-driven wages paid industrial labor, left working people impoverished. These conditions required whole families, not just the head of the
household, to enter the paid labor force. As settlement workers were quick
to discern, the difficulties immigrants encountered in urban work and
habitation were only exacerbated by their cultural dislocation and the
struggle to adjust to American ways.[3]

Hull-House in Chicago and New York's Henry Street Settlement were
important outposts of the American settlement house movement. Impelled to the idea of service by the education she had received and by the
precedent her political father set, Jane Addams, perhaps the best remembered of settlement workers, searched for meaningful engagement of her
skills and sensibilities. During a trip to Europe, Addams was inspired by the
work she saw undertaken at London's Toynbee Hall; she founded Hull-
House with Ellen Gates Starr in 1889. Located in Chicago at Halsted and
Polk Streets, Hull-House bordered on a number of ethnic communities:
Italian, Irish, German, Polish, and Russian Jewish. Addams's peer Lillian
Wald founded a nurses' settlement in New York City in 1893. This became
the Henry Street Settlement, serving the predominantly Jewish, immigrant
neighborhood on the Lower East Side. By taking up residence in workers'
neighborhoods among immigrant people, Addams, Wald, and other settlement workers tried to bridge divides between newcomers and native-born
Americans, to harmonize relations between working-class people and the
middle-class settlers. Working from bases in more than 100 houses by 1900,
and in more than 400 in 1910, settlement people distinguished their efforts
from charity aims and methods. Instead of administering alms or relief,
they offered education and many sorts of services to their neighbors, endeavoring to stimulate "democratic participation and self help." Settlement people observed and documented living and working conditions
in the district, and they used the data they gathered to lobby for labor,
housing, health, and education reform at the local and sometimes national

levels. In this, settlement residents—voluntary workers who filled quasi-professional roles—helped stake out the new domain of social welfare work.[4]

Settlement workers took as a point of departure an "environmental" critique of poverty and urban living. Whereas moral analyses had held sway earlier in the century, pinpointing poor people's deficient character as the source of their distress, social theory increasingly compassed environmental factors as the agents of poverty, degradation, and disease. Settlement workers shared with other groups the belief that only by cleaning up the urban environment could they regenerate American life. Hence the settlement workers' investigation and lobbying over tuberculosis and infant mortality, city water sources and milk supplies, open-air parks and playgrounds, school nurses and lunch programs, child labor and factory conditions. As Allen F. Davis has suggested, settlement houses were extremely successful at catalyzing and drawing attention to social programs that other people and entities then joined or carried further.

It is clear that settlement houses worked actively for reform rather than radical restructuring of society and politics. While supporting and defending laborers' rights to strike, settlement workers typically abhorred violence. And rather than call for the overthrow of government or align with socialist movements, they generally worked for revision or redirection of government responsibilities toward citizens, as in state passage of factory inspection acts or the establishment of a national children's bureau. It's ironic that the settlement movement worked to revitalize "the system" during a period of long-term decline in voting and popular participation in government. The settlement movement's local approach was consistent, however, with such contemporary strategies as NAWSA's campaign to win suffrage in state-by-state contests. And the settlement approach rested squarely within the pattern of voluntary organization so characteristic of middle-class Americans in the nineteenth century.

Despite their commitment to reform rather than structural change on a number of issues, settlements created conditions of possibility for substantially reworking at least one nineteenth-century social structure: women's gender roles. That is, settlement houses constituted sites for exceeding and possibly refiguring the conventional assignment of middle-class women to an identity and subjectivity comprised of piety, purity, domesticity, and obedience. The residential strategy of settlement workers rendered houses "sites" in the most concrete of terms. And, to be sure, its rhetoric of "residence" in neighborhood "houses" and "service" to "neighbors" retained links to earlier constructions of femaleness and domesticity. At the level of ideology, the interjection of middle-class women, numerically significant among settlement workers, into public sphere, quasi-professional work supplied a ground for forging and demonstrating alternatives to the singular, fixed, biologically driven identity assigned women in late-nineteenth-century separate spheres ideology.[5] Further, settlement houses as sites should be comprehended as fluid and shifting configurations, for despite the Progressive era's affinity for bureaucracy formation, settlement houses did not devolve into predictable, well-oiled machines. Their changing practices resulted in part from the turnover among residents: residents spent three years on average in settlement work; they were young people, usually fresh out of college, and their frequent replacement guaranteed fresh input and changing supplies of energy and interests. These were important resources, enabling settlement houses to field flexible, responsive approaches in establishing relationships with neighbors. Settlement leaders prized such resilience for methodological reasons, deeming it both fundamental to and an index of settlements' aptitude for their self-appointed undertaking. Lillian Wald made this clear when reviewing Henry Street club and class work in 1913. "In the Settlement, because of its elasticity, we can do the things that are not possible to more conventionalized forms of education," she wrote on the Settlement's twentieth anniversary. "If the public will continue to encourage us," she proclaimed, "we are ready to go on twenty years more, with the same ardor and the same faith, and not with a fixed program, but moving with our times."[6] Jane Addams wrote with passion on the same point, "The one thing to be dreaded in the Settlement is that it lose its flexibility, its power of adaptation, its readiness to change its methods as its environment may demand."[7]

Settlement houses mobilized their resources and flexible methods to mediate not material conditions alone, but also a perceived strangling of the human spirit that seemed to dog the lives of urban immigrant people. Both Wald and Addams remarked on the debilitating effect of urban life and industrial work upon immigrants' spirits and creativity. In *The House on Henry Street* (1915), for example, Wald wrote

> Cruel and dramatic exploitation of workers is in the main a thing of the past, but the more subtle injuries of modern industry, due to overstrain, speeding-up, and a minimum of leisure, have only recently attracted attention.[8]

Addams wrote more bluntly of immigrants' condition in her 1892 speech "The Subjective Necessity of Social Settlements":

> Their ideas and resources are cramped. The desire for higher social
> pleasure is extinct. They have no share in the traditions and social energy
> which make for progress.[9]

Both agreed that poverty, crowding, child labor, and poor provisions for
recreation sapped immigrants' spontaneity and imagination, leaving untapped an innate longing for beauty they believed to be common to all
people.[10]

Settlement workers diagnosed two other matters of the spirit, or cultural
meaning-making, that seemed to bedevil urban immigrants: conflict between generations within immigrant communities; and the need for immigrants as a group to assimilate, at least functionally, to American ways.
Leaders seized on the connection between children's (lack of) respect for
their immigrant parents and American (lack of) respect for the "dower" the
newcomers brought with them—their cultural practices.[11] Wald wrote
with sympathy:

> Great is our loss when a shallow Americanism is accepted by the newly
> arrived immigrant, more particularly by the children, and their national
> traditions and heroes are ruthlessly pushed aside. The young people have
> usually to be urged by someone outside their own group to recognize the
> importance and value of customs, and even of ethical teaching, when
> given in a foreign language, or [when given] by old-world people with
> whom the new American does not wish to be associated in the minds of
> his acquaintances. This does not apply only to the recent immigrant, to
> whom his children often hear contemptuous terms applied.[12]

But there was no escaping the fact that immigrants needed to assimilate, at
least to some degree. At the loftiest level, assimilation meant the civic
bonding of immigrants to America—their assumption of American values,
participation in the democratic process, and contribution to the progress
of the race. At the practical level, assimilation meant the acquisition of
skills with which immigrants could negotiate everyday life: industrial work
skills and "time discipline" needed to get and keep jobs; sanitary and
domestic skills necessary to cope with tenement life; and English-language
skills required in order to communicate with employers, landlords, and
public authorities. Settlement houses helped immigrants acquire such
skills through specifically designed club and class work. Such work also
assisted in "Americanizing" immigrants—teaching manners, "morals," and
even correct modes of dress and deportment.[13] In *Windows on Henry Street*
(1934) Wald explained why the Henry Street Settlement placed stress on
such activity:

> It seems worth while to note here why we place real importance on the elimination of those superficial qualities which are often more divisive than deeper and more fundamental characteristics. Habits consistent with the conventions of other countries, though varying from our own, often mark as "alien" and "queer" people who might otherwise prove to be sympathetic, and sometimes limit the possibilities of real companionship.[14]

To settlement workers, removal of "superficial" differences facilitated the fundamental goal of forging connections between unlike people. Seen from a Foucauldian point of view, however, such settlement house intervention clearly aimed to "discipline" immigrant people to American ways. Yet, the settlement approach took cold-blooded stock of where power was located in the circulation between capital and labor, native-born and immigrant people. Wald's explanation reflects in part the situation on New York's Lower East Side at the turn of the century. Large numbers of Polish and Russian Jewish immigrants settled in this part of the city, and their Orthodox garb was visually distinctive—prayer shawls and curls for men, wigs for married women, for example. But the issue was larger in scope than New York City. In this period the "new immigration" that streamed into East Coast and Midwest cities flowed largely from eastern and central Europe. Its peoples looked noticeably different from the Irish, Scandinavian, and other western European immigrants—including German Jewish immigrants—that preceded them earlier in the century. Rationales such as Wald's sought to balance respect for immigrant traditions with awareness of the suspicion and nativist prejudice immigrants were likely to encounter.

It was to address such matters of the spirit among immigrants that arts activities were introduced in settlement house curricula. The English settlement example and that country's Arts and Crafts movement, widely emulated in the United States, provided American settlement workers with models for offering instruction in drawing, sloyd, singing, and manual skills. Literature and history clubs met in nearly every settlement, storytelling groups were fixtures, and drama groups were not uncommon. What previous studies have overlooked is that female settlement workers took advantage of the cultural moment to introduce and develop new dance practices in settlement house venues. That is, a specific conjuncture of people, theories, and events positioned women settlers to develop dance practices as direct forms for engagement with pressing Progressive-era problems of immigration, ethnicity, and urbanization. At the same time, the vaunted flexibility of settlement methodology and the cultural staging ground afforded by "residence" in urban neighborhoods empowered women settlers to exceed and refigure public sphere identities for themselves as aesthetic workers and also as social welfare laborers. This dance innovation and refiguring of identities took readily visible form at the Henry Street Settlement, the focus for this and the fourth chapter, and at Hull-House, the subject of the fifth.

THE "ARTS–REFORM" CONNECTION

The strategy of using "arts" curricula in American settlement work drew from at least two different contemporary sources. First, and quite important, was the theoretical currency among settlement workers of John Ruskin's and William Morris's thought and writings. Both these cultural critics drew explicit connections between the character of a society and the quality of the art that the society produced; both linked aesthetic reform to questions of class and economic organization. Commencing in the 1840s with art criticism, Englishman John Ruskin shifted focus in the 1850s to social criticism; he was widely read in the United States even though no authorized American edition of his work appeared until 1890. What Americans grasped from reading their pirated editions was Ruskin's perceptive critique of industrial labor and its debilitating effect on the worker. Ruskin equated industrial division of labor with the "division of man." In reducing artisans to less-skilled "hands," Ruskin insisted, laissez-faire capitalism stripped workers of their capacity for art—their capacity for joy in work. The creative capacity inherent in every worker was dulled by mass production's repetitive tasks and long hours; deprived of their pleasure in the activity of working, industrial laborers turned into machines themselves. Advancing this psychological analysis of work, Ruskin lauded the work processes that created Gothic architecture and urged a return to handicraft labor. Ruskin called for the elite in society to initiate reform: to change the nature of contemporary work processes and restore opportunity for creativity in work. Manufacturers had the further obligation to shape consumption, to demand beauty in public architecture and design. By shaping taste, he believed, the elite would shape character as well; incumbent on the elite was a certain "moral environmentalism."[15]

Without question, Ruskin's vision of top-down, reformative leadership was paternalistic. Yet his writings theorized art as a capacity available to all, a notion that American educators and settlement workers put to use in a variety of ways. William Morris also advanced an egalitarian notion of art, but on quite different grounds. Influenced as a young man by Ruskin's writings, Morris turned from an intended focus on religious engagement to a crusade for beauty and the renovation of the Victorian eye and taste. With a small group of friends he established a decorative arts firm run on a cooperative basis, and he involved himself with artisanal labor and with handicraft. The firm profited and gained renown; commercial decorative arts firms modeled their papers and fabrics on those of the Morris firm. By the 1870s Morris began to despair of the prospects for renewal of art and taste in British capitalist society. Through growing involvement with political questions of the day he came to identify himself as a socialist. Morris called for social revolution to re-establish a situation of equality among all people, asserting that in postrevolutionary society art would be an activity for the whole community, for the many and not the few. Until revolution brought about a new society, he acknowledged, the revival of handicraft promoted by the new Arts and Crafts societies was a noteworthy and encouraging undertaking. Craftsmanship could show the world that "the pleasurable exercise of energies is the end of life and the cause of happiness."[16]

To settlement workers whose personal observation confirmed the premise that industrial labor and capitalist organization degraded workers lives, Ruskin's and Morris's writings offered a rationale and outright encouragement for using arts experiences to tackle the crises of urban immigrant life. Of course, some features of the analysis did not transfer to the United States. Ruskin would not have approved of the public organizational activity that women pursued in settlement work. His 1865 *Sesame and Lilies* expressed the view that women were to be moral guides, while men were to be the active interveners in life. American settlement workers apparently disregarded this stricture while they gave considerable attention to application of other aspects of Ruskin's and Morris's thought. Ruskin study clubs were staples of settlement club curricula; frequent picture exhibitions of Pre-Raphaelite and Old Master work at settlement houses performed the offices of beautifying the environment and enlarging taste. The Arts and Crafts movement found strong support at Hull-House. The Chicago Arts and Crafts Society got its start there, and resident Ellen Gates Starr opened a bookbinding workshop upon her return from study in England with T. J. Cobden-Sanderson. Starr also served as President of Chicago's Public School Art Society, which placed pictures in public school rooms. Jane Addams acknowledged Starr's instrumentality in this area in *Twenty Years at Hull-House*: "Miss Starr always insisted that the arts should receive adequate recognition at Hull House."[17] In their interior decoration, Hull-House and Henry Street Settlement adopted an Arts and Crafts aesthetic of clean lines and fairly spare furnishings: tables, shelves, and mantles uncluttered with mementos; simple window draperies; and handwork such as polished brasses.[18]

Receptivity to the notion of "every one an artist" underpinned such views of the settlement's function as that expressed by Wald in 1913:

> It [the Drama club] also proclaims again the principle that dominates settlements, namely that talents and abilities should be released, and opportunities should be given for expression, for good art, as well as for character.[19]

Combining Ruskinian notions of "joy in work" with received notions of art making as the production of beauty, settlements stipulated that immigrant neighbors were capable of making art themselves, whether it was plying a "genuine craft" in a shop or taking music lessons. Settlements put hybrid theory into practice by making available an array of classes, clubs and workshops in choral and instrumental music, pottery, manual work, drawing, drama, physical training, and dance.[20]

Nothing in Ruskin's or Morris's dicta directly acknowledged or addressed dance as one of the arts whose application in daily life could regenerate modern industrial living. But neither did their writings prohibit consideration or exploration of bodily movement as an artistic practice. A similar situation obtained in a second important seedbed for settlement house incorporation of arts practices—progressive education theory. It is a commonplace in dance history writings to treat John Dewey's educational philosophies as a synecdoche for "Progressive Education," but it should be realized that numerous thinkers and theories comprised a discourse of educational revision from the 1890s to about 1920. These were also years in which many new normal schools were founded, including an ample number of women-only institutions, whose students cut their academic teeth on the contest of ideas and applications in elementary school education. Course work in the new subject of psychology was available for students at four-year colleges, too. Settlement club and class work provided fertile fields for testing pedagogic theories.[21]

Among the theories receiving broad application was the notion of "culture epochs" as a principle for selecting and sequencing materials to be used in common school education. Articulated by the National Herbart Society in the United States, the theory took as its point of departure a "parallelism" between developmental phases of the individual and "the race" (or the human race). In this, culture epoch proponents brought together widely accepted theories of human evolution with findings of a new "physiological psychology" that replaced nineteenth-century faculty psychology. The new psychology proposed that the mind grew and developed in stages. Just as human physiological development was supposed to recapitulate previous phylogenetic stages, so too was psychical development supposed to pass through a series of stages. Culture epoch theory conceived academic curricula as leading children through major stages of intellectual, emotional, and volitional (moral) development. (Education's goal, for the Herbartians, included developing religious and moral strength of character.) The succession of major historical and cultural periods, from past to most recent, supplied the framework for curriculum construction.

Which periods qualified for inclusion? Those which had generated recognized or classic products. Writers frequently quoted Herbart's urging on this point that "Periods that no master described, whose spirit no poet breathed are of little value to the educator."[22] Products took forms that corresponded to phases of children's intellectual development, phases thought to move from sense awareness to imagination, then to hero worship, historical thought, and finally philosophic thought. Thus children might progress from study of fairy tales and myths to the Robinson Crusoe story, legends and heroes' tales, histories, and philosophical works. As culture epoch proponent C. C. Van Liew explained, products from a variety of epochs might do in the early stages of mental development, but as children's capacities for historical and philosophical thinking matured, the demands of their country's institutions required a focus on national culture. In the American context, the Revolutionary War period and early nineteenth centuries would supply appropriate epochs for studying the recent past.[23]

To adequately address the several developmental sequences of the mind, educators were exhorted to select culture epochs that offered "great, connected, and typical portions of subject matter," or thought-wholes.[24] This requirement for broad, linked topoi invoked the allied concern of "correlation," the right relation between disciplines. Here the Progressive-era focus on "efficiency" combined with organicism: with subject fields multiplying in modern scholarship, no sequence could embrace all areas of knowledge.[25] Educators debated which discipline should supply the "core" of the sequence: history-and-literature advocates generally prevailed over proponents of the sciences by claiming that man's decision making properly formed the center of study. Others argued against the blurring of disciplinary boundaries they thought inherent in correlation. In an 1895 conference of the National Herbart Society devoted to scrutiny of culture epoch theory, the correlative emphasis seemed to be in the ascendant. This issue may well have been resolved at the level of local practice.[26]

Three noted institutions put culture epoch theory into practice at the same time that settlement houses were developing programs of club and class work for children. New York's innovative Ethical Culture School employed the culture epoch approach as early as the 1890s, and the Ethical Culture Society sponsored a normal school that trained teachers in kindergarten pedagogy. The Speyer School, the uptown Manhattan demonstration school attached to Teachers College in the first two decades of the twentieth century, used culture epoch planning; so did the laboratory school associated with the University of Chicago's pedagogy curriculum. Rita Wallach (later Morgenthau), who assumed direction of children's work at the Henry Street Settlement soon after 1900, had matriculated in the ECS's normal school. At Hull-House, John Dewey, then Professor of Pedagogy at University of Chicago, was a frequent visitor and speaker. In the 1890s Dewey was still chewing on the idea of culture epochs, and pondered in print whether the approach actually focused on products rather than children, whom he put at the center of the education dynamic.[27]

As fodder for settlement curricula, culture epoch theory offered outright support for the study of literature and pictorial art, and for singing, storytelling, manual work (such as paper cutting and weaving), and dramatization. Advocates of the system made no mention of dance, with one notable exception. In his 1904 *Adolescence*, the avid recapitulationist G. Stanley Hall identified folk dancing as a key activity for adolescents. Starting around 1905, this endorsement supplied pivotal theoretical support for dancing as an after-school athletic activity, a phenomenon treated in chapter 6. When settlement houses mounted their urban residential campaigns in the 1890s, though, culture epoch theory typically bestowed no attention on dance. As a bodily practice that "left behind" few artifacts in periods past, at least in comparison with literature and art, it's not surprising that dance received no recognition as a culture epoch product capable of study. Dance constituted in effect an absence that indexed the culture epoch privileging of "thought" studies over "form" studies: the absence of the body in the academic curriculum, at least as a correlated subject, despite the increasing attention paid to public school physical training in the 1890s. To interested extenders of culture epoch pedagogy, however, the theory created a space for cultural products of the past, keyed to "classic" civilizations and exhibiting recognizable form or genre. The theory created space, in short, for dances of the past. "Greek dances" could be tied to study of the Golden Age, for example, or minuets to the American Revolutionary War era. How to invoke such non-textual "products" for classroom use? Although the theory promoted "developed" culture, giving little incentive for new choreography, in practice the ephemerality of dances past would require imaginative reconstruction and citation of past dance practices. Hence the turn-of-the-century vogue for historical dances ranging from putative Indian (Native American) dances to dances of the classical music suite. (In a related vein, audiences easily assimilated Isadora Duncan's early choreography to "Greek" dancing.) The other alternative was collection via fieldwork of extant "traditional" dances; Cecil Sharp's notation and publication of traditional English Morris dances from 1907 offers an excellent example.[28] In both cases, the dancing which culture epoch theory could embrace operated under the sign of the authentic, of the past in the present. Inherently supportive of the status quo, culture epoch theory might support new consideration of dance, though not new dance.

This absented cultural practice *could* be mobilized, and indeed was, in lived applications and extensions of culture epoch theory in settlement house milieus. It should not be surprising that women—the practitioners stereotypically linked to dance as a bodily practice—took this initiative in settlement house work. At the Henry Street Settlement House, Irene and Alice Lewisohn spearheaded dance and drama experimentation which enjoyed two decades' issue. Scrutiny of the Henry Street Settlement illuminates the opportunities that settlement house milieus afforded for tackling contemporary social welfare problems through innovation in dance and drama, and for fashioning roles for women as innovators of bodily practice in both community and "art" registers, for both "amateur" neighborhood people and settlement workers.

ALICE AND IRENE LEWISOHN

Leonard Lewisohn introduced his daughters to Lillian Wald and the Henry Street Settlement about 1901. This was not unusual in itself, for like his German Jewish contemporaries Jacob Schiff and Henry Morgenthau Sr., Lewisohn was an active supporter of the Settlement. Traveling down Manhattan Island by auto toward the Lower East Side, the young girls were struck by the "exotic" and "foreign" quality of the people and neighborhoods they traversed. Though only about nine and twelve years old at the time, Irene and particularly Alice were impressed with the humanitarian spirit of settlement activities. They subsequently attended the Finch School, a newly established New York City finishing school which stressed the arts as part of its curriculum. Leonard Lewisohn's death in 1902 left the sisters parentless but quite wealthy. In her memoir, *The Neighborhood Playhouse; Leaves from a Theatre Scrapbook*, Alice indicates that she subsequently felt torn between her desire to continue studying drama and her sense of obligation to contribute to the settlement work at Henry Street. The latter sense she shared with many young, college-educated women of the 1890s who had been schooled to make a substantive social contribution and found settlements a new outlet for doing so. The sisters chose Henry Street; first Alice and later Irene turned their energies to work at the settlement as active nonresidents. Neither, however, forwent opportunities to study with other professionals on the side. Alice studied drama with Sarah Cowell LeMoyne, an elocutionist and actress. Alice even performed a small role in *Pippa Passes*, starring Mrs. LeMoyne, during a short run on Broadway in 1906. Reviews of this production exposed Alice's identity, despite her use of a stage name, and trumpeted her considerable financial assets as part of their coverage. Although she doesn't disclose them in her memoir, these circumstances surely confirmed Alice in her commitment to the Henry Street Settlement as a venue whose respectability put her own motives and resources, not to mention talent, beyond question. Of the sisters, Irene was always the one more interested in dance. A draft version of Alice's memoir indicates that the sisters studied the Delsarte system of movement with Genevieve Stebbins, the chief American proponent of the system. Trips abroad in 1910 brought Irene into contact with Japanese Noh as a dance and ritual form, and in 1914 she and Alice witnessed classes and productions using the Dalcroze system of movement at the Dalcroze School in Hellerau, Germany.[29]

The Lewisohn sisters began their club and class work in dance and drama at Henry Street around 1905. Here they joined a network of women doing social welfare work, and also a world of female sociability—one that enabled close collegial, affective, and at times intimate relationships. They worked with other club leaders under the general supervision of Rita Wallach (Morgenthau), director of Work for Girls and Young Women and trainer of club leaders.[30] The activities they formulated for junior girls reveal the direct imprint of culture epoch theory in its articulation of myths and legends as material sequentially appropriate to early elementary-age students, and of nature study as a correlative subject. Alice remembered recounting myths and "age-old rituals of spring" during the storytelling they conducted with club members, and the sisters introduced songs and dancing into the telling of the tales. They gradually moved from leading games to teaching rhythmic movement, and noted the children's "reverent" reaction to the coupling of myths with more structured movement. From these beginnings the Lewisohns created seasonal festivals which seem to have combined aspects of ritual borrowed from Jewish religious celebrations or American civic celebrations with pantomime, dance, song, and imaginative reconstructions of pagan seasonal rituals.[31]

FESTIVALS

Though writers on the Neighborhood Playhouse offer varying dates for the inception of these festivals, it seems clear that one of the first festivals, *Three Impressions of Spring*, was produced in 1905, possibly as early as 1904. It portrayed Greek, Hebrew, and East Indian celebrations of annual springtime ceremonies, in which the death-and-resurrection motif supplied the linkage among three different cultural practices. In a correlative fashion that would have won approval from culture epoch theorists, settlement children worked on costume construction during "manual work" time. They listened during storytelling hours to tales of Ceres and Persephone, stories by Lafcadio Hearn, and translations from the *Mahabarata*; and they learned dances and pantomime in the time more conventionally allotted to games.[32]

A 1905 festival, *Miriam, a Passover Festival*, inaugurated a cycle of Hebrew Ritual Festivals that included A *Midwinter or Chanukkah Festival* and *Tabernacles, or a Thanksgiving Festival*. The *Miriam* festival took biblical texts as its inspiration; thus Bible stories were read and discussed in children's club time. A Russian neighborhood man set the psalms selected by the settlement workers to music of his own composition, and he also coached a chorus of singers. Rita Wallach's account of this festival indicates that the correlative effect extended to the larger community: "How full of vitality were the rehearsals, and how soon the neighborhood was sharing our experience."[33] Irene Lewisohn most probably created the movement materials. These included a garland dance by people "representing children," Miriam's dance with timbrel, and a pantomime by Miriam with a supporting group of maidens enacting thoughts suggested by the spoken texts. Other festivals not part of this cycle utilized little religious reference or content. *Hiawatha*, a spring festival referencing American Indians, was produced in 1908 and again in 1911. Others in this group included the pantomimes *Snow White*, *The Shadow Garden of Shuteye Town*, and *Sleeping Beauty*, the latter interpreted in pantomime as a midwinter myth. *The Frolic of the Holidays* and *The Discontented Daffodil* were produced for the settlement's annual December festivities. *The Revolt of the Flowers* was described as a musical fantasy; an *Evening of*

Russian Music and Slavic Dancing, the only production of its type termed a festival, was probably the occasion for dance pedagogue Louis Chalif's first collaboration with the Lewisohn sisters.[34]

Commingling Ruskinian notions with culture epoch methodology, and aggressively inserting dance as cultural material, the Lewisohn sisters conceived their work as addressing the artistic, spiritual, and social needs of the neighborhood immigrant children. Alice recalled some forty-seven years after the fact that

> From the moment free games gave way to rhythmical movement and relating in a purely imaginative way to the myths, the pandemonium that usually climaxed the game and work period subsided into a calm and reverent mood. The myths we told in the story hour, combined with rhythmic movement and song, had the effect of a magic potion, charming the eager and soothing the wild.[35]

This account echoed the emphasis the settlement house movement placed on cultivating imagination and creativity. Further, the festival approach quite consciously aimed at harmonizing intergenerational tensions in the immigrant community. Rita Wallach revealed as much in her 1906 account of the *Miriam/Passover* festival:

> This festival so modestly conceived, the emphasis always falling on the thought of giving back to the neighborhood through the children, what was its own most beautiful and sacred heritage, received an appreciation and understanding that was beyond the greatest hopes of the originators. The audiences were tense with interest and religious feeling, and one could not but realize that the right note had been struck when one saw the moistened eyes of the "sheitelee" women and the quivering lips of the grey-bearded men.[36]

Historian Selma Berrol, who traces the conflict between Jews of two different eras of immigration to New York—those from Germany and those from eastern Europe—credits the settlement house movement with granting much greater respect to immigrant culture than did such German Jewish Americanizing institutions as the Educational Alliance. George White attributes the same generous attitude to the settlement house movement, citing it as an important influence on casework and intercultural education in the late 1950s.[37]

The cycle of seasonal Hebrew Ritual Festivals, of which *Miriam* formed a part, addressed the problem of devalued immigrant culture by borrowing and shaping for public presentation selected movement, song, dance, and ceremonial elements of Lower East Side Russian Jewish immigrant life. Placing immigrant traditions in a performance context, the festivals tried to publically assign value to immigrant culture and confirm adults in their sense of worth. The festivals also educated second-generation children in elements of their own heritage and possibly strengthened the bond between immigrant generations.[38] As Alice indicated in a 1912 *Playground Magazine* article, the sisters believed that their work freed the emotional force and spiritual energy of the immigrant community. They believed that it helped create "a higher standard of social culture" as well.[39]

Whatever the respect that Henry Street showed for immigrant culture, festivals also contributed to the Americanizing aims of settlement work. As Arthur Holden's 1922 *The Settlement Idea* retrospectively documented, dramatic work was held in appreciative regard for application to such aims:

> Not only is it [drama] an educational force along intellectual and spiritual lines, but it offers first hand to the individual a vision of the possibilities of self development and self equipment for the positive business of everyday existence. To get the force of this, one has to witness the awakening of a drab personality, stirred by the imaginative possibilities and the mock realities of the stage. Through pronouncing words of genius, which are put into one's mouth, one learns the attributes of genius and begins, unconsciously at first, to equip oneself for a fuller and more purposeful part in society . . . to walk upon the stage, to speak to hushed audiences is to awake to a consciousness of power generally unsuspected within the self.[40]

Dramatic activity, in Holden's view, prepared immigrants to negotiate daily life and to conceive a civic role for themselves. Henry Street festival work, in turn, arguably tried to wean immigrant neighbors from their strict Russian Jewish Orthodox roots, diffusing if not eliminating aspects of their cultural identity by linking them to universal symbols of seasonal change. Consider again the *Miriam/Passover* festival, cited above, which Alice Lewisohn Crowley described in some detail:

> Rites, chants and psalms observed during Passover in the orthodox synagogues were incorporated into the body of the festival, not as dogmatic creed, but as a thread upon which to link the spring myth of Israel. It was not a pageant or any attempt at representation. Hemlock boughs provided the setting, the costumes were uniform in cut but dyed by one of the club leaders in a color scale characteristically Eastern. The music was a hybrid collection of themes selected to invoke a mood.[41]

The specific religious character of practically every element of the festival was mediated in some way. The song and dialogue which gave structure to the festival were delivered in English rather than in Yiddish or in the native tongue of the performers. In addition to the chants and "synagogal melodies," for which the festival directors scoured the neighborhood, classical compositions were used to support the dances. And movement vocabulary from Russian folk dance was almost certainly mixed with "classic" dancing, or ballet, and Delsartian gesture. Ceremonial aspects, rather than the theology of the adapted Jewish elements, were emphasized, and symbolic rather than literal representation was stressed. Respect for things Jewish was balanced with concern for modes American, and emphasis on "universal nature symbols" supplied a putative ground on which bonds of "fellowship" might be forged.[42]

Festivals, it seems, constituted strange hybrids, asserting the worth of immigrant culture on one hand yet bridling various aspects of it on the other. The disciplining function of festivals also operated through the intensive preparation required for any and all of these productions. By 1913, weekly Festival Dancing classes were held for three different age-groups, each at least eighteen people strong. In addition to weekly singing, drama, and speech classes, productions required regular group practices. Children performers were coached in diction and pronunciation as well as in posture and movement skills. The demands of ensemble work forced them to practice "cooperation and self discipline." Boys as well as girls felt the structuring effects of such work; although festival work was first developed in the girls department, Irene Lewisohn noted in 1913 that "boys have a large share in every branch of the work from scenery making in carpentry class to acting. They are chosen through their clubs, gymnasium and the social dancing lessons."[43] Across the settlement population, then, assimilation skills and social values were cultivated right alongside experiment with dance and drama.[44]

In 1913, the Henry Street Settlement experimented with its production schedule and mounted three festivals in as many months, rather than the typical single, annual festival. This venture was well received by settlement youths and it stimulated reformulation of the settlement dramatic club. Styling themselves the "Neighborhood Players," the dramatic club produced five plays between 1913 and the 1915 opening of the Neighborhood Playhouse. These included Olive Tilford Dargan's *The Shepherd*, a play of "ideas" dealing with the revolutionary movement in Russia (a subject close to the experience of many settlement neighbors); and John Galsworthy's *The Silver Box*, a drawing-room drama that afforded rich opportunity for characterization. Alice claimed in 1959 that this play, "though set in a

British frame was indigenous to any land," yet features of its mise-en-scène were anything but familiar to the neighborhood immigrants. To master the "Anglo-Saxon" table manners required by the script, the actors met for weekly dinners or tea parties at the Lewisohns' home; the lead actor was coached in wearing a tuxedo at the dress rehearsal.[45] While the Settlement gymnasium had been the customary spot for staging festivals, these plays were presented at Clinton Hall, a community meeting space that the Henry Street Settlement had lobbied hard and raised funds to erect. A twentieth anniversary pageant commanded neighborhood streets for its 1913 performance.[46] It became evident, however, that the demands of play production and the ambitions of the Lewisohn sisters would soon outstrip the resources that Clinton Hall had to offer. Thus the Lewisohns commissioned the design and execution of the Neighborhood Playhouse, located at Grand and Pitt Streets several blocks away from the Settlement. Expanded dance and drama activity in that venue continued to draw on methodologies first employed in the Settlement festivals.

THE FESTIVAL AS GENRE

Why did the Lewisohns' club and class work take the form of "festivals"? Here I speak of the Hebrew religious festivals rather than the pantomime performances which Settlement usage also denominated "festivals," probably because of their annual timing and construction via club and class work rather than their specific content. Answers to this question further situate the Lewisohns' arts practices amidst two other contemporary fields of concern: Progressive education methods, and German Jewish Americans' fears that immense immigration flows would fuel anti-Semitism.

At the most overt level, festivals drew on the actual cultural customs of Russian Jewish immigrants, who comprised the bulk of the neighbors that Henry Street Settlement served. They drew from a body of festivals acknowledged in the Jewish calendar, specifically the pilgrimage holidays of Passover and Sukkot (the Feast of Booths). These constituted two of three "seasonal" festivals that marked milestones in the cyclical agricultural calendar. Pentecost, the third pilgrimage holiday, would form the subject of a 1917 Neighborhood Playhouse festival. The seasonal focus had contemporary parallels: in the Ziegfeld Follies of 1915, one chorus of women represented the twelve months of the year. Historical precedent held as well: Déstouche's Baroque opera-ballet *The Elements* is a case in point. Indeed, drama theory held that tragedy—*tragoedia*—was born of annual Greek festivals honoring the gods. And while the focus on seasonal festivals

allowed the Lewisohns to foreground both the settlement neighbors' traditions and solid theatrical precedent, selection of the pilgrimage holidays
may have held the additional attraction of suggesting a choreographic
strategy: the processional.[47]

The Henry Street Settlement's festival strategy may well have been
influenced by "school festival" productions that the Ethical Culture School
developed. Led by Felix Adler, the Ethical Society had founded the Workingman's school in 1878, realizing in these material terms Adler's conviction that changing the individual was the way to change contemporary
conditions. This tuition-free school for the children of poor working people
eventually admitted paying students; when it added a high school in 1895
it changed its name to the Ethical Culture School. School curricula
applied progressive education models, from instruction in manual training
to the use of culture epoch theory. A child-study group formed by Ethical
Society members in 1888 avidly explored the thinking of educational
psychologist G. Stanley Hall.[48]

The school began in 1890 to produce festivals performed by the students
for teachers, peers, and parents. Percival Chubb, who joined the faculty a
few years later as teacher of English and head of the secondary school
division, made festival work a prominent feature of the curriculum during
his tenure.[49] Chubb strongly advocated a correlation among curricular
subjects quite similar to that of culture epoch theory, and insisted that
festivals reach out to incorporate dance, dramatics, and song into the more
typical mix of literature, languages, history, science, manual studies, and
geography. Chubb classified the several annual festivals into three distinct
categories. Festivals of Thanksgiving, Christmas, and spring or May Day
were intended to arouse a "natural piety" in children, bringing them into
contact with seasonal cycles of death and resurrection, fecundity and
barrenness. The parallel with Henry Street festivals is obvious in this
category. Festivals for Patriots Day (Washington's and Lincoln's birthdays),
Memorial Day, or Independence Day sought to cultivate "human piety" or
appreciation for times past, for historic personages, and for the role "ideas"
played in the past and present. A third type of festival strove to focus
students' "institutional piety," their cognizance of human efforts to forge
social and collective life. Election Day, Memorial Day, Founders Day, and
Graduation Day festivals filled this kind of bill. Chubb's festival taxonomy
thus resonates with Herbartian concerns on the two grounds of culture
epoch sequencing and interest in cultivating ethics as part of pedagogy.
The festival schedule for a given ECS school year would regularly include
seven festivals.[50] While a single class or group of classes might bear chief

responsibility for preparing an assigned festival, the school as a whole participated in the production on the appointed day by singing opening and closing songs, plus others as required. This division of labor fashioned the entire school into a performance community while it promoted the efficiency in production methods so cherished in Progressive-era bureaucracies.

Felix Adler's daughter Ruth Adler Friess remembered the Christmas Festival as a highlight of the school year. Its focus might be a medieval celebration one year, a folk Christmas another. Documents from the period and a summary by Chubb's collaborator in movement materials, Mary G. Allerton, reveal that a range of dance materials was invoked. Morris dances and English country dances, the fruit of recent folklore research, lent themselves immediately to May Day festivals, Allerton maintained. These and other folk dances are heavily represented in photographs. Balleticized arm postures (probably deriving from turn-of-the-century "aesthetic dancing") helped establish the "Greek" character of the "Virtues" played by senior girls in *The Quest*. "Set or formal" dances were also favored; most popular among these were court dances like the minuet, pavane, and gavotte. Pantomime and "symbolic dances" (movement allegories) were widely used with the youngest children.[51]

The ECS festival work was available for scrutiny by Henry Street workers because of their geographical proximity in Manhattan. In addition, Rita Wallach had earned a degree in "elementary education" from the Ethical Society's Normal School, founded in 1898. Most salient of all, however, was the Normal Course in Festival Methods that Percival Chubb and his colleagues offered to the general public in the 1907–08 year. Conducted over the course of twenty weeks, the class treated general theory and outlook of festivals; organization and management; music; dance, gesture, and movement; costume; and art in relation to festivals. The charge for the course—which was aimed at settlement people, playground leaders, and school teachers—was $15. While no records of course subscribers are extant, it seems highly probable that the Lewisohns or Rita Wallach partook of this opportunity to extend their methodological range. These were the very years when Settlement festivals were taking firm shape; given Wallach's previous connection with ECS, it is unlikely she forwent this opportunity.[52]

What effects would have flowed from the ECS stimulus? Comparison of the two groups' practices suggests that some of the dance vocabulary developed by the Henry Street festivals was similar to that used by ECS — notably Russian folk dance material (with the aid of Louis Chalif), and pantomime. English traditional dance and court dance materials did not figure in the Henry Street repertoire, however. Irene Lewisohn adapted Delsartian gesture and perhaps aspects of Japanese Noh dance in her own way, fashioning a movement hybrid rather than reconstructing and reviving traditional forms. After her exposure to the Dalcroze system in 1914, she would draw on this movement source as well. The real salience of Ethical Culture School festivals for the Henry Street festivals, I speculate, lay in their confirmation of dance as an artistic and educational material, the model it provided for the "seasonal festival" theme, and its programatic commitment to cross-curriculum correlation of studies.

The conception of festivals, particularly in their Americanizing dimensions, may well have been fueled by a second factor—tension among New York's earlier German Jewish immigrants and the more recent Russian immigrant Jews. Selection of Passover, Tabernacles, Pentecost, and Channukah as foci for festivals allowed Henry Street festival workers to merge those holidays' Jewish character with mainstream American civil celebrations. The Tabernacles (Booths) festival was expanded to embrace Thanksgiving, and the Channukah festival, in its construction around the symbolism of light, permitted overlap with Christmas celebrations. This strategy allowed festival institutors to hold in creative tension the Jewish, American, and "universal" identifications of their settlement neighbors. Put another way, the beauty—the ethnic specificity—of the form might well lie in the eyes of the beholders: settlement workers or immigrant neighbors. And the gaze that other Americans cast upon newer Russian immigrant Jews deeply concerned German Jewish Americans.

The "uptown" or German Jews had immigrated to America from the 1840s through the 1870s and, in the main, had comfortably established themselves as prosperous members of the middle class. Widely dispersed in the new country and relatively few in number, they were often indistinguishable from other non-Jewish German immigrants who fled political turmoil in those years. Subscribing to the liberal tenets of Reform Judaism, they were disturbed by the distinctive customs of dress and Sabbath keeping which the Orthodox Jews from Russia practiced. As the Lewisohn sisters had noticed on their first trip downtown to visit the Henry Street Settlement, the Russians looked inescapably "exotic" and "foreign" to the uptown Jews; the immigrants' "orientalist" mien threatened to comprise a negative visual definition for all Jewish people. German Jewish antipathy to the newcomers was heightened by the difference in their class positions as well. German Jews were frequently the landlords of Russian Jews, in tenement houses and in leased commercial space. German Jews were major employers of Russian Jews, especially in the garment trades which absorbed so much of New York's immigrant labor. In 1885, for example, German Jews owned more than 97 percent of city garment factories, and their reach extended into other apparel and textile businesses as well. Russian Jewish immigrant labor radicalism disturbed German Jewish capitalists and emphasized the chasm between their economic interests. Of course, the poverty of the immigrants distressed the German Jews even further. The uptown Jews feared that Americans would judge *all* Jews by the negative image which the immigrants presented, and that anti-Semitism would swell in an America that had been blessedly tolerant heretofore. This fear of anti-Semitism was not without basis. In the 1880s, wealthy Jewish people began to encounter discrimination at summer resorts, private girls' schools frequently refused Jewish applications, and some metropolitan clubs rejected Jewish candidates for membership. These social discriminations increased after the turn of the century, with some private schools establishing quotas for Jewish students, and college fraternities barring Jewish members. Surging immigration between 1870 and 1915 created a pressure not unlike that experienced in Prussia, where "oriental" *Ost Juden* fleeing the Pale of Settlement pressed both the national borders and the bourgeois accommodation that emancipated Jews had achieved in Germany.[53]

American German Jews dived into philanthropic work on the predominantly Jewish, Lower East Side in the early twentieth century. Hebrew charities rendered material aid to people being "processed" at Castle Garden and Ellis Island, and then to new residents. Various groups provided monetary aid, shelter for orphans and working girls on their own, health services, even prisoners' aid. Some organizations tried to relocate immigrants to other parts of the country. Many more offered education, with language and civics prominently featured, and emphasized the Americanization of immigrants' dress and behavior. The Educational Alliance, a Lower East Side institution openly devoted to Americanizing immigrants, barred the use of Yiddish on its premises during the 1890s.[54]

Did the German-Russian tension come into play at the Henry Street Settlement? Lillian Wald was of German Jewish parentage, as were Rita Wallach and the Lewisohns. Henry Street received significant financial support from such prominent German Jews as Jacob Schiff, the Morgenthau family, and, before his death, Leonard Lewisohn. Schiff was also a patron of the Educational Alliance, and Wald in *Windows on Henry Street* spoke favorably of the work done there. It seems impossible that Wald and the Lewisohns could have remained untouched by the climate of German

Jewish opinion regarding the Americanizing of immigrants. The reaction of Reform German Jews to the Orthodox immigrants may well help explain the emphasis placed on ritual (or form) rather than theological elements in the *Miriam/Passover* festival discussed above. Similar concern probably informed the Chanukkah festival, in which Jewish religious practices were shown in relation to other cultures' seasonal celebration of the winter solstice. Wald, Wallach, and the Lewisohns all used the rhetoric of "interpretation" to explain the bridging function that settlement festivals tried to effect, but differences are distinguishable among them.[55] Wallach wrote in 1906, "For a long time it has been an ideal of the settlement to have the neighborhood give expression to its own traditions," and "There is a movement underway . . . to make the strangers realize that they have value in our eyes outside their labor-producing power."[56] In 1912 Alice Lewisohn wrote less as the immigrants' appreciator than as one possessing superior vision:

> Besides the desire to widen the vision of the children and to broaden their horizon by giving them an opportunity to glance into other lands and learn to understand other customs and other peoples was the wish to revitalize and interpret for them their own traditions and symbols which to them are without meaning.[57]

Alice's suggestion that immigrants didn't understand their own traditions may be read in the light of ethnic and class differences separating the sisters from the Settlement neighbors. What immigrants didn't comprehend, and what festivals were constructed to assert and illuminate, is that Jewish traditions signify as instances of transhistorical seasonal celebrations and evidences of universal brotherhood. Festivals sustained a nexus, or grounds of commonality, between various Judaisms and world religions, between Americans and immigrants, between German and Russian Jews. The deracination of immigrant Jews that such a strategy could promote, in turn, shares certain concerns with the Ethical Culture movement in its attempts to distance itself from religion per se. Both the ECS "school festival" model and the German-Russian Jewish antagonism contributed independent impulses to the settlement festival strategy, and they reciprocally buttressed each other as well.

The settlement house nexus supplied rationales which gave positive value to dance and drama as mechanisms for engagement with social reform issues. Further, the contemporary sanction accorded settlement house social welfare activities enhanced the sisters' opportunities as women to construct and construe new movement practices for Progressive-era society. When the Lewisohns began their association with Henry Street in 1905 and 1906, St. Denis was still preparing her debut concert of East Indian–inspired dances and Duncan was maturing as an artist in Europe. These two dancers had asserted art status for their work, but the newly claimed terrain was slippery, the battle not yet won.

The Henry Street Settlement, in contrast, was an institution the Lewisohns' father had publically supported and to which he had introduced his daughters. Wald and Wallach gave the Lewisohns support and encouragement, but also freedom to experiment with their favorite art forms in the settlement atmosphere of serious purpose and social responsibility. At Henry Street the sisters worked untroubled by the commercial considerations and expectations of sexual display attached to professional musical theatre. At the same time, their work with children in a reform context intersected then contemporary notions of child nurture as proper to women's role. Thus the settlement house context supplied not only a rationale for incorporating dance into American life, but a platform at Henry Street for launching serious experiment with dance.[58]

From Henry Street to Grand Street: Transfer and Transition to the Neighborhood Playhouse

Having outgrown the Henry Street Settlement facilities, the Lewisohns commissioned design and construction of a new building at 466 Grand Street, several blocks away on the Lower East Side. They moved into the Neighborhood Playhouse in February 1915. The sisters brought to their work in the new venue the rationale for dance and dramatic work conceived at the Settlement. This continuity is confirmed in Alice Lewisohn's October 1915 comments, quoted in the *New York Times*, about the first season at the Playhouse:

> This production [*Jephthah's Daughter*] and those which followed indicated the purpose of the playhouse and gave promise of its ampler fulfillment. For besides the desire to widen the vision of the children and to broaden their horizon by giving them an opportunity to glance into other lands and learn to understand other customs and other peoples, was the wish to revitalize and interpret for them their own traditions and symbols.[1]

The closing lines of this quotation echo Alice's 1912 analysis of the Henry Street festivals' purpose, minus the declaration that immigrants did not comprehend their own rituals. Such intertextuality can be traced in other published statements about the Lewisohns' dance and drama work. What's significant here is the retention of Settlement rhetoric. Since the Playhouse was embraced under the charter of the Henry Street Settlement, the sisters carried with them the aura and sense of legitimacy and respectability which the Settlement had always conferred on their activities. They also benefited from the Settlement's tax status as a nonprofit organization.[2] To their Playhouse work the sisters also transferred the class work methodologies they had developed at the Settlement. That they set their sights beyond the horizon of the neighborhood seems clear as well. As Alice wrote in 1959:

> Although the idea of a new building was to carry further the work of the festivals and plays, its possible scope and value extended beyond our own productions. In fact, we thought of it first as a center for the creative expression of artist, craftsman, and student, not limited strictly to the neighborhood. Even as image, it anticipated the opportunity for the old and the young, the initiated and the potentially gifted in the arts, to contribute their part to an individual adventure in theatre.[3]

From roots sunk deeply in the goals and methods of settlement house work, the Neighborhood Playhouse arose as an arena for the development of dance and drama.[4]

The Dutch Colonial Playhouse, which still stands in 1999, supported in its architectural design an interest in structuring American nationality to which the Settlement festivals had already been party. The auditorium seated about 399 people, who were separated from the stage by a proscenium wall. Harvard theatre professor George Pierce Baker traveled to Grand Street to see the Playhouse's modified "sky dome," a smoothly plastered stage wall that curved around the back and sides of the stage, obviating the need for stretched canvas sky cloths. When the Provincetown Players, another little theatre group founded in 1915, introduced a modified sky dome for its 1920–21 season, the scenic device was still a novelty in the United States. Classrooms, rehearsal rooms, and dressing rooms were located on the floors above the theatre, supplemented by production space in a workshop building on Pitt Street.[5] The Playhouse's location in the heart of the Russian Jewish immigrant district presented an obstacle to New York patrons from outside the neighborhood. Remembering his first visit to the Playhouse in 1924, critic Joseph Wood Krutch situated the Playhouse in theatre world geography:

> The journey to Grand Street in the heart of the great isolated, self-contained, exotic and teeming East Side took one into a world most of us seldom visited on any other occasion and one which was, in many respects, as "foreign" as though it had been located on a different continent.[6]

The Neighborhood Playhouse building in 1989, known as the Henry Street Settlement Playhouse. Photograph by S. F. Tomko.

Orientalist conceptions continued to inform Manhattanites' (not just German Jews') perceptions of the Lower East Side during the 1920s.

For the first several years, the Playhouse scheduled a variety of events. Films, playlets, marionette shows, folk songs, and dance were offered Tuesday through Friday, afternoon through evening. Special children's matinees were held on Saturday and Sunday afternoons, and larger-scale drama and dance works were mounted on Saturday and Sunday evenings. At these weekend evening events, musical or dramatic divertissements typically preceded the feature presentation. On February 24 and 25, 1917, for example, two musicians opened the evening by performing Franck's *Sonata for Piano and Violin*; *The Kairn of Koridwen*, a dance drama in two scenes, followed. Exhibitions were regularly mounted in the Playhouse for viewing by audience members and on these two February evenings, sketches by Herbert Crowley, set designer for *The Kairn* (and Alice Lewisohn's future husband) were displayed. Tickets for the performances cost

$.25 and $.50; in the same era vaudeville tickets typically cost $1 to $2; Broadway tickets $1.50 to $2, and top opera seats $5. In 1920, the Playhouse established a permanent, professional company and scheduled large-scale dance and drama works every night of the week except Monday. Children's performances continued to be weekend afternoon attractions, and the Playhouse functioned as a producing venue through Spring 1927.[7]

Directing Neighborhood Playhouse productions and activities was the same team that had produced Settlement drama productions from 1912 to 1914. Sarah Cowell LeMoyne, until her death in fall 1915, continued to work with Alice and Irene Lewisohn, Agnes Morgan, and Helen Arthur. Morgan, graduate of George Pierce Baker's 47 Workshop at Harvard, frequently wrote or directed plays. She slipped easily into roles of lighting designer and stage manager as well. As had Morgan, Arthur initially worked with the Lewisohns on a volunteer basis; in 1918 Arthur forsook a career with the Schubert organization to become business manager at the Playhouse. Esther Peck, Aline Bernstein, and later Alice Beer worked with costume and scene design; Peck also designed posters and programs. Lily May Hyland served as both dancing class pianist and musical advisor. Several of these skilled women doubled as teachers, enabling the Playhouse to offer instruction in a wide range of theatre crafts. The staff recognized the artisanal qualities and benefits that such instruction might confer. A 1924–25 season pamphlet notes that Playhouse production practices aimed at "restoring some of the medieval devotion to the beauty and sincerity of craftsmanship."[8] Lillian Wald and Rita Wallach Morgenthau served as members of an advisory group, along with Max Morgenthau Jr. — Rita Morgenthau's husband and the sole male granted policy-level input. The roster of producing directors and collaborators clearly establishes what might have gone unremarked about the Settlement drama productions; the Playhouse was a women's enterprise.[9]

That a women's production effort could sustain itself was due in part to changing circumstances in early-twentieth-century American theatre. The Neighborhood Playhouse was one of three "little theatres" that established themselves in New York in 1915 to pursue alternatives to reigning commercial theatre practices. "Intimate theatres" and Symbolist drama had been spawned in France in the 1890s, England enjoyed a little theatre movement, and cabaret flourished in Berlin and Munich. Each of these enterprises tried to reconfigure the nature of theatre practice, the character of dramatic literature, the audience-performer relationship, and forms of sponsorship and patronage. In the United States, the Lewisohns took exception to the realistically staged "well-made plays" that dominated

Broadway, and objected to the profit motive that seemed to drive their construction. These plays were essentially star vehicles and called for supporting actors schooled in "lines of business." They privileged specialization rather than ensemble playing and developed large-scale production techniques.[10]

Traveling in Europe the year before the new Playhouse opened, the Lewisohns drank in evidences of alternative theatrical strategies. In Germany especially, as Peter Jelavich has shown, quests for enlivened "theatricality" drove experiments in drama and cabaret. In Munich and Berlin, theatre theorists thought nineteenth-century drama had come to depend too heavily on texts as the focus of productions, and considered scenic realism a deadening armature. They experimented with ways to "re-theatricalize" productions—invoking greater use of gesture, motion, and voice— and tried to re-equilibrate the balance among these elements. It's possible that the Lewisohns observed some of these ideas set in motion in Max Reinhardt's *Sumurun*, which played New York in January 1912. This production made no use at all of spoken text and instead relied on pantomime, bodily gesture, and movement. During their European tour, the Lewisohns witnessed Max Reinhardt's Berlin production of *A Midsummer Night's Dream* but found more impressive his staging of Wedekind's Symbolist play *Spring Awakening*. They gained exposure to new stagecraft techniques, to changing ideas about song and vocal delivery in theatre, and also to what I would call a mobilizing of actors' embodiment. Visiting the Dalcroze school in Hellerau, Germany, they observed classes and productions emitting "an atmosphere of the Greek gymnasia." In the Dalcroze movement practice, with its emphasis on the bodily generation of rhythm for music and song as well as dance, Irene Lewisohn gained an important source that she would adapt in future Playhouse festival work. In England the Lewisohns witnessed the militant protest tactics of English suffragettes in Christabel and Emmeline Pankhurst's wing of the suffrage movement, another kind of political theatre which mobilized bodily performance in unprecedented ways. This would not have been the Lewisohns' first experience with suffrage spectacle. Suffrage parades and open-air meetings gained increasing visibility in New York suffrage campaigns from 1908, and in 1913 Congressional Committee members of NAWSA aggressively picketed the White House the day before Woodrow Wilson's inauguration. After returning to the United States as World War I broke out, the Lewisohns launched the Playhouse enterprise at a fecund moment for reworking theatre verities, for foregrounding the body as vehicle and creator of theatrical meaning. Not surprisingly, Playhouse productions would never go to the radical lengths that cabaret attained, since the political situations in America and Germany, and the class and gender positions of the two forms' proponents, differed enormously. The motivation to reimagine theatrical performance, however, kindled both endeavors.[11]

Multiple Pursuits

The Neighborhood Playhouse brought the Lewisohns independence from the Henry Street Settlement without severing ties to it. Several emerging motives and lines of development began to strive with one another, to compete for attention within the large Playhouse program. The "neighborhood" motive—releasing immigrant talents and resources, harmonizing relationships with neighborhood people—came into tension with the desire to produce works of art. In her curtain-raising speech at the first Playhouse performance, Lillian Wald sounded the tocsin for continued affiliation with the immigrant community, but she also left room for innovation.

> Above the din of industrialism and the roar of machinery of the city, there rises the hope that a community playhouse, identified with its neighborhood, may recapture and hold something of the poetry and the idealism that belong to its people—not to cling to meaningless fealties because they are old and solemn, but in order to save from ruthless destruction precious inheritance and also to open wide the door of opportunity for the messages, in drama and picture and story and song, that reflect the moral and social and art convictions of our times.[12]

In an issue of the Henry Street *Settlement Journal* devoted to the new Playhouse, Alice Lewisohn echoed settlement sentiment but indexed the strong desire to turn new ground as well:

> We all share in an intense desire to make the Playhouse an expression of the Neighborhood: the place where beauty and poetry may be linked with good will and comradeship; where an art expression may develop independently, untrammeled by convention, unhampered by traditions of the stage.[13]

She was acutely aware that neighborhood responsibility had to be combined with professional standards:

> Yet with all the joy of experimenting, the freedom of creating atmosphere out of plaster, characters out of words, we cannot for a single moment

overlook our responsibility. The responsibility of upholding our standards, justifying our existence as a Playhouse and as players to ourselves and to our community.[14]

Irene was content for a time to develop work in the neighborhood and then "broaden it out to embrace the rest of the city and then the country in the true Settlement spirit." She was enchanted with the possibilities for technical innovation that the Playhouse offered, as indicated in her contribution to the Playhouse issue of the *Settlement Journal*:

> We feel that the Neighborhood Playhouse offers a new field for experimentation in all the technical as well as the artistic branches of theatrical art, and, indeed, may have a small share in welding those two into one. Let us turn our stage hands into artists who shall care for the effect of each tree or shadow as much as the actor shall care for his pronunciation and emotional expression.[15]

Ultimately, the goal of giving expression to the community would conflict with the Lewisohns' aspiration to forge new modes of theatrical expression.

The Lewisohns' class position — their wealth status and social peerage — uniquely positioned them to pursue the several goals that surfaced in the celebratory rhetoric surrounding the Playhouse's inauguration. They essentially bought their way out of the facilities limitations of the Henry Street Settlement. Over the next twelve years, the Lewisohns would sink half a million dollars into the Playhouse. Yet class alone could not have established the female Lewisohns as rightful or appropriate workers — creative workers rather than mere executants — in the dance and drama business. The legitimacy that linkage to the Settlement conferred on their arts experimentation also confirmed their "re-gendering" of dance and drama creation, direction, and management as female pursuits. The Lewisohns' gender marginality in the commercial theatre business made retention of the settlement tie indispensable. The social welfare linkage, together with the conceptualization of dance and drama as forms of social and political engagement, supplied fundamental footing for the new venue.[16]

What resulted from the founders' complex of goals and aspirations was the continuation of festival work, via the Festival Dancers, and re-constitution of the community's amateur Neighborhood Players as a professional company in 1920. The shift toward professional performers dealt in part with realities of working-class life: teenage and adult members who worked in the paid labor force could give concentrated time for rehearsals only on weekends, and not on the Sabbath. The Lewisohns had to pay wages to performers in order to command their rehearsal time on a steady weekday and evening basis. While at least two of these paid performers hailed from the neighborhood, a number came from without. According to Alice, the Playhouse directors held their breath and waited to see how the new plan would affect neighborhood Playhouse participants; they were relieved when it seemed to cause no disturbance.[17] Financing the professional company, in turn, exerted additional pressures. In 1924, the Playhouse introduced a repertory schedule for performances. This scheme was intended to attract additional subscribers; it also offered a wider range of works, which was thought to give performers greater challenges and to keep them interested.

Professional performers and productions did not overwhelm the Neighborhood Playhouse. Rather, amateur performance ran alongside professional presentation. The Junior Neighborhood Players (a children's drama group) and the Festival Dancers, some sixty strong in 1924, continued to train and work as ensembles. Neighborhood children and young adults supplied their principal membership. Each group mounted independent productions, but members were occasionally drawn into performances by the professional company, such as *The Dybbuk* and *Kuan Yin*. Indeed, according to Alice, festival work made all other work at the Playhouse possible. It was in festival methodology that the Lewisohns tried out new relationships between song, speech, bodily movement, and instrumental accompaniment. Class training and the group spirit engendered in long rehearsals for festivals underpinned the gradual achievement of a professional company and a mode of working which privileged ensemble values. The search for a lyric method, to adapt Sartre's phrase, supplied a common experiential bond despite competing interests and production initiatives at the Playhouse.

Production Types

Jephthah's Daughter, the inaugural production at the Neighborhood Playhouse, retained the Settlement emphasis on expressing the neighborhood and affirming neighborhood religious and ethnic heritage. The action of *Jephthah's Daughter* turned on the Book of Judges story in which the warrior Jephthah agrees to lead an army against enemies attacking the people of Mizpeh. He swears that, if victorious, he will sacrifice the first person who comes to greet him on his return. The returning conqueror first meets his own daughter, who leads women of Mizpeh in dance to welcome him. Jephthah is obliged to sacrifice her; after a two-month delay, she finally throws herself upon a fire laid at the community altar. Nine dances were performed in the course of the action, including an excited dance by women who throw jewels at Jephthah's feet when Mizpeh secures his services, a rose dance in which pipers and girls scatter rose leaves in the returning conqueror's path, and a solo torch dance by Jephthah's daughter before she ignites her own fire. A chorus and an orchestra, playing music composed by Lilia MacKay-Cantrell, provided accompaniment. Among the cast of over sixty, Alice Lewisohn took the title role; Irene performed as a maiden of Mizpeh.[18]

The scenario for *Jephthah's Daughter* lent itself to depiction of ritual practice and was clearly congruent with festival precedents at the Henry Street Settlement. Neighborhood reaction was vigorous and mixed, and Alice Lewisohn recalled this production as a kind of nightmare:

> *Jephthah's Daughter* bore much criticism. Our orthodox Jewish neighbors were scandalized at the free interpretation of the Bible text. Caricatures of us appeared in the Yiddish press showing "Miss Neighborhood Playhouse" slamming the door in the face of the Yiddish playwright. The radically inclined were disappointed that the Old Testament was used as source, rather than Andreyev or Gorky, and the conventionally minded were shocked at the bare feet of the dancers. Still another chorus raised its voice in behalf of strictly American culture, protesting that only poor material and no good could come from this East-Side venture. Notwithstanding the criticism and the production's many imperfections, *Jephthah's Daughter* concluded its scheduled run.[19]

These criticisms show that, whatever the producers' goals, the community did not receive their initiatives passively. Belying the social control that historians often attribute to settlement house work, these Lower East Side people responded to the Playhouse production with active interpretive work, making meaning for themselves in no uncertain terms. The community reaction also demonstrates the vitality of bodily representation and its success in engaging issues of community life in 1915. Responses from community members scandalized by *Jephthah's Daughter* indexed ongoing Orthodox resistance to the universalizing efforts of Lewisohn productions. Those who wished to acknowledge Yiddish playwrights faulted the Playhouse for supporting assimilation efforts via their use of English-language texts. A vital Yiddish theatre had existed in New York since the late nineteenth century, sustaining different fictions of what it meant to be Jewish in America, and the *Folksbuehne*, a drama group supported by the socialist Workingman's Circle, set its sights on the new Playhouse as venue for its own productions. Protracted negotiations with the Lewisohns resulted in guest seasons by the *Folksbuehne* at the Playhouse commencing in 1916. The Playhouse itself, however, would produce only a few plays by Yiddish authors, and these were staged in English-language versions.[20] Caricatures that focused on "Miss Neighborhood Playhouse" also censured the gendered nature of the Playhouse enterprise: the temerity of the female producing staff in articulating its own aims and placing them ahead of male-dominated Yiddish theatre organizations and texts. This criticism voiced contemporary gendered ideas about the professional division of labor in commercial theatre. Neighborhood criticism of the performers' bare feet shows that issues of sexuality and bodily economies never lay far from view in live performance. No matter that Duncan and St. Denis had fought battles about bodily display on New York concert stages; ritual references and leading-edge footwear stylings competed with long-standing associations of female sensuality to complicate the reception of dancing neighborhood children and teenagers.

Despite the outcry, neighborhood people continued to participate in Playhouse productions, arguably drawing their own conclusions about the works they performed. Productions fell into several general categories: two of these informed the "lyric drama" for which the Playhouse became known in the 1920s. Personal inclination and the need for efficiency led the Lewisohn sisters to divide up areas of responsibility in their production work. Irene directed the dance training and productions while Alice led the dramatic work. This arrangement did not preclude crossover between the two types of activities; indeed, the Playhouse preached and practiced the unity of the arts in all its productions. Alice and Irene collaborated in directing and choreographing a number of works. All performers, whatever the production, received training in movement, acting, singing, and pantomime skills.

Production types that carried over from Henry Street Settlement days included dramas, dance pantomimes or ballets, and festivals. Plays by English and Irish writers were well represented in the dramatic repertoire, including four works by George Bernard Shaw—this at a time when the Theatre Guild was aggressively introducing Shaw on Broadway.[21] The remainder of the repertoire ranged widely, from authors such as Provincetown Players playwright Susan Glaspell and Symbolist dramatist Mme. Rachilde, to Robert Browning, Eugene O'Neill, Chekhov, and James Joyce. A handful of Yiddish plays was presented in English translation. As Alice Lewisohn remembered it, players and producers strove to develop depth of characterization; matters of diction and vocal delivery received constant scrutiny; and performers were expected to relinquish their personal ambition and stylistic preferences, the better to work as part of a larger whole dedicated to the production. Careful research preceded settings and costume construction. Playhouse dramatic productions pursued scenic realism with some diligence, but on an economic rather than lavish scale.[22] At the same time, the Neighborhood Playhouse proved more receptive than American commercial theatre to realist narratives, "dramas of ideas," new European playwrights, and non-realist drama of a poetic or mythic stripe. The eclectic range of the repertoire was quite in keeping with the approach taken by the Provincetown Players, their contemporary in the American little theatre movement, and by European directors such as Max Reinhardt in Germany and A. E. F. Horniman in the English little theatre movement.[23] The Playhouse's insistence on ensemble values paralleled the emphasis placed on ensemble work by new theatre groups like Ireland's Abbey Theatre.

Playhouse pantomimes and ballets mobilized patterns initiated at the Settlement, where festivals like *Sleeping Beauty*, *Snow White*, and *The Shadow Garden of Shuteye Town* had celebrated seasonal changes using dance and pantomime formats. Productions increased in sophistication and ranged from *Petrouchka* (1916) to *La Boutique Fantasque* (1919–20), *The Royal Fandango* (1921–22), *A Norse Fairy Tale* (1921–22), and *Ritornelle* (1927). Folk plays and Ballets Russes choreographies supplied obvious source material for many of these works. The Lewisohns had viewed the Ballets Russes *Petrouchka* in Europe in 1914, and they mounted the Playhouse version at the same time the touring Ballets Russes presented *Petrouchka* in New York City. Nor were they the only respondents to Ballets Russes models. Gertrude Hoffman pirated Ballets Russes ideas and staged veristic variants of its choreographies before the company ever set foot in the United States.[24] In Alice's view, though, the sisters conceived the work quite differently from the Russians, staging "the Stravinsky score in terms of a purely folk experience." (This lends interesting corroboration to 1990s reappraisals of Stravinsky's music for its articulation of folk sources rather than its modernist momentum.) Collaborating again with the Lewisohns, Russian émigré Louis Chalif choreographed *Petrouchka*'s dances. Alice's memoir clearly suggests that he crafted folk and national material in 1916. Given Chalif's view that classical dancing supplied fundamental grounding for other styles, this material probably bore a balletic imprint. Chalif disseminated a number of dance styles in his New York City career as a pedagogue, and he may have supplied movement resources in other Playhouse pantomimes that called for classical dancing.[25] *Royal Fandango*, for example, struck one journalist as offering authentic ballet technique. This

Gypsy dancers in *Petrouchka*. BILLY ROSE THEATRE COLLECTION, THE NEW
YORK PUBLIC LIBRARY FOR THE PERFORMING ARTS, ASTOR, LENOX AND TILDEN
FOUNDATIONS.

production was surely inspired by the Spanish turn that Ballets Russes repertory took with *The Three-Cornered Hat* and *Cuadro Flamenco* in 1919 and 1922. Ballet was thus one among several techniques available for incorporation into Playhouse movement practices. As did the dramas for Alice, the ballets afforded performance opportunities for Irene, who danced the lead in *Petrouchka* and the Lady with the Fan in *The Royal Fandango*.[26]

Festivals, too, continued as Playhouse productions. Like their Settlement precedents, festivals premiered one season could be recycled during another. This was the case with a November 1915 Thanksgiving festival, "an Autumn Festival Interpreting in Chorus Processionals and in Dances a Thanksgiving for the Elemental Forces." Referring obliquely to ongoing World War I, the action for three of four loosely linked scenes took place at the Temple of Peace. The fourth and closing scene showed "dances and choruses symbolizing the Elemental Forces—Fire, Water, Earth, and Air." The same structure and section titles appeared again in A *Festival*, the February 1916 production celebrating the Playhouse's first anniversary. Another element was added—the Prologue, a citation from Euripides valorizing peace over war. Similar recycling shaped the spring 1918 *Festival of Pentecost* into the fall 1918 *The Feast of Tabernacles*. The fact that Pentecost and Booths (Tabernacles) each marked a different seasonal harvest in the Jewish calendar eased adaptation. Continuing earlier compositional methods, the 1918 harvest festivals built choreographic structure upon processionals and ceremonies of ritual offerings.[27]

Festivals employed large numbers of performers; seventy-eight people drawn from the Festival Dancers, the Neighborhood Players, and the Festival Chorus participated in *The Feast of Tabernacles*. In an October 1918 *Menorah Journal* article, the Lewisohns described the "orchestral" method they used in mobilizing large forces for festival productions:

> The training is approached from an art rather than from a pedagogical standpoint, but emphasis has always been laid upon co-operative effort rather than upon the exploitation of individual talent. Without attempting to challenge comparison with creative art, the Playhouse uses the method of an orchestra where each individual is earnestly endeavoring through honest workmanship to contribute his share to the creation of a thing of beauty.[28]

The orchestra metaphor echoes the musical language used for other contemporary formulations of artistic method: St. Denis's conception of dancers as instruments in a music visualization orchestra, say, or Dalcrozian development of movement rhythms and polyrhythms. These, however, allowed for distinct individuals whose movements harmonize within larger wholes. Festival Dancers, in contrast, were expected to merge their individualities in the larger project. This effect registered visibly for a *Brooklyn Eagle* reviewer covering *Salut au Monde* in 1922, who wrote, "This is hardly a production in which the individual actors seem to be of importance. One is struck rather by the movement of the piece as a whole, as if there were no individual performers behind it."[29] Despite the rhetoric of inclusion, the Playhouse method placed creative control in the hands of the few—the producing staff—and not the many. In combination with the universalizing "seasons" theme, the emphasis on ensemble performance and identity of purpose helped to forge in bodily terms a representation, and possibly a sense, of immigrants belonging to a corporate whole larger than their specific historical or ethnic identities. This political emphasis was not lost in Playhouse festival work, which continued to recruit neighborhood children as Festival Dancers. What assumed increasing weight was the articulation in aesthetic terms of the need for singularity of focus and concentration of forces. Aesthetic resources that had been deployed in Henry Street Settlement festivals to ameliorate social conditions were now put to a second and different use: performers were asked to channel individual resources into "creation of a thing of beauty." These two currents would cycle and contend with each other throughout the Playhouse period.[30]

Irene Lewisohn bore chief responsibility for festival choreography; she was assisted by Blanche Talmud. A neighborhood resident, Talmud grew up performing in the Settlement festivals, becoming an acting and dancing member of the professional company and a dance teacher on the Playhouse staff. She aided Irene in choreographing pantomimes and ballets as well, and was indispensable in working with the Festival Dancers. What was their movement practice like? Alice remembered Irene's dance designs as

> meticulously worked out, nothing left to chance or sudden flair. Inspired by the vision of the exact relationship between movement and music, she could stimulate her group to tune into her values, and in consequence the dancers were ready to mutilate size or ego for a chance to work. The concentrated intensity of a festival rehearsal was electric.[31]

A Dalcroze influence is evident. Alice stated firmly, however, that the Lewisohns made their own use of the materials the Dalcroze system offered. "As Dalcroze himself said, it was a system and not an art form. Later we studied and adapted the method in combination with other techniques for our own group training." Corroborating Alice's memoir, an early Playhouse program reported that movement training embraced "classical, national, and interpretative dancing, of which the festivals and pantomimes are the ultimate expression." The Festival Dancers themselves were enthusiastic fans of the Duncan dancers, who occasionally performed on the Playhouse stage. Thus, no single dance style predominated.[32]

The recollections of modern dance choreographer Helen Tamiris illuminate something of the texture and variety of dance training made available by Lewisohn and Talmud at the Settlement and the Playhouse in the first decades of the century. Born to Russian Jewish immigrant parents on the Lower East Side in 1902, Tamiris lost her mother at an early age. She treasured the dancing opportunities she gained at the Henry Street Settlement as an elementary school girl and then as a high school student. Her induction into dancing classes was accomplished through her brother's girlfriend Eva, secretary to Lillian Wald. Eva made Tamiris a tunic to wear and she attended class in a room draped with "transparent red gold curtains," the walls of which bore "pictures of dancing girls by Botticelli." Classes were taught by Irene Lewisohn

> and occasionally by her favorite pupil—Blanche Talmud . . . Miss Talmud was tall and [A13] slender as a reed and spoke just as Miss Lewisohn did in a soft gentle voice. The dancing was called Interpretative dancing. . . . We danced in a circle facing each other—and Miss Talmud would say—"The Grieg Music." or "Now we'll have Chopin." I liked best what I thought of as strong pieces of music, those with a decided beat — and would lean against the wall to watch the others when the music was dreamy and gentle. . . .[33]

Not long allowed to observe, Tamiris would rejoin the class: "I'd go through the motions of waving my arms in the breeze like a butterfly or run in a soft patter patter across the room [A14] in a diagonal, feeling guilty—as though I was play-acting. . . ."[34]

When Tamiris returned to the settlement after several years away, she wrote, "I was now deeply engrossed in Folk Dancing—It was called Character dancing—and was based on steps taken from the peasant dances of various countries." She also spent time at her high school gymnasium with a teacher "who too loved dancing and was trying to incorporate it into the formal physical training required by the Board of Education." This activity was folk dancing as well, and Tamiris was probably benefiting from the folk dancing instruction offered by the Girls Branch of the Public Schools Athletic League, the subject of chapter 6.[35]

Tamiris's recollections support the conclusion that a variety of movement materials comprised the festival dance class curriculum over time. They also suggest the importance attached to emotional connection, which is also implicit in the remarks of another Neighborhood Playhouse alumna. Sophie Bernsohn Finkle, who performed in Playhouse productions in the mid-1920s, recalls the instruction given by Playhouse teacher Blanche Talmud: "There was no ballet, of course. It was modern dance. You closed your eyes and had a good time. Technique came later." She added, "You did anything—there was no technique." Sophie Maslow, who studied at the Playhouse in the late 1920s, also remembers Talmud as a teacher. "It was a follow through kind of movement, in terms of wavelike movement," she said. Maslow remembers starting one sequence using parallel stance and a deep plié, "which comes up through the feet, through the knees, then hips, with head back, flowing all the way up." Students used "no turnout, no pointed toes, no ballet," and danced "combinations of free flowing movement." The movement practice that the Playhouse forged clearly took advantage of diverse vocabularies and embodiments. During the twelve-year tenure of the Playhouse, productions mobilized elements from Delsarte and Dalcroze techniques; aspects of folk, national, and classical training; influences from Duncan dancing; and input from Bird Larson, for a brief period in the mid-1920s. Among these eclectic resources, different emphases came to the fore at different times and with regard to different productions.[36]

The Festival Dancer Body

Festivals constituted that part of the Playhouse repertoire that embraced transhistorical and idealist themes and settings, and a Symbolist penchant for evoking hidden worlds cloaked by surfaces and exterior reality. Festivals were also the source of an embodiment that the Playhouse used as an icon. To be sure, many types of "bodies" were "made" at the Playhouse in the course of producing plays, pantomimes, ballets, and festivals for twelve years—in one sense, acting or dancing is all about making new, or making anew, characterizations and embodiments. But the Playhouse singled out and circulated one of these embodiments as a representation of its aims and accomplishments: the "Festival Dancer" body captured in a drawing by Playhouse affiliate Esther Peck. Surviving documents show that the Festival Dancer image was printed on Playhouse program covers and as a freestanding handbill. Lillian Wald's 1915 House on Henry Street includes a similar drawing. Peck's Festival Dancers illustrate a 1916 Craftsman ar-

DRAWING BY ESTHER PECK

A FESTIVAL DANCER

𝕿𝖍𝖊 𝕹𝖊𝖎𝖌𝖍𝖇𝖔𝖗𝖍𝖔𝖔𝖉 𝕻𝖑𝖆𝖞𝖍𝖔𝖚𝖘𝖊   466 GRAND STREET
NEW YORK CITY

The image of a Festival Dancer graced various Neighborhood
Playhouse pamphlets, handbills, and performance programs.
NEIGHBORHOOD PLAYHOUSE COLLECTION, THE NEIGHBORHOOD
PLAYHOUSE.

From
a
sketch
of
Isadora
Duncan's
pupils:
By
Esther
Peck,

From
a
sketch
of
East
Side
Russian
children
in
New
York:
By
Esther
Peck.

Renderings of Isadora Duncan dancers (*above*) and Neighborhood Playhouse dancers (*below*) appeared with the article "Dancing and Democracy" in the December 1916 issue of *The Craftsman*.

ticle, "Dancing and Democracy," that compares Playhouse dancing with Duncan dancing.[37] What kinds of meanings did this image negotiate and articulate? The *Craftsman* article, with Peck's sketches of Playhouse and Duncan dancers, helps answer this question. Peck's drawings consistently picture the Festival Dancer as a girl-child, her tunic blousing, girded at hip or breast. The Duncan dancers verge on puberty, long of thigh with waist-nipped tunics. Moving singly or in groups, Festival Dancers handle objects—hand-pipes, slender horn, fabric drapery serving as a cape—and they focus their bodies' effort on the objects at hand. Their arms outstretched, Duncan dancers carry nothing; their limbs' energy attenuates, they catch each other's eye. Festival Dancers assume stances that anchor firmly to the ground; Duncan dancers alight, touch down from airborne motion. Festival Dancers animate shapes; Duncan dancers stream through space. Festival Dancers, in other words, fashioned in bodily terms notions of connection and linkage, forgetfulness of self, and spontaneity and engagement released through task or group orientation. Festival Dancer bodies embodied the hoped-for social effects of reintegrating arts practices into everyday American life. This same embodiment would be turned to account in the lyric drama method forged at the Playhouse, where without relinquishing goals of regenerating social individuals, Playhouse productions would pursue with growing fervor the invigoration of dramatic performance practice.

Lyric Productions

For the production types discussed thus far, and particularly during the first five to seven years of Playhouse activity, the Lewisohns and their collaborators strove to develop a production approach particular to the vehicle. A priori commitment to a specific scenic or movement style was not for them, at least not in theory. By 1922, with the production of *Salut au Monde*, I argue, the Playhouse began to select for performance works which lent themselves to production as "lyric dramas," an approach that privileged bodily movement and choral vocalization in combination with speech for realizing theatrical works. By honing the concept of lyric dramas, the Playhouse placed itself squarely within the orbit of European initiatives to re-theatricalize drama—to animate with movement and voice—that the Lewisohns had witnessed in 1914 and in subsequent trips. Working just as powerfully on their notion of lyric drama, Playhouse production choices reveal, was the circulation of Adolphe Appia's and Gordon Craig's briefs for re-fashioning stage space through light and rhythm. Re-orchestrating the superior position accorded text and speech in conventional American drama, the Playhouse producers amplified the opportunities for movement expression that scenarios afforded, and coordinated song with dance and speech as equally salient devices for mobilizing a vehicle's action and imagery. *Salut au Monde* stands as both the culmination of the festival genre and the juncture of festival with lyric productions. It linked the lyricism of voice and body, long activated by festivals, with dramatic structures at once more legible and less specifically moored in Hebrew ritual roots.[38]

Walt Whitman's poem *Salut au Monde* provided a ready vehicle for Americanizing a production type linked to neighborhood traditions while also invoking "the universal religion of humanity and the brotherhood of man." Work on this production commenced at the end of World War I, and the Festival Dancers performed a preliminary sketch in June 1919. Composer Charles Griffes died in April 1920, however, which delayed completion of the production until Edmund Rickets could orchestrate the score Griffes had left. Taking final form in Spring 1922, this evening-length work comprised a Prologue and three episodes. In addition to Ian Maclaren, who acted the role of Walt Whitman, it required an orchestra of wind and percussion instruments, conducted by Georges Barrère; a singing chorus; featured singers; a chorus of voices that dialogued with Whitman; the Festival Dancers and the Junior Festival Dancers; plus the Neighborhood Players in walk-on roles. The logistics of mounting and rehearsing this work were complicated and the producers acknowledged that its ultimate form was irregular, not completely unified. It was precisely in attempting to use a chorus of voices as an orchestral color, or in interweaving poetic texts with movement discourses, that the producers constructed their lyric method.[39]

Salut au Monde casts the poet as representative of "man's spiritual being," and the action takes him on a spiritual journey. In the Prologue, he experiences a sense of oneness with the cosmic universe, while a color organ throws shifting colors against a huge sphere suggesting Earth. The sphere consists of a circular void formed by a stage-wide set piece cut out in the middle and draped with curtains. During the first episode, the Poet stands at the margin of this void, declaiming verse from *Salut au Monde* in response to unseen voices. His poetic images first summon forces of chaos: depicting the "darkened side of the cosmic sphere," dimly lit forms struggle in confusion as dissonant chords crash round them. Next he calls forces of constructiveness: light grows brighter as laboring bodies perform rhythms of animal husbandry and manufacture. Workers group together to tug an

Salut au Monde, episode one. BILLY ROSE THEATRE COLLECTION, THE
NEW YORK PUBLIC LIBRARY FOR THE PERFORMING ARTS, ASTOR, LENOX
AND TILDEN FOUNDATIONS.

enormous chain across the stage in syncopated rhythm; they push across it a huge wheel, synecdoche for industry. Plying the stage in this manner, forces of rupture and coherence traverse human time and forms of human labor. The episode culminates when young children burst in with "bounding rhythms of play." Five scenes follow for the second episode, wherein Hindu, Hebrew, Greek, Islamic, and Christian religious rituals represent "five manifestations of the divine message." The Islamic scene concludes with a dervish dance—"measured circling movement about an invisible center." Greek "priests" were meant to represent the ecstatic release of Dionysian worship, but extant photographs capture only evidence of composure. Tunic-clad women, rather than priests, are caught in profile, carrying amphoras, a staff, or playing upon pipes. The Hebrew ritual includes singing of the Kol Nidre. The five "ritual" scenes constitute a multiplication of the core materials used in Playhouse festivals, but with the addition of guest performers and the benefit of consultants from various New York communities. The final episode exploits a processional as a choreographic strategy. Here the world's people pass in parade, "enfolded in the banner of human Brotherhood." The Poet, and the audience, are supposed to comprehend this brotherhood as a figure for the unity formed out of diversity in the cosmos.[40]

Following *Salut au Monde*, Playhouse productions increasingly favored lyric productions that exceeded the Hebrew festival formula and promoted admixture of song and dance with speech. Several factors impelled this interest in lyric production. First, the Lewisohns took a sabbatical leave in 1922–23, traveling to Egypt, India, Burma, and Palestine. According to Alice's memoir, the sisters felt the need to regroup, to discover the direction that subsequent Playhouse work would follow. Their quest was simultaneous with the desire of other producing staff, who stayed behind in New York, to investigate the Stanislavski method. Although they were dubious, the Lewisohns gave assent to an experiment conducted during their absence: Richard Boleslavsky used the Stanislavski method with a small group of Neighborhood Players. Two productions that applied the method issued from the experiment; they did not succeed in the Lewisohns' eyes, and work with Boleslavsky did not continue. The Lewisohns understood their sabbatical quest to involve psychological dimensions of performance, and they searched seriously among Eastern traditional practices for the indefinable something that impelled ritual, that constituted mystic communion and fueled a sense of transpersonal connection with unseen cosmic forces. They gained by sabbatical travel exposure to varieties of dance and drama forms. The Boleslavsky venture had threatened to split the producing staff; the Lewisohns marshaled their new resources to secure and invigorate the Playhouse's producing vision, but also to keep pace as a "laboratory" theatre with changing concerns in dramatic theory.[41]

Second, the social imperative that impelled dance and drama work from the days of earliest association with the Henry Street Settlement—the need to manage immigration and assimilation—now waned. The dangers of wartime travel had reduced immigration, and mounting postwar pressures to limit immigration achieved significant success with passage of federal laws in 1921 and 1924.[42] These changing social conditions effectively released the Playhouse from obligations to de-exoticize or defuse the threat posed by immigrant people. The grounds for theatrical innovation could shift from dance and drama as practices of direct social engagement endeavoring to reshape life in industrial society. The Playhouse could now permit itself to revel in fashioning sensuous representations of exotic others and their traditional practices. A third factor consisted in Denishawn constructions of Eastern dances circulating widely in postwar America. These constructions not only supplied models for emulation, but stimulated audience interest in orientalist theatrical fare as well.

The productions the Playhouse mounted following the sabbatical year show the impact of these factors. Significantly, but lost to view unless researchers distinguish among ethnic "Others," new Playhouse productions focused on non-Jewish oriental peoples and customs. The 1923–24 season, for example, produced *An Arab Fantasia*, a vehicle for depicting scenes from bedouin, bazaar, pilgrimage, and Nile-centered Arab life. *The Little Clay Cart*, translated from Sanskrit texts, had already been slated when the Lewisohns embarked on the sabbatical year. They viewed a Hindu version of the play while abroad, and mounted their own rendition for the 1924–25 season. The following season, *A Burmese Pwe* and *Kuan Yin* brought bejeweled sinuousness, swarthy (painted) gamelan players, and suggestive lighting effects to the Playhouse. The sisters' sampling of foreign cultures—their dance, music, narratives, and social groupings—provided materials ripe for synthesis using the lyric method. Their appropriation of age-old ethnic practices enabled them to fashion vehicles for getting at the "roots of theatre" and the "inner pattern" of drama, for accessing elemental ritual forces extant (they believed) in traditional practices. These constructs, experienced through performance, were the Lewisohns' equivalent of psychological dimensions in theatre. Thus, with the 1925–26 production of *The Dybbuk*, the Playhouse could revel in the matters of mysticism and spirit possession that drove this play about Russian Chassidic Jews. And the Playhouse could pursue this angle relatively free of the fear that depicting the "irrational Jew" might provoke anti-Semitic response. Indeed, *The Dybbuk* proved attractive less for the connection between its ethnic subject and Lower East Side neighbors than for its extension of the lyric method. The script, translated and adapted, served as little more than an outline for improvisation, Alice claimed, requiring realization through choreographed gesture, speech, dance, and song. The Beggars' Dance, not surprisingly, played an enhanced part in the Wedding Scene.[43]

"The Grand Street Follies" and Diverging Pursuits

Lyric productions came to fill but also exceed the place accorded festival productions in the Playhouse repertoire, articulating movement, speech, and song in visually and kinesthetically appealing composites. They shared the boards with another genre—the annual revue, or retrospective bill of parodies spoofing repertory from the preceding season. Revues began as private theatrical sketches performed for Lewisohn birthday celebrations, and in 1922 they took the Playhouse stage. Skipping the sabbatical year, revue bills returned in 1924 as an annual installment until the Playhouse closed in 1927. Known as the Grand Street Follies, these revues featured scripts of biting wit written by Helen Arthur and Agnes Morgan. The producing staff performed in these parodies right alongside the Neighborhood Players, and the casting frequently called for cross-dressing and masking. That the Grand Street Follies drew enthusiastic crowds is not really surprising; revue formats proved extravagantly popular in Europe and America in the 1920s. The Ziegfield Follies and John Murray Anderson's Greenwich Village Follies were just two well-known examples of the type. In 1927, Radio City Music Hall would inaugurate its famous chorus line, paralleling the famous Tiller Girls of Berlin revues. Further, The Grand Street Follies at the Neighborhood Playhouse adopted the self-mocking tone that gave European cabaret its appeal in the 1920s. Like that genre, Grand Street Follies bills catered to "those who knew"—audiences familiar with the "straight" versions of Playhouse productions who could grasp the inside jokes. This intertextuality created a sense of intimacy and audience involvement characteristic of little theatre productions in the 1910s. The Grand Street Follies departed, however, from the serious fare and reformist intentions of the Playhouse's own early days. With their smart tone and light-hearted approach, the Follies won adherents who didn't necessarily attend or favor the remainder of the repertory.[44]

The popular and box office success of the Grand Street Follies may well explain the tenor taken by two lyric productions that Irene directed—*Sooner and Later* in 1925, and *Pinwheel* in 1927, one of the last Playhouse productions. These two seemed to strive for contemporary appeal, taking for their focus rituals of modern and futuristic living. Like *Salut au Monde*, urtext for lyric productions, *Sooner and Later* and *Pinwheel* dealt with stages and states of civilizations, correlating the organization of labor—its work and body rhythms—with cultural development. Each required through-composed movement, gesture, song, and text elements. *Sooner and Later* surveyed three societies, in which workers culminated a day's labor by attending or participating in a drama. Primitive tribal people capped their potting, weaving, and tilling by joining in community ritual; frenetic, puppet-like twentieth-century city workers watched a revue; and "crystalline" workers in a futuristic world performed a ritual of geometric patterns, witnessed a Synthetic Mood (a sound, voice, and light prelude), and heard a tabloid radio drama. Of these the tribal world comes off the best: a communal organism vibrant, spontaneous, alive to the moment. The modern city, in contrast, "lives its workers," reducing them to passive consumers of a revue that spectacularizes sameness and repetition (identical showgirls) and blanches cultural difference (peasant dances as leg shows; Spanish dancing as clichéd courtship; jazz as caricatured black dance). *Pinwheel*, two years later, seemed to extract and focus on the puppet world of urban living. The Guy and The Jane stood as "personalized replicas" of the crowd; they were challenged and buffeted by "a fantastic kaleidoscope of scenes, some mad and fluctuant like some dance in a crystal maze, some stark, bleak, and simple." This "loose, staccato, cinematographic play" concluded with the lead couple cast adrift, homeless.[45]

These productions shared none of the joyous, bounding affirmation of *Salut au Monde*. Their modern-day rituals hewed to the dark side of the cosmos, promising decline from primal instinct to pale, brittle uniformity on one hand, and the perpetual motion of a "jerky, gibbet rigadoon," as Alexander Woolcott put it, on the other. Both plumbed veins of satire, excess, and caricature, abetted visually by Donald Oenslager's scene designs; both were understood by viewers to attempt "expressionist" methods. They constituted nothing less, I argue, than naked attempts to stake the popular, contemporaneous ground for lyric productions that had generally immured themselves in traditional materials and cultures. *Sooner and Later* and *Pinwheel* were Irene's salvos fired in an unspoken battle for the helm of Playhouse aesthetic direction and in the more public skirmish for

Sooner and Later, twentieth-century city workers. BILLY ROSE THEATRE
COLLECTION, THE NEW YORK PUBLIC LIBRARY FOR THE PERFORMING ARTS,
ASTOR, LENOX AND TILDEN FOUNDATIONS.

Sooner and Later, the revue. BILLY ROSE THEATRE COLLECTION, THE
NEW YORK PUBLIC LIBRARY FOR THE PERFORMING ARTS, ASTOR, LENOX
AND TILDEN FOUNDATIONS.

audience favor. The Playhouse addressed the latter straightforwardly in a statement "to our subscribers" in the June 1926 program booklet:

> We are sometimes asked by serious minded, art yearning students: "Why does an organization like the Neighborhood Playhouse, that produces *The Dybbuk*, a *Haydn opera*, *The Little Clay Cart*, devote time, energy, and expense to *The Follies?*" And in the same way we are asked by our friends who have a more solicitous, commercial point of view: "When so large a percentage of interest accrues from *The Follies*, when season after season it's a go, why do you venture with uncertain plays, and especially with Repertoire [repertory scheduling]?" And then an analytical observer, studying the theatre asks: "Do you produce for the delight and satisfaction of your audience? Or for your own interests, your own development—using the word 'interests' in the art sense as well as the commercial?"
>
> Now, what would you reply?[46]

Here in a nutshell were the very issues that pricked and pulled the producing staff at the Neighborhood Playhouse. Should the Playhouse take the (high) road of theatrical experiment, whatever the audience appeal of the resulting products, or should it respond to audience preferences, no matter the (low) quality of Follies fare? Was the Playhouse willing, whether ready or not, to stand or fall in the theatrical marketplace, or did it take refuge in its status as a subsidized vehicle for personal research and development? Having subtly rebuked the inquisitive for venturing such questions, the program answered that the Playhouse aimed for diversity and eschewed specialization. That was true enough, but the Playhouse did not survive these and other tensions. It closed its doors as a producing entity in 1927. Even at that, the Playhouse substantially outlived its little theatre peers in New York City. For the Provincetown Players, a year's hiatus for the 1922–23 season resulted in a reworked commercial enterprise. Some four years earlier, the Washington Square Players had folded into the Theatre Guild, which functioned successfully as a Broadway house during the 1920s.[47]

In her memoir of the Playhouse, Alice Lewisohn Crowley cited financial pressure as one of the reasons for closing the Playhouse and rethinking its future. What she did not spell out was the fact that the Lewisohns had spent half a million dollars during the preceding twelve years to support the little theatre. Other reasons were "the increasing handicap of location, the realization that we had outgrown the physical dimensions of the building, the growing intensity of the work." The latter point, again, was understated. During the winter of 1925–26, the Playhouse had run *The Dybbuk* as a weeknight repertory staple, while at the same time preparing a three-part lyric bill to alternate with it in the spring. The burden of maintaining one production and simultaneously preparing new works proved almost unsupportable, and in 1926 Alice, at least, headed into the final year with heavy heart. Such efforts to reconfigure the schedule, in turn, stemmed from the financial reality that the box office for successful works covered only the costs of running the productions, not mounting them, and left no cushion for "failures." Alice claimed that increasing pressure from New York's stagehands' union limited the amount of affordable rehearsal time, and she chafed at the inability to control who worked backstage. She did not mention interpersonal pressures that colored the decision as well. Alice married Herbert Crowley in 1924 and, living abroad, absented herself from Playhouse endeavors for the 1924–25 season. The lure of *The Dybbuk*, which she directed, pulled Alice back in 1925, but she never resumed her former intense involvement with the Playhouse. That Irene increasingly tried to assert herself and her own plans for productions is supported by the timing and tenor of *Sooner and Later* and *Pinwheel*. The split in production directions, publically acknowledged and papered over in the 1926 program, signaled that the equilibrium which once obtained among the producing directors had shifted radically. When the spirit of cooperation declined irreparably, the Playhouse closed.[48]

After reopening at a new location in 1928, the Playhouse limited itself to instruction, as evidenced by its new name, the Neighborhood Playhouse School of Theatre. Rita Wallach Morgenthau was the director and curriculum coordinator, and Irene Lewisohn was a strong adviser. The Playhouse School enlisted Martha Graham and Louis Horst among its faculty and it was there that Horst developed his seminal choreography courses in pre-classic dance forms. Irene Lewisohn continued to pursue dance production activity, albeit as a private individual. She inaugurated a series of annual "Orchestral Dramas" produced at sites like the Manhattan Opera House and Lewisohn Stadium. Performed with professional symphony orchestras, these productions secured the services of dancers Graham, Doris Humphrey, Charles Weidman, Michio Ito, and Benjamin Zemach, active participants in the emerging genre of modern dance choreography and performance. Students from the newly opened Playhouse School were given opportunities to perform in the large supporting casts of these ensemble works. The orchestral dramas warrant separate, detailed study but it should be noted that even in this later incarnation the Neighborhood Playhouse helped support modern dance by offering performing opportunities and visibility to rising artists.[49]

Impacts

If commercial theatre did not adopt the lyric method that the Neighbor-hood Playhouse explored as a producing venue, the fruitage for dance as a concert practice was far more substantial. During its twelve-year tenure on Grand Street, the Neighborhood Playhouse helped consolidate the legiti-macy of expressive dance as an art form and prepared the way for the emergent modern dance in specific ways. First, the Playhouse provided one of the few institutional bases in America for training in expressive dance. Ballet training was available at centers like the Metropolitan Opera Ballet School and Louis Chalif's academy in New York, Ned Wayburn's school excelled in preparing fancy dancers for Broadway productions, and acting academies abounded. The field for expressive dance training was much smaller. The Denishawn school in Los Angeles, offering instruction in an eclectic range of dance styles, was the most commonly recognized center for training. It opened its doors several months after the Neighbor-hood Playhouse commenced operation in 1915. Two of America's most perspicacious and widely cited critics of modern dance soon grasped the significance of Playhouse pedagogy and production for the new genre. John Martin, dance critic for the *New York Times* from 1927 to 1962, wrote in his 1936 *America Dancing* that the Playhouse's influence was second only to that of Denishawn in training and offering performance opportuni-ties to dancers who subsequently worked in modern dance companies. Margaret Lloyd, critic for the *Christian Science Monitor* from 1936 to 1960, echoed the sentiment. Her 1948 *Borzoi Book of Modern Dance* described the Playhouse as "first among pre-natal influences" on modern dance.[50] We may fairly say that consolidation of the Playhouse as a teaching and producing venue abetted the drive for institutional definition that modern dancers had to undertake in the 1920s, founding schools to train dancers but also to fund rehearsal periods, new choreography, and perfor-mance.[51]

The Playhouse training ground bore specific fruit as well: it shaped noted modern dance choreographers and performers Helen Tamiris, So-phie Maslow, and Anna Sokolow. After studying at the Playhouse, Tamiris worked in the corps de ballet at the Metropolitan Opera House and performed in night clubs. She entered the modern dance field with a 1927 concert and won a reputation as a charismatic performer. Her choreo-graphic skills were not as highly esteemed, however, and she remained something of an outsider to the prominent group of Graham, Humphrey, and Weidman. Nevertheless, she tried in diverse ways to bridge the isolation and competition, born of aesthetic differences and marketplace rivalries, that separated leading modern dance innovators. She was instrumental in setting up the short-lived Dance Repertory Theatre, a cooperative production venture, with Graham, Humphrey and Weidman in 1930. She also helped establish the New York branch of the WPA Dance Theatre during the Depression. Sokolow and Maslow both joined Graham's all-female company and subsequently established themselves as choreographers of stature, participating in the leftist dance movement whose "propaganda dances" were derided by the high modernist oracle *Dance Observer*. Long marginalized in master narratives of modern dance, "red" or leftist dance has only in the 1990s begun to receive renewed scrutiny. Sokolow is known also for works of great emotional power and has taught at the Juilliard School in New York for many years.[52]

Tamiris, Maslow, and Sokolow made careers for themselves as choreographers as well as performers, exceeding the bounds of "executant" roles to direct, manage, and create works for their own dance enterprises. In this they carried forward into the next generation the model established by the Playhouse producing staff, and continued the work of re-gendering the theatre world's sexual division of labor. In addition, the choreographers stripped the model of its class determinants. The Playhouse had never run as a collective or communal enterprise; rather, wealth, education, and previous professional experience underpinned the allocation (arrogation) of choreographic and directing activity to the Lewisohns and the producing staff. Not class standing but passion and commitment sustained the arduous excavation of modern dance as a genre in the rocky economics of Depression-era America.

The choreographers' success illuminates matters of ethnicity as well. It debunks the pervasive view that modern dance is a completely indigenous and quintessentially American art form. Rather, these children of Russian immigrant Jews forged important strains in modern dance, incorporating the drive for collective action and passion for socialist theory which circulated in Lower East Side labor organizing and radical politics. Tamiris with her *Negro Spirituals* and Federal Dance Theatre choreographies, and Maslow and Sokolow through their Workers Dance League activity pursued dance making and dance organizing that spoke about and from a community of interest. They comprehended dance as a mode of social and political engagement, thus echoing a motivation for Henry Street and early Playhouse dance and drama work. Theirs was a practice which stressed relationship and intervention, that comprehended dance as social action.

They eschewed "autonomous" art, the precipitation of genius, and the rarefaction of abstract form: the construction of dance modernism which historical accounts have privileged.

Further, the careers of Tamiris, Sokolow, and Maslow provide grist for challenging too easy equations of Progressive-era social welfare work with social control of ethnic immigrants. What Linda Gordon discovered about Boston charity recipients holds for the Lower East Side as well: the relationship is reciprocal; both parties construct meanings for their part in the interchange. Tamiris, Maslow, and Sokolow cannot be construed as passive recipients of Playhouse instruction and representation of exotic others. Instead, they forged distinctive movement idioms and articulated choreographic practices that superceded Playhouse models. They did not become what they portrayed in Playhouse productions, nor did they assimilate conventionalized separate spheres roles of American femininity. They did make their own the example of women's innovation that Playhouse producers had modeled—a gender-budging, socially noncompliant stance. Mediating attempted disciplines, the students turned to their own purpose the tools of the teachers.[53]

As a producing venue, the Neighborhood Playhouse helped develop an audience for serious, expressive dance in America at a time when dance largely meant light entertainment. The Denishawn troupe, the Playhouse's contemporary, toured America on vaudeville and concert circuits from 1915 to the mid-1920s, taking artistic dance to people living outside major cities. It performed frequently in New York City and toured the Orient in 1925 and 1926. Denishawn was thus a name to be reckoned with on a national and international level. The Playhouse was equally instrumental in developing a dance audience, although in the much smaller geographic region of New York City, the acknowledged center of United States theatrical activity. Recognizing its experimental aims, the New York Times and magazines like The Nation and Theatre Arts Monthly covered events at the Playhouse.[54]

Finally, the Playhouse provided a space for probing dance's content. In order to distinguish the new expressive dance from other theatre dance of the day, proponents of the new dance style had to stake out subject matter. In their experiments at the Henry Street Settlement, the Lewisohns had found in the customs of neighborhood people themes suitable for expression through dance. This material they combined with American civic celebrations and imaginative reconstructions of pagan seasonal rites to portray "universal" ritual practices purportedly common to all people. In Playhouse festivals and lyric productions such content was developed much further, to include a number of Eastern cultures. In this the Play-house productions resembled the Denishawn company choreographies, which also drew heavily on non-American cultures. Such material proved attractive to the respective groups for different reasons: the Playhouse was initially stimulated by its contact with immigrant peoples, while St. Denis in particular was motivated by an intense personal mysticism receptive to oriental religions. Both groups clearly appropriated and reworked foreign cultural practices for their own purposes, emulating, it may be said, a time-honored approach of Russian classical ballet as well as the new choreo-graphic practices of Diaghilev's Ballets Russes. Such recourse by the Play-house and Denishawn to foreign cultural materials indexes, I believe, the continuing challenge that new dance makers faced in re-conceptualizing dance as a serious—and native—practice, one that had to make meaning in the face of long-standing cultural linkages between dance and illicit sexual display. Using textbook "orientalist" strategy, innovators framed their new dance via foreign cultural sites and practices. By "othering" dance, they held at bay, but also held up for inspection, a movement prac-tice whose traditional meaning they sought to contest and negotiate in the first decades of the twentieth century. Through appropriation of "other" dance cultures they attempted to alter American perceptions of dance as a native endeavor. But because Denishawn and, increasingly, the Play-house essentialized and exoticized foreign peoples, even when the Play-house asserted universal brotherhood among peoples, innovators failed to redirect or contest American conceptions of foreign people and cultures. Appropriation served at best as an interim strategy, giving emerging mod-ern dance choreographers both a point of departure and a model to vigor-ously rework.[55]

From a base established via connection with the Henry Street Settle-ment, the Playhouse pursued dance and drama work both as a form of social engagement and as an intervention in—a revitalization of—theatre aesthetics. As the relative emphasis given these endeavors shifted over time, the Playhouse negotiated several representations and meanings for immigrant and foreign peoples and practices. At the same time, the Play-house fertilized the emergence of modern dance by offering training, building an audience, and asserting subject matter for expressive dance. The notion of dance as an aesthetic "realm apart" found footing in some dimensions of Playhouse proceedings, but not in all. The master narrative which has historicized modern dance as an autonomous art here stands revealed as an ideological, and not an inevitable, construction.

The Henry Street Settlement–Neighborhood Playhouse nexus also positioned a community of largely female co-workers to collaborate in the creation, direction, production, and business management of the theatrical undertaking they launched. Immigrant children and young adults from the Lower East Side readily took advantage of opportunities to dance and act in Playhouse productions, but the Lewisohns, other professional performers, and city residents from beyond the East Side availed themselves of these experiences as well. Playhouse activity made it possible to conceive dancing and acting as professions, albeit poorly paying ones. As Tamiris, Maslow, and Sokolow demonstrated, children of non-native parents could become constitutors of the new American art form of modern dance. For the wealthy and the working class, the settlement house–playhouse nexus empowered women to innovate in dance, to wrestle with reformulating dance as an American cultural practice, and to construct new professional identities for themselves.

 **Five** Working Women's Dancing,
and Dance as Women's Work:
Hull-House, Chicago
Commons, and Boston's
South End House

"We danced once a week in this carefree class, all winter," wrote Hilda Satt
Polachek, a Russian Jewish immigrant, about social dance classes at Hull-
House. "In June, the class closed for the summer with a gay cotillion. . . .
No matter where the members of the dancing class came from, dingy
hovels, overcrowded tenements, for that one night we were all living in a
fairyland."[1]

After her father died, thirteen-year-old Polachek went to work in a
knitting factory, helping to earn the family living. It was Jane Addams,
founder and leader of Chicago's first settlement, who urged Polachek to
join the social dance classes taught by Mary Wood Hinman: "She thought
I worked too hard and needed some fun."[2] Settlement house dancing
clearly offered this working girl a transporting experience; her recollection
also illuminates the range of dance practices afforded scope by the settlement movement. Teaching and productions at the Henry Street Settlement and Neighborhood Playhouse represented the peak of just one kind
of dance development facilitated by the settlement house movement. No
other Progressive-era settlement house matched the intensity and extent of
the movement practices developed there for theatrical presentation in an
ultimately professional little theatre context. Those areas of Henry Street–
Playhouse dance activity that foregrounded amateur participation and
mobilized movement performance as a form of cultural intervention,
however, resonated readily with concerns catalyzing the settlement move-

ment as a whole. Settlement houses across the country shared the concerns about child welfare, industrial labor, immigration, and assimilation that impelled dance work undertaken at Henry Street and the Neighborhood Playhouse. In addition, settlement workers were responsive to (and in many cases helped to formulate) new critiques of commercial entertainment and to the national movement for systematizing recreation. These strands of maturing social welfare theory further reinforced settlement workers in their drive to promote physical, social, and imaginative outlets for urban dwellers. As was characteristic, settlements experimented with a variety of methods to achieve their goals, and the introduction and exploration of new dancing practices found a ready welcome.

Dancing thus made its way into settlement house curricula under several guises: as a vehicle for social interaction, as a method to secure children's respect for parents' cultures, as fun, and as soul-enriching relief from the deadening impact of monotonous and repetitive industrial labor. The flexible arenas afforded by settlement houses, in turn, allowed dance innovators to participate in the broadly based cultural project consuming contemporary dance makers, writers, and dancers of all types: negotiating differences among and claims made by diverse movement practices. From 1890 to 1920, movement practices were tried and weighed for their social, educational, and aesthetic potential. Here aesthetic potential meant capacity to produce beauty and stir human emotional responses, the latter conceived variously as physiological and psychological. In this period of concentrated scrutiny, aesthetic quality was not yet construed as the special preserve of concert dance, as it would be in master narratives of American modern dance. At the turn of the century, aesthetic qualities could attach to ballroom as well as "folk" or traditional dance, that is, to participant-focused dancing, and also to spectacular or theatrical dancing—which emphasized viewers' reception as much as or more than performers' engagement.

At Hull-House, several types of movement innovation came together in the teaching practice of Mary Wood Hinman. Teaching games, historical dances, folk dances, and ballroom dances to settlement classes, while also laboring at other venues, Hinman consolidated a national professional identity as a dance pedagogue equaled only by that of Elizabeth Burchenal in New York City. Her pedagogy shaped Doris Humphrey, future luminary and choreographer in the new genre of 1920s modern dance. It was Hinman who encouraged Humphrey to journey to the Denishawn School and take on greater challenges. The practices and rationales for dancing that Hinman honed bear the mark of Hull-House's close and sympathetic support for the burgeoning recreation movement and, especially, for the cause of dance hall reform. Construction of social dancing in the settlement context illuminates dance's capacity both for empowerment, as in Hinman's career development and her mentoring of Humphrey, and for Foucauldian discipline, as in attempts to resist change in ballroom dance embodiments and in the heterosexual economy of desire. This cultural moment was indelibly marked by industrial work processes and the new working populations that fueled them. Laboring bodies, particularly women's laboring bodies, focused dance and dancing bodies as exquisite registers and instruments for cultural contest.

Recreation Initiatives and Social Dance Reform at Hull-House

Hull-House workers early established themselves as a community of women reformers. They earned national reputations as they spearheaded investigations and mobilized for change in Chicago's political, economic, and social welfare arenas. Resident Florence Kelley, for example, conducted the research that resulted in Illinois's first factory inspection laws. Governor John Altgeld then appointed Kelley the state's first female factory inspector. Resident Julia Lathrop held a position on the Illinois Board of Charities, analyzing and calling for new organization of state supported institutions. Grace Abbott led the development of the Immigrants' Protective League. Louise de Koven Bowen initiated the Juvenile Protective League, which mediated the relationship between juveniles and the court system. Hull-House was the meeting place for the Dorcas Federal Labor Union and, later, the Illinois Women's Trade Union League. From its founding in 1889, the settlement opened its doors wide to touring speakers and advocates for a variety of causes.[3]

Hull-House workers were deeply concerned with the perils the urban environment posed to immigrant children and working youths. Threats included the visible lack of adequate play space and the frequently irresistible temptations offered by saloons and dance halls. In the 1990s, American fascination with headphones, computer games, and home workout equipment makes it easy to underestimate the seriousness of the "play" or recreation problem at the turn of the twentieth century. But in Chicago as in New York, working-class neighborhoods housed tenements, stables, grocers, retail shops, and sweat shops on the same city blocks. Permeated by meat-packing or brewing smells, thronged streets in densely packed neighborhood blocks nearly precluded play. Rain, mud, and snow choked thoroughfares for almost half the year in northern states and further limited their adaptation for play.

These conditions sparked independent municipal movements in the 1890s and then a nationwide recreation movement, which took the organizational form of the Playground Association of America (PAA). Jane Addams was a leading figure in the PAA and served alongside settlement peers such as Lillian Wald and nationally known physical training professionals such as Luther Halsey Gulick and Joseph Lee. The PAA held its inaugural congress and play day in Chicago in 1907, then shifted to New York City in 1908 and to other major cities in turn. By rotating congress sites the PAA brought delegates face to face with rival cities' existing conditions and newly made provisions for recreation. It adroitly manipulated the public relations capital at its disposal, offering commendation (and potentially condemnation) of publically funded recreation initiatives in the organization's national journal *Playground*. Via year-to-year committee work, the PAA also formulated theories and methods for both municipal and rural recreation practices. This work led to PAA guidelines for a "normal course in play," published in 1910.[4]

Local efforts and then the national recreation movement sought to allocate real estate for use as public playgrounds and to acquire funds to purchase play equipment. Just as important to the PAA was the provision of trained supervisors who could direct playground activities and calibrate them to different groups of users. In characteristic Progressive-era fashion, then, play advocates collected data and identified recreation as a public need, exhorted municipal governments to assume the obligation to meet recreation needs, and defined the skills and professional training that recreation "experts" would need to act as playground staff.

Hull-House took direct action in its earliest years to provide neighborhood recreation in the form of a gymnasium curriculum. "The boys came in great numbers to our provisional gymnasium fitted up in a former saloon," Addams recalled in *Twenty Years at Hull-House*.[5] Dr. Raycroft from the University of Chicago, aided by volunteer students, conducted the initial work until a gymnasium building was completed in 1893. In that same year, settlement pressure secured the transformation of local real estate into a neighborhood playground. A settlement resident publically named and castigated the landlord whose nearby block of tenements and stables lacked sewer connections; touring the property with Addams, the landlord agreed to clear the land for a public playground. He also paid its taxes for fifteen years. Hull-House managed the playground for ten years and then turned it over to the City Playground Commission. Hull-House's efforts were part of the first crucial phase in Chicago public playground development, which proceeded largely as individual efforts by settlements from 1893 to 1897. From 1899 to 1903 play advocates strove to establish playgrounds housed in schoolyards but managed by the vacation school movement. Enabling legislation in the first decade of the new century placed official responsibility and funding authority for playground development in the hands of several district Park Commissions and a Municipal Park Commission, so that when the PAA descended upon Chicago in 1907, President Luther Gulick described the city's South Park Playgrounds as "unparalleled in equipment and scope."[6]

Rose Marie Gyles became director of all Hull-House gymnasium work when new gymnasium facilities were completed. She held this post through at least 1910, and also served as an instructor of women's and girls' classes. To gymnasium work Gyles brought credentials from the Harvard and Chautauqua Summer Schools of Physical Education. In the mid-1890s, these were two of the most prestigious schools in the country for innovative physical training work. After 1896, posts for male instructors to lead men's work frequently were filled by students concurrently pursuing training at the Chicago Y.M.C.A. Training School.[7]

Hull-House Bulletins indicate that men's and women's gymnasium work utilized some of the same activities but pursued different emphases. Men's work included dumbbell practice, heavy apparatus work, and a substantial emphasis on basketball. Women's work was much more varied. In 1896, for instance, a month of women's gymnasium work included: dumbbell drills; German calisthenics; Indian club drills; "free movements"; Swedish movements and games; running jump and standing jump practice; and apparatus work on the rings, horse, and ladder. Following ninety minutes of this work, women could also choose fifty minutes of basketball practice. This eclectic women's curriculum drew from the German Jahn and Swedish Ling systems of exercise then competing for use by educators. Aesthetic or gymnastic dancing—a series of exercises that incorporated ballet foot and arm positions and considerable torso movement—was apparently not taught. Nevertheless, the women's curriculum was very full, and basketball gained increasing popularity with women and girls at the turn of the century. Boys' class work included dumbbell practice and calisthenics. Girls' work focused on dumbbells plus wand, club, and "other apparatus."[8]

Gyles was remembered by Nicholas Kelley, Florence Kelley's son, and with some degree of detail by Hilda Satt Polacheck.[9] Polacheck and her sister scraped together money to buy the recommended girls' gym uniform of bloomers and blouse, although lack of this costume prevented no one from attending, she recalled. Gyles put the sisters "through the paces once a week," but what Polacheck most vividly conveys is the significance that physical training work held for immigrant neighbors:

> The gymnasium was like an oasis in a desert on Halsted Street. Hundreds of boys, who had no other means of recreation, could go to the gymnasium and play basketball till they were so worn out that they could only go home and go to bed.[10]

In other words, Hull-House offered treasured opportunities for bodily cultivation, but in immigrant eyes there was a radical disjunction between demand for recreation and the available community supply.

DANCE HALL REFORM

Polachek's recollections also direct attention to the gendered pursuit of various forms of recreation. If basketball constituted a premier form of play for the "boys" age-group, social dancing and dance halls figured prominently among pursuits followed by older "working girls." To settlement workers, however, commercial dance halls offered an excess supply of inappropriate play. The relationship between dance halls and alcohol was fundamental, and a chief source of danger, they believed; as New York reform leader Belle Israels saw it, dance halls led working girls down the path to promiscuity. In 1908 Israels formed a Committee on Amusements and Vacation Resorts of Working Girls to investigate the dance hall problem, and the impetus she generated stimulated a national reform movement by 1910. Hull-House associate and financial contributor Louise de Koven Bowen took a leading role in Chicago dance hall reform in 1910, a logical extension of her work with the Juvenile Protective League. Jane Addams spoke to the dangers that dance halls presented, first in article form and then in her 1909 compendium *The Spirit of Youth and the City Streets*.[11]

Unlike the contemporary prohibition movement and earlier moral reform (antiprostitution) drives, the dance hall movement did not try to eradicate the object of its concern. Under Israels's leadership, the movement sought regulation through licensing and substitution of model dance halls for disreputable venues. Licensing would prohibit sale of alcohol in public dance halls and require venues' compliance with sanitary, fire, and building codes. What reformers could not secure by law was dance hall

The campaign to clean up urban dance halls mobilized pictorial as
well as textual arguments. Captioned "a low dance hall in New York
City," this photograph appeared with Mrs. Charles Perry Israels's article
"The Dance Hall Problem" in *Playground* magazine, October 1910.
Photograph by Lewis W. Hine. COURTESY GEORGE EASTMAN HOUSE.

patrons' adherence to middle-class codes of conduct for heterosexual sociability. Working girls and young men gained entrance to dance halls simply
by paying admission, and once inside dispensed with formal introductions
that characterized elite balls in the nineteenth century. Girls announced
their interest in dancing by coupling up with a female partner and taking
to the dance floor; prospective male partners broke in on the couple and
carried off the women. Low light levels, unchaperoned balconies, and
proprietors' pressure to buy alcoholic drinks loosened inhibitions and put
girls further at risk, in the view of reformers. Equally problematic were the
rhythms and associated movement styles of the new animal dances. These
promoted close bodily contact between partners and visceral movement in
place of traditional round dance stances with regular rhythms and codified
steps. Reformers turned to "model dance halls" to remedy problems of

etiquette, chaperonage, atmosphere, and dance styles. In these environments, of course, alcohol was excluded as well.[12]

Dance hall reformers clearly shared common analytical ground with the national recreation movement. Observing the neglect of public play space and the physical ravages wrought by unskilled factory labor, both groups believed that the modern industrial economy created a pent-up demand for bodily cultivation that was distinct from the exertion required by paid labor. To their dismay, the state assumed no responsibility for meeting the demand or for monitoring the commercial enterprises that profited from supplying adolescent working youths' demand for recreation. Gesturing toward a modern welfare state, play advocates and dance hall reformers pressed municipal governments to take responsibility for social reproduction in areas where laissez-faire competition failed to benefit consumers as much as producers. While they strove to moderate the effects produced by industrial capitalist organization, it should be noted that they stopped short of calling for structural change.

Articles and books by Addams and Bowen contributed to the dance hall reform movement, which reached its pinnacle between 1910 and 1913. Hull-House participated at the immediate local level as well by sponsoring on Hull-House premises the dances given by settlement clubs. This was a practice shared by settlement houses across the country. To be sure, Hull-House workers had always encouraged their immigrant neighbors' dancing and traditional celebration of native holidays. Living within a square mile of Hull-House in 1893 were people of some eighteen different nationalities, among whom Irish, German, Italian, and Bohemian communities were the largest. Hull-House social clubs, like the German group that met every Thursday evening, offered regular occasions for singing, dancing, and eating together. And when southern Italian men responded in their wives' stead to an invitation from the Women's Club Social Extension committee, "untiring pairs of them danced the Tarantella," sang Neapolitan songs, and performed sleight-of-hand tricks for their hostesses.[13] Hull-House sponsorship of social dances given by settlement clubs was another matter, however. Here the settlement consciously aimed to substitute a chaperoned environment for conditions that obtained in neighborhood saloons, of which there was one for every twenty-six people in the nineteenth ward in 1896.[14] These dances were occasions for courtship among young adults, and nineteenth-century European ballroom forms constituted the dance lexicon. "The parties given by the Hull-House clubs are by invitation," Addams wrote in 1909, and the young people themselves carefully maintain their standard of entrance so that the most cautious mother may feel safe when her daughter goes to one of our parties. No club festivity is permitted without the presence of a director; no young man under the influence of liquor is allowed; certain types of dancing often innocently started are strictly prohibited; and above all, early closing is insisted upon. This standardizing of pleasure has always seemed an obligation to the residents of Hull-House, but we are, I hope, saved from that priggishness which young people so heartily resent by the Mardi Gras dance and other festivities which the residents themselves arrange and successfully carry out.[15]

To her credit, Addams realized that immigrant neighbors might well chafe at the emphasis Hull-House placed on standards and supervision, but the intervention did not abate.

The "standardizing of pleasure" that Addams mentioned was forged in part by scheduled classes offering tuition in social dance skills. These staples of the settlement curriculum "from the earliest days" are identified in Hull-House *Bulletins* and *Year Books* as "dancing classes." Instruction was offered on a fairly steady basis in the late 1890s, although a succession of different teachers led the work. The first evidence of Mary Wood Hinman's involvement appears in fall 1898. *Hull-House Yearbooks* indicate that she had charge of the social dancing instruction through at least September 1907. At first she worked as one of several teachers who led classes. By autumn 1900 she taught all three class levels herself and subsequently worked with assistants whom she directed.[16]

Hinman (1878–1952) taught age-graded classes at Hull-House that mixed members of both sexes. Because no pedagogical records remain from her Hull-House tenure, the methods she used must be extrapolated from her work with private school pupils. She first introduced young children to ballroom behavior and games. When they were able to distinguish "the four necessary [musical] rhythms—that is waltz, two-step, polka and gallop," they were ready for ballroom steps and patterns. Once this work was mastered, young people began to learn "folk" dances like the *Sailor's Hornpipe, Spinning Dance*, and the *Highland Fling*. More complicated folk dances, clogging, reels, or English country dances followed. In classes for young adults she presumably forwent the games.[17]

It was typical of settlement club work that an activity drawing enthusiastic response from one group soon would be tried by others. In the late 1890s, for example, the *Hull-House Bulletin* twice recorded the widespread interest in dramatics among club children. It was not deemed incongruous, accordingly, when the "juvenile gymnasium class" put on a

Mother Goose play in February 1898. In March of the same year, the girls'
gymnasium class presented *Cinderella*.[18] Signaling the success of Gyles
and Hinman's sessions, games and dances were taken up by other Hull-
House clubs and classes. Thus in autumn the United Pleasure Club (for
girls and boys twelve to fourteen years old) outlined its slate of activities for
1900–01. It planned to study literature, art, music, and games, the latter
comprising "marches, physical exercises, dances, contests, sense and trade
games, games illustrating the thought of the day, and dramatization of
stories." Moreover, announced the club, "the four branches [of study] are
not separated, but are developed interdependently, all illustrating the
subject of the day."[19] This plan bears the stamp of Herbartian "correlation
of studies" theories, perhaps echoing the rhetoric of the club's adult advisor. The plan also confirms that gymnasium and dance work were not
confined to specialized classes. Jane Addams illuminated the same point in
describing *The Troll's Holiday*, an operetta given by the music school in
November 1906. "The little brown trolls," she declared, "could never have
tumbled about so gracefully in their gleaming caves unless they had been
taught in the gymnasium."[20] When children in the Hull-House music
classes gave two January 1902 programs of folk songs and dances, clothed
in "national costume," the participants almost certainly had previously
received essential training in Hinman's dancing classes.[21]

At the end of each year's work, Hinman's Hull-House classes gave a
cotillion in which they performed exhibitions of clog, folk, and social
dances. Students from Hinman's classes in other parts of the city frequently
joined the Hull-House pupils on these occasions. The different groups who
participated in cotillions and in the dancing classes that led up to them
made different meanings for folk and social dance practice. Hull-House
residents saw value in the "alternative of group dancing" which cotillions
made available. They emulated Hinman's model in establishing St. Patrick's Day and Mardi Gras cotillions for the settlement's Irish and Italian
neighbors.[22] Hinman, the nonresident pedagogue, believed that her instruction created rapid and demonstrable results among members of the
immigrant community. Children's classes, she wrote in 1909:

> show immediate results in the new interest felt in the old home life of
> their parents. We always teach the foreigners their own dances as far as
> possible. This new bond of sympathy and respect is alone worth a winter's
> work.[23]

Here she drew the same conclusion reached by Lillian Wald and the

Lewisohns at Henry Street, that dance practices could help mitigate inter-generational tensions. She took pride in her students' achievement of kin-esthetic competence and linked the sense of physical mastery with psycho-logical development, citing the "concentrated joy, healthy exercise, grace, interest, control, and the wonderful feeling of self-respect that comes to each child when he has finished a dance and can produce it passably well."[24]

Reactions from immigrant neighbors are hard to come by, with negative responses even rarer. Hilda Satt Polachek's recollections suggest that Hin-man succeeded in forging a warm relationship with her students:

> The dancing class was in the charge of a beautiful, understanding woman. Her name was Mary Wood Hinman and we all loved her. She was always dressed in a gray accordion-pleated skirt, with a blouse of the same material, a red sash, and gray dancing shoes. She floated around that room like a graceful bird. We danced once a week in this carefree class, all winter. In June, the class closed for the summer with a gay cotillion, every bit as gay, if not as elaborate, as the ones staged today to introduce debutantes to society. No matter where the members of the dancing class came from, dingy hovels, overcrowded tenements, for that one night we were all living in a fairyland.[25]

References to Hinman's attire and comparison of the settlement cotillions with debutante balls register Polachek's awareness of professional and class distinctions. What mattered to this adolescent immigrant were the oppor-tunities dancing classes offered to escape quotidian cares and to inhabit—to experience kinesthetically—a fantasy realm, however briefly.

The meanings made for settlement social dancing in these accounts largely hew to the position taken by dance hall reformers, that controlled dance environments provided safe harbors for vulnerable youths. Protec-tionist or fantasy-driven, they constructed a space for sociability carefully removed from the "real world" of commercial entertainment. But we must scrutinize this remove and ask what cultural work was taking place in the fluid space of commercial dance halls. Reconsideration of the social dance debate, I argue, shows that dancing supplied a figure for the larger problem of remapping women's public sphere presence in turn-of-the-century, in-dustrial America. This is a project still unresolved in the 1990s, when debates about women's participation in the paid labor force spawn notions like the "mommy track" on one hand, and demands that welfare mothers find jobs, on the other. In the Progressive era, working women's dancing bodies were important registers for experimenting with the measure of social and sexual autonomy that derived from their wage labor.

REMAPPING WOMEN'S PUBLIC SPHERE PRESENCE

Jane Addams cogently framed the problem of working girls' new autonomy with the first chapter of *The Spirit of Youth and the City Streets*:

> Never before in civilization have such numbers of young girls been suddenly released from the protection of the home and permitted to walk unattended upon city streets and to work under alien roofs; for the first time they are being prized more for their labor power than for their innocence, their tender beauty, their ephemeral gaiety.[26]

In her view, both the journey to work and paid labor itself placed working girls under new obligation to chart their own course where previously family and community members had guided them. Mary Wood Hinman voiced similar anxiety over young people's mobility and also the hope that social dance instruction would dilute the attraction that city streets held for them:

> By letting the young people come for one evening a week in a clean, well-aired hall, with good music, good floor, and rules of politeness and formality maintained, they lose their desire to go elsewhere for this necessary social intercourse. . . . There seems to be no better, quicker, or surer way of obtaining our first hold on the young people we want most to bring off the streets. These young men and women who crave social life seem to have no proper way open to them.[27]

The very autonomy that made women vulnerable, in Addams's and Hinman's eyes, arguably empowered them in another sense. City streets, and the dance halls that opened off them, offered working adolescents a mobile, kinetic domain of self-making. Through dressing adventurously and walking out, working girls tried on new sensibilities and bodily comportments. "As these overworked girls stream along the street," Addams sighed, "the rest of us see only the self-conscious walk, the giggling speech, the preposterous clothing."[28] These walkers in the city were American equivalents of nineteenth-century European flâneurs, with a difference: they were female where their continental counterparts were male.[29] And they strolled and inscribed new urban spaces with their bodies, in contrast to the pens and paintbrushes of Baudelaire and Manet. Arriving without escorts at dance halls, boldly signaling their readiness to dance, and frequently changing partners, working girls revised codes of etiquette and savored peer-group decision making. Accepting men's "treats," and negotiating demands for sexual favors in return, American flâneuses frequently paid the costs of their self-directed odysseys. In an age lacking dependable birth control or easy access to information about it, sexual adventure carried the real risk of pregnancy. Monies borrowed to buy fine clothing, perhaps to purchase time off from work, required repayment in expensive coin. These were payments that settlement workers and dance hall reformers dearly longed to prevent. In all, working girls' self-fashioning and their entertainment choices rendered the public sphere unbearably fluid, messy, and blurred, at least for their elders. The dance hall disregard for chaperonage and formal introductions eroded social boundaries between class groups by removing barriers to entry, denied the moral authority traditionally vested in age, and discounted the leadership of higher classes in matters of decorum. Treating and tribute laid bare the economic organization of heterosexual desire that separate spheres ideology romanticized. In Belle Israels's view, protections afforded by dance hall reform positioned women to compete on more equal terms in a battle of the sexes where men hunted women. Working girls' sallies into commercial dance halls, in contrast, suggest attempts to restructure sexual relations.[30]

In addition, working girls subverted established bodily codes for middle-class female identity in their eager assumption of "tough" dancing styles. Whether animal dances or "foreign" dances like the maxixe, tough dances celebrated passionate embodiment, foregrounding physicality as constitutive of femaleness. This was an association that many elite and middle-class women tried to recast, for its essentialism had been marshaled to constrain women's opportunity, as in access to suffrage or higher education. Adoption of the tango promised to further exoticize immigrant girls and men already stamped as other by virtue of their central or southern European birth or parentage. Tough dancing constituted a return of the barely repressed, so to speak. It complicated the gendered identities that settlement workers, reformers, and new professional women were struggling to establish. It also threatened the negotiated "American" identities that settlement folk strove to achieve for immigrants.

Finally, working girls' strolling and dancing practices blurred the line between domestic and public spaces in separate spheres ideology. As Belle Israels realized, "Three rooms in a tenement, overcrowded with the younger children, make the street a private apartment [for the working girl]. The public resort similarly overcrowded, but with those who are not inquisitive, answers as her reception room."[31] Working girls, in other words, fashioned "privacy" from the resources of public spaces and exposed as a class fiction the analogy between physical space and gendered spheres of activity. By dancing, congregating, strolling, and styling themselves, they performed working-class "multi-bodies" that oscillated between sweated labor and visceral choreographies, between repetitive effort investment and free-flowing malleability. These American flâneuses challenged the rationalist subjectivity that demanded metes and bounds for public sphere presence, and argued with their bodies for changed gender, class, and sexual relations.

Settlement workers and dance hall reformers attempted to eliminate the disorder that working girls' unregulated social dancing set in motion. Their motivations were several: their age and class prerogatives to guide inexperienced—read working-class—rural and immigrant girls in the right disposition of their free time in the city; and their newly constructed, quasi-professional identities as social welfare workers. Stepping in where no publically funded mechanisms existed, these women supplied a "general motherhood of the commonwealth," to use Elisabeth Perry's term. Taking responsibility for social reproduction, they acted as experts qualified to analyze and combat the threats that dancing and dance halls posed to the home—"the foundation of society," in Addams's words—and thus social progress.[32] Settlement workers and reformers acknowledged working girls' industrial wage labor, and the public sphere independence it conferred, because they had to. "The girl announces to the world that she is here," Addams realized. "She demands attention to the fact of her existence, she states that she is ready to live, to take her place in the world."[33] Had it been possible, settlement workers, recreation advocates, and dance hall reformers would have raised the legal minimum age for work, extending further protections to childhood and adolescence rather than treating the latter as an early stage of adulthood. Lacking that power, they acknowledged women's industrial wage labor as a fact of life and deplored the reduction of femininity to its exchange value as bodily labor. They strove to position social dancing within a familial frame of rules, contained sexuality, and adult guidance. Dance hall reform seemed bent on narrowing the terms in which female bodies could circulate.

Laying claim to the streets and commercial entertainments, working-class girls evaded family interpretive frameworks and pursued their social and sexual practices in the public arena, where industrial wage labor had afforded them new responsibilities as well as autonomy. Tough dancing and unregulated dance hall comportments mobilized, in fact, another representation of the body's public exertion. In contrast to sweated labor, this representation was self-authored and pleasurable. What it worried, worked through, and effectively exposed was precisely the circulation of the body's (pleasurable dancing) labor as a medium of commercial and sexual encounter and exchange. Social welfare workers balked at the specter dancing raised of a sociability premised primarily on the sexual exchange of bodily exertion, just as they balked at work practices that depleted workers' bodies with no return of spiritual or imaginative gain. While they could not or did not alter the economic terms for workplace exchange of the body's labor, they did mount a challenge to the "social" exchange of the body's labor. Tough dancing and dance hall comport-ments, for their part, debunked the class-based spatial and temporal dis-tinctions between these "genres" of the body's exertion, laying bare the exchange nexus which underpinned them both. Working girls pressed the limits of their bodies' circulations, remaking themselves, refiguring public and private space, and struggling to recast sexual relations. By means of tough dancing in fast dance halls, numerous Americans grappled with the possibilities and consequences of industrial labor and laissez-faire eco-nomic structures for bodies, class positions, sexualities, and gender roles.

Hinman's Hull-House teaching and the settlement's sponsorship of club dances clearly shared the disciplining thrust of dance hall reform. Admission was screened, settlement residents and parents served as chap-erones, and liquor was outlawed. Dancing classes purveyed a technology of etiquette and established an approved lexicon of dance styles. Otto H. Bacher's sketch of a "German" night at Hull-House suggests that settle-ment supervision still did not prevent girls from coupling up to dance together. But context was everything: while girl-couples danced, mothers lined the room and watched. They lifted cups and chatted, two older men conversed, a child dandled on a knee. Settlement sociability reinstalled social dancing in a family frame.[34]

Settlement dancing and dance hall reform offer a sustaining American case for Michel Foucault's rejection of the "repressive hypothesis," the conjecture that nineteenth-century Europeans put discussion of sexual matters under increasing interdiction. Foucault insists in *The History of Sexuality* that just the opposite occurred; the turn of the century saw a proliferation of discourses about sex and of technologies for monitoring and inciting sexuality.[35] The dance hall reform movement that Belle Israels catalyzed in New York reached a crescendo between 1910 and 1913, explicating the methods used by commercial entertainments in order to

German Night at Hull-House. By Otto Bacher. JANE ADDAMS MEMORIAL
COLLECTION, SPECIAL COLLECTIONS, UNIVERSITY LIBRARY, UNIVERSITY OF
ILLINOIS AT CHICAGO.

justify calls for regulation and substitution.[36] The tools for dance hall
reform, in other words, proliferated discourse about sexuality and inten-
sified connections drawn between dancing and sexuality. In the long run,
however, they succeeded in neither staying change in dance styles nor
divorcing alcohol from dancing sociability (even with Prohibition).

Hinman, Humphrey, and Dance Pedagogy as Women's Work

While dance instruction could be wielded to discipline working girls'
insurgent reformulations of social and sexual exchange, it could also em-
power working women to claim a new professional identity. This was
precisely the potential that Mary Wood Hinman accessed when she took
up dance teaching, first in support of her family, but ultimately as her
livelihood. For much of the history of Western dance, dance pedagogy had
been the purview of men. The careers of Hinman, her student Doris
Humphrey, and her peer Elizabeth Burchenal, discussed in the next chap-

ter, index a major shift in the gendered composition of the dance teaching workforce. They also signaled changing American perceptions and recognition of dance teaching as a quantifiable occupation.

When Hinman secured a teaching position at Hull-House, she had recently become a wage earner for her family. In this she differed radically from Alice and Irene Lewisohn, whose inherited fortune secured them the freedom to undertake dance and drama projects without concern for commercial viability. Occupying a different class position, Hinman made dance teaching her life's work. Financial reverses struck her family around 1894, almost certainly a result of the industrial depression that gripped the country in 1893. It was at this point that Hinman began to teach dancing to the children in her Kenilworth neighborhood. The sources of the movement material which she taught are not clear. Historian Selma Odom suggests that Hinman studied various kinds of dance with Chicago dance teachers, dance callers, and perhaps even people in Chicago's ethnic communities. With this knowledge base Hinman apparently just set up shop as a teacher. She visited Sweden to study folk dances and games at the College of Nääs, and traveled in northern Sweden learning dances. At other times she journeyed to Denmark, Russia, and Ireland, in each case studying and collecting traditional dance material firsthand. She traveled to England in 1909 to study English country dancing and again in 1912 to study English traditional dances with Cecil Sharp at Stratford-on-Avon. In 1914 she observed the application of Dalcroze eurhythmics in the movement staged for *Fête de Juin* in Geneva. Through this travel and study Hinman became one of the first women in the United States to constitute herself as a collector and professional teacher of folk and traditional European dance practices.[37]

Hinman's teaching at Hull-House was but one part of a dance instruction enterprise which she slowly and successfully extended to a number of Chicago schools. A 1909 account of her work, published in Luther Gulick's *The Healthful Art of Dancing*, indicates that in 1900 she began teaching dancing at the University of Chicago Elementary School, the laboratory school founded when John Dewey headed the university's Philosophy Department. She began teaching dance at the University of Chicago High School in 1903. When the University Elementary School merged with the prestigious Francis Parker School in 1906, Hinman continued teaching at the Parker School. She thus enjoyed connection with two nationally known centers for progressive education experiment. Further, she started teaching at the Chicago Latin School for Girls and the University School for Girls in 1905, at the Kenwood Institute in 1906, and at the Electa School in 1907. Hinman was still teaching at all these sites in 1909. Brief economic panics in 1904 and 1907 may well have forced her to occupy this number and combination of teaching posts. No two classes were taught exactly the same way, for Hinman varied the dancing work by the age and gender mix of her classes. Instructing male, female, and mixed groups, she drew from a body of material that included ballroom, gymnastic, clog, English country, and European folk dancing, as well as techniques of courtesy.[38]

Hinman thus became, in the most complete sense, an entrepreneur of the folk dance and social dance teaching business. In addition to her teaching at Hull-House and a number of Chicago private schools, she opened her own Hinman School of Gymnastic Dancing and Folk Dancing around 1904. She was an astute judge of the market for dance instruction, and she knew how to capitalize on Chicago's status as a major Midwestern city located at the hub of a great transportation network. Thus by 1912 she had structured her studio's curriculum to accommodate students living near and far. The Hinman School proffered "private instruction for students from a distance;" and "instruction for groups formed in Chicago but not meeting in the studio." It provided "private half-hour lessons in the studio" for groups of five or more; and instruction in pageants and festivals for groups in distant cities. For the latter, Hinman sent out an instructor who for a one-week period could give up to three hours of daily instruction.[39]

Hinman also launched the Hinman Normal School, which graduated its first trained teacher in 1904. She clearly saw her Normal School training as offering women a vehicle for fashioning a work identity for themselves:

> It is almost impossible to overestimate what this work has meant to the girls. They were not content with the fulfillment of their family or personal obligations, but are striving to respond to the new demand for the welfare of the child of the city or country.[40]

This articulation of work identity references women's separate spheres responsibility to guide and guard children, and extends that charge to sanction public sphere activity and social welfare advocacy. Hinman's students evidently fulfilled this charge by emulating their teacher's model: Hinman wrote in 1909 that each Normal School student "carries a class of her own in some settlement." *Hull-House Year Books* describe Hinman's successor at Hull-House, a Miss Bensinger, as "a former pupil of Miss Hinman." This young woman was probably the Mrs. Irene Bensinger Yahlding listed in a 1917 brochure as a 1907 graduate from the Hinman

Normal School. As Hinman school brochures from the 1910s attest, she continued to cite the educational, social, and creative needs for social and folk dancing which she had formulated in her early work at Hull-House.[41]

Hinman's enterprise extended to publication and national pedagogy leadership and service. As early as 1912, and possibly before, she began to publish instructions and accompanying music for group and solo dances, and for ring games. Her first book of dances and music was published in 1914. She thus joined the likes of Louis Chalif and Elizabeth Burchenal, pedagogues of national and international dance styles whose published work supplied fundamental dance texts for U.S. playground curricula, school festivals, and public school physical training dance instruction. In 1916 and 1917, Hinman gained further professional recognition by being engaged by Columbia University to teach folk and national dancing in summer session classes. During those summer sessions, she taught a class called "Dances for Boys" as well. Dances taught in the latter, she promised, were to "be such as can be taught by the women teachers. Clogs, lilts and jigs together with the English sword dances will be taught."[42] Hinman asserted that hers were the first courses in which tap, a term she used interchangeably with clog dancing, was taught at Columbia. These summer session courses were largely normal courses: affiliation with Columbia inserted Hinman in the primary stream for advanced teacher training in Progressive-era America. At the turn of the century, two-year normal colleges routinely included dance instruction as part of the physical training curriculum. Teachers College, by 1915, and University of Wisconsin, by 1920, had inaugurated classes in natural and educational dancing as part of their baccalaureate curriculums. For post-normal and postbaccalaureate study, however, pedagogues pursued advanced professional training or "stayed current" with rapidly changing dance styles and theories by attending summer sessions like those offered by universities (Columbia, Harvard, and New York University) and private studios (including the Gilbert Studio in New York and Hinman's Chicago school). Starting in 1915, summer camps run by the American Branch of the English Folk Dance Society added another node to this uncoordinated network for normal education. The pattern held true in the 1930s as well, when Bennington College hosted enormously influential summer sessions for modern dance study. Connection with Columbia summer sessions thus helped secure Hinman's professional status even as her pedagogy helped propel dance study and training to new standing as a university-level curricular subject. Finally, Hinman gained national prominence through activity in the premier recreation society of the day, the PAA. She served on the Folk Dancing committee in 1909, and at Luther Gulick's invitation, she spoke during the session on festivals at the 1909 Playground Congress.[43]

CENSUS SIGNALS

Dance instruction's emergence as a Progressive-era profession took statistical shape in national decennial census records for 1910 and 1920. This was in marked contrast with 1900, when census reports for American occupations document the effective absence of dance teaching as an articulated occupational category. The 1900 Professional Service class of occupations distinguishes actors and professional showmen; artists and teachers of art; musicians and teachers of music; and literary and scientific persons, who are further categorized as authors, scientists, librarians, chemists, etc. Professional Service includes other professionals such as dentists and teachers, the latter further disaggregated as "teachers" and "professors in colleges and universities." The catchall category "other Professional service" embraces "veterinary surgeons" and "not specified." Neither dancers nor teachers of dancing receive specific recognition, however. What 1900 records do show is women's strong presence as schoolteachers—those who give instruction up to but not including the collegiate level. Women constituted 74 percent of the school teaching force in 1900, and their preponderance would continue in American education.[44]

In 1910, the absolute number of schoolteachers, and of women schoolteachers, increased; women had grown to 80 percent of the school teaching force. Census occupation records now distinguished "College presidents and professors" as a category separate from "teachers." And, for the first time, the category "teachers" disaggregated "teachers of athletics, dancing, etc." from other kinds of teachers. In this new category, women supplied almost 30 percent and men 70 percent of 3,391 teachers of "athletics, dancing." In 1920, the absolute number of schoolteachers, and of women schoolteachers, had grown again; women constituted 84 percent of the school teaching force. The occupational category "teachers of athletics, dancing" persisted as a disaggregated subcategory of teachers. In 1920 women had climbed to 41 percent, and men had fallen to 59 percent, of teachers of "athletics, dancing."[45]

The constitution of dance teaching as a new occupational category was of course a product of the interplay between responses given by individual workers and the census enumerators' classification of the data they received. I argue that the result of this interplay, the specification of a previously nonexistent category, indexes both a change in American conceptualizations of dance teaching as work, and a significant increase in persons conducting this work.

To be sure, the new occupational category was a gross delimiter. It did not define the content areas of dance and athletics. "Athletics"—as activity concerned with team sports like football and basketball, but also track and field—was substantially changing the face of physical training curricula. "Dance" practices varied widely in the Progressive era. They comprised ballroom dancing (from the waltz to animal dances); aesthetic dancing taught in school physical training courses; and even folk and traditional dancing, taught by people like Hinman in settlement houses, public schools, and private studios. More complicated still, because athletics and dancing were lumped together rather than scrutinized separately, the census data makes it difficult to determine what gendering of these instructional practices was occurring, if any. Gender profiles current in the 1990s prompt the question whether within this occupational category delimited by the Progressive-era censuses, men taught athletics and women taught dancing. But we should not presume that the 1910 census category lumped together unlike instructional practices that were dichotomously gendered, whatever the developments in subsequent years. Instead, we may reasonably weigh this new occupational title as evidence that athletics and dance instruction shared common ground in the Progressive era. The census coupling of athletics with dancing comports with narrative histories of physical education, which document that field's Progressive-era embrace of dance activities. Male physical educators could be expected to teach gymnastics and aesthetic dancing as well as football, just as female physical educators could be expected to teach apparatus work, field hockey, or basketball. Between 1900 and 1920, I suggest, the census coupling limned an instructional domain in which boundaries were indeed permeable, and the exchange fluid, between modes for bodily cultivation explored by physical training; ballroom, folk, and traditional dance vocabularies; and new interpretative dance endeavors. This fluidity empowered Hinman in the 1890s to deploy folk and traditional dance as facets of social dance instruction; a decade later, physical training professionals in New York City schools would just as easily introduce folk dancing as athletic work for girls.

If we stipulate that the occupation was not feminized (not numerically dominated by females) in the Progressive era, we can say several more things about women's work as teachers of "athletics, dancing." First, women's work in the new profession should not be taken as simply continuity with women's contemporary predominance in school teaching. In 1910, when women labored as 80 percent of the country's schoolteachers, women also constituted only 30 percent of teachers of "athletics, dancing." By 1920, women were 84 percent of the country's schoolteachers and 41 percent of teachers of "athletics, dancing." Second, these early-twentieth-century census data make clear that representation of women increased over time to levels more nearly equal with men as teachers of "athletics, dancing." The direction of change for women suggests potential for future feminization of athletics and dance instruction. Between 1900 and 1920, however, women were not numerically preponderant among such teachers.

Differences *among* women teachers of "athletics, dancing" may be identified from data made available in the 1920 census. Whereas earlier records had classified teachers by sex, state, and city (1900), and by color or race, nativity, parentage, and age-group (1910), 1920 data additionally specified female athletics and dancing teachers' marital condition. In terms of age-groups, women teachers 17 to 19 years old outnumbered their male peers 2 to 1; women between the ages of 20 and 24 outnumbered men 1.5 to 1. These ratios varied within age-groups classified by parentage, but women under 25 consistently outnumbered men, regardless of parentage, with one exception. Among foreign-born teachers aged 20 to 24, men outnumbered women 1.2 to 1 (67 males, 53 females). The pattern of female preponderance in youthful age-groups shifted dramatically for teachers 25 or older. In the 25–44 age-group, women's absolute numbers increased over levels in younger age-groups, but men's absolute numbers increased even more. Men now outnumbered women 1.8 to 1. Among teachers 45 to 64 years old, men outnumbered women more than 2 to 1, and among teachers 65 or older, men outnumbered women more than 3 to 1.[46]

The large pattern of female predominance among teachers aged 15 to 24 makes sense in an age when women routinely achieved lower educational levels than men. Young women could legally leave school at age 14 to find employment. If they finished high school at age 16 or 18, and acquired a two-year normal degree, they could easily enter the athletics and dance teaching labor force at age 18, 19, or 20. In America in 1920, however, men were more likely than women to achieve baccalaureate degrees. The time necessary to earn a degree might well cause men to enter the teaching labor force some two to four years later than female athletics and dance teachers. This scenario comports with census figures on men's representation among "athletics, dancing" teachers in the 25–44 age-group; this age-group shows the largest absolute numbers of men relative to other 1920 age-groups.[47] How to explain the anomalous predominance of immigrant male teachers in relation to immigrant female teachers in the 20–24 age-group? The data about immigrants is inadequate to do much more than venture some possible contributing factors. Immigrant men's wealth status or age at arrival (late teens, say) may have posed significant barriers to college entry. Conversely, depending on the cultural tradition in which they matured, immigrant men upon arrival might already have possessed gymnastic, sport, or social dance skills sufficient to enter the athletics and dance teaching market without further training.

Marital status, and period expectations that women would leave the labor force upon marriage, probably also accounts for the shift in preponderance from women to men among teachers aged 25 and above. Among women teachers of "athletics, dancing" in 1920, married women were in the minority in all age-groups. Of 317 women aged 15 to 19, 10 were married; of 1,324 women aged 20 to 24, 120—or 9 percent—were married. Four hundred twenty-two married women comprised 21.5 percent of women teachers aged 25 to 44; 118 married women comprised about 27 percent of women teachers aged 45 and over. Thus, among women, teaching "athletics, dancing" was overwhelmingly an occupation for the single, divorced, or widowed. The difference between the percentage of married women in the 20–24 age-group and in the 25–44 age-group lends support to the view that men surged into athletics and dance teaching at the age by which their women peers would be expected to marry—and also leave the labor force. At the same time, the documented presence in the labor force of married female teachers aged 25 and above confirms the challenge, expressed in other occupational quarters, to conventional wisdom about married women's departure from the workforce. From 1890, married women slowly and incrementally increased their participation in the country's paid labor force, until by 1960 married women constituted 60 percent of the female labor force.[48]

Census figures for 1920 further suggest that among women, teaching "athletics, dancing" had become a profession for American-born white females. Of 4,034 female teachers, by far the largest group was white women native-born of native parents—2,628, or 65 percent. Daughters of immigrants—native-born white women of mixed or foreign parentage—numbered 1,027, or 25 percent of all women teachers. Comparatively, their number was almost two-fifths the number of female teachers born of native parents. Three hundred twenty-two teachers were foreign born, and 55—classified by race rather than country or parents' nativity—were identified as negro. Thus in 1920, 90 percent of female teachers of "athletics, dancing" were white females born in America of native, immigrant, or mixed native-foreign parents.[49]

Mary Wood Hinman's American birth, single status, and early entry into dance teaching as a profession fit the developing occupational profile to a T. Conversely, her publishing, summer session teaching at Columbia, and national recreation organization service helped shape dance teaching as a professional practice. She exemplifies the Progressive-era drive to designate areas of modern urban life in need of new professional expertise, both to solve problems or develop resources, on one hand, and to devise standards for entry into and conduct of professions, on the other. Census assignment to Professional Service status clearly identified dance and athletics instruction as professional training, similar in kind but also recognizably different from the cultivation of singers' and actors' voice production or instrumentalists' digital dexterity and breath management. Swimming this new occupational stream, Hinman was empowered in important part by the rationale that Hull-House and other settlements offered for women's public sphere work: the necessity of extending women's special gifts and moral force to community, municipal, and national arenas where social reproduction received inadequate resources or attention. When this rationale for asserting women's public sphere presence waned, dance teachers and dance makers would have to reformulate their claims. Hinman's protégée Doris Humphrey, trained under the earlier rationale, ultimately reformulated her practice of women's dance work in terms of a modernist ideology.

HINMAN AND HUMPHREY

For a decade, commencing in 1898, Hull-House provided an arena in which Hinman consolidated her professional identity as a dance pedagogue and as a researcher and collector of historical and traditional dance materials. It was during these years that Hinman became Doris Humphrey's first dance instructor. This Chicago girl later performed for a period with the internationally known Denishawn Company; then she constituted herself as a choreographer and prime mover in the new field of 1920s modern dance.

Humphrey (1895–1958) entered the Francis Parker School in 1900; there she started to take dancing class twice weekly with Hinman in about 1903. Humphrey loved the classes, and Hinman praised Humphrey to the girl's mother, urging Julia Humphrey to give her daughter instruction with other teachers as well. By 1911, at age sixteen, Humphrey was assisting Hinman in teaching a weekly class at the Hinman studio. In 1912 she was beginning to give lessons to private pupils at the studio. At the same time, Humphrey circulated to a certain extent in the settlement house orbit. In 1911 she conducted a sewing class at Chicago Commons, a settlement house on Chicago's West Side. In January or February 1913 she performed with her Parker School mate Albert Carroll at a "white fete" at Hull-House. (Carroll joined the Neighborhood Playhouse company in the 1920s.) During her last year at school Humphrey took time off for a performance tour of Santa Fe Railroad club rooms. The same week that she graduated from the Parker School she performed in an exhibition given by Hinman, and, with Carroll, at a private party given by his cousin. Humphrey received encouragement from Hinman to make her own dances, four of which Hinman published. While she was enjoying a holiday on the East Coast the summer after she graduated from the Parker School, Humphrey's prospects changed sharply when the hotel her father managed was sold.[50]

Horace Humphrey retreated into dejection when he lost his job, thrusting his wife and daughter into the position of breadwinners. Julia Humphrey promptly lined up engagements for Doris teaching ballroom and children's dance classes, and provided the piano accompaniment herself. During the first arduous year of this new undertaking, Doris also managed to graduate from the Hinman Normal School. According to Doris, daughter and mother were earning a good living within a year. The Humphrey women proved Hinman to be a professional role model whom other women could imitate with success.[51]

Humphrey performed occasionally during this period. In October 1914, she danced with Albert Carroll at Hull-House but was discouraged that theirs had been brief numbers sandwiched into a dancing party evening rather than a full performance. In 1916 she performed as a soloist for the Chicago Commons Woman's Club. Teaching continued to be her economic mainstay; however, four years of a grueling teaching schedule proved more than enough. It was Hinman who recognized Humphrey's dissatisfaction and encouraged her to study at the Denishawn summer school in Los Angeles. Humphrey enjoyed the 1917 Denishawn sessions enormously, and Ted Shawn invited her to perform in a Zodiac ballet that he planned to tour in vaudeville that fall. Constrained by her mother, Humphrey declined the offer and returned home for another year of teaching. She was back in Los Angeles again in summer 1918, and this time she stayed to become a Denishawn performer and teacher. She handed over her dance teaching to Ethel Moulton, another Chicago girl she met at the summer school. Julia Humphrey continued to accompany the classes for that enterprise. Thus was launched Humphrey's performing career with the Denishawn company; it continued through the mid-1920s. During this period Humphrey at times collaborated with Ruth St. Denis on choreography. Humphrey and Charles Weidman eventually broke with the Denishawn company to establish their own choreographic identities.[52]

As a modern dance choreographer, Humphrey moved away from practices and conceptions of dance that informed her earlier mentors' work. She left Denishawn in 1928, rejecting the conduct of the company enterprise, its (in her view) too ready compromise of artistic standards, and the short leash on which St. Denis and Shawn kept young members who aspired to choreographic innovation. Humphrey also rejected the subjects and the movement materials that Denishawn works treated—mysticism; fiery exoticism; and ritual practices, religious ceremonies, and indigenous dances from foreign and non-Western cultures. In discarding these themes and source materials, she was perforce refusing the practice of Mary Wood Hinman as well. Hinman had mobilized new dance practices by actively researching and collecting extant and historical materials, which she subsequently taught to her students. Hinman was less an inventor than a "selector." Her skill and creativity resided in identifying and assessing movement practices, and in systematically arranging, varying, and calibrating them for appropriate ages, gender groups, and occasions. In keeping with most of her early-twentieth-century peers, she did not develop or disseminate a choreographic theory for creating new work.

Humphrey, in contrast, strove to create *new* movement for dancing. She looked to the human bodies available in her own culture for source material, and theorized dance movement as an arc between the "two deaths" of verticality and horizontality, that is, as a condition of thrilling disequilibrium between two points of stasis. Further, Humphrey was reflexive about her choreographic process, and taught the theory to students at her studio and at Bennington Summer Schools of the Dance. After her performing career concluded, she taught at the Juilliard School. Her method was published posthumously as *The Art of Making Dances*.[53] Where Hinman found integral value in extant and traditional dance materials—resuscitating them in some cases, circulating them more widely in others—Humphrey emphatically privileged the new.

What Humphrey retained from her time spent with Denishawn was a conception of the dance artist as a creature of special sensibility. She extended this notion in her own practice as choreographer, company co-director, and featured performer, and lived her dance-making enterprise as a high-art activity. Humphrey herself perceived the chasm that separated her work and conception of dance making from that of her earliest mentor. The difference between their approaches is illuminated in a letter that Humphrey wrote to her parents in November 1930. Humphrey wrote the letter having recently renewed acquaintance with her old teacher; Hinman had again urged Humphrey to make films of her dances. "I always am stimulated by talking to her," Humphrey wrote,

> although her point of view is as strange to me as the man next door. Her continual interest lies in people, and whatever concerns giving them more of everything they want—my interest lies in making something as beautifully—therefore truly as I can—You can see where these two opinions would clash—She "Why don't you make moving pictures—they'll reach millions of people?" Me "If I did, I would have to make them promise not to cut or change the dances" She "the great thing is to get in touch with people then you can improve the pictures gradually as you go along" Me "The great thing is to do each piece of work well, with no apologies to anybody" And there we are. Two perfectly good points of view with value on both sides—but of course I prefer mine. It's the difference between the humanist and the artist.[54]

Humphrey's assessment is penetrating. Hinman forged her "humanist" approach during a period when innovators introduced dance practices to remedy physical, moral, and spiritual crises precipitated by fundamental changes in industry, immigration, and demography. Some twenty years later, Humphrey launched her enterprise in a society that had weathered a great war, had largely conceded that an industrial economy was there to stay, had choked off immigration, and had seen the professionalization of social welfare work. In radically different social and political circumstances, she constituted her practice in new terms as well: as dance making. Her efforts to forge a career and livelihood as a dance maker partook of the modernist ideology then ascendant, which claimed for "art" an autonomous realm and aesthetic import rather than social welfare instrumentality. Humphrey mobilized dancing as a theatrical, representational practice and presented her work first as a recital and then as a concert form. She strove to perfect her choreographic compositions and to refine her dancers' presentation of them. Dancing practiced in this (high-art) manner was necessarily an exclusive undertaking, requiring long and steady training and rehearsal to achieve aesthetic excellence.

The difference between Humphrey's and Hinman's practices, I argue, index alternative and ultimately competing views of human creativity. Each woman in her own way conceded the individual as the seat of creativity. In Hinman's era, reformist critiques leveled at industrial labor vigorously condemned new work practices because routinized, repetitious, sweated work stripped away the pleasure in work and the potential for imagination and spontaneity it had once offered. Settlement activity aimed to restore individuals to themselves, so to speak. Dancing, in Hinman's practice, affirmed every person's essential creativity. Humphrey's modernist practice positioned creativity as the purview of the few. The capacity to create was still viewed as an individual attribute, to be sure, but only select individuals possessed the quality of genius and the ability to access imaginative truth which were fundamental to artistic creation. Hinman's humanist enterprise aimed to "realize" individuals and release their inherent creativity. Means and ends were quite reversed in Humphrey's undertaking: the few, gifted individuals realized the new modern dance.[55]

Raymond Williams has persuasively argued that recastings of the artist as "genius," and a parallel specialization of artistic production, was put in motion in Western society as a response to the Industrial Revolution. Deprived of traditional sources of patronage and forced into market relations with potential consumers, nineteenth-century "romantic" artists reformulated artistic practice. Previously conducted as a general social activity, art making was now recast as an autonomous special preserve, set aside from daily life. This stance offered artists a base from which to criticize industrial society, although in the long run it left them isolated, and it powerfully inflected early modernist constructions of creativity and the artist's role. The "genius" formulation of artistry was thus readily available to dance innovators from the turn of the century onward. In distinction to it were Progessive-era settlement endeavors, including Hinman's, which pursued the alternative construction of "everyone a creator" in an effort to undo the negative effects of industrial transformation. When this critique faded in the postwar years, and as barriers to women's public sphere and labor force presence changed as well, Hinman's alternative lost salience.[56]

It was Humphrey's approach which garnered broad support for the continuing growth and spread of modern dance choreography and performance through the late 1950s in the United States. But if Humphrey differed in method from her early mentor, the impress of certain settlement house ideas can still be discerned in aspects of her choreographic practice. She made a number of dances about the interactions of people in social groups, a pivotal concern for people like Hinman and Jane Addams, the Lewisohns, Rita Morgenthau, and Lillian Wald. *Day on Earth* depicted in kinetic terms the life cycle of a small family, exploring the relationships among family members of different generations. *New Dance* was a "dance of affirmation from disorganization to organization," fusing a men's group with a women's group, but preserving the individual's relation to the group via solo dancers briefly stating personal themes. *With My Red Fires* tackled societal constraint of romantic love and counterposed the power of the group to that of the individual. *Passacaglia and Fugue in C Minor* rendered in movement terms statements about the harmony of groups and departures from and returns to unity. Such subject matter was substantially different from the music visualizations and oriental dances that the Denishawn Company had popularized in the United States. It also differed from the intense psychological themes that Humphrey's peer Martha Graham explored in works from the 1930s and 1940s. A number of Humphrey's choreographies thus dealt with the dynamics and difficulties of people working and living in societies, a concern which from the first had propelled settlement house people into immigrant neighborhoods.[57]

Chicago Commons, South End House, and Accelerating Folk Dance Work

The folk dance and social dance components in Hinman's Hull-House teaching work showed up in other settlements' curricula as well. Brief consideration of dance work at Chicago Commons and Boston's South End House will confirm a general pattern deduced above: that settlements' methodological fluidity provided positive conditions for women's innovation of new movement practices. Survey of Chicago Commons's and South End House's bodily cultivation work will also illuminate the growing salience of folk dancing as a settlement offering in the 1910s. In these two cases, folk dancing is gendered as a movement practice for females, and instruction in folk dancing is concomitantly imparted by females. Two cases don't constitute a national pattern, of course. Taken in conjunction with Hinman's work, however, they signal the growing attraction of a gendered folk dancing model developed in New York City from 1905 on.

CHICAGO COMMONS

Settlements provided extremely flexible arenas for women's introduction of or experiment with novel movement practices because settlement club and class curricula were driven by residents' and workers' interests. As residents changed, so too could settlement offerings. Rather than see this as disruptive or chaotic, settlement leaders prized the ability to change course quickly. They believed it made them all the more responsive to immigrant neighbors' changing needs. Nowhere was the freedom to shift direction more visible than at Chicago Commons, where early emphasis on Delsartian elocution work was overtaken by a vigorous curriculum of folk dancing. The shift may be read in terms of changing dance fashion, of course, but Americanization and class concerns are also involved.

Chicago Commons was founded by Graham Taylor, an ordained minister who moved to Chicago in 1892 to accept a teaching post at the Chicago Theological Seminary. Taylor accepted the Chicago appointment with the condition that he be permitted to conduct "social-educational work on the field." In Chicago he quickly made the acquaintance of Jane Addams and saw in Hull-House an example of the kind of field work he aspired to do. Taylor founded the settlement with several others in 1894 at a Union Street location on Chicago's West Side; there it served predominantly Irish, German, Scandinavian, and Italian immigrant neighbors. Addams remained an important inspiration to Taylor and served as a trustee of Chicago Commons.[58]

Training and shaping the physical body was recognized from the first as a worthy area of educational work at Chicago Commons. Three different kinds of physical work were offered at the settlement from 1894 to 1920: elocution and Delsarte physical culture; gymnasium work focused on apparatus and drill work; and gymnasium work emphasizing gymnastic and folk dancing. Two of these arenas provided substantial opportunity for women's leadership.[59]

After establishing a free kindergarten for neighborhood children, Chicago Commons inaugurated a formal schedule of classes and club work for the 1894–95 year. This project was called the "Plymouth Winter Night College" because it received substantial funding support from Plymouth Church, located in the area. Classes and clubs met in the late afternoon and evening on weeknights and on Saturday afternoons and evenings. Beginning with the first season of the Plymouth Winter Night College, girls' and young women's elocution, physical culture, and Delsarte work appeared as a regular feature.[60]

Through publication, performance, and personal pedagogy, Genevieve Stebbins had catalyzed circulation of the Delsarte system in the 1880s as an activity for the general public, especially women. Stebbins's books continued to be published as another wave of interest in the Delsarte system swept America in the 1890s. Led by figures like Henrietta and Edmund Russell, this phase focused on the application of Delsartian theory to the aesthetic presentation of the self, home decoration, and virtually all aspects of life. At the same time, the Delsarte system of physical training was being adopted by schools of elocution across the country. Because the system's drills and sequences cultivated "expression," Delsartian gesture could be invoked while delivering dramatic recitations—frequently termed "readings"—or speeches. The two expressional forms that Stebbins had developed as performance vehicles were easily adaptable to school exercises. For statue posing, pupils studied classic marble statuary (or plaster casts) and then assumed the poses with their own bodies, composing tableaus. Delsartian training prepared students to enter into the poses with simultaneous, fluid movements of body parts; once they reached "the climax" of their pictures, they tried to "melt" into the form of a succeeding statue, avoiding jagged or abrupt transitional movements. Pantomimes, on the other hand, added steps and rhythms to Stebbins's expressional exercises, allowing practitioners to communicate a story through a series of plastiques. Historian Nancy Ruyter has identified five leading speech training schools in Boston, Philadelphia, and Chicago whose training was based on the Delsarte system. From one of these, Chicago's Columbia School of Oratory, came instructors who taught elocution at Chicago Commons's Plymouth Winter Night College (PWNC).[61]

Delsartian physical culture and elocution commenced at Chicago Commons in the first term of the PWNC. As part of the 1894–95 winter schedule, Miss Bacock from the Columbia School of Oratory taught Girls' Physical Culture Thursdays at 4 P.M. During the two succeeding years, instructors trained at the Columbia School taught girls' elocution, physical culture, and "Young Ladies Delsarte" classes. By 1897–98, instructors hailed from several different Chicago area oratory schools, and four different weekly classes in elocution were offered. Printed schedules and Chicago Commons brochures for these and succeeding years indicate that most of the elocution teachers were women, and that their pupils were girls and young women.[62]

As with other Chicago Commons educational classes, students paid a nominal sum to support the undertaking. In 1896, for instance, students paid $.25 for ten lessons in manual training, cooking, German, gymnasium drill, sewing class, arithmetic, elocution, and other subjects. A 1904 settlement financial summary indicated that the elocution classes were self-supporting; whether the local speech training schools subsidized the PWNC elocution classes is not known. It is quite possible that some oratory schoolteachers may have completed their training while giving instruction at Chicago Commons. In any event, the settlement and the Columbia School of Oratory enjoyed a mutually supportive relationship. In February 1897, the school gave a benefit performance for Chicago Commons at

Steinway Hall, its headquarters. The program consisted of organ and piano suites, vocal selections, and "readings," the latter surely delivered with Delsartian-molded gesture. In a very tangible way, then, Chicago Commons provided an arena for women's professional work as elocution teachers, and occasional platforms for performances by teachers and their pupils.[63]

Instruction in Delsarte work rapidly exceeded the bounds of formal class work and penetrated the curriculum for Commons girls clubs. Equally significant, settlement club members programmed Delsartian performance materials as part of club entertainments. This was true for the Commons Girls' Progressive Club, whose working-girl members, almost 100 strong in 1898, met weekly to pursue self-culture on the model of middle-class women's culture clubs. Their Fourth Annual Entertainment in April 1898 included two tableaux performed by members themselves: "Flags of the Nations" and "Liberty, Arts, Science and Religion." Performed as the Spanish-American War loomed, these titles suggest that statue posing afforded a bodily register for political positioning. The May 1901 entertainment staged by the Young Women's Progressive Club featured members performing a Greek cymbal drill, a "scarf fantastics" number, and a "Greek tableau."[64]

As Delsartian work reached full throttle, gymnasium work for girls received new impetus around 1901. While formal gymnasium instruction had been available to boys and men since the Commons opened in 1894, girls' work had consisted of weekly calisthenics classes. Shortly after the turn of the century, an initiative staffed by male teachers added apparatus work, games, and basketball to girls' work, with special attention "paid to breathing exercises" (surely a concession to Delsartian ideas) and emphasis given to teamwork. The new methodology, while respectably current, was not the most up-to-date. Missing from the gymnasium work for girls and women was any mention of the gymnastic dancing that had been introduced in the 1890s at leading normal institutions. This gap in the Chicago Commons gymnasium curriculum was filled when Katherine Schofield began to teach girls gymnasium work there in 1905. She directed girls' and women's work at Chicago Commons from 1907 onward and turned girls' work in directions similar to those pursued by Hinman and Burchenal.[65]

Schofield added gymnastic dancing, corrective work, lectures on hygiene, and folk dancing to the drill and apparatus work already part of the gymnasium program for females. One significant product of this expanded work was the inclusion of folk and national dances in the annual May Festivals, a community event that Chicago Commons inaugurated in 1902.[66] In 1906, a settlement brochure proudly reported, the "international night" of singing and dancing national dances was "the high night of the feast." A typical array of exhibition features had also occurred: the cooking school's graduation and exhibit, girls' club broom drill, mothers' shadow comedy, boys' club Indian tribe. But the Commons auditorium was "packed with the men and women of our polyglot people" to see the final exhibition:

> There on the stage were their own representatives to sing and dance in their old-country ways. The graceful delicate dancing of the Italian children, the gay costumes and chivalrous movements of the Norwegians, the plaids and courtesying [sic] of the Scotch grand dames, the Greek whirl of men's skirts, all interspersed by the music of the mandolin club, the chorus of the Choral, and the songs of all nations, lifted all up above their little patriotism and blended all hearts in the neighborly spirit of our American international citizenship.[67]

While the children's dancing was certainly prepared in Schofield's gymnasium classes, that of their parents and neighbors was probably learned in Europe. Girls performed folk songs, games, and gymnastic drills for the 1907 festival, and in 1908 an evening of national dances, called a "kirmess," was again featured. The scheduled dances included a sailor's hornpipe, Italian tarantella (always popular at Chicago Commons), a highland fling, buck and wing, jig, Irish lilt, cachucka, Greek dance, and Swedish Gottland quadrille. The Greek and Scottish dances were probably performed by adults but the remainder were widely taught at the time as children's and young people's dances.[68]

Chicago Commons also participated via folk dancing in larger-scale Chicago and intersettlement events. In August 1908, Chicago Commons took part in the opening exercises for the new West Side park, Small Park No. 1; participants performed three drills and six folk dances. In 1909, Chicago Commons gymnasium girls performed four gymnastic and folk dances in the Chicago Play Festival, an annual variant on the 1907 PAA Play Festival model. Hosted for the first time on the West Side, the 1909 Chicago Play Festival drew more than 3,000 participants and 30,000 observers. In 1910, Chicago Commons participated in folk dancing for the first Neighborhood Play Festival, a similar but smaller-scale and still more local event. The inclusion of national dances in the May Festivals, and the settlement's folk dance participation in city and intersettlement events, must be credited to Schofield and the direction in which she took gymnasium work for females at Chicago Commons. Descriptions of gymnasium work indicate that, even after her death in 1914, folk dancing remained a focus of girls' gymnasium work and a feature of May Festivals through the war years.[69]

Certainly Schofield's expansion of folk dance work at the Commons rode the crest of changing fashions in dance pedagogy. Hinman offered an excellent model at Chicago's Hull-House, and the newly formed Playground Association of America (especially during Luther Gulick's leadership) promulgated folk dancing as civic recreation. But the 1906 May Festival account quoted above raises the further possibility that folk dance work thrived because it performed cultural work on the thorny issue of immigration. In the settlement's view, the dancing, music, choruses, and national songs at that event "lifted all up above their little patriotism and blended all hearts in the neighborly spirit of our American international citizenship." This interpretation of the festival's Americanizing effect is full of transcendental hope and pragmatic faith in neighborliness as a nexus for interaction among differing peoples. It's not at all clear that immigrant neighbors shared this interpretation of the event, nor that the new spirit of citizenship lasted beyond the event itself. This account does index the settlement idea that citizenship, like harmony across class lines, could be forged as a performative act rather than a melting away of essentialized differences. Seen in this light, folk dancing could be considered superior "performative activity" because references to distinctive traditional or national identities that inhered in the movement material itself could be mediated by the way in which folk dancing was staged. Alternatively, folk dancing allowed practitioners to "have it both ways," to hold in tension via performance practice elements of their immigrant and new American identities. The potential for "Americanizing" immigrants was also seen to operate in folk dancing that immigrant neighbors themselves initiated within the settlement frame. An Italian women's group, for example, disregarded convention—and their husbands' wishes—to leave the household and meet weekly at Chicago Commons. Members danced the tarantella as a regular feature of club meetings, a newspaper reporter learned in 1919,

> And now the mothers go on dancing themselves out of individual into social life, out of a narrow rut into citizenship, out of Italy into America. The Commons that set them all a dancing, couldn't it be called a pretty wise tarantula?[70]

As this remark attests, the challenges associated with citizenship were hardly limited to transfer of national allegiance. They extended to immigrants' isolation in ethnic enclaves and gender-constrained patterns of public sociability as well. Written some thirteen years after the first May Festival, in the wake of wartime "100 percent Americanism," and as immigration restriction gathered momentum, this account illuminates the capabilities still attributed to folk dancing. From 1905, as a movement practice introduced and consolidated at Chicago Commons, folk dance instruction offered a potent political instrumentality which Delsartian statue posing or recitation could not match.

Qualitative differences between Delsartian and folk dance movement, which translated into subtle class distinctions, may also have accounted for Chicago Commons's increased emphasis on folk dance. Early-twentieth-century folk dance proponents like Luther Gulick argued folk dance's special suitability for urban children: it demanded the large-muscle group movements and substantial cardiovascular investment necessary for physical maturation and good health. Delsartian physical culture developed a comparatively narrower range of movement; and, despite its emphasis on deep breathing, it would not have elevated heart rates as high. Seen from this perspective, the addition of folk dancing classes brought the settlement in line with leading-edge recreation theory. But folk dance and Delsartian training carried class associations as well. Stebbins and the Russells actively targeted their Delsartian physical culture practice at middle-class and elite women. Its movement style complemented the lifestyle of such women, who were likely to be more sedentary—or better supplied with domestic equipment and servants—than working-class women. Folk dancing, in contrast, took shape at this time as a "general public" practice aimed at ameliorating the lot of urban, immigrant, working-class, and poor children. Its vigorous physiological demands not only matured growing bodies but also suited the physicality demanded of working-class and immigrant people by industrial labor. Certainly Chicago Commons had been adventurous in establishing connections with Chicago oratory schools, and as always, the supply and distinctive interests of club workers powerfully shaped settlement offerings. But did the Commons take advantage of Delsartian modes for bodily cultivation without regard for its class valence—or simply without reflecting upon it? Whatever the motivations at Chicago Commons (and they cannot be determined from extant materials), the subsequent proffering of folk dancing effectively operated to inscribe working-class identity on immigrant girls' bodies.

SOUTH END HOUSE

Boston's South End House offers a related perspective on the rising promi-nence of folk dancing in settlement house curricula. This settlement opened its doors in 1892 as Andover House, operating in a working-class, predominantly Irish neighborhood in the southern part of Boston. The "Andover" reflected the various ties to Andover Theological Seminary felt by Robert A. Woods, the settlement head resident, and Professor William J. Tucker, president of Andover House Association. By 1895, the settlement wished to minimize this sectarian connection and emphasize the tie to its own neighborhood. Thus it changed the name to South End House. From the start, male residents outnumbered female, although a corps of female nonresident Associate Workers grew to more than twenty-five members by 1902. As at other settlements, South End House workers conducted and published (under Robert Woods's direction) detailed studies of neighbor-hood demographics, living conditions, and needs. Woods, with resident worker Albert J. Kennedy, achieved nationwide recognition in the Na-tional Federation of Settlements. The two surveyed United States settle-ment houses and published the *Handbook of Settlements* in 1911.[71]

There is scant evidence of dancing activity per se at South End House between 1892 and 1900. Dancing was reportedly a favorite Saturday after-noon activity of the Merry Times Club, a girls' social club. By 1899, danc-ing appeared consistently in club work for, again, girls twelve to sixteen; it was incorporated into club meetings as one among several activities. Nor could gymnasium activity foster dance, because South End House never implemented a physical training curriculum. The settlement successfully lobbied the city of Boston to establish a public gym for the neighborhood, and when the Ward 9 gym opened in 1900, South End House frequently listed that facility's gymnasium classes in the settlement schedule of clubs and classes.[72]

Starting in 1902, however, South End House actively developed a program of social dance instruction. That first year, a mixed dancing class for young men and women (usually unmarried people over fourteen) met on Saturday night. The residents believed the classes to be a success, and the next year's annual bulletin lauded the disciplining effects that instruc-tion produced:

> In fact there is hardly anything done at the settlement out of which come better results than come from the dancing classes. Both among the young men and the young women, many important points of character can be

made under the head of deportment, which might meet with indifference or recoil if otherwise presented.[73]

Like Hull-House in the same period, South End House linked social dancing to the right ordering of social, including sexual, relations. The settlement experimented with different instruction configurations over the next six years, offering both sex-segregated and mixed social dancing classes for varied age-groups. By 1907, classes achieved steady enrollment and were again routinely mixed; they remained that way through the 1910s.[74]

John Whitman, a resident beloved for his storytelling, launched the first social dancing class in 1903. From 1905 to 1918, however, women supplied leadership and continuity in social dance instruction. For the years 1909 to 1911, Associate Worker Mary Johnson was identified in South End House activity schedules as Director of Dancing. Even when not so identified, Johnson remained a mainstay of social dancing classes from 1905 to 1912. From 1915 to 1918, Aline Murphy, Lucy McLellan, and Ethel Baker consistently led classes. From 1905 to 1918, three times as many women as men participated as social dancing instructors. Eighteen of the women can be identified as Associate Workers and five as female residents. Of the ten male instructors during this fourteen-year period, two are identifiable as Associate Workers and four as residents. South End House maintained a resident fellowship program with Harvard, Dartmouth, and Amherst, and two of the four residents teaching social dance were college fellows. Since the settlement particularly valued social dancing for developing right relationships between the sexes, the presence of men teachers in the classes would have helped establish desirable models for emulation. But the relative involvement of male and female instructors confirms that women established a presence and identity at South End House as social dance instructors.[75]

South End House experimented for a brief period with specialized dancing classes aimed at young girls. During the 1906–07 year, a weekly afternoon "fancy dancing class" was offered for girls aged ten to thirteen. In 1908–09, an evening fancy dancing class was offered, with no gender specified for students; and in 1911 an evening class in Gilbert dancing was available for girls, no age specified. It is difficult to know what kind of movement comprised the so-called "fancy dancing" classes. The term was used freely at the time but without much precision, and South End House class schedules provide no additional details on the class content. Gilbert dancing, in contrast, was well defined. Its originator, Melvin Ballou Gilbert, published articles about the form in a contemporary magazine called

Students from Boston Normal School of Gymnastics, 1906, practicing
"esthetic gymnastics." Melvin Ballou Gilbert began a teaching association
with BNSG in 1898. Photograph by George Brayton. COURTESY OF
WELLESLEY COLLEGE ARCHIVES.

The Director, which he edited. Gilbert dancing was aesthetic dancing; it
utilized ballet techniques, but omitted toe work and added substantial
torso movement. This technique was taught at the school Gilbert established in Boston in 1897 and also at two local, prestigious physical training
institutions: the Boston Normal School of Gymnastics and the Harvard
Summer School of Physical Education. Six of the seven women who
offered the instruction for these three classes at South End House were
Associate Workers whose names do not recur in subsequent years.[76]

A lull in specialty classes ensued, and lasted for several years. When

specialty classes started up again they included afternoon classes in folk dancing for girls. Each year from 1915 to 1918, folk dancing classes were scheduled in addition to the social dancing instruction and the classes in "dancing," of an unspecified nature, regularly made available for girls aged nine to thirteen. As at Hull-House and Chicago Commons, the new instruction was staffed by a corps of female teachers. Ten different women Associate Workers led the folk dancing instruction, none for more than one year at a time. Three of them were affiliated with normal schools for physical training.[77]

The offering of specialty dancing classes, first on an experimental basis and then regularly after 1915, reflects South End House's rapidly changing conception of the needs it should meet and the means it should use. The shift to folk dancing coincided with a mounting perception that preadolescent girls required special attention in settlement work. A 1916 annual South End House pamphlet noted that kindergartens and the recently developed Montessori system provided well for children aged four to seven, and that schools had increasingly turned attention to adolescents. "The pre-adolescent stage has been continuously neglected," it said, arguing that this neglect created a lacuna on which settlement houses should focus:

> Recent psychological research is throwing important new light upon the decisive, life-long results of what may happen in the minds of children when they begin as free individuals, to go forth into the world. A modified and developed form of kindergarten, carefully selected stories, directed reading, spontaneous dramatic expression, simple forms of industrial training, rightly devised athletics for boys and dancing for girls, the right balance of privilege and responsibility, and above all the generous flow of sympathy and confidence in which each child's mind finds its medium of response, — these are the ways by which many of the dangers not only of this period but of oncoming adolescence may be obviated, and many otherwise wasted values be conserved and fulfilled.[78]

South End House's concern to distinguish preadolescents from adolescents followed several years' close scrutiny, throughout the settlement movement, of age-graded settlement work for females. Chicago Commons, for instance, had in March 1910 hosted a conference on girls' club work that was attended by about seventy people from Chicago. A follow-up conference held at Northwestern University Settlement in 1911 focused on work with school-age girls. In December 1911, the National Federation of Settlements issued a questionnaire to canvass nationwide settlement opinion on "the Problem of the Adolescent Girls between Fourteen and Eighteen Years of Age." At Chicago Commons, Schofield was designated to reply to questions posed on the topics "Mixed clubs of Boys and Girls" and "Educational Work," the latter including a specific query on the "value of gymnasium work; folk dancing." In the extant draft of her reply, Schofield praised folk dancing in strong and unambiguous terms.[79] Robert Woods, South End House's head worker, had been directly involved with the 1911 National Federation of Settlements survey. Thus when the Boston settlement in 1915 reorganized its specialty classes to embrace folk dancing, it did so in a context of heightened settlement commitment to developing age-appropriate curricula.[80]

Local conditions exerted an impact on the settlement's shift in priorities as well. South End House had long been concerned to provide "industrial training" for immigrant children. In a 1917 brochure it congratulated itself on the fact that, very largely as a result of settlement initiative, the public schools had recognized their obligation to provide vocational training. The schools' assumption of that work thus "left for the settlements as their special educational field the organization of wholesome and up-building recreation. Here a really educational technique is being developed."[81] In shifting its resources from vocational training to recreation, South End House reflected the contemporary concern with play and leisure that had sparked the formation of groups like the American Pageantry Association and the PAA. And, as the settlement pamphlet announced, it was part of the settlement charter to change programs as circumstances changed. That imperative had been established in the 1880s at Toynbee Hall, the London settlement that had inspired Woods.[82] After assessing the settlement's role among the network of entities that serviced South Boston immigrants, Woods and the South End House settlement force refocused their efforts on a different age group. The addition of folk dancing classes to the schedule in 1915 thus specifically targeted preadolescent girls; by scheduling the classes in the afternoon the settlement effectively precluded older working girls from attending.

Taken together with Hull-House offerings, the movement practices conducted at South End House and Chicago Commons illuminate two significant, shifting patterns in the Progressive-era linkage between women, the body, and dance. First, the record at these settlements confirms the trend, indicated by census data, of women's growing representation among teachers of dancing and athletics. Living cheek by jowl with immigrants in major industrial cities, settlement people realized only too well that the depleting exertion extracted from them in the workplace was only one facet of the body's labor. Settlements thus shouldered considerable responsibility for supplying resources for their neighbors' pleasurable release, expression, and physical training of the body, and they lobbied municipalities to share the burden. The gritty realities of industrial labor and urban crowding, I argue, made bodies a social concern, and settlements' commitments to address these bodies afforded women residents and workers new positions in the public sphere. This new responsibility to protect and shape bodies did not, of course, erase time-honored, less favorable associations of femaleness with the body and its sensuality. But the industrial and urban critiques leveled by the settlement house movement empowered middle-class women to negotiate a broader range of meanings for body-gender linkages attached to their sex. At all three settlements discussed here, women constituted the corps of workers who offered the varied forms of dance instruction. South End House differed from the Chicago settlements in the relative tenure of female dance teachers. Both Hull-House and Chicago Commons enjoyed significant periods when a single teacher guided the work and established the direction of dance instruction. South End House utilized a greater number of dancing teachers and only a few of them taught for periods of any duration. Between 1905 and 1912, Mary Johnson was a constant force in social dance work, while from 1915 to 1918, a trio of female workers supplied steady leadership for the same genre. Not even these patterns of short-term continuity obtained for the South End House folk dancing work begun in 1915; these instructors changed yearly. Whereas Hinman at Hull-House and Schofield at Chicago Commons developed substantial portions of their careers, at South End House dancing teachers moved quickly through the arena that the settlement provided. (Here the South End teachers conformed to the broad settlement pattern, in which college-aged workers stayed one to three years in the field before moving on to other occupations.) The overwhelming preponderance of female dance teachers—social, folk, or Delsartian—at these three settlements confirms and embodies the direction of change revealed by census occupational statistics: women were substantially gaining representation among teachers of athletics and dancing between 1910 and 1920.

Second, and equally significant, the record at Hull-House, Chicago Commons, and South End House signals the accelerating trend toward actively gendering folk dancing as a female-specific *practice*. At Hull-House, Hinman had taught folk dancing within the social dance curriculum, introducing it to boys and young men as well as to girls and young women. At Chicago Commons, in contrast, Schofield presented folk dancing and gymnastic dancing as part of girls' and women's gymnasium class work. A colleague who worked under Schofield's direction, Miss Catlin, was known to incorporate some folk dancing in her mixed gender social dance classes. But the weight and thrust of Schofield's work was to identify folk and gymnastic dancing as a practice for females. South End House hewed to Schofield's Chicago Commons direction. To be sure, the settlement, after trying and abandoning separate-sex social dancing classes, offered mixed classes from 1907 onward. Folk dancing classes, however, were specifically oriented to preadolescent girls. Timing had everything to do with these differences, I argue. South End House introduced folk dancing a decade later than Chicago Commons and almost two decades later than Hull-House. Hinman's work in Chicago gave important early impetus to folk dancing as appropriate settlement work; Schofield, the source of whose own training is unclear, implemented folk dancing as work specifically for girls. By 1915, South End House's straightforward association of folk dancing with girls' work reflected a view of folk dancing as a gendered activity that had slowly consolidated since the early years of the century.

In deploying folk dancing as a female movement practice, Chicago Commons and South End House were advancing a methodology vigorously developed in another quarter altogether. The precedent on which settlement houses surely built was the New York City program instituted in 1905 by the Girls' Branch of the Public Schools' Athletic League. Hinman was well aware of the New York program and regretted Chicago's lack of similar public school support for folk dancing. "The social classes [that I teach] in and around Chicago partially fill the void caused by the Public Schools' failure to realize that dancing is part of a child's heritage," she wrote in 1909.[83] A vehicle for construction of personal and communal identities, Girls' Branch folk dancing also participated in negotiating the Progressive-era linkage between women, the body, and dance.

 Folk Dance, Park Fetes, and
Period Political Values

On clear days in May, early in the twentieth century, hundreds of school-girls tumbled onto the Sheep's Meadow in Central Park. Signaled by a waving flag, they rushed forward in one great tide toward maypoles that had been erected for each of their schools. After running and cheering, they collected themselves in the grassy meadow and commenced a vernal festivity known as a park fete. The opening dance for park fetes was almost always the *Carrousel*, a Swedish singing game. Each group of girls per-forming the *Carrousel* organized themselves around a maypole in two concentric circles. The inner-circle girls linked hands, and the outer-circle girls placed hands on the shoulders of the inner-circle girls standing in front of them. They slid and stamped, first left, then right; they "danced around in circles," remarked one newspaper reporter, "and bewildered the people who were watching them."[1] Following the *Carrousel* the girls shouted their individual school cheers and continued with a series of "folk-dances" from European lands, like an Italian *Tarantella*, or *Sellenger's Round*, an English country dance. Team activities such as the shuttle relay, punch ball, and ball-throwing games alternated with the dances.[2]

A brass band cued the start of the dances, no participant left the area during an activity, and all participants performed the dances at the same time. Presented in this way, a dance like *Reap the Flax* would appear to viewers as fifty or more groups of girls first forming straight-line phalanxes and alternating these formations with single-file chains winding circular patterns, then squares of girls through which dancers wound like thread through spinning wheels, and finally single-file chains winding serpentine patterns. The maypole assigned to each school supplied the spatial point of reference for each group of girls, and established the underlying organization of the dancing field as a whole. In the final *May-pole Dance*, girls encircled the poles once more, then braided bright ribbons around them by dancing in circles of ever-diminishing radius. The winding complete, the girls "unshipped" the poles and carried them off the field, supporting them along their length. At a signal, all the participants ran full tilt toward the bandstand at the center of the meadow, yelling and waving banners emblazoned with their schools' name or the words "Girls' Branch," the name of the sponsoring organization. Stopping just short of the bandstand, the girls cheered Elizabeth Burchenal, the park fete organizer, and sang the *Star Spangled Banner*. Tired and probably dusty, scores of girls then turned homeward with their schoolmates while Boy Scouts on cleanup detail took to the field, picking up litter, stray hair ribbons, and banners left behind.[3]

Park fetes, and the after-school work that prepared them, were sponsored and produced in New York City by a voluntary organization, the Girls' Branch of the Public Schools Athletic League. While settlement house dance practices have effectively been lost to historical scrutiny until the present study, park fetes created lasting cultural images of schoolgirls dancing on the green. At the end of the twentieth century, these images seem so thoroughly "natural" as to obviate analysis. It is precisely such naturalization of females dancing that this chapter will unpack, exposing ways in which Girls' Branch work constructed "folk dancing" and argued issues of power and identity in Progressive-era America. In the selection of dances and organization of fetes, Girls' Branch dancing argued the politically volatile issue of the right relationship between individuals and groups—the part and the whole—in a society grappling with the lived effects of laissez-faire economic ideology and organization. Appropriating European movement materials and addressing immigrants or children of immigrants, it also negotiated issues of ethnicity and national identity in a major American port city. Foregrounding *girls'* activities, Girls' Branch work worried and worked through questions about gender, proffering embodied statements about what it meant to be female in the early 1900s. Further, by association with (and later, through minimal financial support from) New York City's public schools, the production of Girls' Branch dancing located dance in an institutional context at a pivotal time for organization and bureaucracy formation in America. Matters of founding,

"Fifteen Acres of Dancing Girls" reads the caption to this photograph, used as a frontispiece for Elizabeth Burchenal's *Dances of the People* (1913). The image captures the May 14, 1912, park fete held by the Girls' Branch on the Sheep's Meadow in Central Park. The bandstand is visible in the right quadrant of the photo. FROM THE ELIZABETH BURCHENAL COLLECTION, SPECIAL COLLECTIONS, MUGAR MEMORIAL LIBRARY, BOSTON UNIVERSITY.

funding, and conducting the Girls' Branch afforded its inaugurators an instrumentality for asserting political agency. Researching (or collecting) dances, teaching others to teach this material, and publishing choreographies positioned Elizabeth Burchenal to constitute a new professional identity. In important ways, Girls' Branch work participated in early-twentieth-century efforts to recast traditional body-woman-dance linkages.

Founding of and Momentum for Girls' Branch
Folk Dancing

The Girls' Branch was founded amidst a systemwide drive to provide for
the physiological needs of children swelling New York City school rolls at
the turn of the century. The pivotal figure in this drive was Luther Halsey

Gulick (1865–1918), who joined the newly consolidated city school system in 1903 as Director of Physical Training. Gulick revised the physical training offered in all the city's boroughs, in an effort to coordinate it, but found the school day's time frame inadequate to the scope of work he thought necessary. Gulick thus enlisted the aid of prominent New York men to found and fund an after-school athletics enterprise for boys. Charter members of this Public Schools Athletic League (PSAL) included Henry A. Rogers, president of the Board of Education; General George Wingate, a member of the Board of Education; and James A. Sullivan, president of the Amateur Athletic Union, an athletic editor associated with several newspapers, and president of the American Sports Publishing Company, which published Spalding's Athletic Library. Their number also included Charles B. Stover, longtime leader of the Outdoor Recreation League and former resident of New York's University Settlement; and Gustavus Kirby, closely associated with the American Olympic Committee and the Amateur Athletic Union. The PSAL tutored boys in track and field activities during the first year, 1903, and subsequently added team sports. Consciously endeavoring to counter the practice of commercial team sports, with their emphasis on star athletes, the PSAL focused boys' efforts and concentration on team achievement. The PSAL also pitched its work to the "mass" of boys, eschewing the selectivity of school athletics teams that cultivated the talents of the gifted few.[4]

The success of boys' PSAL work prompted consideration of a "girls' branch," which was first broached as an "auxiliary" to boys' work. Jessie Bancroft, a founder of the Girls' Branch, remembered the constitution of the new organization as a contested issue:

> It later came to the organization of a women's auxiliary and the development of athletics for girls . . . At that period in history the term "women's auxiliary" always meant a group to raise money for things the men were doing, and this was the first proposition for the work of the Girls' Branch. But those of us who were on the Girls' Board of Directors at that time did not see it that way. I remember Dr. Gulick discussing the question with me, and that his own sympathies were for the development of the girls' activities. And such, from the start, was the work of this organization.[5]

Bancroft correctly historicized the "women's auxiliary" idea; this model referenced one nineteenth-century mode for voluntary work, in which men made policy and defined agendas, but accepted women's fund-raising support. Many other nineteenth-century voluntary organizations, particularly later in the century, were generated and driven solely by women's activity. Bancroft makes clear that in 1905 a group of determined women directors took this second path. While the very name "Girls' Branch" coded the new organization as a subset of the male, originary PSAL entity, the enterprise that resulted actually constituted a parallel, rather than a subsidiary, practice for girls. Girls' Branch founders included Grace Dodge and Ellin Speyer, wealthy leaders of New York City reform movements. Dodge had supported the founding of the Kitchen Garden Association and subsequent stages of the institutional emergence of Teachers College. She also launched the city's working girls' club movement. Speyer's husband was a prominent supporter of University Settlement, and the couple's contributions made possible the Speyer School, which was connected with Teachers College. Founder Louisa Wingate was the wife of PSAL director George Wingate. With the financial means and organizational momentum supplied by such activist women, the Girls' Branch expanded rapidly as a voluntary organization. The sheer numbers that participated in its dancing made it an enterprise to be reckoned with on the municipal level and also in recreation and physical training circles. From their inauguration in 1908, park fetes grew in size to include, by 1916, more than 50,000 schoolgirls, drawn from all the boroughs in New York City. Elementary, and later high school, girls learned the dances in after-school folk dance clubs organized by the Girls' Branch. Twenty to forty girls formed a club, with one or two clubs functioning at a school. For six months each year, club members met on rooftop playgrounds or in gymnasiums at their schools, playing games and learning dances. Classroom teachers provided the instruction; they in turn had studied how to teach folk dances in classes organized by Elizabeth Burchenal. At first teachers and children from nine schools joined in; by 1916 more than 273 schools took part in the enterprise. Regular newspaper coverage, both stories and photographs, extended public awareness of the park fetes and of the yearly work which they culminated.[6]

How can we account for the Girls' Branch focus on the "education of the girl child," and for the dedication of citywide resources and attention to the young and the female? The child-centered focus of PSAL work—for boys as for girls—sprang from sources that informed contemporary settlement house work as well: the demographic pressures exerted by massive immigration flows into Progressive-era America; and the unsettling, gradual shift from rural to urban residence patterns. In addition, attention paid to boys and girls *as children* culminated a century-long demographic transition in the United States. Between 1800 and 1900 the average number of children born to white women declined from 7.04 to 3.56 nationwide. The reduction was most visible among the middle class and among people who lived in towns and cities, and it constituted a radical change in family size.[7] The decline was accompanied by new ideological emphasis placed on nurturant parenting, an approach which contrasted with eighteenth-century models of more distant, patriarchal parenting. Put simply, fewer children meant proportionally greater resources available for each child within family economies. This normative focus gained an official profile with the 1912 founding of the federal Children's Bureau. In New York City, ideals of child-centered parenting combined with keenly felt population pressures to focus educational, civic, and reform attention on children as a group.

While aimed at children, however, the PSAL developed gender-specific athletics practices for boys and girls. Chief among the distinctions drawn was the allocation of folk dancing to girls' work *as girls' work* and the muting of competition in the conduct of girls' activities. These differences indicate that additional factors drove Girls' Branch "education of the *girl* child" and the focus on dancing. The founding of the Girls' Branch, as narrated by Jessie Bancroft, and its focus on girls among children both indexed and responded to the regnant "separate spheres" ideology of gender roles and the challenges it faced in the first several decades of the twentieth century. By insisting that girls be provided with a separate institutional vehicle for athletics work, Girls' Branch founders confirmed the nineteenth-century value given to sex-segregated congress and domains of activity.[8]

Whatever the certainty that such gender role formulations provided in economically precarious times—and the nineteenth century had been tumultuous in this regard—it must be recognized that performance of these prescriptive gender roles was realizable in distinctly class terms. In New York City, working-class women daily confronted the public world of work when they labored as garment workers, artificial flower makers, milliners, or domestic laborers. Clerical work, which grew by leaps and bounds in the United States from 1880 to 1920, saw an increase of nearly one million female workers between 1910 and 1920.[9] Public and private realms of activity were not neatly separated for these people; prescription clashed with actual practice at a fundamental level.

Protests against separate spheres ideology and resistance to the restrictions it imposed on women's activities proceeded from various groups and class positions during the Progressive era. In New York City, women workers joined the International Ladies Garment Workers Union and also participated in the founding of the Women's Trade Union League, a cross-class coalition supporting labor activism by and for women's gains. Women workers participated vigorously in that city's shirtwaist and cloak maker strikes in 1909 and 1910. State and national campaigns to win female suffrage shifted or adopted new strategies. Alice Paul's Congressional Union (later the Women's Party) forsook state-by-state quests for women's voting rights and labored to secure a federal constitutional amendment. In New York, open-air meetings, marches through Manhattan streets, and even a suffrage pageant in 1914 brought agitation for women's voting rights to public attention. Women were generally succeeding in gaining access to higher education but still struggling for access to professional training and for entry into professional institutions — university posts for female academics and hospital posts for female doctors and surgeons, for example. Through a variety of women-organized reform efforts, middle-class women claimed public sphere roles as extensions of the nurturing roles assigned them by separate spheres ideology.

Such instances of resistance to and recasting of separate spheres ideology demonstrate that the "woman question" was vividly and concretely at issue, in New York City as in the nation. Girls' Branch focus on the girl child partook of this concern. By bringing together schoolgirls in the public spaces of New York City parks, park fetes breached the public-private divide seen in strictly geographical terms. They also destabilized contemporary views of female public spectacularization, which typically labeled as promiscuous the public or commercial bodily display by female orators, suffrage advocates, theatrical performers, and of course sex workers. Park fetes thus mingled and focused contending and changing perceptions about the taxonomy of activities appropriate to females in the Progressive era. They addressed the demarking of realms appropriate to female agency and self-making as well. Park fetes provided annual workings out of the struggle with and about female gender role prescriptions as they intersected contemporary concerns about childhood, immigration and ethnicity, and urban industrial living.[10]

THE FOCUS ON DANCING

Park fete folk dancing provided a physical discourse through which to argue gender and claim public space. But why dancing? Why this activity and not some other? The answers to this are several and proceed, I believe, from a Progressive-era understanding, both intuitively felt and explicit, of the significance of the body in establishing identity. Certainly the physical body commanded increased scrutiny and recognition in the late nineteenth century—the time when a discourse of nature, or evolutionary development, achieved prominence (see chapter 1). To take just one especially relevant example, writer Edward Clarke applied evolutionary logic to issues of gender. Accepting the idea that biology determined destiny, Clarke argued in his enormously influential *Sex in Education* (1873) that higher education put women's health and reproductive potential at risk and thus should not be countenanced.[11] It was on the basis of such evolutionary discourse, along with wartime experiences, that physical training—the cultivation of the human body—gained centrality as a focus of social concern and as an issue of public education. Various systems of physical training had been implemented in public schools since the Civil War, in part as a response to the physical condition of soldiers recruited in that conflict. Growing demand for physical training teachers in the 1880s and 1890s led to the founding of numerous normal schools for physical education. The Sargent Normal School in Boston and the International YMCA Training College, located in Springfield, Massachusetts, were leading institutions of this kind. And the ambitious American Association for the Advancement of Physical Education was formed in 1885 both to theorize the cultivation of the human body and to establish physical education as a professional domain.[12]

As journals and conference reports from the period reveal, the new profession of physical education took as one of its chief responsibilities the analysis of physical training systems suitable for use in public schools. The issue was substantive, for competing systems hailed from a number of different nations and operated on quite different principles. The physical plants available to the public schools had to be taken into consideration as well. Practical implementation of any physical training system met large obstacles in most grade schools. It was common for classroom teachers, rather than trained specialists, to give physical training instruction in the same rooms used to teach academic subjects, and children performed the exercises in the space between desks, in the aisles, or sometimes in the school hallways. In many cases, ten minutes of each hour were given to such instruction, and the focus was on correction of postural defects caused by long hours sitting at school desks. The advent of organized athletics at the end of the nineteenth century, and their rapid commodification in professional sports posed a related problem for evaluation by physical training professionals: could, and should, team sports like football and basketball be added to curricula? In addition, physical training professionals would number significantly among the membership of the PAA (founded in 1906), alongside settlement workers, urban reform activists, and rural play advocates.[13]

A kind of body consciousness thus suffused various turn-of-the-century efforts: the attempt to reconcile religious beliefs and economic thought with evolutionary theory; the crusading work of physical training innovators who demonstrated nationalist concern in weighing foreign systems against new American ones; and the organizational endeavors of recreation reformers. The psychological theories propounded by G. Stanley Hall supplied specific impetus for channeling such body consciousness toward dance as an educational and recreational vehicle in Girls' Branch work. An eminent psychologist and president of Clark University, Hall founded and led the "child study" movement in America. From the early 1890s until about 1910, child study theory and practice attracted enormous popular attention and support, although research psychologists distanced themselves from and finally condemned the movement. Members of state and local teachers associations supplied the backbone of the movement, and physical training professionals numbered among the supporters from the first. Hall tried to extend evolutionary theory to psychic matters and linked cultivation of the body with development of the mind. Speculating that ontogeny recapitulated phylogeny, he declared that individuals' neuro-muscular development recapitulated "race history," or the evolutionary stages of development experienced by race members. Within this framework, males and females recapitulated the physical and psychical differentiation of the sexes and the corresponding divergence of social functions and roles that flowed from these sex differences.[14]

Hall's 1905 treatise *Adolescence* pursued these themes in two-volume detail, recommending revisions and changes in school curricula of the day. These recommendations embraced the importance of exercise to child development. Hall wrote that motor areas were closely "related and largely identical with the psychic," and "muscle culture develops brain-centers as nothing else yet demonstrably does." It followed that to train the muscles was to train the mind; "for the young, motor education is cardinal." Hall identified play as the ideal form of exercise, one in which every movement was "instinct with heredity." When playing, children rehearsed "the activities of our ancestors, back we know not how far, and repeat[ed] their life work in summative and adumbrated ways." Children's play retraced the oldest elements of muscle history first, and as they matured, they enacted progressively more recent history. Hall maintained that the most instinctive, untaught, and nonimitative activities were the most spontaneous and exact expressions of children's motor needs. Hall identified dancing as "one of the best expressions of pure play" and elaborated a number of examples of its use in historical societies. He pinpointed rhythm as a key characteristic of dancing and asserted that rhythmic movement was the source, in some pre-civilized time, of all work, play, and art.[15]

Hall's theories were important because Luther Halsey Gulick drew heavily upon them in numerous articles, speeches, and books that articulated and championed Girls' Branch work. When he invoked Hall's theories, Gulick not only rationalized folk dancing as Girls' Branch work but claimed for it the additional imprimatur of science. The two men knew each other personally as well as professionally, and Hall cited Gulick's writings in Adolescence. Gulick, in turn, echoed Hall's formulation of recapitulation theory and his commendation of dancing. In a 1907 World's Work article, Gulick wrote with Harry Smith of individual development repeating the history of the development of the race, and argued that the child's emotional life logically seeks embodiment in forms that are normal and instinctive to uncivilized people. Dancing, he asserted in Hallian vein, was the most primitive of all the arts and expressed the body's desire for the "rhythmic principle" fundamental to life. A London speech before the 1907 Second International Congress on School Hygiene made clear the psychological dimensions of folk dancing as recapitulation. Here Gulick claimed that folk dance movements formed "an epitome of many of the neuromuscular coordinations which have been necessary to the life of the race. . . . The movements . . . follow long-inherited tendencies toward neuromuscular coordinations that arose under the selective influence of survival."[16]

At the same time, Girls' Branch folk dancing supplied real-world application of Hall's ideas. Throughout the period of his involvement with the child study movement, Hall enjoyed no connection with a laboratory school in which to implement child study findings. In this he lacked a tool available at the University of Chicago to John Dewey, theorist of a social emphasis in education. Dewey's ideas would gain even greater currency as the child study movement receded in popularity. In Adolescence, the fruit of ten years' labor, Hall only minimally specified the kinds of dancing which fit the neuromuscular bill. In that work he described early-twentieth-century social dancing as derelict and called for a work of "rescue and revival" to provide youth with "right dancing," the "completest language of the emotions" and an activity that could "cadence the soul." Six years later in 1911, Hall heaped praise on folk and national dancing in Educational Problems. Girls' Branch work thus demonstrated and promoted Hall's claims for folk dancing's efficacy in physical training.[17]

ELIZABETH BURCHENAL

Elizabeth Burchenal supplied the demand for dancing that Hall theorized and that Gulick seized and promoted. Burchenal brought dance expertise to Girls' Branch work along with vanguard preparation in physical training methods and subjects. After graduating from Earlham College in 1896 with a literature major, Burchenal enrolled in Dudley Sargent's Normal School of Physical Training. Sargent's normal pedagogy was inclusive and exposed Burchenal to a wide range of offerings in the rapidly changing field. These would have included light gymnastics and fancy steps, German as well as Swedish Ling gymnastics, Melvin Ballou Gilbert's "aesthetic dancing," Indian club work, marching, recreational games, and track and field athletics. Theory courses treated anatomy, physiology, hygiene, physics, and child study. By the time she graduated from the two-year program in 1898, Burchenal had also earned a diploma from the Gilbert Summer Normal School. From 1898 to 1903 she found employment in "commercial" physical training jobs: as gymnasium instructor at a children's hospital and at a public gym, and as director of a women's athletic club. During summer 1903 she worked as an instructor at Sargent's Harvard Summer School of Physical Education, since 1887 a prime summer institute for certifying physical training teachers.[18]

Burchenal relocated to New York City and took a teaching position in 1902 with the Horace Mann Schools, the practice schools associated with Teachers College. She remained there through 1905, moving in the orbit of Progressive-education luminaries such as Edward Thorndike, an establisher of educational psychology as a field, and Patty Smith Hill, who challenged the dominance of Froebellian curriculum in kindergarten pedagogy. At Teachers College, Thomas Denison Wood initiated his brand of "natural gymnastics"—which stressed running, jumping, wrestling, and tumbling—in opposition to formal gymnastics work. Wood was as important an innovator in physical training as Hall and John Dewey were in general education theory. John Dewey joined the Columbia University faculty in 1905 and, by means of that institution's curricular arrangements, taught advanced students at Teachers College. Both Thorndike and Hill were involved, to differing degrees, in the child study movement spearheaded by G. Stanley Hall. The movement started to decline in authority and popular reception after 1904, about the time Dewey arrived at Columbia and his views on educational psychology began to gain ascendance. During her three-year tenure teaching at the Horace Mann Schools,

Burchenal would have encountered Hallian psychology even before she applied it in public school work with Luther Halsey Gulick.[19]

That Burchenal taught folk dancing in the Horace Mann curriculum is possible; after relocating to New York City, she began to make trips abroad to collect folk dance. It must be stipulated that Burchenal, like Gulick, used the term "folk dancing" broadly to mean European and North American traditional dances still being performed live in the first two decades of the twentieth century. This notion of folk dancing was fairly elastic; Burchenal at times used it to embrace American contra dances, English country dances, and morris dances "rediscovered" by Cecil Sharp. While perhaps less precise than theorists in the 1990s might wish, the term clearly excluded ballroom or social dances like the turkey trot, new concert dance and "interpretative dance" forms, and "oriental dance"—probably as it was adapted for concert dance presentation. During her childhood in Indiana, Burchenal was introduced to folk dance by her "musical family." Her mother, Mary Day Burchenal, studied at the Peabody Institute in Baltimore, noted for its music academy; her uncle, Willard Gibson Day, Peabody's first graduate, worked as music critic of *The Baltimore American*. During summers, mother and daughter rode horseback in the Virginia mountains, stopping at cabins to visit with the women and "incidentally and surreptitiously to pick up what they could of musical interest." Her father, Charles H. Burchenal, a Republican and former Whig, served one term as District Attorney for the Sixth Common Pleas District of Indiana. Thereafter, he declined pubic office and "gratif[ied] his taste for literature, art and social life." The Burchenal family welcomed numerous visitors from European colleges, dancing with them and singing "songs from the old country." Elizabeth learned to dance at an early age.[20]

Burchenal's adult interest in folk dance revived upon her arrival in New York City and contact there with immigrant people. No account explains satisfactorily how this occurred. Various writers credit her conveyance by friends to a party attended primarily by "baggy men and shawled women only recently come from the other side"; or Burchenal's encounter with "two Russian dancers, sisters, who gave some performances in New York City"; or even Burchenal's "hunt[ing] up the leaders" of immigrant groups in New York and inviting them to teach steps to her Teachers College classes. As early as 1904 she traveled to England where, newspaper accounts assert, on visits to Bampton and Bidford she witnessed morris dancing, which Cecil Sharp had only recently begun to record and publicize. (The actual date may well have been as much as four years later; a

1908 letter from Burchenal to Sharp requested his aid in contacting traditional village dancers.) She traveled frequently to Europe, possibly even
annually from 1906 to 1913, walking and living in rural communities in
Spain, France, Germany, Denmark, Sweden, and Ireland. Her practice
was to not identify herself as American, to learn dances as much as possible
by watching townspeople perform them, and to ingratiate herself with a
community several weeks prior to a festival event being held there, so that
she might be included in the dancing. Her first book, the 1909 *Folk Dances
and Singing Games*, issued from such research, an early mode of what
anthropology terms participant observation methodology.[21]

Burchenal's early field research and Horace Mann Schools teaching
was coeval with the Columbia University summer school courses she
taught in 1904 and 1905. Summer institutes were key nodes for certifying
and distributing new methods and subject matters to professional physical
educators wishing to stay current. Like Sargent's and later Hinman's summer institute work, Burchenal's summer Columbia teaching placed her in
the thick of physical training innovation. The courses were titled "Special
Gymnastics and Swimming" and in 1904 offered "opportunities for teachers who desire special instruction in particular lines of practical work, such
as: Esthetic dancing, Indian clubs, class fencing, swimming, etc." The
same course in 1905 offered "Special gymnastics, dancing, fencing, boxing, and swimming," again with an emphasis on teacher training. Both
times, Burchenal worked as one of two or more teachers assigned to the
course, and her Sargent and Gilbert normal school training equipped her
to give instruction in esthetic dancing, specified for 1904. In 1905, however, the dancing work was not labeled "esthetic," and Burchenal's sister
Emma Howells Burchenal, Elizabeth's "musical half" in later folk dance
labors, worked as an "assistant in physical education" for that session.
These two factors strongly suggest that Elizabeth may have introduced folk
dancing in the summer school curriculum. Lending even greater weight to
this proposition is Gulick's recruitment of Burchenal to teach folk dancing
to New York City schoolchildren on the basis of his familiarity with her
Teachers College work. Burchenal told Gulick's biographer, Ethel Dorgan, that he frequently observed her classes at Teachers College and the
Horace Mann Schools. Jessie H. Bancroft, a member of Gulick's public
school physical training staff from 1903, confirmed that Gulick was familiar with Burchenal's work at Teachers College. Bancroft wrote that Gulick
petitioned Burchenal several times to give up her position there to direct
the newly formulated girls' work with the Public Schools Athletic League.

After Burchenal finally consented, Gulick accompanied her when she delivered her letter of resignation to Teachers College, lest she change her mind.

Gulick's friendship with several Teachers College faculty may have facilitated the acquaintance. Patty Smith Hill, who joined the Teachers College faculty in 1905, was a warmly welcomed visitor in the Gulicks' home, and Thomas Denison Wood had been Gulick's classmate, plus something of a soul mate, at Oberlin College. At the time, Gulick was nationally prominent in the professionalizing discipline of physical training; in 1903 he resigned editorship of the *American Physical Education Review* to assume presidency of the American Physical Education Association, a post he held until 1907. It would have been professionally astute but also quite pleasurable for the gregarious Gulick to visit friends and colleagues at Teachers College to keep abreast of current work.[22]

Gulick and Burchenal thus brought complementary skills to the formulation of Girls' Branch work. Gulick possessed considerable experience in developing and implementing physical training systems, plus theoretical familiarity with Hall's work. He backed the demands of female leaders to create the Girls' Branch as a woman-run organization, and he gave steady, long-term support to folk dancing as the featured activity. Gulick's promotion continued unabated even after 1907, when he left the Public Schools Athletic League for employment with the Russell Sage Foundation. Burchenal, for her part, brought experience as a teacher, in both commercial and academic settings, of a variety of physical training skills, plus a personally developed expertise in teaching folk dance. In its first year, the Girls' Branch experimented with offerings of gymnastics, folk dancing, and athletics (team games and contests of skill). Based on the participation of about 300 girls in nine schools, Girls' Branch administrators concluded that the girls found folk dancing to be the most interesting of the three activities; that, in a given space, more girls could participate in folk dancing than in the other activities; and that folk dancing, unlike athletics and gymnastics, afforded cooperation with other home and school activities. Gymnastics was quickly eliminated as an offering; folk dancing and athletics remained the core activities for years.[23]

Burchenal served as a master teacher, giving free weekly lessons to public school teachers, who in turn spent at least one hour a week for six months leading girls' athletic clubs organized at their schools. The teachers' classes lasted about twenty weeks; club work at public schools was expected to start by November and to occur within the fall-to-spring academic calendar. From the outset, the Board of Education granted the Girls' Branch permission to use public school facilities after the close of the school day, and the organization scheduled slates for both indoor and outdoor activities. The Girls' Branch in turn provided a salary for Burchenal, as Assistant Secretary and Instructor in folk dancing and athletics, to direct the work. It also bore the costs of running athletics meets, which included the provision of judges to supervise other officials, score cards, and pins and trophies for winning clubs. By 1908, the Board of Education signaled its approval of Girls' Branch activity at an even more fundamental level—it incorporated folk dancing into the physical training syllabus for the city school system. By 1909, the board announced that teachers could receive credit for voluntary work as girls' clubs instructors. In November 1909, the board appointed Burchenal Inspector of Girls' Athletics, and shouldered her salary. With this action the board legally and financially linked itself to the Girls' Branch. In succeeding months the Board of Education continued to formally acknowledge Girls' Branch views as policy standards for city school conduct of girls' physical training.[24]

The conclusions the Girls' Branch drew from its first-year scrutiny of athletics options illuminate ways in which its after-school practice incorporated elements of several Progressive-era drives. The first finding, that girls found folk dancing to be the most interesting of the activities provided, ratified folk dancing as educationally and psychologically sound methodology. Since the 1890s, Herbartian educational theory had taken children's expression of interest to be an index of an activity's suitability. In Hall's voguish psychology, interest confirmed an activity's "racially old" validity. The second finding, that, in a given space, more girls could participate in folk dancing than in the other activities, evidenced Progressive-era concerns with efficiency and productivity. These were matters of absorbing interest for those structuring large-scale industrial or recreational enterprises. The third finding—that folk dancing, unlike athletics and gymnastics, afforded cooperation with other home and school activities—reflects the recognition by Girls' Branch sponsors that after-school folk dancing could bridge the prescriptive realms of public and private spheres for females. It seems clear that such bridging was expected to be conservative, to weigh on the side of preserving the separate spheres status quo. Yet accounts of Girls' Branch work and of the year-end, culminating park fetes reveal that folk dancing provided a flexible practice for struggling with, troubling, and contesting issues of social order and ethnicity, as well as gender.[25]

Worrying Power

How did folk dancing address, trouble, argue, and worry these and other issues of power and the allocation of resources in Progressive-era society? In what ways did technical vocabularies, choreographic forms, or movement qualities embody political concerns or propose alternative arrangements? One of the most palpable problems that the Girls' Branch introduced folk dancing to redress was the failure of urban dwelling conditions and public schools to provide necessary and adequate resources, conditions, and guidance for children's bodily development and healthy play. Factors that put children's health at risk included design of school desks, length of school days, and lack of appropriate spaces for play and for physical training activities.[26] Gulick and the Girls' Branch were not alone in formulating an urban environmental critique: the inadequate and unequal distribution of fundamental resources for safe play—sunlight, air, and square footage—motivated several contemporary regeneration efforts in New York City. The Outdoor Recreation League, a tenement reform movement, and city settlement houses each campaigned in their orbits, and collaborated across domains, to secure more and better-sited parks, improved dwelling places, and additional playgrounds and gyms. As noted earlier, these reform efforts aimed to ameliorate conditions of city living resulting from industrial labor and laissez-faire economic competition. They did not challenge the generating causes.[27]

Gulick's writings specify several particular features of folk dancing that made its movement vocabulary particularly suitable for addressing urban resource and school regimen problems. First and foremost, folk dancing required large-muscle movement. Since the effects of exercise were experienced by the body "in proportion to the number of foot-pounds of energy expended," he wrote, this large-muscle use made folk dancing an extremely efficient means to achieve health. It also produced a big impact on circulation and respiration. Folk dancing not only realized these gains, but also proved capable of accommodating large numbers of children—clustering girls in couples, lines, circles, and other group formations—while requiring relatively small amounts of space.[28]

Gulick thus wed an ideology of efficiency, one that resonated strongly with contemporary applications in mass production technology as well as domestic management, to the privileging of "health" that undergirded demands for and supplies of physical training as a cultural practice. This turn-of-the-century construction of folk dancing confirms the late-twentieth-century theoretical recognition of the body as "the very site of material inscription of the ideological . . . , the ground where socio-political determinations take hold and are real-ized," as Teresa de Lauretis has put it.[29]

What goes understated in the claims made by Gulick for folk dancing is the degree to which such dancing permitted Girls' Branch work to distance itself from European systems of physical training imported in the previous century. A competing system such as Swedish Ling calisthenics, for example, surely offered the muscular, circulatory, and respiratory benefits that Gulick extolled in folk dancing. However, the Swedish system was faulted in American physical training literature for relying on drills directed by an instructor barking commands to keep activity going. It thus introduced a rigidity and authoritarianism at odds with Hallian values of spontaneous and instinctive play. And although Gulick never made the point in print, the conduct of a folk dance, once learned, could remain in the hands and feet of the girls dancing it, with memory of sequence and musical cues from the accompanying score supplying the "directives." The German Jahn system of physical training eluded criticisms of inflexibility, to an extent, because it combined certain amounts of free play with other structured work on specialized apparatuses. The need to acquire apparatuses for each and every school, however, made the system costly to implement.[30]

Testimony by Jessie Bancroft reveals ways in which folk dancing satisfied another methodological criterion that other systems failed to meet:

> the happiness that came to the little children of the East side through the folk dancing. Up to that time their serious, sad, unsmiling faces were noted by all visitors to the schools, who could but feel a great depression from it. This unchildlike seriousness was the aftermath of pogroms and massacres and exile. But after the folk dancing came, the smiles crept over those little faces like sunshine after a cloud, and brought some, at least, of their childhood's rightful heritage of laughter and joyousness.[31]

References to "serious, sad, unsmiling faces," "unchildlike seriousness," and "childhood's rightful heritage of laughter and joyousness" confirm the Girls' Branch subscription to an ideology of play-filled, carefree childhood (an ideology that the PAA would reinforce) and a moral sense that children possessed "rights." Citing "pogroms and massacres and exile" as the source of East Side children's grim miens, Bancroft indirectly acknowledges the immigration and population pressures threatening a widely held social construction of childhood. She reports that folk dancing provides the solution, and she likens it to sunshine. Transformations wrought by folk dancing are spontaneous, like weather changes, she implies; the unpredictabilities of climate comport with the impetuous, unplanned qualities of instinctive play.

In the characteristics it offered as a movement vocabulary—the scale, vigor, and ongoingness of its motions; the possibility it held out for spontaneous, relatively independently sustained execution and enjoyment—folk dancing thus gave bodily presence to ideologies of health, efficiency, and even a certain American nationalism, at the same time that the Girls' Branch was wielding these practices to mediate certain effects of urban living and a burgeoning industrial economy. Girls' Branch folk dancing mingled recuperative strategies with remonstrative gestures. But it stopped short of calling for fundamental change in the generating structures of those effects.[32]

FIGURING SOCIAL ORDER

In other ways, Girls' Branch park fetes asserted the need to rethink Progressive-era modes of social organization, notions of individual personhood, and the laissez-faire principles that underpinned them. At their advent in Revolutionary-era America, principles of laissez-faire economic competition had promised that the general good would be won through the free competition of individual actors in a self-regulating market. Although it was a radical doctrine at that time, by the end of the nineteenth century the conservative implications of laissez-faire economic and political organization had become clear to players operating from a variety of positions. Railroad management, the first to exploit new techniques of bureaucratic organization, also had been among the first to discover the costs of unrestrained competition, turning then to oligopolistic models of deploying capital. On the opposite side of the economic relationship, labor forces during the nineteenth century quickly discovered the disabling effects of an ideology that identified workers as singular units, collective action among whom was legally limited or disallowed as infringement upon individual rights. Farmers during the 1890s supported features of the Populist platforms like community ownership of storage elevators, the subtreasury plan, and inflationary free silver measures because they offered some instruments, collectivities, and leverage to individual producers in negotiating brutally competitive international markets for agricultural products.

In social terms as well, the "free agency " promised by capitalist organization had seemed to augur freedom from traditional limitations on aspiration, opportunity, and position that had characterized earlier models of corporate, hierarchical, reciprocally responsible societies. In the nineteenth century, however, amidst cycles of economic booms and panics, the flourishing of separate spheres ideology, and continuing social struggles over race, it became clear that successful achievement of such free agency was heavily weighted toward white males, even if economic security was unpredictable for most. The costs and benefits of pure competition, the possibilities of "individual agency," and the procedures for effecting right relationships between individuals and collectivities animated political and economic debates as industrial development achieved the mass production stage and the country's population became increasingly urban.

That human bodies bore the brunt of these contesting issues was clear to labor activists, to community workers, and to schoolteachers and administrators in New York City. Gulick saw in the selection and organization of after-school athletics the opportunity to work out through bodily interactions better balanced relationships between individuals and the groups in which they functioned. Support for this view, clearly proceeding from preoccupation with race history, could be found in Hall's *Adolescence*:

> . . . [play's] social function develops solidarity and unison of action between individuals. The dances, feasts, and games of primitive people, wherein they rehearse hunting and war and act and dance out their legends, bring individuals and tribes together.[33]

At the outset, Gulick and the founders of Girls' Branch work rejected free play because strong youths could realistically be expected to take the floor with games and stunts, displacing the weaker and less aggressive children to the edges of the room or playground, where they would engage in more passive play. A few children would reap the full physical benefit intended for the many; only organized play could ensure the equal distribution of benefit. The loss of freedom and individual choice that this decision entailed was more apparent than real, Gulick explained:

> We are only beginning to learn what freedom means. It is not the privilege of doing, irrespective of everybody else, what one wants to do. That would make the tramp the ideally free man. Freedom lies in the recognition and joyful acceptance of relationships. In organized play, where every child is a unit in a larger, mutually responsible, and mutually

responsive whole, all reach a higher and more significant stage of indi-
vidualized freedom than is possible on the unorganized, free-for-all
playground.[34]

The playground stood as a microcosm of society in this formulation; the
physical was clearly connected to the political. And relationships, that stuff
of everyday life in which women were supposed by separate spheres theory
to excel, constituted the kinetic substance of "freedom." By singling out
relationships in this way, Gulick's words made a claim for female agency in
the construction and dynamic functioning of social order. Also operating
in the Girls' Branch institution of folk dancing is the recognition, to which
theorists have come (again) in the 1980s and 1990s, that the "political"
could not be defined solely as "having to do with state power."[35]

The number and distribution of dancers participating in a park fete gave
kinetic and visual shape to Girls' Branch concerns about connections
between individuals and the collective. The dances required groups of
individuals or couples to perform the same steps and gestures simultaneously. Girls' Branch handbooks stipulated that group dances should not
be performed by fewer than ten girls, and that no soloists should be singled
out. To be sure, leaders of lines were required at times, but they emerged
from and dissolved back into the group. With the exception of the basketball throw, the games interspersed among the dances in the course of a park
fete were all team games or relays. Handbook descriptions of park fetes
consistently claimed that, by design, it was impossible to distinguish individual girls among the many. Park fetes thus embodied and facilitated
realization of individual qualities through combined effort in group activity rather than through performance as heightened presentation of particular sensibilities, personalities, or emphasized figures. This position was
reinforced, summarized, and finalized in the traditional closing dance of
the park fete; the *May-pole Dance* was incapable of execution without the
cooperation of individual girls in a single unified process.[36]

The forms created in the course of various folk dances realized in spatial
terms the emphasis Girls' Branch work placed on integration of individuals
and groups. *Reap the Flax* and *May-pole Dance*, described above, create
recognizable patterns as they progress: lines, circles, and serpentines for the
former; concentric circles for the latter. The English morris dance *Lauda-
num Bunches* deploys sets of six girls, each set arrayed in parallel lines of
three dancers, for much of its duration. A sense of the importance of
recurring forms such as these can be gained by reconstructing park fete
dances recorded in Elizabeth Burchenal's publications. A typical dance

description provides a piano transcription of the music and a breakdown of the choreography into several sections. The analysis of each section includes textual descriptions of step units to be performed (slides, hops, stamps, turnings); relationships and physical contact among the girls (hands on shoulders, taking hands, for instance); and characterizations of the spirit and brio that should animate the movements. Occasional photographs interspersed throughout the text frequently select moments in the dance when activity coalesces into geometrical shapes. Most of these photos appear to have been made on occasions other than park fetes, with photos from 1909 and the next several years taken on rooftop play areas or ground-level playgrounds.[37]

Choreographic emphasis on geometric form was intersected by, at times mediated by, the quality of the effort exhibited in the girls' dancing. This intersection must be discerned from a second type of photograph. Newspaper coverage of park fetes regularly featured photographs, typically taken either at close range or from distant vantage points. It is the long-shot photos that seize the *May-pole Dance* in its crystalline moments, girl-bodies etching closely dotted circles, circles bulging into ovals with the curvature of the camera lens. The fixing of moments that close-up shots offer, however, brings the viewer up short. Here clarity departs and flurry abounds. Bodies framed at full length, or sometimes from the waist up only, reveal their smiles, swaying torsos, stretching limb-reach, throat-bared heads. These photos reinscribe the tumult of the field, the horizontal multiplications of efforts, the absence of overarching, vertical panoptic control, the abandon released.[38]

No park fete photograph that I have found captures these two kinds of experiences in a single image; they crash against each other most powerfully in the mind's eye of the reader. Photos from Burchenal's textbooks, however, do show schoolgirls suffused with abandon as they figure the shapes of folk dance choreographies: one's head turns rightward, another's body arches back, for instance, as all *Reap the Flax*. This composite of information about the effort qualities that informed performances of folk dance choreographies indexes, I believe, the extent to which individual variation persisted within the group focus of park fete dancing. Folk dancing didn't press little girls into uniform molds, in other words; it accommodated their individual agencies as they moved into and out of group forms. Embodied here were the very concerns that troubled economic relations, constructions of gender identities, and race relations in the early twentieth century. Park fetes proposed that solutions to the dilemma were inherently dynamic and unstable, possible in local situations but also full of contradictory impulses.

MAKING "AMERICANS"

The prose of Girls' Branch handbooks, the pleasures of the dancing field reproduced for newspaper consumption, and other evidences of folk dance practices privilege the utopian effects claimed for folk dancing. But a gritty side to Girls' Branch practice loomed as well, one which worried issues of assimilating ethnic others into American culture. Grainy photographs and earnest texts signaled appropriation, sorting, even bowdlerizing of foreign dance practices. They press us to ask what linkages folk dancing created between bodily and ethnic identifications and the political ordination or ranking of those ethnicities.

A rare glimpse of folk dancing from the participant's remembered perspective may be gleaned from the recollections of modern dance choreographer-dancer Helen Tamiris. Her autobiographical writings, cited earlier in connection with the Henry Street Playhouse, make fleeting, fond reference to public school folk dancing activities that must have been Girls' Branch work:

> All my spare time, often deliberately cutting a geometry or Latin class, I spent in the gymnasium with my instructor, who too loved dancing and was trying to incorporate it into the formal physical training required by the Board of Education. Both at the [Henry Street] settlement and here, I was now deeply engrossed in Folk Dancing—It was called Character dancing—and was based on steps taken from the peasant dances of various countries.[39]

Tamiris's recollection signals the period perception that Girls' Branch folk dancing brought to the United States the peasant dances of foreign countries. It should be remembered that the Girls' Branch organized in the period shortly following United States acquisition of the Philippines and Guam. Seen from one point of view, Girls' Branch activity constituted another instance of American imperial reach, colonizing or appropriating the indigenous dance materials of other, "peasant" (read inferior) cultures.

In her work as a folk dance collector and teacher, Burchenal certainly aimed to immerse herself in contemporary practices of Western European traditional movement practices. By her own account, she attempted to live among the people in towns and festivals that she visited, learning dances firsthand and performing them with native people whenever possible. She frequently traveled in the company of her sister, whose musical expertise was pressed into service when Burchenal later published collected textual notations of the dance materials she gathered.[40] But in many respects, Girls' Branch stagings of the materials she collected and taught seemed to make only limited reference to the originals. Girls' Branch guidelines strictly enjoined girls in participating clubs from wearing special costumes. Everyday school dress was the rule, with ribbons or perhaps a sash allowed to distinguish the clubs one from another. "Folk" or "ethnic" dress, however, was in no way attempted.[41] Acoustic matters were handled in a similar vein. The music for park fetes was supplied by brass bands and no effort was made to replicate the instrumentation or texture of the "native" accompaniment that served this dance material in its European context. Burchenal's published books of notated dances provide piano reduction scores for each dance; these music scores were certainly used for club work at the school level. By 1916, the Victor Phonograph Company published recordings of her instruction book tunes; the instrumentation was supplied by military and brass bands.[42] Perhaps most significantly, the mixed-gender performance of couple dances was not reproduced in Girls' Branch club work and park fete performances. Girls danced with girls—no heterosexual coupling took place. Linguistic evidence from Burchenal's texts published during her tenure with the Girls' Branch suggests that girls danced *as* girls. The instructions identify dancers by assigning numbers to each girl or to the spatial position each occupied in a group or "set" configuration. Or the directions refer to the two girls who form a couple as "partners." These strategies substituted gender-neutral references for mentions of a "man's" part or "woman's" position, effectively absenting male roles from the conception of Girls' Branch folk dancing. From the lexicon of instructional terms to the execution of the choreography, the heterosexual gendering of these dances and their European models were downplayed in park fete realizations. These evidences confirm that the Girls' Branch clearly chose to adopt a revisionist practice of costume, music, and gendered performance in the years of Burchenal's association with it.

To be sure, the Girls' Branch utilized this revisionist practice—this bowdlerization—to achieve specific social and political goals. Reliance on everyday dress rather than "ethnic" costume sought to reinforce the sense of community and common purpose among the girls. It took into account as well the economic circumstances of working-class families that might not permit the annual purchase of a special dress for intraschool meets or park fetes. The decision not to replicate specific instrumentations for folk dances was probably made for economic reasons, while the absenting of male performers and erasure of male roles in the conception of folk dances indexes the conscious effort to perform gender and to gender dance performance as female.

The promoters' goals aside, did Girls' Branch folk dancing strike immigrant people as bowdlerized? Correlation of schools participating in Girls' Branch folk dancing with their geographic location on Manhattan Island shows, for example, that a good two-thirds of the schools involved from 1909 through 1913 were located on New York's Lower East Side, a locus for working-class, immigrant people who labored in several different sweated trades at the turn of the century.[43] In these neighborhoods, first-generation adults, if not their American-born children, arguably retained acquaintance with European dance practices. According to Luther Gulick, spectators attending a 1908 Girls' Branch demonstration "shared in the fun, nodding delighted heads and tapping responsive feet to the familiar rhythms, and rapturous comments in nearly every language of Europe mingled with the frequent applause."[44] Whatever had been expurgated, something of a familiar practice remained recognizable to immigrant parents of Girls' Branch participants. Put another way, parents made a meaning for the dancing they viewed that conceivably differed from the Girls' Branch meaning: the tenor of Gulick's comments suggests that parents grasped the Old World provenance of the dancing and assigned value to it. But this was Gulick's view; to find a first- or second-generation immigrant voice, we circle back to Tamiris's recollections. It can be argued that the interpretive community that viewed park fetes was itself multiple and heterogeneous; Girls' Branch renderings of European dance materials could at one and the same time reference, even sample, an "authentic" original and construct a new practice. As was the case with Chicago Commons May Festivals, Girls' Branch park fetes can be viewed as proffering performative experiences of ethnic identity that held in tension European movement sources and American pressures exerted upon them.

The revisionist features of Girls' Branch practice might also be seen as homogenizing or Americanizing the European dances taken as source material. At one level, the lack of variation in costume and instrumentation would tend to make the dances look and sound more alike, leaving difference to be discerned primarily at the rhythmic and kinetic levels. Here, indeed, one form of "homogenization" can be seen at work. But to argue this point alone—that distinctive features were blurred and that European dances were dissolved into American dance as a means of managing or controlling the influx of immigrant peoples—neglects the contemporary perception in many quarters that the United States *lacked* tradition, lacked a heritage of dance and other cultural forms with which Europe was replete. America was young, as nations go, and had acquired a reputation for emphasizing material acquisition. Settlement workers, who were daily brought into contact with the cultural practices of their immigrant neighbors, decried the situation. The pageantry movement responded to a felt lack of historic national identity by producing at the regional level community-based re-enactments of historical events. The Arts and Crafts movement and the museum movement responded in their different ways to the search for and constitution of an artistic and historical heritage.[45] Gulick himself hopefully proclaimed the potential for folk dancing to give the country "a national life far richer, deeper, and more beautiful than one where the main emphasis in education was upon bare intellectual training for the purposes of 'practical success.'"[46] Thus, Girls' Branch folk dancing can be seen as constructing an American sense of tradition through the experiencing of dance materials unique to the floods of immigrants making new lives in America in the early twentieth century. Rather than simply assimilating European materials to an American tradition or dancing urtext, Girls' Branch folk dancing may be seen as making an urtext—the making of Americans, as Gertrude Stein might have put it.

There is no small irony in an approach that would construct the "American" heritage from materials and practices borne by and embodied in the outsiders, the immigrants, the newcomers to the country. The contemporary case of England, another country scrutinizing its heritage and seeking a distinctive national identity, supplies useful perspective on the American endeavor. England experienced its revivals of traditional music and traditional dance at the turn of the century, but for different reasons, and it turned to "indigenous" British materials such as sword, morris, and country dancing.[47] It is startling and important to understand in this light that the American privileging of European folk dancing denied and left unrecognized the presence and cultural practices of African Americans, long resident in the land. It left unremarked as well the more recent flows of Asian immigrants to the West Coast. Further, the bulk of the folk dances presented in park fetes were drawn from northern and western Europe—not from southern and eastern Europe, the countries of origin for the so-called "new immigration" of the Progressive era.[48] At the same time that folk dancing constituted an American tradition through dancing, it sorted and ranked the ethnic heritages that comprised the newfound sense of history. Folk dancing confirmed the political priority assigned to people and practices of Anglo-Saxon derivation, granting only occasional place, and thus status, to dances from Italy, Bohemia, or Russia. In failing to acknowledge black and Asian peoples and practices as folk sources for the work of cultural construction, Girls' Branch dancing reinforced the contemporary social and political erasure of these people.

TROUBLING GENDER

Park fetes also turned the disciplinary powers of folk dancing to the work of worrying and constructing Progressive-era gender roles. Throughout the Progressive era, women laid claim to a variety of activities in the supposedly male public sphere, thereby contesting the boundaries of gender roles assigned by separate spheres ideology. Girls' Branch park fetes participated in this laying claim to public space, but in a carefully delimited way: fetes were structured to assert female presence without dissolving into male modalities. Thus, as the culminating event of a year's work, park fetes were structured as celebrations rather than competitions. This was in decided contrast with boys' work, which featured competitive athletic meets as early as 1903. To be sure, the Girls' Branch did sanction limited competition in the form of intraschool folk dance and athletic meets. But it never permitted competition *between* schools. Further, the criteria used for judging in-school meets similarly constrained the nature of the competition that was permitted and placed emphasis on communal responsibility. Specifically, "memory" and "form" remained the two stable criteria through time. "Skill," a criterion articulated in 1908, had been dropped by 1914. Even the conditions for participating in PSAL activities contributed to a construction of public sphere dancing that carefully differentiated female and male behavior. Eligibility requirements stressed high grades in effort, deportment, and proficiency for boys' and girls' work alike in 1909–10, the year of the third annual fete. The Girls' Branch revised the requirements the following year, however, deciding that eligibility would be entirely at the discretion of school principals. Boys' participation continued to be predicated on their competitive standing in the categories of behavior and academic accomplishment. This validation of boys' competition was confirmed by the athletic work itself, which promoted fierce interschool competition between clubs.[49] Girls' participation hinged instead on a principal's subjective evaluation of their worthiness, further reinforcing the cooperative, conciliatory group spirit promoted by the competition-minimizing framework erected for folk dancing.

Park fetes thus claimed a place for women in the public sphere, relinquishing the separateness of the domestic sphere but not the distinctive qualities assigned females by separate spheres ideology nor the practice of same-sex affiliation. Moving beyond the confines of schools and their physical plants, fetes brought girls into the vernal spaces of urban parks carved out of—and in opposition to—the surrounding commercial and industrial city. Here dancing girls held in tension the competing demands of individual and group agency in a laissez-faire society. As had a number of Progressive-era reform efforts, park fetes capitalized on women's presumed difference to direct attention to social and political problems. In addition, the pastoral settings reinforced connections between generativity in the natural world and women's reproductive roles in the social world. Folk dancing, then, was deeply involved in both contesting and elaborating a taxonomy of female-appropriate activities at a time of climax, and impending crisis, for gender roles fashioned by separate spheres ideology.

Girls' Branch work also exerted pressure on this taxonomy by making canny use of structural means. Park fete organizers fully appreciated the allure of public spectacles and they were equally sensitive to the commercialization that characterized contemporary professional sporting events. Thus they prepared park fetes carefully, trying to counter the commodification that attached to other forms of public female dancing such as burlesque performance and Broadway dancing.[50] They sought to resist commodification and commercialization by controlling the content of dances—no ballroom or "spectacular" dances for school girls—and by scheduling fetes during afternoon hours, which were working hours for most of the public. They neither issued nor sold tickets to the events. In these efforts they proved fairly successful—contemporary photographs suggest that on-site viewers were relatively few, and that no single viewing position could take in the totality of the event.[51]

In addition, the very organization of the Girls' Branch as a teaching and producing enterprise offered an enlarged framework and set of functions susceptible to women's agency and self-making. At the moment of its founding, the female organizers of the Girls' Branch resisted efforts to make it a ladies auxiliary, on the early-nineteenth-century model, for the male-focused Public Schools Athletic League. They aligned themselves instead with models for postbellum voluntary organizations that pursued female-articulated goals while spending woman-raised monies. The Girls' Branch consistently obtained the cooperation of New York City's Park, Education, and Baths Departments in conducting the fetes, combining private with municipal resources to provide a public service to city schoolchildren.[52] By selecting Burchenal to develop the repertoire of dances and methods for transmitting it, this woman-centered structure also positioned Burchenal to constitute a professional identity as a folk dance collector and teacher. In operating annual folk dancing programs and planning year-end park fetes, the Girls' Branch enterprise staked out public sphere territory as a bureaucracy relying in large part on the guidance of a folk dance expert. Bureaucratization and concession to specialists, characteristic of business management strategies as well as new electoral politics in the Progressive era, provided the structural means with which Girls' Branch patrons and producers constituted themselves as a public instrumentality, a force for social and cultural action.

Contesting and constituting a taxonomy of women's public sphere activities in this variety of ways, Girls' Branch work gendered folk dancing as female and it generated an all-female corps of folk dancing producers. Not only did females embody contending Progressive-era political and gender ideals as performers of folk dances, but women also imagined, formulated, and constructed folk dance practice as teachers and administrators. This empowered female instructors under Burchenal's direction to gain and claim expertise as folk dance educators, thereby making inroads into the male-preponderant ranks of athletics and dance teachers. Like Burchenal, numerous women writers found publishers for folk dance, singing game, and rhythmic play instruction books gauged to children's needs. This marked expansion of the primarily male-authored nineteenth-century dance manual market.[53] Like the gendering of folk dance performance as female, the mobilizing of women as folk dance producers promoted reconsiderations of the body-woman-dance linkage. As configured through Girls' Branch work, this linkage constituted a positive good for women and dance in the Progressive era because folk dancing had successfully asserted a social instrumentality for raising and worrying social and political concerns.

SITUATING DANCING

Girls' Branch work acted to situate folk dancing in a rapidly shifting field of dance practices. Girls' Branch after-school classes and yearly park fetes—together with the rationale for folk dancing that Gulick penned in many articles—constructed a definition for dancing as a cultural practice that was distinct from commercial dance hall, ballroom, and theatre dance of the day. Comprised of several strands of signification, this dancing was populist, scientific, universalist, and nostalgic.

Folk dancing's populism inhered in its accessibility, its availability to nearly every moving body. According to Gulick and Hall, the body as aesthetic material was within range of "almost everyone"; the rhythmic instinct fundamental to play was common to all people and present without question in dancing. Dance was the art activity most capable of execution by the great number of "normal" people, and it met the needs of schoolchildren, immigrants interacting with native-born Americans, and even society as a whole in its search for aesthetic expression. Dancing thus constituted a perfect, and nearly perfectly available, form of art expression. This position resonated clearly with the Ruskinian notion of "every person an artist," and Gulick himself made the connection to Ruskin's theories. After-school clubs and park fete dancing put this populism into practice. Mobilizing dancing as the prerogative of the many, the Girls' Branch consciously distinguished its practice from concert dance presentations being pioneered by contemporary American performers like Isadora Duncan, Loie Fuller, and Ruth St. Denis, each of whom cast her career in the "genius" mold. The inclusive Girls' Branch stance was consistent with both the contemporary critique of specialization in industrial economy and the changing conception of "culture" at the end of the nineteenth century. Raymond Williams, in *Culture & Society*, limned the shift from culture identified as a special set of practices and body of knowledge that offers a "court of appeal," to culture conceived as a whole way of life. The dancing that the Girls' Branch mobilized acknowledged not only the capability of schoolchildren to contribute to the cultural life of the nation but also the necessity that they do so.[54]

Folk dancing wore the mantle of "science" in the sense that its theoretical rationale, articulated and voiced by Gulick, applied the psychological theory of neuromuscular recapitulation. By 1910, new methods started to supersede the child study movement. Education theory turned toward consideration of children's social engagement as part of the learning process, looking to John Dewey as an important leader. Hall himself went on to become a supporter of Sigmund Freud's psychology, bringing the great man to Clark University in 1911 for his first American appearance. Nevertheless, in its heyday, recapitulation theory and the child study movement supplied Gulick and Girls' Branch work with what may be called leading-edge support for folk dancing; as a social practice it enjoyed the imprimatur of science.[55]

Though folk dancing was populist and forward-looking, its theorized heritage in "racially old" activities also rendered it a universalist and in some ways nostalgic social practice. By linking folk dancing to activities characteristic of "primitive" peoples, Gulick—and Hall before him—connected dancing to the naive, preindustrial stages of human civilization. The joy and spontaneity it produced resulted from neuromuscular heritages thought to be universally present in human beings. It is easy to understand the attractiveness of such theorizing in an era of unprecedented immigration flows. The notion of a universal kinship derived from the physical or instinctual likeness of humans offered hope for the integration of newcomers into American society. Gulick thought he saw this kinship performing just such harmonizing offices when he witnessed the 1908 fete in Central Park, with its variety of folk dances from different European countries. Indeed, the Girls' Branch regulations expressly favored "distinctive national and folk-dances of traditional origin" and deprecated invented dances, which they felt to "weaken" the value obtained from a dance.

At the same time, folk dancing helped salve a contemporary nostalgia for eras past. Gulick consistently lauded folk dances as having "a significance rooted in the history, customs, traditions, and even religion of the people," and he decried the lost centrality of such dances in a people's social life. Gulick shared with others of his day a longing for past forms and practices of social communion. He should not be thought antimodern, however, in the sense that T. J. Jackson Lears has attributed to Henry Adams and proponents of the Arts and Crafts movement. Gulick longed not so much to turn back the clock as to make the past vitally instant in the present. He wished to infuse forward-moving American society with the social spirit inherent in earlier modes. This social spirit valorized mutuality, cooperation of individuals within social wholes, and responsiveness of the whole to the parts. It is not difficult to see how such nostalgia complemented Progressive-era reformist drives for municipal ownership of utilities, institution of city manager forms of administration, and creation of referendum and recall mechanisms. In its kinetic forms and in its promotion by Gulick, Girls' Branch work presented folk dancing as a participatory cultural practice which reached widely through American class levels as well as through human history—through space and time.[56]

Progressive-era folk dancing indexed the salience of the body as a site for inscribing relations of power, and the potency of dance practices for troubling and negotiating meanings. Girls' Branch folk dancing prospered, I believe, because it held in tension several oppositions in American culture. It offered an instrumentality for working through tensions about the nature of subjectivity—including questions about whether to characterize social identification as independent, individual agency or as group membership and action. It supplied a means for addressing concerns about national identity—for questioning whether people should look to unmarked "American" or to richly marked "European" materials as the sources for identity as a country. And it provided a mode for performing gender—for worrying the possibilities for and limitations of autonomy in a gender role for women that disavowed self-assertion and competition.

The positive valence it accorded the woman-body-dance linkage would prove temporary and volatile. During the Progressive era, the constitution and gendering of folk dance as a bodily discourse simultaneously disciplined female bodies to a status of subordinate difference and garnered increased social effectivity for dancing bodies on the basis of that difference. The privileging of women's difference that separate spheres ideology spawned would decline in the 1920s, however, and with it the gender-specific rationale for women's intervention and claim to instrumentality in public social and political domains. Tamiris and her peers in the new genre of modern dance—Doris Humphrey, Martha Graham, Sophie Maslow, and Hanya Holm, along with others—would have to negotiate new meanings for female-gendered dance practices in their time. Seen from the 1990s, the functionalization of dance for establishing Americans' sense of a national heritage has proven largely unique to the Progressive era. Nevertheless, early-twentieth-century gendering of dance performance and instruction as a female practice, in which Girls' Branch activity played a significant part, has had lasting effects.

Conclusion

The movement practices scrutinized in these pages have illuminated dance as an instrumentality for cultural intervention. In Progressive-era America, new dance practices provided substantive vehicles for social engagement, particularly for attempts to manage massive flows of immigrant people. Dance innovation also afforded dynamic grounds for interchange and jockeying among class groups. Riddling these lines of engagement, dance provided a medium for negotiating matters of gender.

Early in this century, middle-class Americans articulated new kinds of dance practices in order to pursue several different cultural aims. On the East Coast and in the Midwest, settlement workers like those at Hull-House, Henry Street, Chicago Commons, and South End House dived into neighborhood residence and volunteer social welfare work to acknowledge the swelling demographic presence of immigrant Europeans. They strove to assist their new "neighbors" in functionally assimilating—learning basic language and conduct skills necessary to gain jobs—but also in gaining knowledge of American culture and political heritage, to further their participation in democratic living. At settlements and through Girls' Branch athletics, the dancing classes and the club work addressed perceived needs for immigrant children's imaginative play and bodily cultivation, nurturing human capacities that industrial work and urban living were thought to damage. Festivals and productions at the Neighborhood

Playhouse and Girls' Branch park fetes strove to blend "foreign" with native materials, winning "American" status for immigrant practitioners through dance. In the 1990s we may recognize the considerable sleight of hand exerted in "making Americans" from borrowed and re-fashioned immigrant ritual and dance practices. Settlement workers and folk dance leaders like Mary Wood Hinman and Elizabeth Burchenal both acknowledged and admired the traditions and heritages that new immigrants brought with them. These self-constituted middle-class workers keenly felt the absence of comparable traditions and roots for modern America, and creatively tried to fashion a past from other (European) traditions. This fashioning was in every way re-constitutive; it selected, arranged, and appropriated for its own ends rather than attempting to reinstall European "originals." It pursued its own kind of "authenticity," however. By accessing European traditions, middle-class American cultural workers believed they tapped into "racially old," primal ways of being in the world that were saturated with capacities for feeling, spontaneity, and imagination. They believed these capacities were being steadily leached from quotidian existence by its very conditions of possibility: industrial labor, urban congregation and density, and geographic mobility enacted by immigration and rural-to-urban migration.

These middle-class interventions on behalf of immigrants exerted disciplining force as well. Settlement workers and after-school folk dance leaders justified their work in part on the basis of its ability to harmonize relationships among first- and second-generation immigrants. Citing and re-circulating traditional dance in their programs for immigrant clients, American cultural workers sought to acquaint the young with the values and practices of older immigrants, practices that children frequently shrugged off in their negotiation of the new country. Here middle-class interveners tried to shore up the nuclear family as the organizing node for American culture, an effort that continues to have political resonance, if not demographic presence, in 1990s America. Also disciplinary in intent was settlement house participation in drives for dance hall reform. Here middle-class women, who justified their new public sphere social welfare work on the basis of women's special moral sensibility, strove to limit or channel the uses that adolescent working girls made of public sphere entertainment spaces. They also tried to contain the embodiments—and sexualities—afforded by tough dancing styles and by working girls' dance hall etiquette. Middle-class workers ultimately lost the battle about dance styles as middle-class youth adopted the new embodiments with enthusiasm. The dance hall reform drives reveal, however, the contest for class leadership—the ability to impose discipline—argued through dance and matters of the body.

Middle-class efforts to contain dance hall behaviors and embodiments of course expose the agency of working-class girls, a self-authorization historians have only recently come to acknowledge. In their zest for attending dance halls, for walking out on city streets, and for negotiating treats and tribute, working girls threw into relief the contradictory social codes governing the primary domains of their bodily exertion. For early-twentieth-century labor markets drank up females' labor as well as males', and unions wrestled with women's demands for participation. Women's activity in these domains gave the lie to the class fiction spun by separate spheres ideology, which assigned women to the home and domesticity and men to the world of work and politics. Further, adolescent working girls' self-styling, walking out, and exploration of new dance embodiments exposed the romanticization of heterosexual courtship maintained by elite and middle-class groups. Trading treats and tribute for bodily experiences in new kinetic domains, working girls revealed the exchange nexus as the basis common to both sweated labor and the heterosexual economy of desire. In their way, working-class girls limned and tried to remap women's public sphere presence. This remapping was not resolved in the Progressive era; indeed, women's public space sexuality and embodiment continue to be read as ambiguous and contextually defined, nowhere more so than in criminal trials for rape.

Managing working-class immigrant people, or attempting to do so, middle-class American women endeavored to rewrite their gender roles as well. Pressing and extending nineteenth-century separate spheres ideology to its limits, they took action in the public sphere in settlements and via the Girls' Branch programs to formulate and consolidate professional occupations for themselves: as social welfare workers, as dance pedagogues, as authors of dance instruction books. Middle-class women like Hinman and Burchenal began to wrest from men the effective monopoly on dance teaching, a pattern of development that has continued into the late twentieth century.

Certain elite women, too, pursued this assertion and performance of public sphere agency. The wealthy Lewisohns financed their Neighborhood Playhouse work largely with inherited monies, and they used the opportunity to direct, choreograph, and perform. By linking their work with settlement house goals and legitimacy, they countered earlier models of elite women's conduct that shunned commercial theatrical work. The well-heeled sponsors of the Girls' Branch voluntary organization similarly asserted a public sphere role for themselves. They created the supply for a demand not met by municipal government, one not even conceived as local government's obligation.

Further, from the 1890s to the 1910s, a number of elite women assertively claimed the position of custodians of culture, that is, arbiters of cultural production and taste. Men of wealth had founded and funded institutions of brick and mortar: libraries, museums, and universities. They also supported large-scale arts institutions like new symphony orchestras. Elite women of their cohort bid for recognition as judges and sponsors of new dance practices introduced by Isadora Duncan and Ruth St. Denis. The women's culture club movement provided a middle-class example of this kind of claim. At the elite level, the cream of New York and Chicago high society constituted itself as adjudicators of what might be danced, and recognized as dance, at the turn of the century in America. Their public sphere assertion supported Duncan and St. Denis in prying female dancing loose from exclusive association with ballet girls of yore; it positioned new female soloists to trouble masculinist practices of viewing as well.

Within different class positions, and at junctures of cross-class interaction, then, new dance practices created areas of liminality, opportunities for re-registering ethnic, class, and gender "givens." Newly fashioned dance initiatives also troubled and contested crucial issues of social order and conceptions of polity. Festivals and Festival Dancers at the Neighborhood Playhouse instated ideas about linkage and relationship as promising principles for sorting social relationships. Girls' Branch park fetes put into question contending contemporary emphases on competitive individualism, on one hand, and on corporate communal wholes, on the other. Park fetes, Playhouse festivals and lyric productions, Commons May fetes, working girls' dance hall behaviors, and salon performances by Duncan and St. Denis: each of these constituted events capable of being read differently by their several kinds of viewers or consumers. Settlement workers and immigrant parents alike could read festivals, fetes, and theatrical productions as negotiations of ethnic difference. Made of kinetic materials, staged periodically, these events constituted ongoing remakings and remappings of what it might mean to be American. Although scheduled fairly regularly, their very instability afforded a dynamic tension of competing claims. This was a resolution without fixity or permanent "marking," one suited to the fluidity of the historical moment. And it was a resolution that mobilized performative rather than essentialized notions of citizenship and identity. While reformers read working-class dance halls as venues of female vulnerability, adolescent girls played them as realms for self-fashioning, a self-making that was rapidly emulated by middle-class youth. Salon performances by Duncan and St. Denis certainly offered the featured dancers much-needed platforms for asserting difference from commercial dance hall embodiments. To their male salon viewers these soloists may have looked for all the world like specially served-up specimens from the Great White Way. To their elite women sponsors, however, the soloists arguably brought together in one embodiment the special spiritual sensibility and the sensuous physicality long assigned to women as separate poles on the continuum of what it meant to be female. In their several forms, these nodes, these liminal events, nurtured subsequent development and career staking by women in the 1920s and 1930s genre of modern dance, for practitioners born to immigrant families—Sokolow, Tamiris, and Maslow—and not simply natives such as Humphrey, Graham, and Weidman. In diverse ways, treading a variety of platforms, new Progressive-era dance practices created conditions of possibility for change: for reconsidering principles of social order, for negotiating demographic expansion and cultural difference, for multiplying embodiments and sexualities available to women.

Of the several legacies left by new Progressive-era dance practices, though, the gender legacies remain distinctly equivocal. What turn-of-the-century dance activity won was reconsideration and recasting of received views on the body-woman-dance linkage. It definitely confirmed women in their role as numerically preponderant executants of dance. Beyond this historical continuity, it effectively and aggressively asserted women's claims to dance innovation and direction, roles typically allocated to men in dance's sexual division of labor. Further, women in the Progressive era made substantial inroads against men's previous dominance in dance teaching, setting that profession well on the way to becoming a female occupational domain. Female sponsors of new dance practices instated themselves as cultural custodians, negotiating fluid class configurations within their wealth stratum while empowering new female soloists to refigure dance as an aesthetic enterprise. The gains for women's constitution of, participation in, and sponsorship of dance have earned dance a feminized aspect, one sometimes bemoaned by women presently in the field. In 1990s American modern and experimental dance, both purveyors and consumers, leaders and followers, teachers and students, are predominantly female. Choreography has become a shared domain. In America's (still) patriarchal culture, leadership by men connotes significance and power; leadership by women implies secondary status. In the long run, women's achievement of predominance in dance occupations, even their ascendance as choreographers, has won subordinate status for dance as well. (Still) coupled with gender, dance remains caught in the male-female binary. This study illuminates ways in which women began to gain a predominance that has proven so fraught.

I have proposed a new way of looking at dance in the Progressive era, as an instrumentality for cultural intervention. In that period, production of dancing was keyed to demographic and industrial change, to mounting stresses placed on the sex-gender system, and to America's world position as quasi-isolationist, only lately drawn into imperial reach through the Spanish-American war. What we might call a Progressive-era ideology of engagement, a conception of dance as a socially invested practice, differed strikingly from a modernist ideology of "autonomy" that informed 1920s and 1930s modern dance. In this conception, dance existed independent of immediate social application or utility. To be sure, the notion of autonomous dance, or art for art's sake, had circulated during the Progressive era, and certainly contributed to Duncan's and St. Denis's conceptions of their practice. The ideologies of engagement and autonomy co-existed during the period. Each had its persuasiveness, each had its audiences. The modernist autonomy conception gained ascendancy, I argue, in relation to changing historical conditions in America. First and foremost, a shattering war had tried America and changed the world. By the early 1920s, immigration restriction had become law. With flows of foreign-born people in check, the need to manage assimilation receded as a priority. And as the Neighborhood Playhouse repertory makes visible, attention could be turned to representation of exotic others with less thought given to dangers of compromising hard-won acceptance of ethnic "others." Even this strategy was superseded by 1930s modern dancers like Humphrey, Graham, and Weidman, who had found Denishawn's preoccupation with exotic others stifling. What new modern dance choreographers rejected was the by then conventionalized "foreign" material; they actually resembled Progressive-era innovators in aiming to make dances that dealt with their time.

The star for a notion of autonomous modern dance also rose in response to the changing reception granted industrial labor and a burgeoning consumer economy. By the 1920s, an industrial economic organization was clearly here to stay in America. Streamline Moderne, the new architecture and design style, celebrated the surge and dynamism of modern industry and the quickening pace of urban work and social life. When the bubble burst and the country's greatest depression descended, paeans to American nationality did not urge retreat to a preindustrial era. The sharpness, angularity, and tension of Martha Graham's choreography, so difficult at first for contemporary viewers to understand, similarly put into play qualities of a maturing machine age, as did 1930s International style architecture.

So too had ideas about sexuality and gender shifted. Increasing circulation of Freud's theories in America refigured notions of what it was that bodies contained or deployed or needed to "express." Woman's achievement of suffrage in 1920 did not change the way politics were conducted, as some had predicted. Rather, women's suffrage figured in the long-term decline in voting by the electorate as a whole. Further, the singular focus for political action with which suffrage drives had welded together women of markedly different class and ethnic positions dissipated in the 1920s. And, where one important argument had previously pressed women's political and public sphere agency on the basis of their (separate spheres) difference from men, a renewed claim was made for such agency on the basis of women's equality with men. Thus the 1920s saw the first campaign for passage of an Equal Rights Amendment. The competing claims of difference and equality are still at issue in the 1990s; what was important for dance innovation, I believe, was the diminution of women's claim to public sphere activity on the basis of special sensibility. The equality claim could comport easily with ideas of modernist autonomy: good dance is good dance, one might argue, regardless of the sex of its producer. At the turn of the century, dance innovation rode the wave of sallies into the public sphere on the basis of women's difference. In the 1920s, women dance makers could claim participation on the basis of aesthetic qualification, not gender.

Shifts in the relative cultural positions of dance ideologies carried with them changes in conceptions of human creativity. For Progressive-era cultural producers like the Lewisohns or Mary Wood Hinman, the new dance practices they introduced acted to release capabilities attributed to individuals, notably their imagination and spontaneity. These qualities of being were available to all people and could be expressed—that is, activated—with a modicum of instruction. The new modern dance also located creativity in the individual person. However, only the gifted few were thought to possess the genuine talent requisite for making and performing dances. According to this ideology, a small number of individuals gave form to—released—dance.

Inherent in these opposed conceptions of creativity are different theories of the dance work, of what it comprises. Dances mounted in Girls'

Branch park fetes or in Neighborhood Playhouse festivals took extant materials and selected, arranged, and sequenced them for performance. Burchenal and Hinman made their careers in part as collectors of valuable traditional materials; the Lewisohns joined together materials derived from Dalcroze and Delsarte techniques, classic and national dances, and even Duncan dancing as it circulated in New York City. What mattered for these uses was the producers' acuity in selection, their calibration of material to appropriate age-grades, their consolidation of dances past and dance's past by re-circulating traditional dances. In contrast, the modernist ideology of autonomy privileged choreography, the making of new dance, the discovery of uncharted bodily materials, the theorizing of sequencing and arrangement. Graham, Tamiris, Sokolow, Humphrey, and Weidman marshaled human physical capacities to construct distinctive movement vocabularies and choreographic approaches. Invention was all important. This difference between Progressive-era approaches and modernist ideologies is thrown into sharp relief by the transit the Neighborhood Playhouse made in the late 1920s. The Playhouse focused its energies on production until it closed its doors in 1927. Among the numerous classes it offered in theatre arts, the dance classes centered on movement techniques. Rehearsals for festivals and lyric productions were led by the directors, although dancers were expected to improvise at times and contribute to Irene Lewisohn's movement designs. At no time was choreography taught as part of the curriculum. This changed when the Playhouse re-opened as a teaching enterprise under Rita Wallach Morgenthau's direction. Martha Graham was engaged early to teach movement, but more important still, Louis Horst began to teach composition. Principles employed at the Neighborhood Playhouse inform his *Pre-classic Dance Forms*; Horst dedicated the volume "to Irene Lewisohn, whose foresight first made possible new experiments in these old forms." Horst's theoretical impress and disciplining weight was certainly felt by Martha Graham, and his methodology was disseminated in years to come through instruction he gave at Bennington Summer Schools of the Dance and at the Juilliard School. The large point is that articulation of choreography as a theoretical domain distinguished the new modernist dance from Progressive-era dance innovation; the two tracked different game.

Or at least, that's what master narratives of modern dance would have us believe. Those narratives have privileged the choreographic principles and works articulated by Graham, Humphrey, Weidman, and émigré Hanya Holm. They've largely written Helen Tamiris out of the record; her choreography was not evaluated as equally significant, and her animal ease, even voluptuousness, in performance seemed suspect. And they've made little of her attempts at collective action, from Dance Repertory Theatre's short-lived joint performance seasons to the 1936 Dance Congress. Also marginalized until recently have been the work of leftist dance groups and choreographers. While Anna Sokolow and Sophie Maslow certainly cut their spurs in Graham's all-female company, they also participated in American workers' dance groups of the 1930s. This side of their practice was left quiet, one suspects, in the wake of Communist-baiting and then McCarthyism, from the late 1930s to the 1950s. The fact remains, however, that the new genre of modern dance did include dance practices aimed at social engagement. Choreographically, leftist dance groups addressed economic and racial problems in American culture. Left-wing pedagogical enterprises like the New Dance Group offered modern dance technique and composition classes at cheap prices; a populist move, this made the knowledge bases of new dance that much more accessible.

What this study of Progressive-era dance innovation enables, then, is a close scrutiny of the narratives that have been spun for twentieth-century American dance. It liberates turn-of-the-century dance practices from consignment to quaintness, and from even more damning status as merely predecessor developments to the new genre of modern dance. It illuminates dance's salience for troubling, contesting, and confirming issues of grave political and social moment in the United States. And it throws into question the absence (erasure) of dance's instrumentality from modernist narratives of modern dance history. Promoting reappraisal of ideologies and actual practices mobilized by new dance, this study positions us to query dance's past anew. It should help us to weigh the past in the present as well.

Full citations are given for first references in each chapter, and shortened citations thereafter.

Introduction

1. Robert Allen, *Horrible Prettiness: Burlesque and American Culture* (Chapel Hill: University of North Carolina Press, 1991), 159–62.

2. See, for example, the collection of articles, edited by Lynn Garafola, devoted to "dancing on the left" in *Studies in Dance History* 5, no. 1 (Spring 1994); Ellen Graff, *Stepping Left: Dance and Politics in New York City, 1928–1942* (Durham, N.C.: Duke University Press, 1997); Stacey Prickett, "From Workers' Dance to New Dance" and "Dance and the Workers' Struggle," in *Dance Research* 7, no. 1 (Spring 1989): 47–64, and 8, no. 1 (Spring 1990): 47–61, respectively.

3. See Griselda Pollock, *Vision and Difference: Femininity, Feminism and Histories of Art* (London: Routledge, 1988), especially 1–17. Also Janet Wolff, *The Social Production of Art* (New York: St. Martin's Press, 1981); Hal Foster, preface to *Vision and Visuality*, ed. Hal Foster (Seattle: Bay Press, 1988), ix–xiv; Craig Owens, "The Discourse of Others: Feminists and Postmodernism," in *The Anti-Aesthetic*, ed. Hal Foster (Seattle: Bay Press, 1983), 57–82; Peter Burger, *Theory of the Avant-Garde*, trans. Michael Shaw (Minneapolis: University of Minnesota Press, 1984/92).

4. Rhys Isaac, *The Transformation of Virginia 1740–1790* (Chapel Hill: University of North Carolina Press, 1982), 78–87. Histories of black peoples and cultures have been prominent among studies of the U.S. that have given weight to dance. See Albert J. Raboteau, *Slave Religion: The "Invisible Institution" in the Antebellum South* (New York: Oxford University Press, 1978); Sterling Stuckey, *Going*

through the Storm: The Influence of African American Art in History and *Slave Culture: Nationalist Theory & the Foundations of Black America* (both New York: Oxford University Press, 1994 and 1987, respectively); Lawrence W. Levine, *Black Culture and Black Consciousness; Afro-American Folk Thought From Slavery to Freedom* (New York: Oxford University Press, 1981). Proceeding from a dance perspective, Lynne Fauley Emery's *Black Dance in the United States from 1619 to 1970* remains the most comprehensive account to date (New York: Dance Horizons, 1980; 2d rev. ed. Princeton Books, 1988), updating later-twentieth-century developments with a chapter by Brenda Dixon Stowell. See also Brenda Dixon Gottschild, *Digging the Africanist Presence in American Performance; Dance and Other Contexts* (Westport, Conn.: Greenwood Press, 1996); John Perpener, "The Seminal Years of Black Concert Dance" (Ph.D. diss., New York University, 1992).

1. Bodies and Dances in Progressive-era America

1. Important studies of the Progressive era which make clear the period's wrenching dislocations and pattern shifts include Richard Hofstadter, *The Age of Reform* (New York: Vintage Books, 1955); Robert H. Wiebe, *The Search for Order 1877–1920* (New York: Hill and Wang, 1967); Gabriel Kolko, *The Triumph of Conservatism; A Reinterpretation of American History, 1900–1916* (New York: The Free Press, 1968); Daniel T. Rodgers, "In Search of Progressivism," in *The Promise of American History; Progress and Prospects,* ed. Stanley I. Kutler and Stanley N. Katz (Baltimore: Johns Hopkins University Press, 1982).

2. For studies of economic and industrial change in nineteenth- and early-twentieth-century America see Herbert G. Gutman, *Work, Culture & Society in Industrializing America* (New York: Vintage Books, 1977); Alice Kessler-Harris, *Out to Work; A History of Wage-Earning Women in the United States* (New York: Oxford University Press, 1982); Sean Wilentz, *Chants Democratic; New York City & the Rise of the American Working Class, 1788–1850* (New York: Oxford University Press, 1984); Nick Salvatore, *Eugene V. Debs; Citizen and Socialist* (Urbana: University of Illinois Press, 1982); Glenn Porter, *The Rise of Big Business, 1860–1910* (Arlington Heights, Ill.: Harlan Davidson, 1973); Melvin Dubofsky, *We Shall Be All: A History of the IWW* (Chicago: University of Chicago Press, 1969); Melvyn Dubofsky, *Industrialism and the American Worker, 1865–1920,* 2d ed. (Arlington Heights, Ill.: Harlan Davidson, 1985); David Brody, *Steelworkers in America, the Non-Union Era* (Cambridge: Harvard University Press, 1960).

3. On immigration flows and immigrants' reception in postbellum and early-twentieth-century America see John Higham, *Send These to Me; Immigrants in America,* rev. ed. (Baltimore: Johns Hopkins University Press, 1984); Higham, *Strangers in the Land; Patterns of Nativism 1860–1925* (New York: Atheneum, 1985). See *Twelfth Census of the United States taken in the Year 1900. Census Reports. Volume One: Population,* Part 1 (Washington, D.C.: United States Census Office, 1901), table 24, pp. 651, 668–69.

4. For changing farm conditions see Hofstadter, *The Age of Reform;* Lawrence Goodwyn, *The Populist Moment; A Short History of the Agrarian Revolt in America* (New York: Oxford University Press, 1978). Wiebe, *The Search for Order,* makes

clear changing conceptions of community and loss of clear senses of order and ordination.

5. See Goodwyn, *The Populist Moment*; Hofstadter, *The Age of Reform*; Rodgers, "In Search of Progressivism," 116.

6. Periodization is a necessarily arbitrary practice. Nonetheless, the Progressive era should not be thought limited to those years in which the Progressive Party actively participated in American electoral politics. I take a broad view of the Progressive era as limned by its aggressive reformist drives and its shattering demographic changes. I purposefully date the Progressive era back to 1890 in order to foreground women's leadership in reform initiatives such as the settlement house movement (Jane Addams and Ellen Gates Starr founded Hull-House in 1889, Lillian Wald the Nurses Settlement in 1893) and the temperance movement (as in the broadly based, grassroots organization, the Women's Christian Temperance Union). I date the end of the era, a difficult decision in any case, to 1920, not because women's suffrage was then achieved but because postwar rethinking of social relations, including gender roles, combined with economic instability, mounting immigration restriction efforts, and shifting patterns of political participation to substantively change people's conceptions of the state, their ability to affect it through activism, and hence their own social roles.

7. Hofstadter applied the term "status anxiety" in *The Age of Reform*; Wiebe coined the second term with *The Search for Order*.

8. William R. Leach, "Transformations in a Culture of Consumption: Women and Department Stores, 1890–1925," *Journal of American History* 71 (September 1984): 319–42. See also Richard Wightman Fox and T. J. Jackson Lears, *The Culture of Consumption; Essays in American History, 1880–1980* (New York: Pantheon Books, 1983).

9. Chapter 2 treats separate spheres ideology in detail.

10. Chapters 3 and 5 address the settlement house movement.

11. Michael McGerr, "Political Style and Women's Power, 1830–1930," *Journal of American History* 77 (December 1990): 864–85; Lisa Tickner, *The Spectacle of Women; Imagery of the Suffrage Campaign 1907–14* (London: Chatto & Windus, 1987); Nancy Cott, *The Grounding of Modern Feminism* (New Haven: Yale University Press, 1987); Ellen Carol Dubois, *Harriot Stanton Blatch and the Winning of Woman Suffrage* (New Haven: Yale University Press, 1997). Classic studies of woman suffrage are Aileen Kraditor, *The Ideas of the Woman Suffrage Movement 1890–1920* (New York: Columbia University Press, 1965); Eleanor Flexner, *Century of Struggle; The Woman's Rights Movement in the United States* (1959).

Susan A. Glenn, *Daughters of the Shtetl; Life and Labor in the Immigrant Generations* (Ithaca: Cornell University Press, 1990), 173–76, 207–16, 222–27, 237–42. Useful studies of women's labor activism in New York include Ann Schofield, "The Uprising of the 20,000: The Making of a Labor Legend," in *A Needle, a Bobbin, a Strike; Women Needleworkers in America*, ed. Joan M. Jensen and Sue Davidson (Philadelphia: Temple University Press, 1984), 167–82; Nancy Schrom Dye, *As Equals and as Sisters: Feminism, the Labor Movement, and the Women's Trade Union League of New York* (Columbia: University of Missouri

Press, 1980); Dye, "Creating A Feminist Alliance: Sisterhood and Class Conflict in the New York Women's Trade Union League, 1903–1914," *Feminist Studies* 2 (1975): 24–38; Alice Kessler-Harris, "Where are the Organized Women Workers?" *Feminist Studies* 3 (1975): 92–110; Kessler-Harris, *Out to Work: A History of Wage-Earning Women in the United States* (Oxford: Oxford University Press, 1982), 142–79. See also Abraham Cahan, *The Rise of David Levinsky* (1917; reprint, New York: Harper Torchbooks, 1960); Edith Wharton, *The House of Mirth* (1905; reprint, New York: Penguin American Library, 1985).

12. William H. Chafe, *The American Woman; Her Changing Social, Economic, and Political Roles, 1920–1970* (New York: Oxford University Press, 1972), 80, 128–29; Gerda Lerner, ed., *Black Women in White America; A Documentary History Edited by Gerda Lerner* (New York: Vintage Books, 1973), 193–215; Jacquelyn Dowd Hall, *Revolt Against Chivalry; Jessie Daniel Ames and the Women's Campaign Against Lynching* (New York: Columbia University Press, 1979).

13. See, for example, Cynthia Russett, *Darwin in America; The Intellectual Response 1865–1912* (San Francisco: W. H. Freeman, 1976); Russet, *Sexual Science; The Victorian Construction of Womanhood* (Cambridge: Harvard University Press, 1989); Martha Verbrugge, *Able-Bodied Womanhood; Personal Health and Social Change in Nineteenth-Century Boston* (New York: Oxford University Press, 1988); Edward Clarke, *Sex in Education* (Boston: James R. Osgood, 1887).

14. Upton Sinclair, *The Jungle* (1905; reprint, New York: New American Library, 1980), 43–44.

15. On garment industry work conditions see Glenn, *Daughters of the Shtetl*, 98–106, 136, 138–39.

16. Davis, *Spearheads for Reform*, 60–83; Jacob Riis, *How the Other Half Lives* (New York: Macmillan, 1890); Glenn, *Daughters of the Shtetl*, 54–60; Anzia Yezierska, *Bread Givers* (1925; reprint, New York: Persea Books, 1975); Jane Addams, *Twenty Years at Hull-House* (1910; reprint, New York: New American Library, 1981), 200–10; Lillian Wald, *The House on Henry Street* (New York: Henry Holt, 1915).

17. Luther H. Gulick, director of physical training for turn-of-the-century New York City schools, wrote eloquently about school conditions in Gotham—see chapter 5. Municipal conditions are evoked in *Physical Training; A Full Report of the Papers and Discussions of the Conference Held in Boston in November, 1889*, reported and edited by Isabel C. Barrows (Boston: Press of George H. Ellis, 1890).

18. Allen F. Davis, *Spearheads for Reform; the Social Settlements and the Progressive Movement 1890–1914* (New York: Oxford University Press, 1967), 63–70; Dominic Cavallo, *Muscles and Morals; Organized Playgrounds and Urban Reform, 1880–1920* (Philadelphia: University of Pennsylvania Press, 1981). See *Charities and the Commons* 18 (August 3, 1907) for additional information and a report on the first PAA Congress.

19. Known first by the term "physical culture," systems of bodily exercise were later embraced by the term "physical training." In the early twentieth century, use of the locution "physical education" signaled the growing professionalization of exercise practitioners and their incorporation into education curriculums. The change in nomenclature accurately indexes change in conception of the practices themselves. See Luther Halsey Gulick, "Physical Education; A New Profession,"

Proceedings of the American Association for the Advancement of Physical Education at its Fifth Annual Meeting Held at Cambridge and Boston, Mass., April 4 and 5, 1890 (Ithaca, N.Y.: Andrus & Church, 1890): 59–66.

20. The notion of an "extensive body" is my own. Discussion of the several physical training systems pursued in this and following paragraphs draws useful information from now-classic histories of physical education. See Ellen W. Gerber, *Innovators and Institutions in Physical Education* (Philadelphia: Lea & Febiger, 1971); Norma Schwendener, *A History of Physical Education in the United States* (New York: A. S. Barnes, 1942); Emmett A. Rice, John L. Hutchinson, and Mabel Lee, *A Brief History of Physical Education*, 4th ed. (New York: Ronald Press Co., 1958); Fred Eugene Leonard, *A Guide to the History of Physical Education*, 3d ed. (London: Henry Kimpton, 1947/52). Useful as well are the cogent characterizations of various systems advanced at the 1889 conference, documented in *Physical Training; A Full Report*. See also Harvey Green, *Fit for America; Health, Fitness, Sport and American Society* (New York: Pantheon Books, 1986).

On the Jahn system specifically, see Leonard, *A Guide to the History of Physical Education*, 231–54, 294–314; Fred Eugene Leonard, "Friedrich Ludwig Jahn, and the Development of Popular Gymnastics (Vereins-Turnen) in Germany. II." *American Physical Education Review* (March 1905): 1–19. See also three articles in the collection *Turnen and Sport; the Cross-Cultural Exchange* (New York: Waxmann Publishing, 1991): Janice A. Beran, "The Turners in Iowa, USA: Promoters of Fitness and Shapers of Culture"; Rainer Grossbroehmer, "German Influences on the North American System of Gymnastics Teachers' Training: The NAGU Normal College"; and Roland Naul, "Studies of the Turner System by an American: Fred E. Leonard's Visits to Germany, 1896, 1900/01, 1913."

21. Schwendener, *A History of Physical Education*, 125–26, offers confirmation of my man-machine notion: apparatus work as a base for complicated performance requiring approach and dismount. A chart inserted in *Mind and Body* (May 1894), n.p., adds specifics on the German system to those provided by Leonard and Schwendener. On the Jahn group orientation see *Mind and Body* chart (exercises of attention where the single member is but a part of the whole: tactics, rhythmical motions); Schwendener, 40–51. Leonard, "Friedrich Ludwig Jahn," 2–3, references games and squads in German antecedents.

22. Green, *Fit for America*, 193; William G. Riordan, "Dio Lewis in Retrospect," *Journal of Health, Physical Education, Recreation* (October 1960): 46–48; Dio Lewis, *The New Gymnastics for Men, Women, and Children*, 3d ed. (Boston: Ticknor and Fields, 1862).

23. See Schwendener, *A History of Physical Education*, 105, for movement into the void left by Lewis's death. Hartwig Nissen, *A B C of the Swedish System of Educational Gymnastics a Practical Hand-book for School Teachers and the Home* (New York: Educational Publishing Company, 1892); Verbrugge, *Able-Bodied Womanhood*, 149–55, 165; Betty Spears, *Leading the Way: Amy Morris Homans and the Beginnings of Professional Education for Women* (New York: Greenwood Press, 1986).

24. On corseting and silhouettes, see Lois Banner, *American Beauty* (Chicago: University of Chicago Press, 1983). See also handbooks of New York City's Girls'

Branch of the Public Schools Athletic League, for advertisements of women's sports dress run by sporting supply companies like Spalding's Athletic Company. Banner points to popularization by the 1890s of an "athletic" body for women, which she analyzes in terms of silhouette. My analysis of physically cultivated bodies also addresses movement and spatial qualities promoted by specific systems.

25. For areas Sargent tested, see Leonard, *A Guide to the History of Physical Education*, 286–87. On his system, see Dudley Allen Sargent, *An Autobiography*, ed. Ledyard W. Sargent (Philadelphia: Lea & Febiger, 1927); Clarence B. Van Wyck, "The Harvard Summer School of Physical Education 1887–1932," *The Research Quarterly* 13 (December 1942): 403–31. Green uses the descriptor "all around, healthy young men" in *Fit for America*, 205.

26. See Hazel Wacker, "The History of the Private Single-Purpose Institutions which Prepared Teachers of Physical Education in the United States of America from 1860–1958," 3 vols. (Ph.D. diss., New York University, 1959).

27. See *Physical Training; A Full Report*; Spears, *Amy Morris Homans*; Verbrugge, *Able-Bodied Women*.

28. Nancy Lee Chalfa Ruyter, *Reformers and Visionaries; The Americanization of the Art of Dance* (New York: Dance Horizons, 1979), especially 15–30; Genevieve Stebbins, *The Delsarte System of Expression*, 6th ed. (1902; reprint, New York: Dance Horizons, 1977); Katherine M. Adelman, "Statue-Posing in the Late Nineteenth Century Physical Culture Movement," *Proceedings 5th Canadian Symposium on the History of Sport and Physical Education 1982* (Toronto: School Physical and Health Education, University of Toronto, 1982).

29. On reclining and falls see Stebbins, *The Delsarte System of Expression*, 165–67; Peggy Pendennis, "A Craze for Delsarte: Society Leaders Who are in Love with its Mysteries," *New York World*, August 16, 1891, p. 15.

30. Lewis Erenberg's *Steppin' Out; New York Nightlife and the Transformation of American Culture, 1890–1930* (Westport, Conn.: Greenwood Press, 1981) must be noted as one of the earliest studies to take the "dance craze" seriously. Julie Malnig's *Dancing til Dawn; A Century of Exhibition Ballroom Dancing* (Westport, Conn.: Greenwood Press, 1992) is one of the most recent works to historicize the dance craze. Kathy Peiss's *Cheap Amusements; Working Women and Leisure in Turn-of-the-Century New York* (Philadelphia: Temple University Press, 1986) explores working-class dance practices as they functioned in the larger domain of commercialized leisure.

31. Erenberg in *Steppin' Out*, and Marshall and Jean Stearns in *Jazz Dance; The Story of American Vernacular Dance* (New York: Schirmer, 1968), identify West Coast/Barbary Coast developments that stimulated social dance innovation. Lynne Fauley Emery's *Black Dance in the United States from 1619 to 1970* (1972; 2d rev. ed, Princeton, N.J.: Princeton Books, 1988) and Katrina Hazzard-Gordon's *Jookin'; The Rise of Social Dance Formations in African-American Culture* (Philadelphia: Temple University Press, 1986) consider social dance among blacks in Progressive-era America—the former at the survey level.

Because New York registered the several impacts of immigration, variable industrialization, and urban crowding, and because it also served as the nation's center for theatrical production—topics of special concern in this book—studies of changes in that city's social dancing practices offer particularly useful, if inevitably partial, ground for situating the dance renaissance and its production of bodies. It's clear that more monographic and book-length work is needed to begin to assess in a scholarly way synchronic trends and differences among regions and groups, not to mention diachronic changes.

32. Erenberg, *Steppin' Out*, 20; Peiss, *Cheap Amusements*, 88–114.

33. Peiss, *Cheap Amusements*, 93–96; Erenberg, *Steppin' Out*, 20–22.

34. Of course, events programmed to benefit charity or other causes departed from this noncommercial format, but they are the exception that helps establish the rule. Erenberg, *Steppin' Out*, 10–13, 33–41, 55.

35. Erenberg, *Steppin' Out*, 75–79, 113–42; Malnig, *Dancing til Dawn*, 7–10.

36. Erenberg, *Steppin' Out*, 79, 83–85, 149; Irene and Vernon Castle, *Modern Dancing* (New York: Harper & Brothers, 1914), 155–59. Conclusions regarding consumers and producers are my own.

37. Period sources suggest that at least three principal dance types were predominant in turn-of-the-century ballrooms. In middle-class and elite ballrooms, quadrilles placed four male-female couples along the four sides of a square formation, with any number of squares or "sets" occupying the floor simultaneously. In a typical quadrille, dancers moved through five "figures" separated by musical interludes for resting and chatting. While completing each figure, dancers interacted with each other: giving and taking hands; changing places with others; promenading through space in star, cross, circle, and chain patterns. Although women and men frequently figured with same-sex members of couples standing opposite them in the square, they always returned to their partners; men assisted or guided women in several of the steps. Thus, despite their profile as group dances, quadrilles emphasized the "couple" as the fundamental unit of organization. The waltz, common to working-class dancers as well as elite and upper-class people, featured couples as well. Whereas the man and woman stood side by side in a quadrille couple, when waltzing they faced and clasped each other in the "round dance position." Each couple was independent, but pursued, as did every other couple, a counterclockwise course around the floor. Cotillions — sometimes called Germans — offered elite and middle-class dancers formats for playing party games. (Creating no little confusion for historians, "cotillion" was the word given to quadrille-format dances in the early nineteenth century. The shift to the term "quadrille" was accomplished by the 1840s.) My knowledge of these dance practices is informed by movement study with noted dance reconstructor and period-style choreographer Elizabeth Aldrich, Aldrich's *From the Ballroom to Hell; Grace and Folly in Nineteenth-Century Dance* (Evanston, Ill.: Northwestern University Press, 1991), and insights derived from my work as a reconstructor of early-eighteenth-century French and English social and theatre dances.

38. Erenberg, *Steppin' Out*, 149–50, and Peiss, *Cheap Amusements*, 100–101, describe the waltz, but the close reading of waltzing supplied by this chapter is my own. In addition to sources cited in note 37, my analysis is informed by period dance manuals such as Dodworth's *Dancing* (New York: Harpers, 1885) and my own experiences dancing a range of reconstructed nineteenth-century waltz variations.

39. See Peiss, *Cheap Amusements*, for spieling and tough dancing (100–103),

and for reform discourse (98–100, 104); Julian Ralph, *Scribners* 20 (July 1896): 18, cited in Peiss 101–02. I owe acquaintance with zweifachers to Bob Fraley's Palo Alto, California, country dance calling, and to Matthew Larson.

40. Erenberg, *Steppin' Out*, 150–55; Peiss, *Cheap Amusements*, 100–03. I gained experience with ragtime dances under Elizabeth Aldrich's tutelage at the International Early Dance Institute.

41. Erenberg, *Steppin' Out*, 158, 163; Irene and Vernon Castle, *Modern Dancing*, 3–7, 38, 40–41, 83–84; Irene Castle, *Castles in the Air* (1958; reprint, New York: Da Capo Press, 1980), 87–89, 113.

42. Peiss, *Cheap Amusements*, 105–06, 108–14.

43. Erenberg, *Steppin' Out*, 135–37.

44. That the spectacularization of public dancing might have obtained in working-class dance halls is also possible. There too the table sitters became performers, although the greater remove of tables from the dance floor and the absence of exhibition dancers made the status shift from consumer to producer less explicit.

45. Irene and Vernon Castle, *Modern Dancing*, 17, 37–41, 176.

46. At the level of gestalt, the court-derived lineage of ballet and the noble personages that peopled classical ballet plots resonated with the aristocratic carriage the Castles achieved, and tried to cultivate in their elite students. Both ballroom and ballet dancing placed structural emphasis on the male-female couple. While the grand pas de deux format of classical ballet allotted each dancer a virtuoso solo, the opening adagio and concluding coda reinforced the couple as normative. The Castles' masterful resistance to the improvisatory capabilities of the 1910s animal dances reinforced a dyad in which the male led and the female followed. The twinned efforts of the two were requisite to painting a harmonious picture.

47. On ballet in nineteenth-century America see Lillian Moore, *Echoes of American Ballet*, ed. Ivor Guest (New York: Dance Horizons, 1976) (148 for Metropolitan Opera Ballet school); Barbara Barker, *Ballet or Ballyhoo; The American Careers of Maria Bonfanti, Rita Sangalli and Giuseppina Morlacchi* (New York, Dance Horizons, 1984); and articles by Lillian Moore and Marian Hannah Winter in *Chronicles of the American Dance; From the Shakers to Martha Graham*, ed. Ivor Guest (1948; reprint, New York: Da Capo, 1978), 103–88. On ballet girls see Robert C. Allen, *Horrible Prettiness; Burlesque and American Culture* (Chapel Hill: University of North Carolina Press, 1991). Anne Ellis, *The Life of an Ordinary Woman* (1929; reprint, Lincoln: University of Nebraska Press, 1980), 126–27, 226–28, indicates the impact itinerant dance masters exerted on her mining community. For 1910 commentary on Pavlova and Mordkin in New York City, see *The Dance Writings of Carl Van Vechten*, ed. Paul Padgette (New York: Dance Horizons, 1980), 95–102.

48. Fokine, Nijinsky, and Massine are emphasized here as Ballets Russes choreographers during the 1910s; in the 1920s, Bronislava Nijinska and George Balanchine were equally important. Studies of the Ballets Russes are legion; see, for example, informative works by Lynn Garafola, *Diaghilev's Ballets Russes* (New York: Oxford University Press, 1989); Joan R. Acocella, "Symbolism and Modernism: The Response of European Intellectuals to the Fin-de-Siècle Element in the

Prewar Diaghilev Ballet," *Proceedings Society of Dance History Scholars* (1983): 142–51; *Bronislava Nijinska; Early Memoirs*, trans. and ed. Irina Nijinska and Jean Rawlinson (New York: Holt, Rinehart & Winston, 1981); Nesta MacDonald, *Diaghilev Observed by Critics in England and the United States 1911–1929* (London: Dance Horizons & Dance Books, 1975). On Gertrude Hoffman, see Dawn Lille Horowitz, *Michel Fokine* (Boston: G. K. Hall, 1985), 40–41; Barbara Naomi Cohen, "The Borrowed Art of Gertrude Hoffman," *Dance Data* 2 (1977): 2–11.

49. *Dance Writings of Carl Van Vechten*, 97–98, 101.

50. Natalia Roslavleva, *Era of the Russian Ballet 1770–1965* (London: Victor Gollancz, 1966), 153, 165–66, suggests that the Moscow-school training of men like Mordkin, Volinine, and Novikoff accounts for the "manly" style they brought to male roles in the first several decades of the twentieth century. All three were, at various points, partners to Pavlowa. Deborah Jowitt, *Time and the Dancing Image* (New York: William Morrow, 1988), 121, notes a similar masculinization of male roles in 1910s Ballets Russes repertory.

51. Duncan, St. Denis, and Fuller are discussed in considerable detail in chapter 2.

52. Troy and Margaret West Kinney, *The Dance; Its Place in Art and Life* (1914; reprint, New York: Tudor Publishing Co., 1936), 288; Caroline and Charles H. Caffin, *Dancing and Dancers of Today; The Modern Revival of Dancing as an Art* (1912; reprint, New York: Da Capo Press, 1978).

2. Constituting Culture, Authorizing Dance

1. Substantial literature exists on separate spheres ideology and women's culture in the U.S. See, for example: Barbara Welter, "The Cult of True Womanhood 1820–1860," *American Quarterly* 18 (Summer 1966): 131–75; Nancy Cott, *The Bonds of Womanhood; Woman's Sphere in New England, 1780–1835* (New Haven: Yale University Press, 1977); Kathryn K. Sklar, *Catharine Beecher; A Study in American Domesticity* (New Haven: Yale University Press, 1973); Mary Ryan, *Cradle of the Middle Class; The Family in Oneida County New York 1790–1865* (Cambridge: Cambridge University Press, 1981); Alice Kessler-Harris, *Out to Work: A History of Wage-Earning Women in the United States* (New York: Oxford University Press, 1982); Nancy Schrom Dye, *As Equals and as Sisters; Feminism, the Labor Movement and the Women's Trade Union League* (Columbia: University of Missouri Press, 1980); Aileen Kraditor, *The Ideas of the Woman Suffrage Movement 1890–1920* (New York: Columbia University Press, 1965); Ruth Bordin, *Woman and Temperance; The Quest for Power and Liberty, 1873–1900* (Philadelphia: Temple University Press, 1981).

2. Carroll Smith-Rosenberg escapes the majority of these problems in "The Female World of Love and Ritual; Relations Between Women in Nineteenth-Century America," *Signs* 1 (Autumn 1975): 1–29. Her investigation of intimate, enduring bonds between women in nineteenth-century same-sex relationships has lent strength to the concept of a women's culture, although Smith-Rosenberg never employs the term herself, preferring "female world," the locution used in the title of her well-known article. Drawing on a sample of letters written by middle-

class people from a range of geographical regions, occupations, and wealth levels, Smith-Rosenberg describes a female world of close-knit, affective relationships in which a particular, perhaps even essential, female mode of relating to other women is available to all middle-class women. Smith-Rosenberg is a careful delimiter of her study's subjects and findings; because she structures variation into her research design, her conclusion about a common mode of homosocial relationship thus carries greater weight. Other historians have been less cautious in assimilating her findings to a concept of a commonly held women's culture; the result is that the homogeneity implicit in the theorizing of women's culture is reinforced.

3. Paula Baker, "The Domestication of Politics: Women and American Political Society, 1780–1920," *Journal of American History* 89 (June 1984): 644. Works dealing with political culture include Daniel Walker Howe, *The Political Culture of American Whigs* (Chicago: University of Chicago Press, 1979); Howe, "The Evangelical Movement and Political Culture in the North during the Second Party System," *Journal of American History* 77 (March 1991): 1216–39; Jean Baker, *Affairs of Party; The Political Culture of Northern Democrats in the Mid-Nineteenth Century* (Ithaca: Cornell University Press, 1983); Eric Foner, *Free Labor, Free Soil, Free Men; The Ideology of the Republican Party Before the Civil War* (New York: Oxford University Press, 1970).

On consumer culture see William R. Leach, "Transformations in a Culture of Consumption: Women and Department Stores, 1890–1925," *Journal of American History* 17 (September 1987): 319–42; Richard Wightman Fox and T. J. Jackson Lears, *The Culture of Consumption: Critical Essays in American History, 1880–1980* (New York: Pantheon Books, 1983).

For conceptualizations of culture in labor histories, see for example: Herbert Gutman, *Work, Culture and Society in Industrializing America 1815–1919* (New York: Vintage Books, 1976); Sean Wilentz, *Chants Democratic: New York City and the Rise of the American Working Class 1788–1850* (New York: Oxford University Press, 1984); Alice Kessler-Harris, *Out to Work: A History of Wage-Earning Women in the United States* (New York: Oxford University Press, 1982); David Montgomery, "Workers' Control of Machine Production in the Nineteenth Century," *Labor History* 17 (1976): 485–509; Paul Faler and Alan Dawley, "Working-Class Culture and Politics in the Industrial Revolution: Sources of Loyalism and Rebellion," *Journal of Social History* 9 (1975): 466–80. E. P. Thompson's *The Making of the English Working Class* (New York: Vintage Books, 1963) helped catalyze conceptions of culture in U.S. labor history.

4. *The End of American Innocence; The First Years of Our Own Time 1912–1917* (New York: Alfred A. Knopf, 1959), Henry May's pathbreaking relocation of a major shift in American history to the pre– rather than post–World War I era, offers substantial analysis of the "genteel tradition" in literature. Thomas Bender's *New York Intellect; A History of Intellectual Life in New York City, from 1750 to the Beginnnings of Our Own Time* (Baltimore: Johns Hopkins University Press, 1987), focuses on the life of the mind and its institutional vectors, and thus necessarily relies on literature as a primary form of culture and expression. Concentrating specifically on Progressive-era developments, Robert Crunden's *Ministers of Reform; The Progressives' Achievement in American Civilization, 1889–1920* (New

York: Basic Books, 1982) considers among other figures writers, painters, an architect, and a composer. Lawrence Levine's recent synthetic *Highbrow/Lowbrow; The Emergence of Cultural Hierarchy in America* (Cambridge: Harvard University Press, 1988) turns attention to easel art, Shakespearean drama, and band and symphony music throughout the nineteenth and early twentieth centuries. The arts which Levine treats have been more thoroughly assessed in earlier concentrated studies like Neil Harris's *The Artist in American Society; The Formative Years 1790–1860* (New York: George Brazilier, 1966); David Grimsted's *Melodrama Unveiled; American Theater and Culture, 1800–1850* (Chicago: University of Chicago Press, 1968); and Frank Rossiter's *Charles Ives and His America* (New York: Liveright, 1975).

5. T. J. Jackson Lears, *No Place of Grace; Antimodernism and the Transformation of American Culture 1880–1920* (New York: Pantheon, 1981); Eileen Boris, *Art and Labor; Ruskin, Morris, and the Craftsman Ideal in America* (Philadelphia: Temple University Press, 1986); Helen Lefkowitz Horowitz, *Culture & The City; Cultural Philanthropy in Chicago from the 1880s to 1917* (Lexington: University Press of Kentucky, 1976); Kathleen D. McCarthy, *Noblesse Oblige; Charity & Cultural Philanthropy in Chicago, 1849–1929* (Chicago: University of Chicago Press, 1982). See also McCarthy's *Lady Bountiful Revisited: Women, Philanthropy, and Power* (New Brunswick, N.J.: Rutgers University Press, 1990).

6. Indispensable scholarship on Fuller includes Sally R. Sommer, "Loie Fuller: From the Theater of Popular Entertainment to the Parisian Avant-Garde" (Ph.D. diss., New York University, 1979); and Clare de Morini, "Loie Fuller—The Fairy of Light," in *Chronicles of the American Dance; From the Shakers to Martha Graham*, ed. Paul Magriel (New York: Da Capo, 1978), 203–20. Sommer gives 1862 as the year of Fuller's birth, 6–7.

7. Loie Fuller, *Fifteen Years of A Dancer's Life, With Some Account of Her Distinguished Friends* (Boston: Small, Maynard & Co., 1913), 20–23; Sommer, "Loie Fuller," 9–11, 18–20, 23; Loie Fuller, holograph page, no title, n.d., Loie Fuller Papers 1892–1913 (hereafter Fuller Papers 1892), folder 34, item 34–1, Dance Collection, New York Public Library for the Performing Arts (hereafter DCNYPL).

8. de Morini, "Loie Fuller," 204, 206–09; Sommer, "Loie Fuller," 24–48 passim, 68, 79, 126, 182, 185, 213, 215.

9. Sommer, "Loie Fuller," 11–12, 15, 19–20.

10. Sommer, "Loie Fuller," 18. On the Crusade see Ruth Bordin, "'A Baptism of Power and Liberty': The Women's Crusade of 1873–1874," *Ohio History* 87 (1978): 393–404; Ruth Bordin, *Woman and Temperance; The Quest for Power and Liberty* (Philadelphia: Temple University Press, 1981), 15–33; [Eliza Daniel] Mother Stewart, *Memories of the Crusade; A Thrilling Account of the Great Uprising of the Women of Ohio in 1873, against the Liquor Crime*, 2d ed. (Columbus, Ohio: William G. Hubbard & Co., 1889); Jack S. Blocker Jr., *'Give to the Winds Thy Fears': The Women's Temperance Crusade 1873–1874* (Westport, Conn.: Greenwood Press, 1985).

On contemporary receptivity to temperance agitation see also Jed Dannenbaum, "The Origins of Temperance Activism and Militancy Among American Women," *Journal of Social History* 15 (Winter 1981): 235–52. On formation of the

WCTU, see Bordin, *Woman and Temperance*; *Minutes of the First Convention of the National Woman's Christian Temperance Union, 1874*, Woman's Christian Temperance Union Annual Meetings Minutes files (Joint Ohio Historical Society—Michigan Historical Collections—W.C.T.U. Microfilm Edition [hereafter Joint M/F Edition], roll 1).

11. Bordin, *Woman and Temperance*, 45–48, 57–58, 118–19; Frances E. Willard, *Woman and Temperance* (Hartford, Conn.: Park Publishing Co., 1883), 636–40. See also the *Minutes* for the First (1874: 33, 39), Second (1875: 55–56, 64–66, 73), Third (1876: 97, 105–13), and Fourth (1877: 197) Conventions of the National Woman's Christian Temperance Union, all in Woman's Christian Temperance Union Annual Meetings Minutes files (Joint M/F Edition, roll 1).

12. Fuller's *Fifteen Years of a Dancer's Life* recounts neither this temperance lecture nor the 1875–77 touring stints in which she also gave temperance speeches. See Sommer, "Loie Fuller," 18, 20–23; Fuller, holograph page, no title, n.d., Fuller Papers 1892, folder 34, item 34–1, DCNYPL; Loie Fuller, "Before Many Years Were Over, I had attended many lectures . . . ," unpublished autobiography typescript and holograph pages, n.d., Loie Fuller Papers 1914–1928 (hereafter Fuller Papers 1914), microfilm reel 3, folder 204, items C–9–204.1 through 204.12, DCNYPL).

13. On women in antebellum temperance movements, see Dannenbaum, "The Origins of Temperance Activism"; Ian R. Tyrrell, "Women and Temperance in Antebellum America, 1830–1860," *Civil War History* 28 (June 1982): 128–52; Ian R. Tyrrell, *Sobering Up; From Temperance to Prohibition in Antebellum America, 1800–1860* (Westport, Conn.: Greenwood Press, 1979), 67–68, 159–90, 279; W. J. Rorabaugh, *The Alcoholic Republic; An American Tradition* (New York: Oxford University Press, 1979), 257. For remarks on public speaking, see Mother Stewart, *Memories of the Crusade*, 29, 66.

14. Sommer, "Loie Fuller," 19; Fuller, "Before Many Years," autobiography typescript, n.d., page 3, Fuller Papers 1914, m/f reel 3, folder 204, item C–9–204.10, DCNYPL.

15. Sommer, "Loie Fuller," 18, 23.

16. Thorough scholarship on Ruth St. Denis can be found in Christena L. Schlundt, *The Professional Appearances of Ruth St Denis & Ted Shawn; A Chronology and an Index of Dances 1906–1932* (New York: New York Public Library, 1962); Suzanne Shelton, *Divine Dancer; A Biography of Ruth St. Denis* (Garden City, N.Y.: Doubleday & Co., 1981); Nancy Ruyter, *Reformers and Visionaries; The Americanization of the Art of Dance* (New York: Dance Horizons, 1979). See also Elizabeth Kendall, *Where She Danced* (New York: Alfred A. Knopf, 1979). On the course of St. Denis's early career, see Shelton, *Divine Dancer*, 22–33, 38–43, 49–52.

17. Ruth St. Denis, *An Unfinished Life* (New York: Harper & Brothers, 1939), 56, 65–70; Shelton, *Divine Dancer*, 53, 55–58.

18. "The following ladies appreciating the beauty of the Oriental Dances of Radha . . . ," printed program, in Denishawn Collection—Scrapbooks—Clippings, microfilm reel 11 (hereafter cited as DCS m/f reel 11), Dance Collection, New York Public Library for the Performing Arts, and in Ruth St. Denis—Pro-

grams and Announcements 1900–1930, folder 1 1900–1910 (hereafter cited as RSDPA), DCNYPL.

Also, "Bringing Temple Dances from the Orient to Broadway," *New York Times*, March 25, 1906, 2d Magazine section, p. 2; Henry Tyrrell, "Yes, Society DID Gasp When 'Radha' in Incense-Laden Air 'Threw off the Bondage of the Earthly Senses,'" *The World*, March 25, 1906, DCS m/f reel 11; "No Rude Men May Gaze Upon These Sensuous Dances," newspaper clipping [dated only as 1906], Ruth St. Denis Reserve Dance Clipping File–1919 (hereafter cited as RSDRDC), DCNYPL; "East Indian Dances," undated newspaper clipping, DCS m/f reel 11; "Society Gasps at Oriental Dances," undated newspaper clipping, DCS m/f reel 11; "Young Dancer Charms Society," *Herald*, March 23, 1906, RSDRDC.

St. Denis, *An Unfinished Life*, 71; Shelton, *Divine Dancer*, 56; Schlundt, *Professional Appearances*, 11.

19. Henry Tyrrell, "Yes, Society DID Gasp," DCS m/f reel 11.

20. Ibid.

21. "Bringing Temple Dances from the Orient to Broadway," *New York Times*, March 25, 1906, 2d Magazine section, p. 2.

22. Horowitz, *Culture & the City*, 55; Boris, *Art and Labor*, 59, 62, 76–80, 100, 119, 121; Lears, *No Place of Grace*, 66–73.

23. Rossiter, *Charles Ives*, xi, 12, 24–44; McCarthy, *Noblesse Oblige*, 33, 36–37, 50, 95, 175; Karen J. Blair, *The Clubwoman as Feminist; True Womanhood Redefined, 1868–1914* (New York: Holmes & Meier Publishers, 1980), 118, 28.

24. "Bringing Temple Dances from the Orient to Broadway," *New York Times*, March 25, 1906, 2d Magazine section, p. 2. For data on the club movement, see Blair, *The Clubwoman as Feminist*; Theodora Penny Martin, *The Sound of Our Own Voices: Women's Study Clubs, 1860–1910* (Boston: Beacon Press, 1987); Mary I. Wood, *The History of the General Federation of Women's Clubs for the First Twenty-two Years of its Organization* (New York: The History Department, General Federation of Women's Clubs, 1912; Farmingdale, N.Y.: Dabor Social Science Publications, 1978); Caroline French Benton, *Woman's Club Work and Programs or First Aid to Club Women* (Boston: L. C. Page & Co., 1913). See also Blair's *The Torchbearers: Women and Their Amateur Arts Associations in America, 1890–1930* (Bloomington: Indiana University Press, 1990).

25. St. Denis, *An Unfinished Life*, 74; "Entertain for Thursday Club," *New York Herald*, April 6, 1906, DCS m/f reel 11; "Weird Dancer Whirls at Saterlee Party," *New York American*, April 6, 1906, DCS m/f reel 11.

26. For the People's Symphony benefit see "An East Indian Matinee in aid of the People's Symphony Concerts . . . will be given . . . April 24, 1906 . . . ," printed announcement in RSDPA; "East Indian Matinee in Aid of the People's Symphony Concerts, The Waldorf Astoria, Tuesday Afternoon April Twenty-Fourth 4:40 O'Clock," printed program in RSDPA; "An East Indian Matinee in Aid of the People's Symphony Concerts will be Given at the Waldorf-Astoria Tuesday Afternoon, April 24th at 4:30 o'clock," printed program in DCS m/f reel 11.

People's Symphony trustees who were also present at St. Denis's Thursday Evening Club appearance include Mrs. Francis P. Kinnicut, Gustav E. Kissel, Mrs. Douglas Robbinson, Mrs. H. Fairfield Osborn, and Charles T. Barney.

For the Barney benefit at the Belasco Theatre, see "Fashionable Set at Radha Dances," *New York Herald*, April 28, 1906, DCS m/f reel 11; "Large Audience Attends Benefit at Belasco Theater," *Washington Post*, April 28, 1906, DCS m/f reel 11; "Gives Oriental Dances," undated newspaper clipping, DCS m/f reel 11; "Only Appearance of the Great Indian Dancer Radha," printed program in DCS m/f reel 11 and in RSDPA. The *Washington Times* linked St. Denis's appearance with her recent New York successes in "Radha, Indian Dancer, in Hospital Benefit," April 26, 1906, DCS m/f reel 11.

For the benefit held at Fenway Court see "Barefooted Maiden Gives Society Folk a New Thrill," *Boston Post*, May 8, 1906, DCS m/f reel 11; "Fenway Court, Wednesday May 2, 1906, Entertainment in Aid of Holy Ghost Hospital for Incurables, Cambridge Massachusetts," printed program in RSDPA; "Social Life," *The Sunday Herald*, May 6, 1906, DCS m/f reel 11.

See also Schlundt, *Professional Appearances*, 11; St. Denis, *An Unfinished Life*, 74–75; Shelton, *Divine Dancer*, 58.

27. On Washingtonian women's work with alternative entertainments see Tyrrell, *Sobering Up*, 176–78. The literature on women's antislavery activism is large; for one treatment of the connection between abolition and women's rights activism, see Gerda Lerner, *The Grimké Sisters from South Carolina; Pioneers for Women's Rights and Abolition* (New York: Schocken Books, 1973). On women's growing equal rights sentiment within temperance movements see Tyrrell, "Women and Temperance," 144–48.

28. Schlundt, *Professional Appearances*, 14–18; Shelton, *Divine Dancer*, 92, 105, 107.

29. Sources for named entertainments are found in DCS, all m/f reel 11.

On the Lydig entertainment see "Lydigs to Stage 'Judith' at Home," *Morning Telegraph*, January 24, [1913]; untitled news item, *Town Topics*, January 30, 1913; "Players from France Brought by Mrs. Ly[dig] for Remarkable [headline broken]," *Press*, [1913].

On the Tiffany fete see "Egyptian Fete Closed New York's 'Season [headline broken]," *Philadelphia Inquirer*, February 8, 1913; "Mr. Tiffany's Egyptian Fete Scene of Splendor [headline broken]," *Herald*, February 5, 1913; "Gorgeous Pageant at Tiffany Studio," [unidentified newspaper], n.d.

On the Armours' entertainment see untitled news item, *Club Fellow*, August 6, [1906]; Newspaper clipping fragment, "One of the experiences of the imaginative child," *Tribune*, August 3, n.d.

On the Kansas City and Chicago study clubs, see untitled news item, *Musical Leader*, December 11, 1913; "Kansas City Schubert Club Entering Twenty-First Season," *Musical Courier*, November 26, 1913; "Fine Audience for Ruth St. Denis at First Concert," *Kansas City Post*, November 24, 1913; "A Morning of Ruth St. Denis," *Kansas City Star*, November 24, [1913]; "'Morning of Music' at Baltimore, Nov. 24," [Kansas City, Mo.] *Journal*, November 16, 1913; "Chansons En Crinoline Resumed," *Musical Leader*, December 11, 1913.

For the York Harbor event, see "Ruth St. Denis to Appear at Mid-Summer Festival," [Portsmouth, N.H.] *Herald*, August 4, 1913; "Ruth St. Denis in York Harbor Dance," [Boston] *American*, August 13, 1913; "Hindoo Dances for York Harbor's Fete," [Boston] *Herald*, August 3, 1913; "Ruth St. Denis to Dance,"

[Portland, Maine] *Press*, July 24, 1913; "Boston Cottager at York Harbor Interested in Fete," [Boston] *Herald*, July 27, 1913; "York Awaits Ruth St. Denis," [Boston] *American*, July 27, 1913.

For St. Denis's appearance at Mrs. Potter Palmer's charity ball, see "Ruth St. Denis Will Dance for Charity," *Ocean*, December 14, 1909; "Fortunes in Gems Watched by Army of Guards," [1909].

For St. Denis's participation in the Christmas Fund benefit, see "Program" [printed program]; "More Stars for Xmas Benefit," *New York American*, December 18, 1913; "Xmas Show at Princess Triumph," *New York American*, December 19, 1913, p. 6.

Schlundt, *Professional Appearances*, 17–18; Shelton, *Divine Dancer*, 95; St. Denis, *An Unfinished Life*, 134–35, 147–48.

30. "Dr. Anna Shaw Enjoys Maxixe," *Evening Sun*, March 3, 1914, DCS m/f reel 11; "Dr. Shaw Enjoys New Wrinkle," *Morning Telegraph*, March 3, 1914, DCS m/f reel 11; "Dr. Shaw Had Her Party," *Evening Post*, March 3, 1914, DCS m/f reel 11. Shaw's remarks are quoted in "Anna Howard Shaw Wishes She Could Dance Like Ruth St. Denis," [New Britain, Conn.] *Herald*, March 4, 1914; and "Twinkling Toes Tantalize Dr. Shaw on Her Birthday," *Tribune*, March 3, 1914, both DCS m/f reel 11.

31. "Dr. Anna Shaw Enjoys Maxixe," *Evening Sun*, March 3, 1914; Dr. Shaw Had Her Party," *Evening Post*, March 3, 1914; "Dr. Shaw Enjoys New Wrinkle," *Morning Telegraph*, March 3, 1914.

32. On Duncan's childhood, early professional experiences, and launching as a dance soloist in America, see Isadora Duncan, *My Life* (London: Victor Gollancz, 1928), 1–56; Paul Hertelendy, "Isadora's Childhood; Clearing Away the Clouds," *Dance Magazine* 51 (July 1977): 48–50; Nesta MacDonald, "Isadora Reexamined; Lesser-known Aspects of the Great Dancer's Life, 1877–1900, Part One" *Dance Magazine* 51 (July 1977): 51–54; Frederika Blair, *Isadora; Portrait of the Artist as a Woman* (New York: McGraw-Hill, 1986), 1–38; Ruyter, *Reformers and Visionaries*, 33–41; Allan Ross MacDougall, *Isadora: A Revolutionary in Art and Life* (New York: Thomas Nelson, 1960), 1–47; Deborah Jowitt, *Time and the Dancing Image* (New York: William Morrow, 1988), 69–82; "Isadora Duncan Returns to Scene of First Triumphs," *Chicago Sunday Tribune*, November 29, 1908, Society/Editorial/Drama sect., p. 3. Ann Daly's *Done into Dance: Isadora Duncan in America* (Bloomington: Indiana University Press, 1995) gives important insight into American tours that Duncan made later in her career.

33. *The Director*, March 1898, asserts Duncan's support by society patrons in "Emotional Expression," 109–11; the October-November 1898 issue provides female sponsors' names in "Narcissus and Other Scenes," and in an extract from *Town Topics* (September 15): 272–74. Page numbers in this and succeeding notes reference the reprint edition of *The Director* (December 1897–November 1898) published by Dance Horizons, n.d.

34. Duncan, *My Life*, 50–51; MacDougall, *Isadora*, 39; "Society Notes," *New York Times*, March 25, 1898, p. 7; *The Director* (March 1898): 109. Note that *The Director* quotes from a February 20, 1898, *New York Herald* review.

35. Duncan, *My Life*, 51; Program, "Rubaiyat of Omar Khayyam, Done Into Dance by Isadora Duncan, Newport Sept 8, 1898," in Duncan, *Isadora. Programs*

1898–1929, microfilm *MGZB-Res (hereafter Duncan Programs), DCNYPL; *The Director* (September 1898): 254.

36. "What is Doing in Society," *New York Times*, March 15, 1899, p. 7; "Isadora Duncan as the Only Real Society Pet," *Broadway Magazine* [June 1899]: 143 and photos ff., in Duncan, Isadora. Reserve Dance Clipping File (hereafter Duncan Clippings), microfilm #ZBD–170, DCNYPL. "Miss Duncan's\[torn]\She Is to Illustrate a Lecture\[torn]\Omar Khayyam," newspaper fragment, n.p, (hand-dated [incorrectly, I believe] 1898), Duncan Clippings, DCNYPL. Daly, too, reads the cabinet cards in *Done into Dance*, 47–49, 59.

37. "A Soulful Function," unidentified newspaper clipping, ([hand-dated April 19, 1899]), Duncan Clippings, DCNYPL. Despite the support shown by society women in the April benefit, Duncan had little luck soliciting society women on an individual basis for travel funds.

38. Ruyter, *Reformers and Visionaries*, 33.

39. "Isadora Duncan as the Only Real Society Pet," *Broadway Magazine* [June 1899].

40. Frederic Cople Jaher, "Nineteenth-century Elites in New York and Boston," *Journal of Social History* 6 (1972): 32–77; Frederic Cople Jaher, "Style and Status: High Society in Late Nineteenth-Century New York," in *The Rich, the Well Born, and the Powerful*, ed. Jaher (Urbana: University of Illinois Press, 1973), 258–84; Wallace Evan Davies, "Caroline Webster Schermerhorn Astor" in *Notable American Women 1607–1950*, eds. James, James, Boyer (Cambridge: Harvard University Press, Belknap Press, 1971), 1: 62–4; Dixon Wecter, *The Saga of American Society 1607–1937* (New York: Charles Scribner's Sons, 1937).

41. Davies, "Astor"; Janet W. Buell, "Alva Belmont: From Socialite to Feminist," *The Historian* (February 1990): 219–34; Wallace Evan Davies, "Marian Graves Anthon Fish," *Notable American Women*, 1: 620–21.

42. "Isadora Duncan as the Only Real Society Pet," *Broadway Magazine* [June 1899].

43. Karen Halttunen, *Confidence Men and Painted Women; A Study of Middle-Class Culture in America, 1830–1840* (New Haven: Yale University Press, 1982); Joseph Roach, "Theatre History and the Ideology of the Aesthetic," *Theatre Journal* 41, no. 2 (May 1989): 155–68.

44. On American Delsartism see Ruyter, *Reformers and Visionaries*, 17–30.

45. Robert Allen, *Horrible Prettiness: Burlesque and American Culture* (Chapel Hill: University of North Carolina Press, 1991). The videotape *Trailblazers of Modern Dance* includes short snatches of ballet girls performing at the turn of the century (Merrill Brockway and Judy Kinberg, producers, WNET-TV, 1977).

46. Shelton parses the American Orientalism vogue in *Divine Dancer*, 54–56; Edward W. Said's *Orientalism* (New York: Vintage Books, 1979) illuminates the political and cultural othering which Orientalist constructions perform.

47. Ann Daly, "Dance History and Feminist Theory: Reconsidering Isadora Duncan and the Male Gaze," in *Gender in Performance: The Presentation of Difference in the Performing Arts*, ed. Laurence Senelick (Hanover, N.H.: University Press of New England, 1992), 239–59.

48. Daly, "Dance History and Feminist Theory;" Susan Manning, *Ecstasy and the Demon: Feminism and Nationalism in the Dance of Mary Wigman* (Berkeley:

University of California Press, 1993). Classic statements of gaze theory include Laura Mulvey, "Visual Pleasure and Narrative Cinema," in *Art After Modernism: Rethinking Representation*, ed. Brian Wallis (New York: New Museum of Contemporary Art, 1984), 361–73; E. Ann Kaplan, "Is the Gaze Male?" in *Powers of Desire*, ed. Ann Snitow, Christine Stansell, and Sharon Thompson (New York: Monthly Review Press, 1983), 309–27. Efforts to problematize, wriggle free from the grasp of, or expose the heterosexual underpinnings of the male gaze include Mary Anne Doane, "Film and the Masquerade: Theorizing the Female Spectator," *Screen* 3–4 (October 1982): 74–87; Doane, "Masquerade Reconsidered: Further Thoughts on the Female Spectator," *Discourse* 11, no. 1 (Fall-Winter 1988–89): 42–54; Diane Fuss, "Fashion and the Homospectatorial Look," *Critical Inquiry* (Summer 1992): 713–37. On the gaze and vision in art historical representations, see Griselda Pollock, *Vision and Difference: Femininity, Feminism and Histories of Art* (London: Routledge, 1988), especially chapter 3.

49. Jonathan Crary, "Modernizing Vision" and "Discussion," in *Vision and Visuality*, ed. Hal Foster (Seattle, Wash.: Bay Press, 1988), 29–44, 45–49.

50. Manning, *Ecstasy and the Demon*, 127, 99, 35.

51. Jane Sherman and Christena L. Schlundt, "Who's St. Denis? What Is She?" *Dance Chronicle* 10 (1987): 305–29.

52. MacDougall, 45–46, 52.

53. MacDonald, "Isadora Reexamined," 55–57, 60–64; MacDougall 52–53.

54. Henry James, *The Bostonians* (1886; reprint New York: Vintage Books, 1991).

55. James, *The Bostonians*, 54–55, 186, 207, 210, 230, 244, 249, 308, 314, 363.

56. James, *The Bostonians*, 239.

57. James, *The Bostonians*, 189, 112, 395.

58. James, *The Bostonians*, 125.

3. The Settlement House and the Playhouse

1. Alice Lewisohn Crowley, *The Neighborhood Playhouse; Leaves from a Theatre Scrapbook* (New York: Theatre Arts Books, 1959), 40–41. Crowley's memoir was composed after the Playhouse ceased functioning as a production house. She indicates that she made at least two attempts to write a memoir prior to preparing the published volume, and she thanks several individuals for assistance with assemblage and editing tasks (xxiii). While she disclaims any "direct aim to evaluate these 'memories' from a psychological angle," she acknowledges the insights of C. G. Jung (xxiii). The frequent metaphoric references she makes to ancestral roots or images, for example, or to spontaneous release and release values, suggest that familiarity with psychoanalytic discourse informed her interpretive framework.

2. On the settlement house movement see Mina Carson, *Settlement Folk; Social Thought and the American Settlement Movement, 1885–1930* (Chicago: University of Chicago Press, 1990); Allen F. Davis, *Spearheads for Reform; The Social Settlements and the Progressive Movement 1890–1914* (New York: Oxford University Press, 1967); Judith Trolander, *Professionalism and Social Change; From the Settlement House Movement to Neighborhood Centers 1886 to the Present*

(New York: Columbia University Press, 1987); Henry C. Adams, ed., *Philanthropy and Social Progress, Seven Essays* (New York: Thomas Y. Crowell & Co., 1893); Jane Addams, *Twenty Years at Hull-House* (1910; reprint, New York: New American Library, 1981); Samuel A. Barnett, "The Settlement Movement, III: Education by Permeation," *Charities and The Commons* 16 (May 5, 1906): 186–88; Werner Picht, *Toynbee Hall and the English Settlement Movement*, rev. ed. (London: G. Bell & Sons, 1914); Robert A. Woods and Albert J. Kennedy, *Handbook of Settlements* (New York: Charities Publication Committee, 1911); Arthur Holden, *The Settlement Idea, A Vision of Social Justice* (New York: MacMillan, 1922); William E. McLennan, "Democracy and the Settlement," *Social Forces* 4 (June 1926): 769–73; Lorene M. Pacey, *Readings in the Development of Settlement Work* (New York: Association Press, 1950); *Settlements and Their Outlook; An Account of the First International Conference of Settlements* (London: P. S. King & Son, 1922); George C. White, "Social Settlements and Immigrant Neighbors, 1886–1914," *Social Service Review*, 33 (March, 1959): 55–66.

On immigration see Selma C. Berrol, "In Their Image: German Jews and the Americanization of the *Ost Juden* in New York City," *New York History*, 63 (October 1982): 421; Lloyd P. Gartner, "Immigration and the Formation of American Jewry, 1840–1925," *Journal of World History*, 11 (1968): 297–312.

3. Moses Rischin, *The Promised City: New York's Jews 1870–1940* (Cambridge: Harvard University Press, 1962), 20, 33; Mary Beth Norton, David M. Katzman et al., *A People and A Nation; A History of the United States, vol. 2: Since 1865* (Boston: Houghton Mifflin, 1982), A–15.

4. White, "Social Settlements," 56; Davis, *Spearheads for Reform*, 12; Lillian Wald, "The Henry Street (the Nurses) Settlement, New York," *Charities and the Commons* 16 (April 7, 1906): 35–41; Wald, *The House on Henry Street* (New York: Henry Holt & Co., 1915); Wald, *Windows on Henry Street* (Boston: Little, Brown, 1934).

5. Kathryn Kish Sklar analyzes the sources of settlement women's social power in "Hull House in the 1890s: A Community of Women Reformers," *Signs* 10 (Summer 1985): 658–77. See also Stephen Kalberg, "The Commitment to Career Reform: The Settlement Movement Leaders," *Social Service Review* 49 (December, 1975): 608–28; John P. Rousmaniere, "Cultural Hybrid in the Slums: The College Woman and the Settlement House, 1889–1894," *American Quarterly* 22 (Spring 1970): 45–66.

6. *Report of the Henry Street Settlement 1893–1913* (New York: The Henry Street Settlement, 1913), 20, 27, holding of the Neighborhood Playhouse School of Theatre, New York City (this Neighborhood Playhouse Collection cited hereafter as NPC).

7. Addams, *Twenty Years at Hull-House*, 98.

8. Wald, *The House on Henry Street*, 210.

9. Jane Addams, "The Subjective Necessity for Social Settlements," (1892) in *Philanthropy and Social Progress*, ed. Adams, 5, 44.

10. Addams, *Twenty Years at Hull-House*, 260, 265.

11. See Wald, *The House on Henry Street*, 186, for the term "dower."

12. Wald, *The House on Henry Street*, 303.

13. White, "Social Settlements" 56; James Daugherty, "Jane Addams: Culture

and Imagination," *Yale Review* 71 (April, 1982): 363–79; Addams, "Subjective Necessity," in Adams, ed., 23, 26; Wald, *The House on Henry Street*, 310, 308, 93; Addams, *Twenty Years at Hull-House*, 272; Wald, *Windows on Henry Street*, 16, 157.

14. Wald, *Windows on Henry Street*, 16.

15. Roger B. Stein, *John Ruskin and Aesthetic Thought in America, 1840–1900* (Cambridge: Harvard University Press, 1967), 263–65; John Ruskin, *The Stones of Venice* (London: Smith, Elder & Co., 1853; facsimile reprint, New York: Garland Publishing, 1979), 2: 161, 163, 165; Ruskin, "Modern Manufacture and Design," in *The Works of John Ruskin*, ed. E. T. Cook and Alexander Wedderburn (New York: Longmans, Green & Co., 1905), 16: 338, 344 (hereafter cited as Ruskin, *Works*); John Ruskin, *Unto This Last* (London: Smith, Elder & Co., 1862), 33–35, 47, 102, 144; "Traffic," Ruskin, *Works* 18: 436. See also John D. Rosenberg, *The Darkening Glass; A Portrait of Ruskin's Genius* (New York: Columbia University Press, 1961), 152–60; Eileen Boris, *Art and Labor; Ruskin, Morris, and the Craftsman Ideal in America* (Philadelphia: Temple University Press, 1986), especially 3–7.

16. William Morris, "How I Became a Socialist," *William Morris; Selected Writings and Designs*, ed. Asa Briggs (New York: Penguin Books, 1962), 33–37 (hereafter cited as Morris, *Selected Writings*); "'A Rather Long-Winded Sketch of My Very Uneventful Life,'" Morris, *Selected Writings*, 32; William Morris, "The Lesser Arts. Delivered Before the Trades' Guild of Learning, December 4, 1877," *The Collected Works of William Morris*, ed. May Morris (New York: Longmans, Green & Co., 1914) 22: 22, 25–26 (hereafter cited as Morris, *Collected Works*); "The Worker's Share of Art," Morris, *Selected Writings*, 140–43; "The Revival of Handicraft. An Article in the 'Fortnightly Review,' November 1888," Morris, *Collected Works* 22: 341; "The Arts and Crafts of To-day. An Address Delivered in Edinburgh Before the National Association for the Advancement of Art in October, 1889," Morris, *Collected Works* 22: 373. See also Boris, *Art and Labor*, 7–28.

17. Addams, *Twenty Years at Hull-House*, 258.

18. Rosenberg, *The Darkening Glass*, 164; "Sesame and Lilies" in Ruskin, *Works* 18: 121–23; Stein, *John Ruskin and Aesthetic Thought in America*, 259–60; Arthur Mann, *Yankee Reformers in the Urban Age; Social Reform in Boston, 1880–1900* (Chicago: University of Chicago Press, 1954; Midway Reprint, 1974), 219–24; Boris, *Art and Labor*, especially 45–47, 73, 105, 180–85; Addams, *Twenty Years at Hull-House*, 221, 257–58, 261, 275; Wald, *The House on Henry Street*, 12, 78, 182. On the Arts and Crafts movement, see also Lionel Lambourne, *Utopian Craftsmen; The Arts and Crafts Movement from the Cotswolds to Chicago* (London: The Architectural Press Ltd, Astragal Books, 1980); T. J. Jackson Lears, *No Place of Grace; Antimodernism and the Transformation of American Culture 1880–1920* (New York: Pantheon Books, 1981), 60–96.

19. *Report of the Henry Street Settlement 1893–1913*, 21.

20. See, for example, Addams, *Twenty Years at Hull-House*, 259–73; Helen Horowitz, *Culture & the City; Cultural Philanthropy in Chicago from the 1880s to 1917* (Lexington: University Press of Kentucky, 1976), 128–40.

21. On Progressive education issues see Michael Katz, *Class, Bureaucracy, and Schools; The Illusion of Educational Change in America* (New York: Praeger Pub-

lishers, 1971), 3–55; Lawrence A. Cremin, *The Transformation of the School; Progressivism in American Education 1876–1957* (New York: Vintage Books, 1964), 1–22; David Tyack and Elisabeth Hansot, *Managers of Virtue; Public School Leadership in America, 1820–1980* (New York: Basic Books, 1982); Lawrence A. Cremin, David A. Shannon, and Mary Evelyn Townsend, *A History of Teachers College Columbia University* (New York: Columbia University Press, 1954); Dorothy Ross, *G. Stanley Hall; The Psychologist as Prophet* (Chicago: University of Chicago Press, 1972); *John Dewey: The Middle Works, 1899–1924, v. 1: 1899–1901*, ed. Jo Ann Boydston (Carbondale and Edwardsville: Southern Illinois University Press, 1976); *The Early Works of John Dewey, 1882–1898, v. 5: 1895–1898, Early Essays*, ed. Jo Ann Boydston (Carbondale and Edwardsville: Southern Illinois University Press, 1972); Merle Curti, *The Social Ideas of American Educators* (Totowa, N.J.: Littlefield, Adams & Co., 1978).

22. C. C. Van Liew, "The Educational Theory of the Culture Epochs, Viewed Historically and Critically," 117, in *The First Year Book of the Herbart Society*, reprinted in *The National Herbart Society Yearbooks 1–5, 1895–1899* (New York: Arno Press, 1969).

23. Van Liew, "Educational Theory of the Culture Epochs," 118.

24. Ibid, 117.

25. Ibid.

26. See *The First Year Book of the Herbart Society*, reprinted in *The National Herbart Society Yearbooks 1–5, 1895–1899* (New York: Arno Press, 1969).

27. "Rita Wallach, Social Worker, 84," obituary, *New York Times*, April 9, 1964, p. 13; John Dewey, "Interpretation of the Culture-Epoch Theory" (1896), reprinted in *The Early Works of John Dewey, 1882–1989*, 5: 247–53.

28. Percival Chubb, et al., *Festivals and Plays in Schools and Elsewhere* (New York: Harper & Bros., 1912), 62; Maud Karpeles, *Cecil Sharp, His Life and Work* (London: Routledge & Kegan Paul, 1967). Duncan's early *Dance Idylls* were set to "pre-classic" forms, as Louis Horst would term them; see programs from 1903 to 1905 in Duncan, Isadora. Programs 1898–1929, microfilm *MGZB-Res, Dance Collection, New York Public Library for the Performing Arts (hereafter DCNYPL).

29. The dating of the girls' introduction to the Henry Street Settlement is addressed most directly in Crowley, *The Neighborhood Playhouse*. The remarks are still ambiguous, however, with only the death of the father during this period independently dated. Two possible scenarios can be constructed from a close reading of the text. First, the girls visited the Settlement in 1900; Alice began her association there in 1901; Leonard Lewisohn died in 1902; Irene subsequently joined Alice in her Settlement work. The second interpretation, presented here, emerges more straightforwardly from Alice's elliptical narrative: the girls visited Henry Street in 1901; Leonard Lewisohn died in 1902; Alice began her association with the Settlement in 1903; Irene followed subsequently.

For additional biographical data see Marian Rich, "Lewisohn, Irene," *Notable American Women, 1607–1950*, ed. Edward T. James (Cambridge: Harvard University Press, Belknap Press, 1971) 2: 400–02; "Irene Lewisohn," *Women of Achievement* (New York: House of Field, 1940), 117; "Lewisohn, Leonard," *The National Cyclopaedia of American Biography* (New York: James T. White and Co., 1939)

27: 464–65; author's telephone interview with Rodney O. Felder, former President of Finch College, March 8, 1985.

For the Finch School see 19–20, for Delsarte see 31–32, both in Alice Lewisohn Crowley, "Growing Into Theatre: The Story of the Neighborhood Playhouse," (typescript, the Neighborhood Playhouse School of Theatre, 1941), NPC. On Dalcroze exposure, see Crowley, *The Neighborhood Playhouse*, 37; on Noh, see Crowley, 86; Robert L. Duffus, *Lillian Wald, Neighbor and Crusader* (New York: MacMillan Co., 1939), 139–40. On Alice's debut in *Pippa Passess*, see "Miss Lewisohn, Millionaire Girl, Has Gone on Stage Here," *New York Evening Journal*, November 14, 1906, p. 5, in "Alice Lewisohn, Locke Collection Envelope 1170," Billy Rose Theatre Collection, New York Public Library for the Performing Arts (hereafter cited as Locke Collection); "Girl Millionaire, Her Secret Out, Will Not Give Up Work on Stage," *New York Evening Journal*, November 16, 1906, p. 6, Locke Collection; "With $2,000,000, Girl is Paying to Act in Play," clipping from unidentified newspaper, November 15, 1906, Locke Collection.

30. Relationships among female workers and residents could operate in several registers. In *The Neighborhood Playhouse*, Alice makes clear the force of Wald's example at the Settlement and the deep, abiding affection that the "Leading Lady" inspired. In correspondence ca. 1906–10 preserved in Lillian Wald's papers, Blanche Wiesen Cook emphasizes the intimacy of relationships with Wald. Kathryn Kish Sklar has argued with reference to Hull-House in the 1890s that the decision to remain single positioned women to reconstruct their gender identities. For Jane Addams and a core of resident colleagues, refusal to marry enabled refusal "to replicate their class identity through marriage." At Henry Street, Alice Lewisohn did not marry until 1924, some twenty years later; Irene never did. The woman-centered community there provided crucial support for the sisters' self-fashioning as directors, authors, and even performers of dance and drama. Rita Wallach (1880–1964) married Max Morgenthau Jr., cousin of Henry Morgenthau Jr., who would be Secretary of the Treasury under Franklin D. Roosevelt. They divorced in 1928. When the Lewisohns re-opened the Neighborhood Playhouse as a School of the Theatre, Rita Morgenthau served as director. See Crowley, *The Neighborhood Playhouse*, 4–7; Cook, "Female Support Networks and Political Activism: Lillian Wald, Crystal Eastman, Emma Goldman," in *A Heritage of Her Own*, ed. Cott and Pleck (New York: Simon and Schuster, 1979), 412–42, especially 420–24; Sklar, *Florence Kelley and the Nation's Work: the Rise of Women's Political Culture, 1830–1900* (New Haven: Yale University Press, 1995), 186–87, 192. See also Carol Smith-Rosenberg, "The Female World of Love and Ritual: Relations Between Women in Nineteenth-Century America," *Signs* 1 (Autumn 1975): 1–29.

31. Crowley, *The Neighborhood Playhouse*, 17–19; Crowley "Growing into Theatre," 34.

32. Crowley, *The Neighborhood Playhouse*, 16–22; *Report of the Henry Street Settlement 1893–1913*; Alice Lewisohn, "Religious Seasonal Festivals," *Playground* 6 (December 1912): 328, 326; Rita Teresa Wallach, "The Settlement Movement IV: The Social Value of the Festival," *Charities and the Commons* 16 (June 2, 1906): 315–19.

33. Wallach, "Social Value of the Festival," 318–19.

34. My chronology of festivals and their typing is heavily influenced by *Report of the Henry Street Settlement 1893–1913*, and 1911–12 and 1913 issues of *The Settlement Journal* (a publication produced by Henry Street Settlement club members), both in NPC. For Chalif, see Crowley, *The Neighborhood Playhouse*, 42.

35. Crowley, *The Neighborhood Playhouse*, 17–18.

36. Wallach, "The Social Value of the Festival," 319.

37. Selma C. Berrol, "In Their Image," 428; White, "Social Settlements," 616.

38. *Report of the Henry Street Settlement 1893–1913*, 39–40; Crowley, *The Neighborhood Playhouse*, 16–22.

39. Alice Lewisohn, "Religious Seasonal Festivals," 324, 328.

40. Holden, *The Settlement Idea*, 54.

41. Crowley, *The Neighborhood Playhouse* 18–19.

42. Alice Lewisohn, "Religious Seasonal Festivals," 326. My dissertation argued that ballet or "classic" dancing provided one of the movement resources used in Henry Street Settlement festivals, 90, and that ballet technique was visible in Playhouse pantomime ballets such as *Petrouchka* and *The Royal Fandango*, 111. See Tomko, "Women, Artistic Dance Practices, and Social Change in the United States, 1890–1920" (Ph.D. diss., UCLA, 1991). Recognition of ballet as a movement material gains support from Melanie Blood's finding of technique class notes by Irene Lewisohn that used ballet vocabulary, and by Blood's reading of Lewisohn's choreographic notes/sketches for *Jephthah's Daughter*. See Blood, "The Neighborhood Playhouse, 1915–1927; A History and Analysis," 2 vols. (Ph.D. diss., Northwestern University, 1994), 258–59, 263–68, 386–87. Blood notes that "the only specifically dated technique class notes are from the 1909–10 year, though some may be from other years, and the same cards may have been used in future years."

43. *Report of the Henry Street Settlement 1893–1913*, 41.

44. *The Repertory Idea* (New York: The Neighborhood Playhouse, 1927), n.p.; *Report of the Henry Street Settlement 1893–1913*, 41.

45. According to Alice Owen's chronology—"Productions of the Neighborhood Playhouse," 252, in Crowley, *The Neighborhood Playhouse*—the three other plays were *Womenkind* (Wilfred Wilson Gibson), *The Price of Coal* (Harold Brighouse), and *Ryland* (Thomas Wood Stevens and Kenneth S. Goodman).

46. The twentieth anniversary pageant "marked our only experience in pageantry" wrote Crowley in *The Neighborhood Playhouse*, 13, clearly trying to distinguish the sisters' work from that popular movement. Cf. Naima Prevots, *American Pageantry* (Ann Arbor: UMI Research Press, 1991), 118.

47. Brooks Atkinson, *Broadway*, rev. ed. (New York: Limelight Editions, 1970), 47, 106; Leo Trepp, *The Complete Book of Jewish Observance* (New York: Behrman House, 1980); Theodor H. Gaster, *Festivals of the Jewish Year* (New York: William Morrow, 1974); "Calendar" and "Festivals" entries in *The Encyclopedia of Judaism*, ed. Geofrey Wigoder (New York: Macmillan, 1989), 145–46 and 263–65. Also useful is Barbara Kirshenblatt-Gimblett, "*Contraband*: Performance, Text and Analysis of a *Purim-shpil*," *The Drama Review* 24 (September 1980): 5–16.

48. On the founding of the Ethical Society, its development, and Ethical

Society schools, see Howard B. Radest, *Toward Common Ground; The Story of the Ethical Societies in the United States* (New York: Frederick Ungar Pub. Co., 1969); Horace L. Friess, *Felix Adler and Ethical Culture: Memories and Studies*, ed. Fannia Weingartner (New York: Columbia University Press, 1981); Benny Kraut, *From Reform Judaism to Ethical Culture: The Religious Evolution of Felix Adler*, Hebrew Union College Monograph 4 (Cincinnati: Hebrew Union College Press, 1979).

49. Radest, *Toward Common Ground*, 187. The pride of place given ECS festivals may seem distinctly at odds with the Ethical Society's aversion to religious ritual and historical ceremonial practices. Part of the strangeness, and appeal, of the new society that Adler founded in 1878 lay in the way it distanced its services from Reform Judaism, the religion in which Adler, son of Temple Emanu-El's Rabbi, was reared. At Ethical Society meetings, a lecturer spoke, rather than a rabbi or minister, and he dressed in street clothes. Organ music was provided, as in Reform Judaism services, but the congregation did not sing. One of the problems the society had to work out was how to deal with marriages, deaths, and births, occasions for which members were wont to value ceremony. Chubb, an Englishman, had circulated in English Ethical circles surrounding Stanton Coit, who experimented with adding an altar to Ethical services, dressing as lecturer in clerical robes, and using responsive readings during meetings (Radest, *Toward Common Ground*, 72–77). Adler and other American leaders of Ethical Societies looked askance at such development of ritual forms but did not prohibit it. Adler himself delivered major Christmas and Easter addresses to Ethical Societies, exploring the "contemporary symbolic meaning of those festivals for the modern age" (Kraut, *From Reform Judaism*, 176). Adler's family adopted Christmas celebrations, but not the Christian religious meaning of the occasion. Emphasizing the ethical thread in specifically religious practices, Adler acknowledged human needs for symbolic festivals and, while shunning historically contingent ritual, found contemporary symbols appropriate (Kraut, *From Reform Judaism*, 176). Perhaps the grounding of Chubb's festivals in literary and historical epochs, rather than ritual religious practice, delivered them from a "ritual" aspect, although their emphasis on communal expression strained at the Ethical insistence on molding the individual.

50. Chubb et al., *Festivals and Plays*, 41–52.

51. Radest, *Toward Common Ground*, 137; Mary C. Allerton, "Dancing in the Festival," in Chubb et al., *Festivals and Plays*, 261–68. ECS festival programs and announcements may be found in Ethical Culture Fieldston School Archives, Record Group 2, Box 36. See the files "Festivals, Annual Exhibits ("Open School"), Drama: 1898–1910" and "Festivals, Annual Exhibits ("Open School"), Drama: 1910–1914," also the bound volume "Ethical Culture School, A Book of the Festival, 1888–1906." The Archives (hereafter ECFSA) are housed at the Tate Library on the Fieldston campus of the Ethical Culture Fieldston School, New York City. See also Chubb's pamphlet "The Function of the Festival in School Life," Ethical Pamphlets no. 9, n.d., Record Group 2, Box 36, ECFSA.

52. For announcements and a syllabus for the Normal Course see Record Group 2: Box 36, and the file "Scrapbook 1905–10" [internally and contradictorily labeled "Scrap Book to 1917"] in Box 34, ECFSA. From the look of the syllabus,

Normal Course materials found their way fairly directly into the 1912 publication of *Festivals and Plays,* by Chubb and his colleagues.

53. Useful works on German Jews, Russian Jews, and the two waves of immigration to America include Selma Berrol, "Education and Economic Mobility: The Jewish Experience in New York City, 1880–1920," *American Jewish Historical Quarterly* 65 (March 1976): 257–71; Berrol, "Germans versus Russians; An Update," *American Jewish History* 73 (December 1983): 142–56; Berrol, "In Their Image," 417–33; John Higham, *Send These to Me, Immigrants in Urban America,* rev. ed. (Baltimore: Johns Hopkins University Press, 1984); Rischin, *The Promised City,* 95–111; Norman L. Friedman, "German Lineage and Reform Affiliation: American Jewish Prestige Criteria in Transition," *Phylon* 26 (Summer, 1965): 140–47; Gartner, "Immigration and the Formation of American Jewry," 297–312; Jeffrey S. Gurock, "Jacob A. Riis: Christian Friend or Missionary Foe? Two Jewish Views," *American Jewish History* 71 (September 1981): 29–47; S. E. Aschheim, "Caftan and Cravat," in *Political Symbolism in Modern Europe: Essays in Honor of George L. Mosse,* ed. Seymour Drescher et al. (New Brunswick, N.J.: Transaction Books, 1982), 81–99. For specific matters of dress, the garment trade, and social discrimination, see Higham, *Send These to Me,* 117, 127–34; Berrol, "Germans versus Russians," 155.

54. Chief among the German Jewish organizations were: United Hebrew Charities, Hebrew Sheltering and Guardian Society, the Hebrew Orphan Asylum, and the Clara de Hirsch Home for Working Girls. See Rischin, *The Promised City,* 101–11; Peter Romanofsky, "'. . . To Rid Ourselves of the Burden . . .': New York Jewish Charities and the Origins of the Industrial Removal Office, 1890–1901," *American Jewish Historical Quarterly* 64 (June 1975), 331–43; Deborah Dash Moore, "From Kehillah to Federation: the Communal Functions of Federated Philanthropy in New York City, 1917–1933," *American Jewish History* 68 (December 1978): 131–46.

55. Davis, *Spearheads for Reform,* 12; "Leonard Lewisohn," *The National Cyclopaedia of American Biography,* 465; "Mitchell Advocates Settlement Work," *New York Times,* February 1, 1914, sec. 3, p. 4; "Henry St. Settlement Celebrating Its 20th Birthday," *New York Times,* June 1, 1913, sec. 5, p. 9; Wald, *Windows on Henry Street,* 23, 47, 117; Berrol, "In Their Image," 427–29; Wald, *The House on Henry Street,* 308.

56. Wallach, "The Social Value of the Festival," 318.

57. Alice Lewisohn, "Religious Seasonal Festivals," 325.

58. Crowley, *The Neighborhood Playhouse,* 12–13; Robert L. Duffus, *Lillian Wald, Neighbor and Crusader* (New York: MacMillan Co., 1939), 139–40.

4. From Henry Street to Grand Street

1. "The Neighborhood's Year," *New York Times,* October 10, 1915, sec. 6, p. 7.

2. Alice Lewisohn Crowley, *The Neighborhood Playhouse: Leaves from a Theatre Scrapbook* (New York: Theatre Arts Books, 1959), xx.

3. Crowley, *The Neighborhood Playhouse,* 35.

4. Lillian Wald, *Windows on Henry Street* (Boston: Little, Brown, 1934), 166; Crowley, *The Neighborhood Playhouse,* 36, 38.

5. The Playhouse architects were Harry Creighton Ingalls and F. Burrall Hoffman Jr. The *New York Times*, January 25, 1915, p. 9, credits these men with the design of Winthrop Ames's Little Theatre as well. On the theatre and seating, see Crowley, *The Neighborhood Playhouse*, 76–82; on the sky dome, see "Minute Visits in the Wings," *New York Times*, February 28, 1915, sect. 7, p. 5; Robert K. Sarlos, *Jig Cook and the Provincetown Players; Theatre in Ferment* (University of Massachusetts Press, 1982), 128.

6. Krutch, introduction to Crowley, *The Neighborhood Playhouse*, xi.

7. Brooks Atkinson, *Broadway*, rev. ed. (New York: Limelight Editions, 1990), 4–5, 120; Crowley, *The Neighborhood Playhouse*, 36, 44–45; "Biblical Fete to Open Playhouse," *New York Tribune*, January 25, 1915, p. 9; "The Neighborhood Playhouse" (New York: The Neighborhood Playhouse, n.d. [1915]), n.p., Neighborhood Playhouse Collection (hereafter NPC); Program bill for *The Kairn of Koridwen*, February 24 and 25, 1917, NPC; "The Neighborhood Playhouse" (New York: The Neighborhood Playhouse, n.d. [1924–1925 season, also retrospective]), n.p., NPC.

8. "The Neighborhood Playhouse," (New York: The Neighborhood Playhouse, n.d. [1924–1925 season]), n.p., NPC; Crowley, *The Neighborhood Playhouse*, 31, 51, 84; Doris Fox Benardete, "The Neighborhood Playhouse in Grand Street" (Ph.D. diss., New York University, 1949), 62, 79, 90, 95; "Morgan, Agnes," *The Biographical Encyclopedia & Who's Who of the American Theatre*, ed. Walter Rigden (New York: James H. Heinemann, 1966), 693; Margaret M. Knapp, "Morgan, Agnes," *Notable American Women in the American Theatre; A Biographical Dictionary*, ed. Alice M. Robinson, Vera Mowry Roberts, and Milly S. Barranger (New York: Greenwood Press, 1989), 666.

9. On the advisory group, see "Biblical Fete to Open Playhouse," *New York Tribune*, January 25, 1915, p. 9. On collaborators, see Crowley, *The Neighborhood Playhouse*, 30–33. Over time, male staff filled some technical positions at the Playhouse.

10. On the little theatre movement, see Kenneth Macgowan, *Footlights Across America; Towards a National Theatre* (New York: Harcourt, Brace & Co, 1929); Jack Poggi, *Theater in America: The Impact of Economic Forces 1870–1967* (Ithaca: Cornell University Press, 1966); Edward Reed, "The Organized Theatres," *Theatre Arts Monthly* 18 (October 1934): 785–93; Sarlos, *Jig Cook*, 1–8; Garff B. Wilson, *Three Hundred Years of American Drama and Theatre* (Englewood Cliffs, N.J.: Prentice-Hall, 1973). On stars and "well-made plays," see Atkinson, *Broadway*, 21–39, 49–59; Oscar G. Brockett, *History of the Theatre*, 5th ed. (Boston: Allyn and Bacon, 1987), 492–93.

11. Peter Jelavich, *Berlin Cabaret* (Cambridge: Harvard University Press, 1993); Jelavich, *Munich and Theatrical Modernism; Politics, Playwriting, and Performance 1890–1914* (Cambridge: Harvard University Press, 1985); Brigitte Kueppers, "Max Reinhardt's *Sumurun*," *The Drama Review* 24 (March 1980): 75–84; Crowley, *The Neighborhood Playhouse*, 36–38; Nancy Cott, *The Grounding of Modern Feminism* (New Haven: Yale University Press, 1987), 53–63; Ellen DuBois, "Working Women, Class Relations, and Suffrage Militance: Harriot Stanton Blatch and the New York Woman Suffrage Movement, 1894–1909," *Journal of American History* 74 (1987): 53–57; Lisa Ticknor, *The Spectacle of*

Women; Imagery of the Suffrage Campaign 1907–14 (London: Chatto & Windus, 1987); Dubois, *Harriot Stanton Blatch and the Winning of Woman Suffrage* (New Haven: Yale University Press, 1997), chapters 4, 5, 6.

12. "Miss Lillian D. Wald Speaks at the Neighborhood Playhouse," *The Settlement Journal*, Playhouse Number (March-April 1915): 3, NPC.

13. Alice Lewisohn, "Random Thoughts Suggested by the Playhouse," *The Settlement Journal*, Playhouse Number (March-April 1915): 7, NPC.

14. Alice Lewisohn, "Random Thoughts," 7.

15. Irene Lewisohn, "The Playhouse as an Experimental Laboratory," *The Settlement Journal*, Playhouse Number (March-April 1915): 14, NPC.

16. Rich, "Lewisohn, Irene," 400–402; "Miss Irene Lewisohn is Dead; Aided Social Settlement Work," *New York Herald Tribune*, April 5, 1944, p. 22.

17. Both Blanche Talmud and Lily Lubell had danced in Henry Street Settlement festivals; see *The Repertory Idea* (New York: The Neighborhood Playhouse, 1927), n.p. While not from the New York neighborhood, Albert Carroll had performed in Hull-House theatre productions and danced in Chicago with Doris Humphrey, student of Hull-House dance innovator Mary Wood Hinman. See chapter 5 in this book.

18. Crowley, in *The Neighborhood Playhouse*, provides an overview of the variety of dance and dance-related productions mounted at the Playhouse. Particularly helpful is Alice Owen's appendix to the same work, "Productions of the Neighborhood Playhouse," 252–60. See also Melanie Blood, "The Neighborhood Playhouse 1915–1927; A History and Analysis" (Ph.D. diss., Northwestern University, 1994); Maida Castelhun Darnton, "A Playhouse of Wide Interests: Plays, Festivals and Pantomimes at the Neighborhood Playhouse," *Survey* 53 (Jan. 1, 1925): 395–401, 423–24; Thomas H. Dickinson, "Ten Years of the Neighborhood Playhouse," *American Review* 2 (March 1924): 134–41; "Second Year of the Neighborhood Playhouse," *Playground* 10 (July 1916): 129–31; Oliver M. Sayler, "The Neighborhood Playhouse," *Theatre Arts Magazine* 6 (January 1922): 15–19; Anne Sprague MacDonald, "The Neighborhood Playhouse," *Dance Observer* 5 (December 1938): 144–45. Program bill for *Jephthah's Daughter*, February 12–14 and 20–21, 1915, NPC; typescript scenario *MGZT *Jephthah's Daughter*, n.d. [1915], Dance Collection, New York Public Library for the Performing Arts (hereafter DCNYPL).

19. Crowley, *The Neighborhood Playhouse*, 40–41.

20. I thank Judith Brin Ingber for bringing to my attention David Lifson's *The Yiddish Theatre in America* (New York: Thomas Yoseloff, 1965). See 221–22, on the Neighborhood Playhouse, 214–41, for the *Folksbuehne*. See also Leon Crystal, "The Yiddish Theater" and "The Yiddish Art Theatre," *The Universal Jewish Encyclopedia*, 236–39. For Neighborhood Playhouse accommodation, see Crowley, *The Neighborhood Playhouse*, 61, and Alice and Irene Lewisohn, "A Festival at the Neighborhood Playhouse," *Menorah Journal* (October 1918): 313. S. Ansky's *The Dybbuk*, produced at the Playhouse during the 1925–26 season, must count in addition to S. Asch's *With the Current* (1915–16 season) and D. Pinski's *Little Heroes*, the latter mentioned by Irene Lewisohn but not reflected in Owen's chronology (*The Neighborhood Playhouse*, 252–60.)

21. Atkinson, *Broadway*, 61–65, 214 ff.

22. David Belasco's theatrical realism provides an excellent contemporary example of lavish means devoted to scenic realism. His work as a producer also illustrates the Victorian dilemma of theatre committed to innovative technical experiment and visual realism, but reliant on melodramatic texts and action favored in the preceding century.

23. Brockett, *History of the Theatre*, 559, 575, 597ff.; Jelavich, *Berlin Cabaret*.

24. For correspondences between NP productions and Ballets Russes repertory, see Alice Owen's chronology in Crowley, *The Neighborhood Playhouse*; the chronology appendix 1 to Arnold Haskell and Walter Nouvel, *Diaghileff; His Artistic and Private Life* (1935; reprint, New York: Da Capo, 1978), 331–44; Lynn Garafola, *Diaghilev's Ballets Russes* (New York: Oxford University Press, 1989), 65–66 and 399–415 (appendix C). On Hoffman, see Barbara Naomi Cohen, "The Borrowed Art of Gertrude Hoffman," *Dance Data* 2 (New York: 1977): 2–11.

25. Crowley, *The Neighborhood Playhouse*, 41–43. Inclusion of "classical" training among Playhouse dance classes is indicated by a May 20th, 1916, program pamphlet (NPC) inviting National Federation of Settlements guests to *A Night at an Inn* and *Petrouchka*. Evidence of Chalif's diverse choreographic and arrangement skills was readily apparent in the dance "divertissements" presented by the "Chalif Dancers," along with the Neighborhood Dancers, as the opening salvos for two previous *Petrouchka* performances, March 18 and 19, 1916 (program pamphlet, NPC). Since the choreography for these seven dances is uncredited in extant program data, their style must be deduced from the titles and performers' names, familiarity with contemporary works and artists, and knowledge of Chalif's professional practice. Thus *The Swan*, danced by Miss Gardiner to music by Saint-Saens, was almost certainly modeled on Fokine's famous choreography for Anna Pavlowa; *Valse Caprice*, with music by Rubinstein, danced by Miss Gardiner and Mr. Grymes, was probably an exhibition social dance in the vein of Ruth St. Denis or the Castles. These had to be Chalif choreographies performed by his students. In contrast, Playhouse regulars Blanche Talmud and Bertha Uhr performed *Dance Interpretation*, [Haydn's] *Second Symphony*; Talmud and Playhouse affiliate Albert Carroll danced Liszt's *Hungarian Rhapsody No. 2*. The former "interpretative" dance probably took inspiration from Isadora Duncan's approach to high-art concert music; the folk material anchoring the latter, arguably choreographed by Chalif, was typical of a second emphasis dating from Settlement festival days. The public exposure afforded his own pupils might well have motivated Chalif's agreement to collaborate with the Lewisohns. On classical training as fundamental ground, see *The Chalif Text Book of Dancing, Book 3 Greek Dancing* (New York: the author, 1920), 25–28.

26. Program pamphlet for *A Fairy Tale* and *The Royal Fandango*, The Neighborhood Playhouse, December 31, 1921, and January 1, 1922, NPC; H. B. L., "Guinea Pig Among Playhouses," *New York Times*, May 1, 1921, sec. 3, pp. 11, 30.

27. Program bill for *Thanksgiving*, November 27 and 28, 1915; program bill for *A Festival*, February 27, 1916; program pamphlet for *A Festival*, February 12, 1916; program bills for *A Festival of Pentecost*, May 25 and 26, 1918; program bill for *The Feast of Tabernacles*, November 30 and December 1, 1918; all NPC.

28. Alice and Irene Lewisohn, "A Festival at the Neighborhood Playhouse," *Menorah Journal* (October 1918): 311–12.

29. N.a., "Salut au Monde," *Brooklyn Eagle*, May 12, 1922, n.p., in Salut au Monde—Clippings, Billy Rose Theatre Collection, New York Public Library for the Performing Arts (hereafter TCNYPL); Alice and Irene Lewisohn, "A Festival at the Neighborhood Playhouse," 312.

30. Alice and Irene Lewisohn, "A Festival at the Neighborhood Playhouse," 312.

31. Crowley, *The Neighborhood Playhouse*, 21.

32. Crowley, *The Neighborhood Playhouse*, 37; Program pamphlet, "Invitation Performance tendered by the Henry Street Settlement to the National Federation of Settlements," May 20, 1916, NPC.

33. "Tamiris in Her Own Voice: Draft of an Autobiography," transcr., ed., annot. Daniel Nagrin, *Studies in Dance History* 1 (Fall-Winter 1989–90): 4–7, 53.

34. "Tamiris in Her Own Voice," 7.

35. "Tamiris in Her Own Voice," 8. Depending on the year that Tamiris graduated from high school, she may have taken class at the Neighborhood Playhouse building on Grand Street. In this memoir, she consistently refers to the Henry Street Settlement.

36. Author's telephone interview with Sophie Bernsohn Finkle, January 21, 1989; author's telephone interview with Sophie Maslow, January 14, 1989; "The Festival Dancing Classes," in *The Settlement Journal* (December 1912): 5, NPC; Program pamphlet, "Invitation Performance tendered by the Henry Street Settlement to the National Federation of Settlements," May 20, 1916, NPC; *The Neighborhood Playhouse School of the Theatre; October 5, 1937 to May 16, 1938*, in New York City—The Neighborhood Playhouse—Catalogs, Announcements, etc., DCNYPL.

Bird Larson, a Playhouse teacher in the mid-1920s, brought background in anatomy and physical education instruction to her work. Discussions with Playhouse alumnae have not yielded information about her teaching. Maslow's peer Anna Sokolow joined Playhouse classes about 1925. Sokolow's biographer Larry Warren describes Talmud's movement quality as "a softer style than the intense and emotionally demanding one Martha Graham would soon be exploring, closer to the work of Isadora Duncan as seen in a performance by Irma Duncan and a group of her Russian students at the Manhattan Opera House in December 1928. After their visit, flowing scarves and movements beckoning to the wind were very much in evidence in Playhouse dance classes." Larry Warren, *Anna Sokolow; The Rebellious Spirit* (Princeton, N.J.: Princeton Book Co., Dance Horizons, 1991), 16. Data I have gathered confirms Warren's sense of the softness of Talmud's movement for the period before 1928 as well. Graham and Duncan represent extremes of the effort spectrum in dance movement; Warren's comparison of Talmud to Duncan is instructive in indicating the end of the spectrum toward which Talmud inclined. Use of fabrics was also prevalent in St. Denis's Denishawn teaching and music visualizations of the late 1910s.

37. Crowley, *The Neighborhood Playhouse*, 37; Esther Peck sketch printed as freestanding handbill, n.d., NPC; Program pamphlet, "Invitation Performance tendered by the Henry Street Settlement to the National Federation of Settlements," May 20, 1916, NPC; Wald, *The House on Henry Street*, 183; "Dancing and

Democracy; Illustrated from Drawings by Esther Peck," *The Craftsman* 31 (December 1916): 224–32.

38. Melanie Blood addresses lyric dramas in "The Neighborhood Playhouse," 236. The analysis presented here is my own.

39. Darnton, "Playhouse of Wide Interests," quotation 398; Crowley, *The Neighborhood Playhouse*, 121–32; "Music: Griffes Airs for Whitman," *New York Times*, April 30, 1922, sec. 7, p. 3; "The Neighborhood Playhouse" (New York: The Neighborhood Playhouse, n.d. [1924–1925 season]), n.p., NPC; "Seen on the Stage," clipping from incompletely identified magazine article [*Vogue*, July 15–], in "Incidental dances. Salut au Monde," DCNYPL. My analysis of *Salut Au Monde*'s structure incorporates program booklet data, which differs from Crowley in the sequencing of events.

40. Crowley, *The Neighborhood Playhouse*, 121–32; Program for *Salut au Monde*, April 22, 1922, file MWEZ/+ n.c. 10,307 in Neighborhood Playhouse Collection of Scrapbooks, TCNYPL.

41. Crowley, *The Neighborhood Playhouse*, 133–35, 165–71. While they understood their quest to involve psychological dimensions of performance, it is not at all clear how they defined these dimensions. On the other hand, the Lewisohns definitely distinguished their approach from the Stanislavski method then in vogue in New York.

42. Higham, *Send These to Me*, 48–58.

43. Crowley, *The Neighborhood Playhouse*, 133–34, 207, 213. Also useful is Pearl Fishman, "Vakhtangov's *The Dybbuk*," *The Drama Review* 24 (September 1980): 43–58.

44. Crowley, *The Neighborhood Playhouse*, 116–20; Jelavich, *Berlin Cabaret*; "Productions of the Neighborhood Playhouse," in *The Neighborhood Playhouse 1923–1924 Season*, *MGZB Neighborhood Playhouse New York City Souvenir Program Grand Street Follies 1923–4, DCNYPL; Emanual Eisenberg, "And in the Beginning," 3–4 in *The Grand Street Follies*, 1929 ed. [souvenir booklet], with file MWEZ/ + n.c. 16,904 in Neighborhood Playhouse Collection of Scrapbooks, TCNYPL.

45. Crowley, *The Neighborhood Playhouse*, 228–31, and photos between 234 and 235. On *Sooner and Later*, see Stephen Rathburn, "New Bill at Neighborhood," *The Sun*, April 1, 1925, in Clippings Scrapbooks T-NBL, 1924–5, vol S-Z, TCNYPL; *Neighborhood Playbill Season 1924–5*, no. 4 [*The Legend of the Dance* and *Sooner and Later*], NPC; and scenarios in NCOF p.v. 321, DCNYPL, and MWEZ/ + n.c. 10,316, TCNYPL. On *Pinwheel*, see reviews by Alexander Woolcott, "The Stage," *World*, February 1, 1927; Brooks Atkinson, "The Play," *New York Times*, February 4, 1927; Percy Hammond, "The Theaters," *Tribune*, February 4, 1927; Frank Vreeland, "Farragoh's Farrago," *Telegram*, February 4, 1927; all in Clippings Scrapbooks T-NBL, 1926–7 vol. N-Q, TCNYPL. Chunks and fragments of script sketches and lines may be found in MWEZ + n.c. 10,296, TCNYPL. In an author's note to *Pinwheel* (New York: John Day Co., 1927), Francis Farragoh indicates changes made to his play for its Neighborhood Playhouse staging.

46. See Woolcott for "jerky, gibbet rigadoon." "To Our Subscribers," in *Neigh-*

borhood Playbill Season 1925-6, no. 4 [The Grand Street Follies, June 1926], 8, NPC.

47. Sarlos, *Jig Cook*, 138-52; Atkinson, *Broadway*, 133-35, 210 ff.

48. Crowley, *The Neighborhood Playhouse*, 219-20; 237; "Miss Irene Lewisohn is Dead," *New York Herald Tribune*, April 5, 1944, p. 22; "Alice Lewisohn a London Bride," *New York Times*, December 16, 1924, p. 25. Doris Fox Benardete speculates that tensions grew between the sisters and that the spirit of cooperation declined specifically among the sisters and the two other principal staff, Helen Arthur and Agnes Morgan. Benardete, "The Neighborhood Playhouse in Grand Street: An Abridgement [of a dissertation, NYU, 1949]" (New York: New York University, 1952), 4-5; Benardete, "The Neighborhood Playhouse in Grand Street," Ph.D. diss., 555-57, 572-76, 602-08; Rich, "Lewisohn, Irene," 401.

49. Crowley, *The Neighborhood Playhouse*, 240-41, 246-49; Rich, "Lewisohn, Irene," 401; Helen Ingersoll, "Orchestral Drama," *Theatre Arts Monthly* 12 (August, 1928): 591-94; "The Great World Theatre," *Theatre Arts Monthly* 6 (June 1928): 381-82; John Martin, "The Dance: Programs of Symphonic Music," *New York Times*, May 12, 1929, sec. 9, p. 11; John Martin, "The Dance: A New Synthesis," *New York Times*, February 16, 1930, sec. 9, p. 10; J. Brooks Atkinson, "Dance and Music in Dramatic Form," *New York Times*, February 21, 1930, p. 23; John Martin, "The Dance: Anniversary," *New York Times*, September 22, 1940, sec. 9, p. 8; Warren, *Anna Sokolow*, 19-22. Dorothy Bird recalls 1930s study at the Neighborhood Playhouse School of Theatre in Bird and Joyce Greenberg, *Bird's Eye View: Dancing with Martha Graham and on Broadway* (Pittsburgh: University of Pittsburgh Press, 1997), 61-88.

50. Both writers observed that dance activity at the Playhouse grew out of settlement work conducted at the Henry Street Settlement House but neither they nor later historians probed these settlement house roots. See John Martin, *America Dancing* (New York: Dodge Publishing Co., 1936), 160-65; Margaret Lloyd, *The Borzoi Book of Modern Dance* (1949; reprint, New York: Dance Horizons, 1974), 302.

51. Elizabeth Kendall, *Where She Danced* (New York: Alfred A. Knopf, 1979), 7; Suzanne Shelton, *Divine Dancer; A Biography of Ruth St. Denis* (Garden City, N.Y.: Doubleday & Co., 1981), 126; Christena L. Schlundt, *The Professional Appearances of Ruth St. Denis & Ted Shawn; A Chronology and an Index of Dances 1906-1932* (New York: New York Public Library, 1962), 23-24; Ned Wayburn, *The Art of Stage Dancing* ([n.d.]; reprint, New York: Belvedere Publishers, 1980), 35-37; Barbara Naomi Cohen, "Modern Americanized Ballet," *Dancescope* 14, no. 3 (1980): 29-35, and "Fancy Dancing and Tap & Stepping," *Dancescope* 14, no. 1 (1979): 34-47. Cohen's recent publication is "Ned Wayburn and the Dance Routine: From Vaudeville to the Ziegfeld Follies," *Studies in Dance History* 13 (1996).

52. Schlundt, *Tamiris: A Chronicle of Her Dance Career 1927-1955* (New York: New York Public Library, 1972), 10, 14, 40; Lloyd, *Borzoi Book*, 214-21, 173-78, 183-86; Warren, *Anna Sokolow*.

53. Linda Gordon, "Family Violence, Feminism, and Social Control," *Feminist Studies* 12 (Fall 1986): 453-78.

54. Christena L. Schlundt, *Professional Appearances of Ruth St. Denis & Ted*

Shawn, 23, 73; Crowley, *The Neighborhood Playhouse*, 117, xv–xvi; Wald, *Windows on Henry Street*, 171.

55. Crowley, *The Neighborhood Playhouse*, 254, 258–59; Schlundt, *Tamiris*, 7, 28. For access to 1930s modern dance, scholars have traditionally consulted biographies and autobiographies of individual choreographers. For a period survey, see Lloyd's *Borzoi Book of Modern Dance*. See also Sali Ann Kriegsman, *Modern Dance in America: The Bennington Years* (Boston: G. K. Hall, 1981); Ellen Graff, *Stepping Left: Dance and Politics in New York City, 1928–1942* (Durham, N.C.: Duke University Press, 1997); Susan Foster, *Reading Dancing: Bodies and Subjects in Contemporary American Dance* (Berkeley: University of California Press, 1986); Mark Franko, *Dancing Modernism/Performing Politics* (Bloomington: Indiana University Press, 1995); John O. Perpener, "The Seminal Years of Black Concert Dance" (Ph.D. diss., New York University, 1992).

5. Working Women's Dancing, and Dance as Women's Work

1. Hilda Satt Polachek, *I Came a Stranger: The Story of a Hull-House Girl*, ed. Dena J. Polacheck Epstein, introduction by Lynn Y. Weiner (Urbana: University of Illinois Press, 1989), 77.

2. Polachek, *I Came a Stranger*, 76–77.

3. Kathryn Kish Sklar, "Hull House in the 1890s: A Community of Women Reformers," *Signs* 10 (1985): 658–77; Sklar, *Florence Kelley and the Nation's Work: The Rise of Women's Political Culture, 1830–1900* (New Haven: Yale University Press, 1995), 171–205; Jane Addams, *Twenty Years at Hull-House* (1910; reprint, New York: New American Library, 1981). See entries on Kelley and Lathrop by Louise C. Wade, in *Notable American Women, 1607–1950*, 3 vols., ed. Edward James, Janet Wilson James, and Paul Boyer (Cambridge: Harvard University Press, 1971), 2: 316–19 and 370–72; Louise de Koven Bowen, *Growing Up with a City* (New York: MacMillan, 1926). Notices of meetings of the Dorcas Federal Labor Union and the Illinois Women's Trade Union League are found, passim, in *Hull-House Bulletins*, Hull-House Association Records, Special Collections, the University Library, University of Illinois at Chicago (hereafter cited as HHAR). See also Stuart Hecht, "Hull-House Theatre: An Analytical and Evaluative History" (Ph.D. diss., Northwestern University, 1983).

4. Dominick Cavallo, *Muscles and Morals: Organized Playgrounds and Urban Reform, 1880–1920* (Philadelphia: University of Pennsylvania Press, 1981); *Charities and the Commons* 18 (August 3, 1907), a large section of which was devoted to "The Playground Meeting," 471–565. Also useful are monthly issues of *Playground* magazine and annual *Yearbooks* for the PAA from 1907 and the 1910s.

5. Addams, *Twenty Years at Hull-House*, 114.

6. Addams, *Twenty Years at Hull-House*, 205–06; E. B. DeGroot, "Recent Playground development in Chicago," *Proceedings of the 2nd Annual Playground Congress and Yearbook* (New York: Playground Association of America, 1908), 148–54. Also related are A. W. Beilfuss, "Municipal Playgrounds in Chicago," *Proceedings of the 2nd Annual Playground Congress and Yearbook*, 255–63. *Hull-House Year Book* (September 1, 1906[–]September 1, 1907): 29–32, HHAR; *Hull-House* [Year Book] (May 1, 1910): 31–33, HHAR.

7. On Gyles's and male instructors' credentials, see for example *Hull-House Bulletin* (December 1, 1896): 3; *Hull-House Bulletin* (April 1, 1897): 3; *Hull-House Bulletin* (December 1, 1897): 4; *Hull-House Bulletin* (March 1898): 3; all in HHAR.

8. *Hull-House Bulletin* (January 1896): 4, HHAR. German and Swedish exercise systems are treated in chapter 1 of this book. For the Swedish Ling system, see Hartwig Nissen, *A B C of the Swedish System of Educational Gymnastics; A Practical Hand-book for School Teachers and the Home* (New York: Educational Publishing Company, 1892). On the Swedish and German systems, see Deobold B. Van Dalen and Bruce L. Bennett, *A World History of Physical Education; Cultural, Philosophical, Comparative*, 2d ed. (Englewood Cliffs, N.J.: Prentice Hall, 1971), 399–400, 417–18; Emmett A. Rice, John L. Hutchinson, and Mabel Lee, *A Brief History of Physical Education*, 4th ed. (New York: Ronald Press Co., 1958), 215–21; and Nancy Lee Chalfa Ruyter, *Reformer and Visionaries: The Americanization of the Art of Dance* (New York: Dance Horizons, 1979), 85–88.

9. Nicholas Kelley, "Early Days at Hull House," *Social Service Review* 28 (December 1954): 428; Polacheck, *I Came a Stranger*, 77.

10. Polacheck, *I Came a Stranger*, 77.

11. Elisabeth I. Perry, "'The General Motherhood of the Commonwealth': Dance Hall Reform in the Progressive Era," *American Quarterly* 37 (Winter 1985): 719–33; Elisabeth I. Perry, *Belle Moskowitz; Feminine Politics and the Exercise of Power in the Age of Alfred A. Smith* (New York: Oxford University Press, 1987); Ann Wagner, "Terpsichore and Taxi-Dancers: American Anti-Dance Attitudes," *Proceedings Society of Dance History Scholars* (Ninth Annual Conference, City College, City University of New York, February 14–17, 1986): 217–27. Belle Lindner Israels, "The Way of the Girl," *Survey* 22 (July 3, 1909): 486–97; n.a., "Making Model Dance Halls a Paying Proposition," *New York Times*, November 10, 1912, Magazine section, p. 11.; Louise de Koven Bowen, "Dance Halls," *Survey* 26 (June 3, 1911): 383–87; n.a., "Regulating Dance Halls," *Survey* 26 (June 3, 1911): 345–46; Louise de Koven Bowen, *Growing Up with a City*, 122–24; Addams, *Twenty Years at Hull-House*, 242–44; Jane Addams, "Some Reflections on the Failure of the Modern City to Provide Recreation for Young Girls," *Charities and the Commons* (December 5, 1908): 365–68; Jane Addams, *The Spirit of Youth and the City Streets* (New York: Macmillan Co., 1909).

12. Several types of dance halls were in operation, according to Belle Lindner Israels in "The Way of the Girl." These included "inside" halls, dance space cleared away inside saloon premises; "outside" halls or casinos, premises available for rent for public or private parties; and dancing academies, advertised as centers of paid instruction but also the locale for regularly scheduled "receptions" at which students mixed with paying customers. Brewers and some immigrant communities frequently balked at strictures on the sale of alcohol. See Perry, "'The General Motherhood of the Commonwealth,'" 722, 727. For more information on regulation and "model dance halls," see "Licensing Dance Halls in Denver," *Survey* 28 (September 28, 1912): 788–89; n.a., "Model Dance Halls Here," *New York Times*, February 17, 1909, p. 4.; n.a., "East Siders Like Model Dance Hall," *New York Times*, February 6, 1910, p. 8.; and citations in n. 11.

On the role played by dancing academies, plus the much-debated new dance styles, see accounts and exchanges generated in New York City: n.a., "Dancing Academies: Some Possibilities," *Charities and the Commons* (February 27, 1909): 1018–19; Henry Moskowitz, "Dancing Academies; Not Regulated or Inspected, they are Subject to Gross Abuses" [letter to the editor], *New York Times*, April 7, 1909, p. 10; Maurice Mouvet, "Maurice and the New Dances; Disclaims Importing or Teaching Improper Steps" [letter to the editor], *New York Times*, January 25, 1912, p. 10; n.a., "Turkey Trot Lures Rubinstein Club," *New York Times*, January 24, 1912, p. 11; n.a., "It was the 'Chicken Trot' and not the 'Turkey Trot' that was danced at the Rubinstein Club," *New York Times*, January 25, 1912, p. 1; n.a., "Charity Ball Bars the Turkey Trot," *New York Times*, February 7, 1912, p. 11; n.a., "Pastors Approve Ban on the Tango," *New York Times*, January 5, 1914, p. 5; n.a., "Uphold the Tango, Mrs. Israels and Miss De Wolfe Call It a Beautiful Dance," *New York Times*, January 5, 1914, p. 5.

13. Addams, *Twenty Years at Hull-House*, 249; Florence Kelley, "Florence Kelley Comes to Stay," and Nora Marks and Ellen Gates Starr, "Two Women's Work, Tenements, and a Name," both in *100 Years at Hull-House*, ed. Mary Lynn McCree Bryan and Allen F. Davis (Bloomington: Indiana University Press, 1990), 18–19.

14. Ernest C. Moore, "The Social Value of the Saloon," in *100 Years at Hull-House*, 49.

15. Addams, *Twenty Years at Hull-House*, 243–44.

16. *Hull-House Year Book* (1906–1907): 27–29; *Hull-House Bulletin* (November 1898): 3; *Hull-House [Year Book]* (May 1, 1910): 28; *Hull-House Bulletin* (January and February 1899): 3; *Hull-House Bulletin* (November and December 1899): 4; *Hull-House Bulletin* (Autumn 1900): 3; all in HHAR.

17. See the account of Hinman's current and past teaching activity that Luther H. Gulick published in *The Healthful Art of Dancing* (New York: Doubleday, Page & Co., 1910), 73–95, especially 81–85. For "necessary rhythms" see 81. Hinman's account, plus remarks by teachers of folk dancing, public school teachers and principals, and playground supervisors appear in chapter 4 and were supplied in response to a questionnaire on folk dancing circulated by Gulick. See also Polacheck, *I Came a Stranger*, 77; *Hull-House Year Book* (1906–1907): 27–28, HHAR.

18. *Hull-House Bulletin* (January and February, 1898): 7; *Hull-House Bulletin* (March 1898): 3; *Hull-House Bulletin* (April and May, 1898): 3; all in HHAR.

19. *Hull-House Bulletin* (Autumn 1900): 9–10, HHAR.

20. *Hull-House Bulletin* (1905–06): 4, HHAR; Addams, *Twenty Years at Hull-House*, 273.

21. *Hull-House Bulletin* 5, no. 1 (Semi-Annual, 1902): 5, HHAR.

22. *Hull-House Year Book* (1906–1907): 27–28, HHAR.

23. Hinman in Gulick, *Healthful Art of Dancing*, 76.

24. Hinman in Gulick, *Healthful Art of Dancing*, 77.

25. Polacheck, *I Came a Stranger*, 77.

26. Addams, *Spirit of Youth and the City Streets*, 5.

27. Hinman in Gulick, *Healthful Art of Dancing*, 75–76.

28. Addams, *Spirit of Youth and the City Streets*, 8.

29. Mary P. Ryan regards late-nineteenth-century male journalists as another kind of American flâneur; see *Women in Public; Between Banners and Ballots,*

1825–1880 (Baltimore: Johns Hopkins University Press, 1990), 61. Christine Stansell explores Bowery Gals' self-fashioning in antebellum New York City; see *City of Women; Sex and Class in New York 1789–1860* (New York: Alfred A. Knopf, 1986), 86, 93–101.

30. Israels, "Way of the Girl," 495.

31. Israels, "Way of the Girl," 486–87.

32. Addams, *Spirit of Youth and the City Streets*, 31. A long passage, 30–31, makes this point several times: "We exalt the love of the mother and the stability of the home, but in regard to those difficult years between childhood and maturity we beg the question and unless we repress, we do nothing. We are so timid and inconsistent that although we declare the home to be the foundation of society, we do nothing to direct the force upon which the continuity of the home depends."

33. Addams, *Spirit of Youth and the City Streets*, 8.

34. Marks and Starr, "Two Women's Work, Tenements, and a Name," 19. This sketch is signed "Otto H. Bacher '92."

35. Michel Foucault, *The History of Sexuality, Volume 1: An Introduction,* trans. Robert Hurley (New York: Vintage Books 1990). See especially chapter 1.

36. On subsequent development of the national movement see Perry, "'General Motherhood of the Commonwealth,'" 729–33, and "Licensing Dance Halls in Denver."

37. On Hinman's training and her family's economic situation, see Selma Landen Odom, "Sharing the Dances of Many People: The Teaching Work of Mary Wood Hinman," *Proceedings Society of Dance History Scholars* (Tenth Annual Conference, University of California, Irvine, February 13–15, 1987): 64–74. Odom dates Hinman's work at Nääs 1907. Other sources are *Hinman School of Gymnastic and Folk Dancing* [ca. 1912], n.p., Dance Collection, New York Public Library for the Performing Arts (hereafter DCNYPL); *Hinman School of Gymnastic and Folk Dancing* [ca. 1914], n.p., DCNYPL; *Hinman School of Gymnastic and Folk Dancing* [1917], in "Swedish Book: Materials Relating to the Career of Mary Wood Hinman," n.p., Doris Humphrey Collection (hereafter cited as DHC), item Res3-Z8, DCNYPL; typescript biographical statement, n.a., n.d. [1917 or later], DHC, item Res3-Z12.5, DCNYPL. A *Fête de Juin* account is in the "Swedish Book" loose-leaf notebook, DHC, folder Res3-Z7, DCNYPL.

38. These institutional affiliations are detailed by Hinman in Gulick, *Healthful Art of Dancing*, 75–95. Hinman taught interpretative dancing to her studio and private school students, but probably not in her settlement house classes, where the premium was placed on group participation.

39. Odom, "Sharing the Dances," 67; *Hinman School of Gymnastic and Folk Dancing* [ca. 1912], n.p., DCNYPL.

40. Hinman in Gulick, *Healthful Art of Dancing*, 94–95; *Hinman School of Gymnastic and Folk Dancing* [ca. 1912], DCNYPL.

41. Hinman in Gulick, *Healthful Art of Dancing*, 95; *Hull-House [Year Book]* (May 1, 1910): 28; *Hinman School of Gymnastic and Folk Dancing* [1917], n.p., DHC, item Res3-Z8. Hinman discusses the value of folk dancing in the 1912, 1914, and 1917 *Hinman School of Gymnastic and Folk Dancing* brochures.

42. See Odom, "Sharing the Dances," 68–69. Hinman dance instructions available for purchase are listed in *Hinman School of Gymnastic and Folk Dancing*

[ca. 1912], n.p., DCNYPL. See also typescript biographical statement, n.a., n.d. [1917 or later], DHC, item Res3-Z12.5, NYPL; *Columbia University Bulletin of Information, Summer Session Announcement,* 16th Series, no. 11 (April 1, 1916), 223–24, 226, and *Columbia University Bulletin of Information, Summer Session Announcement,* 17th Series, no. 12 (May 3, 1917), 172–73, 175, both in Columbia University Archives and Columbiana Library; *Hinman School of Gymnastic and Folk Dancing* [1917], n.p., DHC, item Res3-Z8, DCNYPL.

43. Mary Wood Hinman, "Educational Possibilities of the Dance," offprint of her article in *The Journal of Health and Physical Education* 5 (April 1934), DHC, item Res3-Z11.6, DCNYPL; *Proceedings of the Third Annual Playground Congress and Yearbook 1909* (New York: Playground Association of America, 1910), 316. Hinman's remarks are reprinted in the *Proceedings,* 447–50, in the report of the Session on Festivals, 442–50. On curricular additions at Teachers College and University of Wisconsin, see Ruyter, *Reformers and Visionaries,* 111, 117–23.

44. *Twelfth Census of the United States taken in the Year 1900. Census Reports. Volume Two: Population,* Part 2 (Washington, D.C.: United States Census Office, 1902), table 91 p. 505, table 93 p. 520. Dancers may well be counted among actors, and possibly among other, "not specified" professional services. While for dancers the lack of recognition persists in the 1910 and 1920 censuses, dance teachers start to be singled out as early as 1910, signaling, I would argue, conceptualization of dance teaching as different from performance, and suggesting greater absolute numbers of teachers than dancers, although the latter must remain conjecture.

45. For 1910, see *Thirteenth Census of the United States Taken in the Year 1910. Population 1910: v. 4, Occupation Statistics* (Washington, D.C.: Government Printing Office, 1914), table 1 p. 93. For 1920, see *Fourteenth Census of the United States Taken in the Year 1920. Population 1920: v. 4, Occupations* (Washington, D.C.: Government Printing Office, 1923), chapter 2, table 4 p. 42.

46. *Fourteenth Census (1920), Population v. 4,* chapter 4: table 6 pp. 392–93, table 7 p. 403, table 8 p. 412, table 9 p. 421; table 10 p. 430. Teachers of "athletics, dancing" are not disaggregated for Indians, Chinese, Japanese, and other Non-White Persons; see tables 15 p. 739 and 16 p. 740.

47. *Fourteenth Census (1920), Population v. 4,* chapter 4, table 6 pp. 392–93.

48. *Fourteenth Census (1920), Population v. 4,* chapter 6, table 10 p. 706; *The Statistical History of the United States from Colonial Times to the Present,* introduction and user's guide by Ben J. Wattenberg (New York: Basic Books, 1976), series D 49–62, p. 133.

49. *Fourteenth Census (1920), Population v. 4,* chapter 6, table 11 p. 714, table 12 p. 722, table 13 p. 730, table 14 p. 737.

50. Two essential sources on Humphrey are Marcia B. Siegel, *Days on Earth; The Dance of Doris Humphrey* (New Haven: Yale University Press, 1987), and Selma Jeanne Cohen, *Doris Humphrey; An Artist First* (Middletown, Conn.: Wesleyan University Press, 1972), the latter being Humphrey's autobiography, edited and completed by Cohen. On Humphrey's early training with Hinman, see Siegel, *Days on Earth,* 21–22, 24 and Cohen, *Doris Humphrey,* 11–12. Doris Humphrey (spelled Humphreys) is listed as a nonresident worker in *Chicago Commons 1894–1911,* 62, Pamphlet Collection, box 2, folder "Chicago Com-

mons 1899–1925," Social Welfare History Archives, University of Minnesota, Minneapolis, Minn. (hereafter cited as SWHA). Her work with a Commons sewing club is indicated in Doris Humphrey to "Dearest Aunty May" [Mrs. A. C. Walker], January 8, 1911, DHC, item C 235.4, DCNYPL.

On Humphrey's teaching, settlement house connections, and performing, see Doris Humphrey to "Dear Aunty May" [Mrs. A. C. Walker], [postmark October 31, 1911], DHC, items C235.1 and C235.2; Doris Humphrey to "My dearest Aunty May" [Mrs. A. C. Walker], [postmark October 23, 1912], DHC, items C237.1 and C237.2; Doris Humphrey to "Dearest Aunty May" [Mrs. A. C. Walker], January 8, 1911, DHC, item C235.4; Doris Humphrey to "Auntie May" [Mrs. A. C. Walker], February 7, 1913, DHC, item C239.2; Cohen, *Doris Humphrey*, 22–23; Siegel, *Days on Earth*, 24–6; Doris Humphrey to "Aunty May" [Mrs. A. C. Walker], June 17, 1913, DHC, item C239.4; Odom, "Sharing the Dances," 69. Sale of the hotel is recounted in Cohen, *Doris Humphrey*, 25.

51. Cohen, *Doris Humphrey*, 25–26, 28. Humphrey's name appears among the "Graduates from the Hinman School" listed in *Hinman School of Gymnastic and Folk Dancing* [1917], n.p., DHC, item Res3-Z8, DCNYPL.

52. Doris Humphrey to "Dear Auntie May" [Mrs. A. C. Walker], [postmark October 16, 1914], DHC, items C240.5 and C240.6, DCNYPL; *Yearbook Chicago Commons Woman's Club 1914–15*, Graham Taylor Manuscripts, Chicago Commons—Records of the founding, history and growth of the Chicago Commons, 1894—date, box 1911–1917, folder 1914, Newberry Library; Cohen, *Doris Humphrey*, 26–27, 30–33; Siegel, *Days on Earth*, 30–37.

53. See *The Art of Making Dances* (New York: Grove Press, 1959).

54. Doris Humphrey to "Dearest ones" [Mr. and Mrs. H. B. Humphrey], [postmark November 24, 1930], DHC, items C279.5 and C279.6. Odom cites this passage in "Sharing the Dances"; the interpretation given here is my own.

55. Among Humphrey's peers in the new modern dance, Tamiris was exceptional in her efforts to stimulate cooperative collective action. She succeeded for a short time with Dance Repertory Theatre; see Christena L. Schlundt, *Tamiris; A Chronicle of her Dance Career 1927–1955* (New York: New York Public Library, 1972), 14, 16–23.

56. Raymond Williams, *Culture & Society: 1780–1950* (New York: Columbia University Press, 1983), 30–48.

57. The Humphrey quotation is from "New Dance," 145, in *Dance as a Theatre Art*, 2d ed., ed. Selma Jeanne Cohen and Katy Matheson (Princeton, N.J.: Princeton Book Co., 1992). The interpretation of Humphrey's dances given here is derived from my viewing of films and reconstructions of the dances, and from analyses of Humphrey's works. See, for example, Siegel's eloquent discussions of Humphrey dances in *Days on Earth*.

58. Graham Taylor, *Chicago Commons through Forty Years* (Chicago: Chicago Commons Association, 1936), 4–6, 313; Allen Davis, *Spearheads for Reform; The Social Settlements and the Progressive Movement 1890–1914* (New York: Oxford University Press, 1967), 13.

59. "Physical Culture," *Chicago Theological Seminary*, n.d., 49–51, in Graham Taylor Manuscripts, Chicago Commons—Records of the founding, history and

growth of the Chicago Commons, 1894—date (hereafter cited as GTMCC Records), box 1894–1898, folder 1894, Newberry Library (hereafter cited as NL).

60. On the Plymouth Winter Night College see *Chicago Commons; A Social Settlement*, January 1896, GTMCC Records, box 1894–1898, folder 1897, NL. Delsarte and physical culture offerings are spelled out in "Chicago Commons Plymouth Winter Night College Schedule of Classes, Lectures and Clubs," [1894–1895], Graham Taylor Mss., Chicago Commons Scrapbooks for the early period (hereafter cited as GTMCC Scrapbooks), NL.

61. Ruyter, *Reformer and Visionaries*, 20–30; Genevieve Stebbins, *Delsarte System of Expression*, 6th ed. (New York: Edgar S. Werner Publishing & Supply Co., 1902; New York: Dance Horizons, 1977), 401–13, 457–61.

62. During the 1895–96 year, Miss Davis and Miss Skinner, from the Columbia School, taught girls' elocution and physical culture classes. Miss Amalia Schweitzer, trained at the American Conservatory, taught a Saturday class specifically labeled as "Young Ladies' Delsarte" the same year. Miss Mary M. Mason, trained at Northwestern University School of Oratory, appears on the fall 1896 schedule along with Julia Davis; male colleague Archie Turner, also trained at Columbia School of Oratory, taught a girls' elocution class as well. "Chicago Commons Plymouth Winter Night College Schedule of Classes, Lectures and Clubs," [1894–1895], GTMCC Scrapbooks, NL; "Chicago Commons Plymouth Winter Night College Schedule of Classes, Clubs and Lectures," [1895–1896], GTMCC Records, box 1894–1898, folder 1894, NL; "Chicago Commons, November 1896. Schedule of Classes, Clubs and Lectures, Fall Term 1896," GTMCC Scrapbooks, NL; "Schedule of Classes, Clubs and Lectures Winter Term 1897–8," in *Chicago Commons—Its Work and Its Needs, Special Circular January, 1898*, GTMCC Records, box 1894–1898, folder 1898, NL.

63. Cost of lessons is indicated on schedules, see "Chicago Commons, November 1896. Schedule of Classes, Clubs and Lectures. Fall Term 1896," GTMCC Records, box 1894–1898, folder 1896, NL. For the financial statement see "1894–1904 Tenth Anniversary Summary of the Work of Chicago Commons," GTMCC Records, box 1904–1910, folder 1904, NL.

Teachers' affiliations are listed parenthetically on PWNC schedules. It is not clear whether these were institutions from which the teachers had previously graduated or at which they were currently matriculating. In either case, the Commons teaching opportunity provided real-world teaching experience and professional recognition.

For the Columbia School benefit, see *Chicago Commons Relief Fund Benefit* program, GTMCC Records, Box 1894–1898, folder 1897, NL. A later indication by Graham Taylor of the cooperative relationship with Columbia School of Oratory is found in "Report of the Work of Chicago Commons for the year ending September 30, 1916," Chicago Commons Papers, Box 5, folder "Annual and other reports 1908–28," Chicago Historical Society.

On occasion, elocution teachers whose affiliation is not identified staged recitals of their pupils at the Chicago Commons Auditorium. Pupils of Mary E. Rafferty and Rose E. Rafferty performed at Chicago Commons in 1901 (Mary) and in 1902 and 1904 (Rose). In the 1901 recital, a series of twenty-six Delsarte poses capped a program of piano and vocal numbers, recitations, and solo dances by guest fancy dancer Miss Anna O'Neil. See "Recital Given by Pupils of Miss Mary A. Rafferty . . . October 15th, 1901," GTMCC Records, box 1899–1903, folder 1901, NL; "Recital by pupils of Miss R. E. Rafferty at Chicago Commons . . . February 28, 1902," GTMCC Scrapbooks, NL; "Dramatic Recital given by Pupils of Miss Rose E. Rafferty at Chicago Commons April 19, 1904," GTMCC Scrapbooks, NL.

64. "The Girls' Clubs," *Chicago Commons; A Social Settlement*, [1899], 14, GTMCC Records, box 1899–1903, folder 1899, NL; "Fourth Annual Entertainment Given by Girls' Progressive Club of Chicago Commons, at Scandia Hall, April 25th, 1898," GTMCC Scrapbooks, NL; "May Entertainment of the Progressive Club of Chicago Commons . . . May 23rd, 1901," GTMCC Records, box 1899–1903, folder 1901, NL.

65. Early evidence of increasing girls' gymnasium work is found in *Supplement, The Commons* (December 1901), 6, GTMCC Records, box 1899–1903, folder 1901, NL. For Todd and Burt, see *Chicago Commons Its Work for the Ninth Winter 1902–1903*, GTMCC Records, box 1899–1903, folder 1902, NL. Quotation from *Chicago Commons A Social Center for Civic Co-operation*, December 1904, 25–26, Pamphlet Collection, box 2, folder "Chicago Commons 1899–1925," SWHA. For Schofield see "Katherine Schofield 1881–1914," uncredited typescript, GTMCC Records, box 1911–1917, folder 1914, NL. No data has yet been found on Schofield's dance and gymnasium training, though it is known that she was born in Buffalo, New York. While she may have known about Hinman's ongoing work in Chicago, it's not clear that she was aware of Elizabeth Burchenal's work directing folk dancing as after-school athletics for New York City public school girls. One of Schofield's colleagues at Chicago Commons in 1908 and 1909, a Miss Catlin who taught social dance classes, may have been a graduate of Hinman's Normal School. A 1909 Commons brochure notes that Catlin's classes varied the "regular" social dance material studied with folk dances, a procedure which Hinman utilized in her teaching.

A list of Hinman Normal School graduates is given in *Hinman School of Gymnastic and Folk Dancing* [ca. 1912], DCNYPL. Schofield's name is not among those listed, but a Miss Elsie Abigail Catlin is named as graduating in 1908. The Hinman brochure also states that "the dancing in the majority of the social settlements of Chicago is also either directly supervised by her [Hinman] or by some of her graduates." Was the Hinman graduate Catlin the Chicago Commons Catlin? Complete confirmation would require further evidence. Only the surname is given for Miss Catlin in *Chicago Commons Council* (November 22, 1909): 3, and in the pamphlet "Chicago Commons . . . Fifteenth Winter, 1908–9," GTMCC Records, box 1904–1910, folders 1909 and 1908, NL. Schofield's name is entered in a list of residents at Chicago Commons while Catlin's is not; the latter may well have been a nonresident worker. See Chicago Commons Papers, box 55, folder "Lists of Residents 1894–1932," Chicago Historical Society.

66. "Chicago Commons . . . Fifteenth Winter, 1908–9," GTMCC Records, box 1904–1910, folder 1908, NL. For May Festival data, see "First Annual May Festival Chicago Commons May 9–10, 1902," and "Second Annual May Festival

Friday and Saturday, May 8 & 9, 1903," in GTMCC Records, box 1899–1903, folders 1902 and 1903, NL.

67. *Autumn News Letter 1906 Chicago Commons*, 3, GTMCC Records, box 1904–1910, folder 1906, NL.

68. See "Thirteenth Annual May Festival and Loan Exhibit of Paintings . . . May 10th, 11th and 12th, '07," typed page "[May Festival] Program of Kirmess, May 2, 08," and "Fourteenth Annual May Festival . . . April 30 – May 2, 1908," all in GTMCC Records, box 1904–1910, folders 1907 and 1908, NL. Shortly after the May Festivals were inaugurated in 1902, they began to be erroneously labeled as if they had commenced when Chicago Commons opened in 1894.

69. On settlement house interest in city parks and on the 1907 PAA meeting in Chicago, see Davis, *Spearheads for Reform*, 60–65; Graham Romeyn Taylor, "How They Played at Chicago," *Charities and the Commons* 18 (August 3, 1907), 471–80. On Chicago Commons's participation in various play events, see "Program Opening Exercises for Small Park, No. 1 . . . August 1st, 1908," GTMCC Records, box 1904–1910, folder 1908, NL; "Our 'Gym' Girls," *Chicago Commons Council* (November 8, 1909): 3, GTMCC Records, box 1904–1910, folder 1909, NL; "First Annual Neighborhood Play Festival . . . May 7th, 1910," GTMCC Records, box 1904–1910, folder 1910, NL; *Chicago Commons Council* (May 2, 1910): 3, GTMCC Records, box 1904–1910, folder 1909, NL.

Schofield's successors in girls' gymnasium work included Mildred Evans, from 1917 to 1919, and a Miss Tyrrell, beginning as early as December 1918. See "1916–1941. Minutes of Staff Meeting," October 1917, October 1918, October 1919, and December 9, 1918, GTMCC Records, box 1911–1917, folder 1916, NL. May Festival literature continues to show emphasis on folk dancing; see GTMCC Records, boxes 1911–1917 and 1918–1922, passim, NL.

70. Ruth Russell, "Tarantula, Tambourine and Tarantella," *The Daily News*, January 4, 19[19], n.p., GTMCC Records, box 1918–1927, folder 1919, NL.

71. Alfred Boer, *The Development of USES: A Chronology of the United South End Settlements – 1891–1966* (Boston: United South End Settlements, 1966), 3, 6–9; Robert A. Woods, ed., *The City Wilderness; A Settlement Study* (Boston: Houghton, Mifflin & Co., 1898), especially 33–57. For women Associate Workers in 1902, see *South End House Report 1902*, 46, in United South End House Settlements Collection, box 4, folder Freestanding Annual Reports, Social Welfare History Archives (hereafter cited as USESC, SWHA).

72. Boer, *Development of USES*, 11; and the following *South End House Association Annual Reports*, all found in USESC, box 4, folder South End House Annual Reports 1895–1901, SWHA: *Eighth Annual Report* (January 1900), 2, 16; *Ninth Annual Report* (February 1901), 15–16; *Seventh Yearly Report* (February 1899), 5–6; *Sixth Yearly Report* (January 1898), 15.

73. *South End House Report 1903*, 8, USESC, box 4, folder Freestanding Annual Report 1903, SWHA.

74. See annual schedules for classes and clubs in *South End House Report 1902*, 40, USESC, box 4, folder Freestanding Annual Report 1902, SWHA; [*South End House Report 1905*] [cover missing; title page dated February 1905], 43–44, USESC, box 4, folder Freestanding Annual Report 1905, SWHA; *South End*

House Report 1906, 39, 41, USESC, box 4, folder Freestanding Annual Report 1906, SWHA; *South End House 1892–1907,* 48–49, USESC, box 4, folder Freestanding Annual Report 1907, SWHA.

75. Boer, *Development of USES,* 12; *South End House Report 1902,* 40. On Johnson, see *South End House 1909,* 42, Pamphlet Collection, box 1, folder South End House 1909, SWHA; *South End House 1910,* 32, USESC, box 4, folder Freestanding Annual Report 1910, SWHA; *South End House 1911,* 30, USESC, box 4, folder Freestanding Annual Report 1911, SWHA. For Murphy, McLellan, and Baker, see *South End House 1915,* 36–37, USESC, box 4, folder Freestanding Annual Report 1915, SWHA; *South End House 1916,* 31, USESC, box 4, folder Freestanding Annual Report 1916, SWHA; *South End House 1891–1916* (April 1917), 33, USESC, box 4, folder Freestanding Annual Report 1917, SWHA; *South End House 1918,* 31, 33, USESC, box 4, folder Freestanding Annual Report 1918, SWHA. Figures and affiliations for social dancing instructors are compiled from annual South End House reports for the years 1902, 1903, 1905–1908, 1910–1918, all in USESC, box 4, dated folders for Freestanding Annual Reports, SWHA, and from *South End House 1909,* Pamphlet Collection, box 1, folder South End House 1909, SWHA. On university fellowship programs at South End House, see Boer, *Development of USES,* 11–12.

76. *South End House 1892–1907,* 48, 61; *South End House 1909,* 42, 52, 54; *South End House 1911,* 30, 45. On Gilbert dancing see Ruyter, *Reformer and Visionaries,* 91; *The Director* 1, nos. 1–10, December 1897–November 1898, bound facsimile reprint of the first ten issues of the magazine *The Director* (New York: Dance Horizons, 1987).

77. On the folk dancing classes, see *South End House 1915,* 35, 53; *South End House 1916,* 30, 49; *South End House 1891–1916* (April 1917), 31, 52; *South End House 1918,* 28, 53–54.

78. *South End House 1916,* 12.

79. "Conference of Girls' Club Workers," *Chicago Commons 1894–1911,* 24–25, Pamphlet Collection, box 2, folder "Chicago Commons 1899–1925," SWHA. In a typescript reply to the questionnaire, Schofield wrote, "Formal gymnastic alone will not hold a girl. There must be some form of organized play. Play is far more important than mere muscular activity. It is the most natural and the most potent expression of the girl's personality. Folk dancing supplies this great need. It gives to young people interesting and beautiful group activities and adds to the social resources for the leisure hour. It helps to make life more vivid, happy and wholesome. The spread of the folk dance is significant because of the effect it has had upon the two-step and waltz." See *National Federation of Settlements Schedule on the Problem of the Adolescent Girl Between Fourteen and Eighteen Years of Age,* December 1911, and "Schedule on the Problem of the Adolescent Girl Between Fourteen and Eighteen Years of Age," [typescript reply to questionnaire], both in GTMCC Records, box 1911–1917, folder 1911, NL.

80. *South End House 1916,* 12, 49; *South End House 1915,* 53; *South End House 1891–1916,* 52.

81. *South End House 1891–1916* (April 1917), 7.

82. *South End House 1891–1916* (April 1917), 11.

83. Hinman in Gulick, *Healthful Art of Dancing,* 91.

6. Folk Dance, Park Fetes, and Period Political Values

1. "5,000 Schoolgirls Dance on the Green," *Brooklyn Daily Eagle*, May 19, 1915, Picture and Sporting sec., p. 5.

2. See, for example, *Folk-Dances and Singing Games* (New York: G. Schirmer, 1909); Elizabeth Burchenal, ed., *Official Handbook of the Girls' Branch of the Public Schools Athletic League of the City of New York, 1914–1915* (New York: American Sports Publishing Co., 1914).

3. "5,000 Schoolgirls Dance on the Green," *Brooklyn Daily Eagle*, May 19, 1915.

4. On the origins of the PSAL, see Burchenal, *Handbook 1914–1915*, 15; Ethel Dorgan, *Luther Halsey Gulick* (Washington, D.C.: McGrath Publishing Co. & National Recreation and Park Assoc., 1934), 79–80, 91, 98; biographical sketches "James E. Sullivan" and "Dr. Luther Halsey Gulick," in Jessie H. Bancroft, *Girls' Athletics for Elementary, High and Collegiate Grade Being the Official Handbook of the Girls' Branch of the Public Schools Athletic League of the City of New York 1910–1911* (New York: American Sports Publishing Co., 1910), n.p., also 11; Jessie H. Bancroft, "Contributions of Dr. Luther Halsey Gulick to the Public Schools of New York City," *American Physical Education Review* 28, no. 7 (September 1923): 338.

On PSAL organizers, participants, and activities, see "Public Schools Athletic League. New York City," *The Playground* (August 1908): 12–15; Selma Berrol, "William Henry Maxwell and a New Educational New York," *History of Education Quarterly* 8 (1968): 215–28; Luther H. Gulick and Harry J. Smith, "Dancing as a Part of Education; Happy Results of Rhythmic Play by New York School Children," *The World's Work* 14, no. 6 (October 1907): 9445–52; "Remarks by Lee F. Hanmer, Director of Recreation Dept., Russell Sage Foundation," *American Physical Education Review* 28 (October 1923): 382–83; "Public Schools Athletic League," *The Playground* 3, no. 11 (February 1910): 14; Helen Storrow, review of *The Healthful Art of Dancing*, by Luther Halsey Gulick, *The Playground* 4, no. 10 (January 1911): 353–54; Benjamin Rader, *American Sports: From the Age of Folk Games to the Age of Spectators* (Englewood Cliffs, N.J.: Prentice-Hall, 1983), 157–60; J. Thomas Jable, "The Public Schools Athletic League of New York City: Organized Athletics for City School Children, 1903–1914," in *The American Sporting Experience: A Historical Anthology of Sport in America*, ed. Steven A. Riess (New York: Leisure Press, 1984): 219–38.

5. Bancroft, "Contributions," 338, 340. Also asserting the women-grounded inspiration for and founding of the Girls' Branch is the short descriptive pamphlet "Girls' Branch Public Schools Athletic League," n.p., 1907, in Scrapbook, Elizabeth Burchenal Collection, Special Collections, Mugar Memorial Library, Boston University. Accounts of the Girls' Branch founding, published in the annual handbooks, confirm the mutual sympathy and confidence shared by Gulick and the Girls' Branch women founders. See, for example, Burchenal, *Handbook 1914–1915*, 15–16.

6. On instruction classes and teacher participation, see Bancroft, *Handbook 1910–1911*, 18, 88–89. On girls' participation, see Gulick and Smith, "Dancing as

a Part of Education," 9449; Luther Gulick, *The Healthful Art of Dancing* (New York: Doubleday, Page & Co., 1910), 46–47; Jessie H. Bancroft, "Contributions of Dr. Luther Halsey Gulick to the Public Schools of New York City (Concluded)," *American Physical Education Review* 28, no. 8 (October 1923): 378; "Athletics for Public School Girls in New York City," *The Playground* 4, no. 1 (April 1910): 33. Annual handbooks are a primary source of participation data; see Bancroft, *Handbook 1910–1911*, 88–89; Burchenal, *Handbook 1914–1915*, 17, 26; Elizabeth Burchenal, ed., *Official Handbook of the Girls' Branch of the Public Schools Athletic League of the City of New York, 1915–1916* (New York: American Sports Publishing Co., 1915), 29, 34; Elizabeth Burchenal, ed., *Official Handbook of the Girls' Branch of the Public Schools Athletic League of the City of New York, 1916–1917* (New York: American Sports Publishing Co., 1916), 30–31, 37; Elizabeth Burchenal, ed., *Official Handbook of the Girls' Branch of the Public Schools Athletic League of the City of New York, 1917–1918* (New York: American Sports Publishing Co., 1917), 32, 37.

7. Robert V. Wells, "Demographic Change and the Life Cycle of American Families," *Journal of Interdisciplinary History* 2 (Autumn 1971): 272–82; Daniel Scott Smith, "Family Limitation, Sexual Control, and Domestic Feminism in Victorian America," in Nancy F. Cott and Elizabeth Pleck, *A Heritage of Her Own* (New York: Simon & Schuster, 1979): 222–45; Nancy Woloch, *Women and the American Experience* (New York: Alfred A. Knopf, 1984): 271–76.

8. On separate spheres, see chapter 2, and sources in nn. 1–2; Woloch, *Women and the American Experience*, 113–26.

9. William H. Chafe, *The American Woman: Her Changing Social, Economic, and Political Roles, 1920–1970* (New York: Oxford University Press, 1972), 55.

10. For women's work and suffrage activity, see Pleck, "A Mother's Wages": Income Earned Among Married Italian and Black Women, 1896–1914," in *A Heritage of Her Own*, ed. Cott and Pleck, 367–92; Alice Kessler-Harris, *Out to Work: A History of Wage-Earning Women in America* (New York: Oxford University Press, 1982); Susan A. Glenn, *Daughters of the Shtetl; Life and Labor in the Immigrant Generation* (Ithaca: Cornell University Press, 1990), 167–73; Nancy Schrom Dye, *As Equals and as Sisters: The Labor Movement and the Women's Trade Union League of New York* (Columbia: University of Missouri, 1980); Eleanor Flexner, *Century of Struggle: The Women's Rights Movement in the United States* (Cambridge: Harvard University Press, 1959); Aileen Kraditor, *The Ideas of the Woman Suffrage Movement 1890–1920* (New York: Columbia University Press, 1965); Ellen Carol Dubois, *Feminism and Suffrage: The Emergence of an Independent Women's Movement in America 1848–1869* (Ithaca: Cornell University Press, 1978); Nancy Cott, *The Grounding of Modern Feminism* (New Haven: Yale University Press, 1987), 26–28, 53–59. On suffrage pageants, see Naima Prevots, *American Pageantry; A Movement for Art and Democracy* (Ann Arbor: UMI Research Press, 1990), 211; Michael McGerr, "Political Style and Women's Power, 1830–1930," *Journal of American History* 77 (December 1990): 864–85.

11. Edward Clarke, *Sex in Education* (Boston: James R. Osgood, 1987); Mabel Newcomer, *A Century of Higher Education for Women* (New York: Harper, 1959), 28–29.

12. Historians useful in understanding the state of physical training include Ellen W. Gerber, *Innovators and Institutions in Physical Education* (Philadelphia: Lea & Febiger, 1971); Norma Schwendener, *A History of Physical Education in the United States* (New York: A. S. Barnes, 1942); Harvey Green, *Fit for America; Health, Fitness, Sport and American Society* (New York: Pantheon Books, 1986); Benjamin Rader, *American Sports*; Martha Verbrugge, *Able-Bodied Womanhood; Personal Health and Social Change in Nineteenth-Century Boston* (New York: Oxford University Press, 1988); Hazel Wacker, "The History of the Private Single-Purpose Institutions which Prepared Teachers of Physical Education in the United States of America from 1860–1958," 3 vols. (Ph.D. diss., New York University, 1959); Betty Spears, *Leading the Way: Amy Morris Homans and the Beginnings of Professional Education for Women* (New York: Greenwood Press, 1986); Emmett A. Rice, John L. Hutchinson, and Mabel Lee, *A Brief History of Physical Education*, 4th ed. (New York: Ronald Press Co., 1958); William G. Riordan, "Dio Lewis in Retrospect," *Journal of Health, Physical Education, Recreation* (October 1960): 46–48; Earle F. Zeigler, "Historical Perspective on Contrasting Philosophies of Professional Preparation for Physical Education in the United States," *Canadian Journal of History of Sport and Physical Education* 6 (May 1975): 23–42. Relevant works by period participants include Dio Lewis, *The New Gymnastics for Men, Women, and Children*, 3d ed. (Boston: Ticknor and Fields, 1862); Dudley Allen Sargent, *An Autobiography*, ed. Ledyard W. Sargent (Philadelphia: Lea & Febiger, 1927); Luther Halsey Gulick, "Physical Education; A New Profession," *Proceedings of the American Association for the Advancement of Physical Education at its Fifth Annual Meeting Held at Cambridge and Boston, Mass., April 4 and 5, 1890* (Ithaca, N.Y.: Andrus & Church, 1890): 59–66.

13. *Physical Training; A Full Report of the Papers and Discussions of the Conference Held in Boston in November, 1889*, reported and edited by Isabel C. Barrows (Boston: Press of George H. Ellis, 1890); Gulick and Smith, "Dancing as a Part of Education." See Dorgan, *Luther Halsey Gulick*, for the PAA's first president; also *Charities and the Commons* 18 (August 3, 1907), for additional data and report on the first PAA Congress.

14. Nancy Lee Chalfa Ruyter devotes considerable discussion to Hall's theories in *Reformers and Visionaries: The Americanization of the Art of Dance* (New York: Dance Horizons, 1979), 96–100. Connections between Gulick and Hall, theoretical and personal, may be discerned in Gulick and Smith, "Dancing as a Part of Education," 9451; Bancroft, "Contributions of Dr. Luther Halsey Gulick," 340. On the child study movement, see Dorothy Ross, *G. Stanley Hall; The Psychologist as Prophet* (Chicago: University of Chicago Press, 1972), 279–308.

15. G. Stanley Hall, *Adolescence; Its Psychology and Its Relations to Physiology, Anthropology, Sociology, Sex, Crime, Religion and Education*, 2 vols. (New York: D. Appleton & Co., 1905), 1: 132, 202–03, 211, 213.

16. Ruyter, *Reformers and Visionaries*, 97–98; Ross, *G. Stanley Hall*, 359; Gulick and Smith, "Dancing as a Part of Education," 9451; Gulick, *Healthful Art of Dancing*, 137.

17. Hall, *Adolescence* 1: 214; G. Stanley Hall, *Educational Problems*, 2 vols. (New York: D. Appleton and Co., 1911), 1: 58–60.

18. At the time Burchenal was enrolled, Sargent's Normal School was known

as Dr. Sargent's Normal School of Physical Training and Sanatory Gymnasium for Women and Children. See Hazel Wacker, "The History of the Private Single-Purpose Institutions which Prepared Teachers of Physical Education in the United States of America from 1860–1958," 49.

Clarence Van Wyck's monograph on Sargent's Harvard Summer School of Physical Education (HSSPE) provides the most comprehensive indication of the breadth of work Sargent offered physical training students. From its founding in 1887, HSSPE listed course work in light gymnastics and fancy steps, taught by Christian Eberhard; these classes were probably derived from the German system of Ludwig Jahn. From 1893 to 1914, Hartwig Nissen, a pioneer in introducing Swedish Ling gymnastics in the U.S., taught the system and a class in massage. Sargent brought Melvin Ballou Gilbert, developer of "aesthetic dancing," to the summer school in 1893. This movement material, also called gymnastic dancing, combined ballet foot positions, turnout of the legs, and arm positions with isolation of body parts and drill-like repetition. Here was forged an important connection between physical education and dance; Gilbert taught his material at HSSPE for fifteen summers. Jennie Wilson, a graduate of Sargent's normal school, taught Indian club work along with gymnastics; Carl Schrader taught marching tactics; and Harry P. Clarke taught recreational games. Boxing, fencing, and track and field athletics were also taught, as were courses for coaching intramural athletics. See Dudley Allen Sargent, *An Autobiography*, ed. Ledyard W. Sargent (Philadelphia: Lea & Febiger, 1927), 208–12; Clarence B. Van Wyck, "The Harvard Summer School of Physical Education 1887–1932," *The Research Quarterly* 13 (December 1942): 408–11, 424–25; Hartwig Nissen, *A B C of the Swedish System of Educational Gymnastics; A Practical Hand-book for School Teachers and the Home* (New York: Educational Publishing Company, 1892).

From 1898 to 1899 Burchenal worked as gymnasium instructor at the Boston Children's Hospital, and from 1898 to 1900 as an instructor at the Charlesbank gymnasium in Boston. Starting in 1900, she served for two years as physical director of the Chicago Women's Athletic Club, and during summer 1903 as an instructor at Sargent's Harvard Summer School of Physical Education. See *Teachers College Announcement 1905–06*, 20, Department of Special Collections, Milbank Memorial Library, Teachers College, Columbia University (hereafter SCMMMLTC).

19. On Teachers College, see James Earl Russell, *Founding Teachers College; Reminiscences of the Dean Emeritus* (New York: Bureau of Publications, Columbia University, 1937), 57–66; Lawrence A. Cremin, David A. Shannon, and Mary Evelyn Townsend, *A History of Teachers College Columbia University* (New York: Columbia University Press, 1954), 37–58; Schwendener, *History of Physical Education*, 126; Lawrence A. Cremin, *The Transformation of the School; Progressivism in American Education 1876–1957* (New York: Vintage Books, 1964), 169–75.

On Hall and the child study movement, see Ross, *G. Stanley Hall*, 279–308, 342–67.

For Burchenal's HMS teaching, see *Teachers College Announcement 1905–1906*, 20, SCMMLTC. That the Horace Mann elementary school scheduled physical training as part of each grade's yearly work should not be a surprise. This curriculum included games, dances, and "simple class gymnastics," plus "individual corrective work" in grades one through three; athletic games, and class and individual work in grade four; gymnasium work plus daily classroom calisthenics and brief breathing exercises "in connection with phonic drill" in grade five; gymnasium, schoolroom, and out-of-doors work in grades six, seven, and eight; and "attention to personal hygiene" and "the meaning of temperance" in grades seven and eight. Photographs of physical training work published in Horace Mann Schools bulletins for 1902–03 and 1905–06 show girls performing wand drills and a mixed class straining in a position of attention—images which could easily have illustrated gymnasium work of the three preceding decades. But the course work described above—detailed in a 1902–03 curriculum statement—reveals a balance of the "old" with the "new," of systematized gymnastics and apparatus work with athletics, games, and out-of-doors work. This represented a leading-edge curricular position in 1902, and Burchenal was at the center of it. She taught physical training to elementary and high school students in the Horace Mann Schools through December 1905. See Schwendener, *History of Physical Education*, 125–27; *Outline of Course of Study for the Horace Mann Kindergarten and Elementary School 1902–1903*, 8, 11, 13, 15, 18, 20, 22, 24, SCMMLTC; *Horace Mann Schools [Bulletins], 1902–1903* and *1905–1906*, n.p., SCMMLTC; *Officers' Records*, vol. "B," SCMMLTC. Neither HMS bulletins nor Teachers College *Announcements* include Burchenal in faculty lists for the 1902–03 years. In subsequent faculty listings in these same sources, her brief employment summary has her work at Teachers College commencing in 1902. Data in Burchenal's *Officers' Records* personnel history indicates payment for her for teaching in 1902–03. Her services were probably secured after 1902–03 bulletins and announcements were printed.

20. "Mrs. C. H. Burchenal" *New York Times*, January 8, 1932, p. 21; "Burchenal, Charles H.," *American Biographical Archive* (New York: Saur, 1986–), fiche 218, frames 145–46; Emma Bugbee, "Elizabeth Burchenal Advocates Folk Dances to Relax War Nerves," *New York Herald Tribune*, May 31, 1943, p. 9. See also Marilyn B. Weissman's Burchenal entry in *Notable American Women; The Modern Period*, ed. Barbara Sicherman et al. (Cambridge: Harvard University Press, Belknap Press, 1980), 121–22. Until about 1915, Girls' Branch *Handbooks* hyphenated the term folk-dance. This chapter regularizes the spelling as folk dance, except as required in quoted material.

21. Frances Drewry McMullen, "Folk Dances for Fox Trots," *The Woman Citizen* (June 1927): 27; Bugbee, "Elizabeth Burchenal Advocates Folk Dances," 9; Gertrude E. S. Pringle, "This Girl Teaching the Whole Continent Folk-Dancing," *Toronto Star Weekly*, March 18, 1922, p. 20. Pringle's article dates this visit to England to a summer two years before Burchenal began work with the PSAL; this could be either 1903 (Burchenal resigned from TC in December 1905) or 1904 (Burchenal began work with PSAL in January 1906). An undated brochure about the American Folk Dance Society, founded by Burchenal in 1916, lists one of its activities—research and collection of folk dances, music, costumes, games, and festivals—as "in progress since 1904." *American Folk Dance Society*, n.p., n.d., in Photographs Box, Elizabeth Burchenal Collection, Special Collections, Mugar

Memorial Library, Boston University. For Burchenal's letter to Sharp (September 1, 1908), see Cecil Sharp Correspondence Collection, Box 1, Vaughan Williams Memorial Library, Cecil Sharp House, London, England.

On Burchenal's collecting practice, see "To Tramp Europe Learning Dances," *New York Herald*, June 28, 1911, p. 9; "Girls' Branch of Public Schools Athletic League has Set New Standards for Girl Athletes," *New York Herald*, February 9, 1913, Magazine section, p. 2; "American Girl Teaches Folk Dancing to Ireland," *New York Times*, September 28, 1913, Magazine section, p. 5; "Power Behind Success of 'America's Making' Tells Difficulties of Directing Pageants," *The* [New York City] *Sun*, January 10, 1922, p. 22.

22. *Columbia University, Bulletin of Information, Summer Session Announcement 1904*, 57, and *1905*, 51, Columbia University Archives and Columbiana Library. The announcement for Summer 1906 does not list Burchenal among the faculty, although a course description for the course she taught previously retains her name. Data in her personnel history indicate she resigned January 1906, so it is unlikely that she actually taught during Summer 1906. *Officers' Records*, vol. "B," SCMMLTC.

Gulick had from 1887 developed the department of physical training at the International YMCA Training School in Springfield, Massachusetts. In 1900 he took the position of principal at the Pratt School in New York City, and in 1903 accepted appointment as Director of Physical Training in New York City's newly consolidated school system. His editorship of the *American Physical Education Review* commenced in 1901. Following his AAPE presidency, he accepted employment with the Russell Sage Foundation. Dorgan, *Luther Halsey Gulick*, 18–19, 85–86, 134; "Association Presidents Through the Years 1885–1960," *Journal of Health, Physical Education and Recreation* 31 (April 1960): 64; Schwendener, *History of Physical Education*, 124; Jessie H. Bancroft, "Contributions," 340.

23. Gulick, *Healthful Art of Dancing*, 36–38; Bancroft, *Handbook 1910–1911*, 88; Bancroft, "Contributions (Concluded)," 378.

While the date is not clear, evidence suggests that the Girls' Branch also adopted the questionnaire method utilized in Hallian child study research, conducting a survey of physical training professionals around the country to determine those activities deemed most suitable for girls work.

24. In December 1909, the Board of Education formed a committee on Athletics charged with oversight of public school athletics not conducted during school hours. This committee as a matter of policy referred "to the Girls' Branch for recommendation on matters relating to girls' athletics." In April 1910, the Board of Education adopted as policy a set of Girls' Branch resolutions on the proper aims and conduct of folk dancing. On school facilities, Burchenal's salary, and Board of Education policies, see Gulick, *Healthful Art of Dancing*, 45–48; Gulick and Smith, "Dancing as a Part of Education," 9445–46; Bancroft, *Handbook 1910–1911*, 19, 29, 33, 35, 46–48, 86; Burchenal, *Handbook 1914–1915*, 24, 74, 107, 143; "Athletics for Public School Girls in New York City," *The Playground* 4, no. 1 (April 1910): 31; Dorgan, *Luther Halsey Gulick*, 83; "Girls' Branch of Public Schools Athletic League has Set New Standard for Girl Athletes," *New York Herald*, February 9, 1913, sec. 2, p. 2

In the first year, about thirty-eight teachers took advantage of the free Girls'

Branch training class. By 1907–08, 374 teachers led 11,270 girls in athletics clubs at 175 schools. Burchenal and a group of assistants taught six teachers' instruction classes that year and supervised the after-school work of the Girls' Branch. In 1909–10, the year the Board of Examiners announced that credit would be awarded for teachers' after-school participation, the number of teachers involved doubled, and instruction reached over 16,000 girls. In 1913–14, 26,909 girls and 733 teachers participated. By 1916–17, when Burchenal took a leave of absence due to illness, over 50,000 girls and 960 teachers were taking part in 500 clubs organized at 273 schools. Ten teachers' instruction classes were taught that year and the preceding year. On instruction classes and teachers, see Bancroft, *Girls' Athletics 1910–1911*, 18, 88–89. On girls' participation see Gulick and Smith, "Dancing as a Part of Education," 9449; Gulick, *Healthful Art of Dancing*, 46–47; Bancroft, "Contributions (Concluded)," 378; "Athletics for Public School Girls in New York City," *The Playground* 4, no. 1 (April 1910): 33. Annual handbooks are a primary source of participation data; see Bancroft, *Handbook 1910–1911*, 88–89; and Burchenal-edited *Handbooks* for 1914–1915 (17, 26); 1915–1916 (29, 34); 1916–1917 (30–31, 37); 1917–1918 (32, 37).

25. Gulick, *Healthful Art of Dancing*, 36–38.

26. Gulick, *Healthful Art of Dancing*, 102, 115, 131–32, 135–36; Gulick and Smith, "Dancing as a Part of Education," 9445, 9447–48.

27. See Allen F. Davis, *Spearheads for Reform; The Social Settlements and the Progressive Movement 1890–1914* (New York: Oxford University Press, 1967), 60–71.

28. Gulick and Smith, "Dancing as a Part of Education," 9447–48; Gulick, *Healthful Art of Dancing*, 102–09.

29. Teresa de Lauretis, "Feminist Studies/Critical Studies: Issues, Terms, and Contexts," in *Feminist Studies/Critical Studies*, ed. de Lauretis (Bloomington: Indiana University Press, 1986), 11–12.

30. See chapter 1 for system features; for criticisms leveled at them, see *Physical Training; A Full Report*, ed. Barrows.

31. Bancroft, "Contributions," 381.

32. Gulick, *Healthful Art of Dancing*, 102, 115, 131–32, 135–36; Gulick and Smith, "Dancing as a Part of Education," 9445, 9447–48.

33. Hall, *Adolescence*, 1: 233.

34. Gulick and Smith, "Dancing as a Part of Education," 9446–47.

35. Linda Gordon, "What's New in Women's History," in *Feminist Studies/Critical Studies*, 25.

36. Burchenal, "A Dance Around the May-Pole," *Woman's Home Companion* 37 (April 1910): 5, 66. See also Bancroft, *Handbook 1910–1911*, 12, and Burchenal-edited *Handbooks* for 1914–1915 (pp. 74–78), 1915–1916 (45), and 1916–1917 (89).

37. See Burchenal's *Folk-Dances and Singing Games* (1909). Her publishing career was substantial, beginning in 1908 and continuing through the 1930s with revisions and reissues of earlier books. By the 1920s and 1930s, photo subjects came to include adults as well as girls dancing, frequently captured in indoor settings or, when out of doors, adjacent to entrances or stairways.

38. See, for example, "When 7,000 School Girls Danced Around Eighty-Two

May Poles in Central Park," *New York Times*, May 25, 1913, Picture sec., part 1, pp. 4–5.

39. *Tamiris in Her Own Voice: Draft of an Autobiography*, transcr., ed., annot. Daniel Nagrin, *Studies in Dance History* 1, no. 1 (Fall-Winter 1989–90), 9.

40. Again, it is possible that Burchenal learned dances from immigrant people in New York City as well. See p. 192 above.

41. See *Folk-Dances and Singing Games* (1909). Photographic examples show that, while Girls' Branch dress consistently adhered to the standards mentioned above, other groups with whom Burchenal worked, in the 1910s as well as the 1920s and 1930s, dressed in "ethnic" or European costumes, or facsimiles of them.

42. *The Victrola in Physical Education, Recreation and Play* (Camden, N.J.: Educational Department, Victor Talking Machine Co., 1918). In the same period, provision of music for revivalist English traditional dance events demonstrated more than a little fluidity. Historian Pruw Boswell has found that morris teams dancing in England's Lancashire Plain from 1890 danced to "any available local brass band," because they maintained no bands of their own, nor a single musician attached to them. The American Branch of the English Folk Dance Society ran summer camps in Eliot, Maine (1915), and Amherst, Massachusetts (1916, 1917); solo violin accompaniment is documented in numerous photographs. Clearly the "tradition" itself was in flux, at least in matters musical, and Girls' Branch practice partook of the same fluidity. See Pruw Boswell, "Trends in Morris Dancing on the Lancashire Plain from 1890," *Traditional Dance* 5/6 (1988): 4–5; also Scrapbooks of the English Folk Dance Society–American Branch, Country Dance and Song Archives, now held by University of New Hampshire, Special Collections Department.

43. Schools and Lower East Side locations were correlated with the *New York Directory 1909–1910*, vol. Resh-Z (New York: Trow Directory, Printing and Book Binding Co., 1909), and *Atlas of the City of New York, Borough of Manhattan, vol. 1, Battery to 14th Street to 1906, Corrected to May 1909* (Philadelphia: G. W. Bromley & Co., 1909).

44. Gulick, "Teaching American Children to Play: Significance of the Revival of Folk Dances, Games and Festivals by the Playground Association," *The Craftsman* 15 (November 1908): 195–96. This event was scheduled for conferees at a New York City PAA Congress.

45. See Jane Addams, *Twenty Years at Hull-House* (1910; reprint, New York: New American Library, 1981); Eileen Boris, *Art and Labor: Ruskin, Morris, and the Craftsman Ideal in America* (Philadelphia: Temple University Press, 1986); Neil Harris, "The Gilded Age Revisited: Boston and the Museum Movement," *American Quarterly* (Winter 1962): 545–66; Naima Prevots, *American Pageantry: a Movement for Art and Democracy* (Ann Arbor: UMI Research Press, 1990). G. Stanley Hall voiced a view of America's need to establish traditions in *Educational Problems*, 2 vols. (New York: D. Appleton and Co., 1911) 1: 60–61.

46. Gulick and Smith, "Dancing as a Part of Education", 9452.

47. For several perspectives on the English traditional dance revival, see Maud Karpeles, *Cecil Sharp: His Life and Work* (London: Routleldge & Kegan Paul, 1967); Dave Harker, *Fakesong: the Manufacture of British "Folksong" 1700 to the*

Present Day (Philadelphia: Open University Press, 1985); and *Traditional Dance*, vols. 1 (1981), 2 (1982), and 5/6 (1988).

48. See John Higham, *Strangers in the Land; Patterns of American Nativism 1860–1924*, 2d ed. (New Brunswick: Rutgers University Press, 1988); Selma Berrol, "In Their Image: German Jews and the Americanization of the *Ost Juden* in New York City," *New York History* 63 (October 1982): 417–33; Berrol, "Germans versus Russians: An Update," *American Jewish History* 73 (December 1983): 142–56; Moses Rischin, *The Promised City; New York's Jews 1870–1940* (Cambridge: Harvard University Press, 1962); Lawrence Levine, *Black Culture and Black Consciousness: Afro-American Folk Thought from Slavery to Freedom* (New York: Oxford University Press, 1977).

49. Bancroft, *Handbook 1910–1911*, 93; Jable, "The Public Schools Athletic League," 219–38.

50. On burlesque, see Robert Allen, *Horrible Prettiness; Burlesque and American Culture* (Chapel Hill: University of North Carolina Press, 1991). Theodore Dreiser offers a period view of Broadway dancing in *Sister Carrie; A Novel* (New York: Harper, 1912).

51. See Bancroft, *Handbook 1910–1911*, 46–47, 52; Burchenal, *Handbook 1914–1915*, 35–36, 41, 74–77; Burchenal, *Handbook 1915–1916*, 45, 87–89.

52. See Bancroft, *Handbook 1910–1911*, 48, 83, 86–88; and Burchenal, *Handbooks* for 1914–1915 (16–17, 24–25, 37, 74–77), 1915–1916 (27–28, 37), 1916–1917 (27–30) and 1917–1918 (29–31).

53. Mary Wood Hinman's publications confirm this point: *Music for Hinman Gymnastic Dancing* (Chicago, 1911), and the five-volume *Gymnastic and Folk Dancing* series (New York: A. S. Barnes Co., ca. 1916 to 1930). The latter treated *Solo Dances* (vol. 1), *Couple Dances* (2), *Ring Dances* (3), *Group Dances* (4), and *Clogs and Jigs* (5). See Caroline Crawford, *Folk Dances and Games* (New York, 1912), also published by A. S. Barnes, which fielded a "Folk Dance and Game Book" series. In addition, women authored numerous Progressive-era dance and game books for kindergarten pedagogy.

54. Gulick, *Healthful Art of Dancing*, 4, 140; Raymond Williams, *Culture & Society: 1780–1950* (New York: Columbia University Press, 1983), xviii, 30–48, 130–58.

55. Ross, G. *Stanley Hall*, 341–45, 355–56, 358–60; Michael Steven Shapiro, *Child's Garden; The Kindergarten Movement from Froebel to Dewey* (University Park: Pennsylvania State University Press, 1980), 126–30.

56. Gulick and Smith, "Dancing as a Part of Education," 9451; Gulick, *Healthful Art of Dancing*, "Introduction," n.p. Gulick invoked the Greek ideal in his early work with the YMCA; see Green, *Fit for America*, 214; Bancroft, *Handbook 1910–1911*, 52; Gulick, "Teaching American Children to Play," 197.

COLLECTIONS CONSULTED

The Billy Rose Theatre Collection, New York Public Library for the Performing Arts, New York City
> Locke Collection
> Neighborhood Playhouse Collections

Boston University, Mugar Memorial Library, Special Collections
> Elizabeth Burchenal Collection

Chicago Historical Society
> Chicago Commons Papers

Columbia University Archives and Columbiana Library
> Columbiana Collections

The Dance Collection, New York Public Library for the Performing Arts, New York City
> Denishawn Collection
> Doris Humphrey Collection
> Loie Fuller Papers
> Neighborhood Playhouse materials

Neighborhood Playhouse School of the Theatre, New York City
> Neighborhood Playhouse Collection

Newberry Library
> Graham Taylor MSS., containing Chicago Commons Papers

Social Welfare History Archives, University of Minnesota, Minneapolis
> United South End Settlements Collection
> Pamphlet Collection
> United Neighborhood Houses Collection

Teachers College, Columbia University, Milbank Memorial Library, Department of Special Collections

University of Illinois at Chicago, University Library, Special Collections
> Hull-House Association Records

Vaughan Williams Memorial Library, Cecil Sharp House, London, England
> Cecil Sharp Correspondence Collection

INDEX

Page numbers in italic type refer to illustrations.

Linda J. Tomko

Associate Professor of Dance at the University of
California, Riverside, is President of the Society of
Dance History Scholars (SDHS), and Co-Director of
the annual Stanford University Summer Workshop in
Baroque Dance. In 1997 she won the Gertrude
Lippincott Prize, awarded by SDHS, for her article
"Fete Accompli," published in *Corporealities*.